Modern C++ Design

The C++ In-Depth Series

Bjarne Stroustrup, Editor

"I have made this letter longer than usual, because I lack the time to make it short."
—BLAISE PASCAL

The advent of the ISO/ANSI C++ standard marked the beginning of a new era for C++ programmers. The standard offers many new facilities and opportunities, but how can a real-world programmer find the time to discover the key nuggets of wisdom within this mass of information? **The C++ In-Depth Series** minimizes learning time and confusion by giving programmers concise, focused guides to specific topics.

Each book in this series presents a single topic, at a technical level appropriate to that topic. The Series' practical approach is designed to lift professionals to their next level of programming skills. Written by experts in the field, these short, in-depth monographs can be read and referenced without the distraction of unrelated material. The books are cross-referenced within the Series, and also reference *The C++ Programming Language* by Bjarne Stroustrup.

As you develop your skills in C++, it becomes increasingly important to separate essential information from hype and glitz, and to find the in-depth content you need in order to grow. The C++ In-Depth Series provides the tools, concepts, techniques, and new approaches to C++ that will give you a critical edge.

Titles in the Series

Accelerated C++: Practical Programming by Example, Andrew Koenig and Barbara E. Moo

Applied C++: Practical Techniques for Building Better Software, Philip Romanik and Amy Muntz

The Boost Graph Library: User Guide and Reference Manual, Jeremy G. Siek, Lie-Quan Lee, and Andrew Lumsdaine

C++ Coding Standards: 101 Rules, Guidelines, and Best Practices, Herb Sutter and Andrei Alexandrescu

C++ In-Depth Box Set, Bjarne Stroustrup, Andrei Alexandrescu, Andrew Koenig, Barbara E. Moo, Stanley B. Lippman, and Herb Sutter

C++ Network Programming, Volume 1: Mastering Complexity with ACE and Patterns, Douglas C. Schmidt and Stephen D. Huston

C++ Network Programming, Volume 2: Systematic Reuse with ACE and Frameworks, Douglas C. Schmidt and Stephen D. Huston

C++ Template Metaprogramming: Concepts, Tools, and Techniques from Boost and Beyond, David Abrahams and Aleksey Gurtovoy

Essential C++, Stanley B. Lippman

Exceptional C++: 47 Engineering Puzzles, Programming Problems, and Solutions, Herb Sutter

Exceptional C++ Style: 40 New Engineering Puzzles, Programming Problems, and Solutions, Herb Sutter

Modern C++ Design: Generic Programming and Design Patterns Applied, Andrei Alexandrescu

More Exceptional C++: 40 New Engineering Puzzles, Programming Problems, and Solutions, Herb Sutter

Modern C++ Design

Generic Programming and Design Patterns Applied

Andrei Alexandrescu

✦ Addison-Wesley

Boston • San Francisco • New York • Toronto • Montreal
London • Munich • Paris • Madrid
Capetown • Sydney • Tokyo • Singapore • Mexico City

The publisher offers discounts on this book when ordered in quantity for special sales. For more information, please contact:

Pearson Education Corporate Sales Division
201 W. 103rd Street
Indianapolis, IN 46290
(800) 428-5331
corpsales@pearsoned.com

Visit AW on the Web: www.awprofessional.com

Library of Congress Cataloging-in-Publication Data
Alexandrescu, Andrei.
   Modern C++ design : generic programming and design patterns applied /
Andrei Alexandrescu.
     p. cm. — (C++ in depth series)
   Includes bibliographical references and index.
   ISBN 0-201-70431-5
   1. C++ (Computer program language)   2. Generic programming (Computer science)
I. Title. II. Series.
QA76.73.C153 A42   2001
005.13'3—dc21   00-049596

ISBN 0-201-70431-5

Text printed in the United States on recycled paper at RR Donnelley Crawfordsville in Crawfordsville, Indiana

19th Printing   January 2011

Contents

Foreword by Scott Meyers   xi

Foreword by John Vlissides   xv

Preface   xvii

Acknowledgments   xxi

Part I   Techniques   1

Chapter 1   Policy-Based Class Design   3
  1.1   The Multiplicity of Software Design   3
  1.2   The Failure of the Do-It-All Interface   4
  1.3   Multiple Inheritance to the Rescue?   5
  1.4   The Benefit of Templates   6
  1.5   Policies and Policy Classes   7
  1.6   Enriched Policies   12
  1.7   Destructors of Policy Classes   12
  1.8   Optional Functionality Through Incomplete Instantiation   13
  1.9   Combining Policy Classes   14
  1.10   Customizing Structure with Policy Classes   16
  1.11   Compatible and Incompatible Policies   17
  1.12   Decomposing a Class into Policies   19
  1.13   Summary   20

Chapter 2	**Techniques**	**23**
2.1	Compile-Time Assertions	23
2.2	Partial Template Specialization	26
2.3	Local Classes	28
2.4	Mapping Integral Constants to Types	29
2.5	Type-to-Type Mapping	31
2.6	Type Selection	33
2.7	Detecting Convertibility and Inheritance at Compile Time	34
2.8	A Wrapper Around `type_info`	37
2.9	`NullType` and `EmptyType`	39
2.10	Type Traits	40
2.11	Summary	46
Chapter 3	**Typelists**	**49**
3.1	The Need for Typelists	49
3.2	Defining Typelists	51
3.3	Linearizing Typelist Creation	52
3.4	Calculating Length	53
3.5	Intermezzo	54
3.6	Indexed Access	55
3.7	Searching Typelists	56
3.8	Appending to Typelists	57
3.9	Erasing a Type from a Typelist	58
3.10	Erasing Duplicates	59
3.11	Replacing an Element in a Typelist	60
3.12	Partially Ordering Typelists	61
3.13	Class Generation with Typelists	64
3.14	Summary	74
3.15	`Typelist` Quick Facts	75
Chapter 4	**Small-Object Allocation**	**77**
4.1	The Default Free Store Allocator	78
4.2	The Workings of a Memory Allocator	78
4.3	A Small-Object Allocator	80
4.4	Chunks	81
4.5	The Fixed-Size Allocator	84
4.6	The `SmallObjAllocator` Class	87
4.7	A Hat Trick	89
4.8	Simple, Complicated, Yet Simple in the End	92
4.9	Administrivia	93
4.10	Summary	94
4.11	Small-Object Allocator Quick Facts	94

Part II	**Components**	**97**
Chapter 5	**Generalized Functors**	**99**
5.1	The Command Design Pattern	100
5.2	Command in the Real World	102
5.3	C++ Callable Entities	103
5.4	The Functor Class Template Skeleton	104
5.5	Implementing the Forwarding Functor::operator()	108
5.6	Handling Functors	110
5.7	Build One, Get One Free	112
5.8	Argument and Return Type Conversions	114
5.9	Handling Pointers to Member Functions	115
5.10	Binding	119
5.11	Chaining Requests	122
5.12	Real-World Issues I: The Cost of Forwarding Functions	122
5.13	Real-World Issues II: Heap Allocation	124
5.14	Implementing Undo and Redo with Functor	125
5.15	Summary	126
5.16	Functor Quick Facts	126

Chapter 6	**Implementing Singletons**	**129**
6.1	Static Data + Static Functions != Singleton	130
6.2	The Basic C++ Idioms Supporting Singleton	131
6.3	Enforcing the Singleton's Uniqueness	132
6.4	Destroying the Singleton	133
6.5	The Dead Reference Problem	135
6.6	Addressing the Dead Reference Problem (I): The Phoenix Singleton	137
6.7	Addressing the Dead Reference Problem (II): Singletons with Longevity	139
6.8	Implementing Singletons with Longevity	142
6.9	Living in a Multithreaded World	145
6.10	Putting It All Together	148
6.11	Working with SingletonHolder	153
6.12	Summary	155
6.13	SingletonHolder Class Template Quick Facts	155

Chapter 7	**Smart Pointers**	**157**
7.1	Smart Pointers 101	157
7.2	The Deal	158
7.3	Storage of Smart Pointers	160
7.4	Smart Pointer Member Functions	161

7.5	Ownership-Handling Strategies	163
7.6	The Address-of Operator	170
7.7	Implicit Conversion to Raw Pointer Types	171
7.8	Equality and Inequality	173
7.9	Ordering Comparisons	178
7.10	Checking and Error Reporting	181
7.11	Smart Pointers to const and const Smart Pointers	182
7.12	Arrays	183
7.13	Smart Pointers and Multithreading	184
7.14	Putting It All Together	187
7.15	Summary	194
7.16	SmartPtr Quick Facts	194
Chapter 8	**Object Factories**	**197**
8.1	The Need for Object Factories	198
8.2	Object Factories in C++: Classes and Objects	200
8.3	Implementing an Object Factory	201
8.4	Type Identifiers	206
8.5	Generalization	207
8.6	Minutiae	210
8.7	Clone Factories	211
8.8	Using Object Factories with Other Generic Components	215
8.9	Summary	216
8.10	Factory Class Template Quick Facts	216
8.11	CloneFactory Class Template Quick Facts	217
Chapter 9	**Abstract Factory**	**219**
9.1	The Architectural Role of Abstract Factory	219
9.2	A Generic Abstract Factory Interface	223
9.3	Implementing AbstractFactory	226
9.4	A Prototype-Based Abstract Factory Implementation	228
9.5	Summary	233
9.6	AbstractFactory and ConcreteFactory Quick Facts	233
Chapter 10	**Visitor**	**235**
10.1	Visitor Basics	235
10.2	Overloading and the Catch-All Function	242
10.3	An Implementation Refinement: The Acyclic Visitor	243
10.4	A Generic Implementation of Visitor	248
10.5	Back to the "Cyclic" Visitor	255
10.6	Hooking Variations	258
10.7	Summary	260
10.8	Visitor Generic Component Quick Facts	261

Chapter 11	**Multimethods**	**263**
11.1	What Are Multimethods?	264
11.2	When Are Multimethods Needed?	264
11.3	Double Switch-on-Type: Brute Force	265
11.4	The Brute-Force Approach Automated	268
11.5	Symmetry with the Brute-Force Dispatcher	273
11.6	The Logarithmic Double Dispatcher	276
11.7	FnDispatcher and Symmetry	282
11.8	Double Dispatch to Functors	282
11.9	Converting Arguments: static_cast or dynamic_cast?	285
11.10	Constant-Time Multimethods: Raw Speed	290
11.11	BasicDispatcher and BasicFastDispatcher as Policies	293
11.12	Looking Forward	294
11.13	Summary	296
11.14	Double Dispatcher Quick Facts	297
Appendix	**A Minimalist Multithreading Library**	**301**
A.1	A Critique of Multithreading	302
A.2	Loki's Approach	303
A.3	Atomic Operations on Integral Types	303
A.4	Mutexes	305
A.5	Locking Semantics in Object-Oriented Programming	306
A.6	Optional volatile Modifier	308
A.7	Semaphores, Events, and Other Good Things	309
A.8	Summary	309
Bibliography		**311**
Index		**313**

Foreword

by Scott Meyers

In 1991, I wrote the first edition of *Effective* C++. The book contained almost no discussions of templates, because templates were such a recent addition to the language, I knew almost nothing about them. What little template code I included, I had verified by e-mailing it to other people, because none of the compilers to which I had access offered support for templates.

In 1995, I wrote *More Effective* C++. Again I wrote almost nothing about templates. What stopped me this time was neither a lack of knowledge of templates (my initial outline for the book included an entire chapter on the topic) nor shortcomings on the part of my compilers. Instead, it was a suspicion that the C++ community's understanding of templates was about to undergo such dramatic change, anything I had to say about them would soon be considered trite, superficial, or just plain wrong.

There were two reasons for that suspicion. The first was a column by John Barton and Lee Nackman in the January 1995 C++ *Report* that described how templates could be used to perform typesafe dimensional analysis with zero runtime cost. This was a problem I'd spent some time on myself, and I knew that many had searched for a solution, but none had succeeded. Barton and Nackman's revolutionary approach made me realize that templates were good for a lot more than just creating containers of T.

As an example of their design, consider this code for multiplying two physical quantities of arbitrary dimensional type:

```
template<int m1, int l1, int t1, int m2, int l2, int t2>
Physical<m1+m2, l1+l2, t1+t2> operator*(Physical<m1, l1, t1> lhs,
                                         Physical<m2, l2, t2> rhs)
{
    return Physical<m1+m2, l1+l2, t1+t2>::unit*lhs.value()*rhs.value();
}
```

Even without the context of the column to clarify this code, it's clear that this function template takes six parameters, none of which represents a type! This use of templates was such a revelation to me, I was positively giddy.

Shortly thereafter, I started reading about the STL. Alexander Stepanov's elegant library design, where containers know nothing about algorithms; algorithms know nothing about containers; iterators act like pointers (but may be objects instead); containers and algorithms accept function pointers and function objects with equal aplomb; and library clients may extend the library without having to inherit from any base classes or redefine any virtual functions, made me feel—as I had when I read Barton and Nackman's work—like I knew almost *nothing* about templates.

So I wrote almost nothing about them in *More Effective* C++. How could I? My understanding of templates was still at the containers-of-T stage, while Barton, Nackman, Stepanov, and others were demonstrating that such uses barely scratched the surface of what templates could do.

In 1998, Andrei Alexandrescu and I began an e-mail correspondence, and it was not long before I recognized that I was again about to modify my thinking about templates. Where Barton, Nackman, and Stepanov had stunned me with what templates could *do*, however, Andrei's work initially made more of an impression on me for *how* it did what it did.

One of the simplest things he helped popularize continues to be the example I use when introducing people to his work. It's the CTAssert template, analogous in use to the assert macro, but applied to conditions that can be evaluated during compilation. Here it is:

```
template<bool> struct CTAssert;
template<> struct CTAssert<true> {};
```

That's it. Notice how the general template, CTAssert, is never defined. Notice how there is a specialization for true, but not for false. In this design, what's *missing* is at least as important as what's present. It makes you look at template code in a new way, because large portions of the "source code" are deliberately omitted. That's a very different way of thinking from the one most of us are used to. (In this book, Andrei discusses the more sophisticated CompileTimeChecker template instead of CTAssert.)

Eventually, Andrei turned his attention to the development of template-based implementations of popular language idioms and design patterns, especially the GoF* patterns. This led to a brief skirmish with the Patterns community, because one of their fundamental tenets is that patterns cannot be represented in code. Once it became clear that Andrei was automating the generation of pattern *implementations* rather than trying to encode patterns themselves, that objection was removed, and I was pleased to see Andrei and one of the GoF (John Vlissides) collaborate on two columns in the C++ *Report* focusing on Andrei's work.

In the course of developing the templates to generate idiom and pattern implementations, Andrei was forced to confront the variety of design decisions that all implementers face. Should the code be thread safe? Should auxiliary memory come from the heap, from the stack, or from a static pool? Should smart pointers be checked for nullness prior to dereferencing? What should happen during program shutdown if one Singleton's destructor tries to use another Singleton that's already been destroyed? Andrei's goal was to offer his clients all possible design choices while mandating none.

*"GoF" stands for "Gang of Four" and refers to Erich Gamma, Richard Helm, Ralph Johnson, and John Vlissides, authors of the definitive book on patterns, *Design Patterns: Elements of Reusable Object-Oriented Software* (Addison-Wesley, 1995).

His solution was to encapsulate such decisions in the form of *policy classes*, to allow clients to pass policy classes as template parameters, and to provide reasonable default values for such classes so that most clients could ignore them. The results can be astonishing. For example, the Smart Pointer template in this book takes only 4 policy parameters, but it can generate over 300 different smart pointer types, each with unique behavioral characteristics! Programmers who are content with the default smart pointer behavior, however, can ignore the policy parameters, specify only the type of object pointed to by the smart pointer, and reap the benefits of a finely crafted smart pointer class with virtually no effort.

In the end, this book tells three different technical stories, each compelling in its own way. First, it offers new insights into the power and flexibility of C++ templates. (If the material on typelists doesn't knock your socks off, it's got to be because you're already barefoot.) Second, it identifies orthogonal dimensions along which idiom and pattern implementations may differ. This is critical information for template designers and pattern implementers, but you're unlikely to find this kind of analysis in most idiom or pattern descriptions. Finally, the source code to Loki (the template library described in this book) is available for free download, so you can study Andrei's implementation of the templates corresponding to the idioms and patterns he discusses. Aside from providing a nice stress test for your compilers' support for templates, this source code serves as an invaluable starting point for templates of your own design. Of course, it's also perfectly respectable (and completely legal) to use Andrei's code right out of the box. I know he'd want you to take advantage of his efforts.

From what I can tell, the template landscape is changing almost as quickly now as it was in 1995 when I decided to avoid writing about it. At the rate things continue to develop, I may *never* write about templates. Fortunately for all of us, some people are braver than I am. Andrei is one such pioneer. I think you'll get a lot out of his book. I did.

Scott Meyers
September 2000

Foreword

by John Vlissides

What's left to say about C++ that hasn't already been said? Plenty, it turns out. This book documents a convergence of programming techniques—generic programming, template metaprogramming, object-oriented programming, and design patterns—that are well understood in isolation but whose synergies are only beginning to be appreciated. These synergies have opened up whole new vistas for C++, not just for programming but for software design itself, with profound implications for software analysis and architecture as well.

Andrei's generic components raise the level of abstraction high enough to make C++ begin to look and feel like a design specification language. Unlike dedicated design languages, however, you retain the full expressiveness and familiarity of C++. Andrei shows you how to program in terms of design concepts: singletons, visitors, proxies, abstract factories, and more. You can even vary implementation trade-offs through template parameters, with positively no runtime overhead. And you don't have to blow big bucks on new development tools or learn reams of methodological mumbo jumbo. All you need is a trusty, late-model C++ compiler—and this book.

Code generators have held comparable promise for years, but my own research and practical experience have convinced me that, in the end, code generation doesn't compare. You have the round-trip problem, the not-enough-code-worth-generating problem, the inflexible-generator problem, the inscrutable-generated-code problem, and of course the I-can't-integrate-the-bloody-generated-code-with-my-own-code problem. Any one of these problems may be a showstopper; together, they make code generation an unlikely solution for most programming challenges.

Wouldn't it be great if we could realize the theoretical benefits of code generation—quicker, easier development, reduced redundancy, fewer bugs—without the drawbacks? That's what Andrei's approach promises. Generic components implement good designs in easy-to-use, mixable-and-matchable templates. They do pretty much what code generators do: produce boilerplate code for compiler consumption. The difference is that they do it within C++, not apart from it. The result is seamless integration with application code.

You can also use the full power of the language to extend, override, and otherwise tweak the designs to suit your needs.

Some of the techniques herein are admittedly tricky to grasp, especially the template metaprogramming in Chapter 3. Once you've mastered that, however, you'll have a solid foundation for the edifice of generic componentry, which almost builds itself in the ensuing chapters. In fact, I would argue that the metaprogramming material of Chapter 3 alone is worth the book's price—and there are ten other chapters full of insights to profit from. "Ten" represents an order of magnitude. Even so, the return on your investment will be far greater.

John Vlissides
IBM T.J. Watson Research
September 2000

Preface

You might be holding this book in a bookstore, asking yourself whether you should buy it. Or maybe you are in your employer's library, wondering whether you should invest time in reading it. I know you don't have time, so I'll cut to the chase. If you have ever asked yourself how to write higher-level programs in C++, how to cope with the avalanche of irrelevant details that plague even the cleanest design, or how to build reusable components that you don't have to hack into each time you take them to your next application, then this book is for you.

Imagine the following scenario. You come from a design meeting with a couple of printed diagrams, scribbled with your annotations. Okay, the event type passed between these objects is not char anymore; it's int. You change one line of code. The smart pointers to Widget are too slow; they should go unchecked. You change one line of code. The object factory needs to support the new Gadget class just added by another department. You change one line of code.

You have changed the design. Compile. Link. Done.

Well, there is something wrong with this scenario, isn't there? A much more likely scenario is this: You come from the meeting in a hurry because you have a pile of work to do. You fire a global search. You perform surgery on code. You add code. You introduce bugs. You remove the bugs . . . that's the way a programmer's job is, right? Although this book cannot possibly promise you the first scenario, it is nonetheless a resolute step in that direction. It tries to present C++ as a newly discovered language for software architects.

Traditionally, code is the most detailed and intricate aspect of a software system. Historically, in spite of various levels of language support for design methodologies (such as object orientation), a significant gap has persisted between the blueprints of a program and its code because the code must take care of the ultimate details of the implementation and of many ancillary tasks. The intent of the design is, more often than not, dissolved in a sea of quirks.

This book presents a collection of reusable design artifacts, called *generic components*, together with the techniques that make them possible. These generic components bring their users the well-known benefits of libraries, but in the broader space of system architecture. The coding techniques and the implementations provided focus on tasks and issues that traditionally fall in the area of design, activities usually done *before* coding. Because of their high level, generic components make it possible to map intricate architectures to code in unusually expressive, terse, and easy-to-maintain ways.

Three elements are reunited here: design patterns, generic programming, and C++. These elements are combined to achieve a very high rate of reuse, both in the horizontal and vertical "markets" of software design. In the horizontal dimension, a small amount of library code implements a combinatorial—and essentially open-ended—number of structures and behaviors. On the vertical dimension, the generality of these components makes them applicable to a vast range of programs.

This book owes much to design patterns, powerful solutions to ever-recurring problems in object-oriented development. Design patterns are distilled pieces of good design—recipes for sound, reusable solutions to problems that can be encountered in many contexts. Design patterns concentrate on providing a suggestive lexicon for designs to be conveyed. They describe the problem, a time-proven solution with its variants, and the consequences of choosing each variant of that solution. Design patterns go above and beyond anything a programming language, no matter how advanced, could possibly express. By following and combining certain design patterns, the components presented in this book tend to address a large category of concrete problems.

Generic programming is a paradigm that focuses on abstracting types to a narrow collection of functional requirements and on implementing algorithms in terms of these requirements. Because algorithms define a strict and narrow interface to the types they operate on, the same algorithm can be used against a wide collection of types. The implementations in this book use generic programming techniques to achieve a minimal commitment to specificity, extraordinary terseness, and efficiency that rivals carefully handcrafted code.

C++ is the only implementation tool used in this book. You will not find in this book code that implements nifty windowing systems, complex networking libraries, or clever logging mechanisms. Instead, you will find the fundamental components that make it easy to implement all of the above, and much more. C++ has the breadth necessary to make this possible. Its underlying C memory model ensures raw performance, its support for polymorphism enables object-oriented techniques, and its templates unleash an incredible code generation machine. Templates pervade all the code in the book because they allow close cooperation between the user and the library. The user of the library literally controls the way code is generated, in ways constrained by the library. The role of a generic component library is to allow user-specified types and behaviors to be combined with generic components in a sound design. Because of the static nature of the techniques used, errors in mixing and matching the appropriate pieces are usually caught during compilation.

This book's manifest intent is to create generic components—preimplemented pieces of design whose main characteristics are flexibility, versatility, and ease of use. Generic components do not form a framework. In fact, their approach is complementary—whereas a framework defines interdependent classes to foster a specific object model, generic components are lightweight design artifacts that are independent of each other, yet can be mixed and matched freely. They can be of great help in *implementing* frameworks.

Audience

The intended audience of this book falls into two main categories. The first category is that of experienced C++ programmers who want to master the most modern library writing techniques. The book presents new, powerful C++ idioms that have surprising capabilities, some of which weren't even thought possible. These idioms are of great help in writing high-level libraries. Intermediate C++ programmers who want to go a step further will certainly find the book useful, too, especially if they invest a bit of perseverance. Although pretty hard-core C++ code is sometimes presented, it is thoroughly explained.

The second category consists of busy programmers who need to get the job done without undergoing a steep learning investment. They can skim the most intricate details of implementation and concentrate on *using* the provided library. Each chapter has an introductory explanation and ends with a Quick Facts section. Programmers will find these features a useful reference in understanding and using the components. The components can be understood in isolation, are very powerful yet safe, and are a joy to use.

You need to have a solid working experience with C++ and, above all, the desire to learn more. A degree of familiarity with templates and the Standard Template Library (STL) is desirable.

Having an acquaintance with design patterns (Gamma et al. 1995) is recommended but not mandatory. The patterns and idioms applied in the book are described in detail. However, this book is not a pattern book—it does not attempt to treat patterns in full generality. Because patterns are presented from the pragmatic standpoint of a library writer, even readers interested mostly in patterns may find the perspective refreshing, if constrained.

Loki

The book describes an actual C++ library called Loki. Loki is the god of wit and mischief in Norse mythology, and the author's hope is that the library's originality and flexibility will remind readers of the playful Norse god. All the elements of the library live in the namespace Loki. The namespace is not mentioned in the coding examples because it would have unnecessarily increased indentation and the size of the examples. Loki is freely available; you can download it from http://www.modernpcdesign.com.

Except for its threading part, Loki is written exclusively in standard C++. This, alas, means that many current compilers cannot cope with parts of it. I implemented and tested Loki using Metrowerks' CodeWarrior Pro 6.0 and Comeau C++ 4.2.38, both on Windows. It is likely that KAI C++ wouldn't have any problem with the code, either. As vendors release new, better compiler versions, you will be able to exploit everything Loki has to offer.

Loki's code and the code samples presented throughout the book use a popular coding standard originated by Herb Sutter. I'm sure you will pick it up easily. In a nutshell,

- Classes, functions, and enumerated types look LikeThis.
- Variables and enumerated values look likeThis.
- Member variables look likeThis_.
- Template parameters are declared with class if they can be only a user-defined type, and with typename if they can also be a primitive type.

Organization

The book consists of two major parts: techniques and components. Part I (Chapters 1 to 4) describes the C++ techniques that are used in generic programming and in particular in building generic components. A host of C++-specific features and techniques are presented: policy-based design, partial template specialization, typelists, local classes, and more. You may want to read this part sequentially and return to specific sections for reference.

Part II builds on the foundation established in Part I by implementing a number of generic components. These are not toy examples; they are industrial-strength components used in real-world applications. Recurring issues that C++ developers face in their day-to-day activity, such as smart pointers, object factories, and functor objects, are discussed in depth and implemented in a generic way. The text presents implementations that address basic needs and solve fundamental problems. Instead of explaining what a body of code does, the approach of the book is to discuss problems, take design decisions, and implement those decisions gradually.

Chapter 1 presents policies—a C++ idiom that helps in creating flexible designs.

Chapter 2 discusses general C++ techniques related to generic programming.

Chapter 3 implements typelists, which are powerful type manipulation structures.

Chapter 4 introduces an important ancillary tool: a small object allocator.

Chapter 5 introduces the concept of generalized functors, useful in designs that use the Command design pattern.

Chapter 6 describes Singleton objects.

Chapter 7 discusses and implements smart pointers.

Chapter 8 describes generic object factories.

Chapter 9 treats the Abstract Factory design pattern and provides implementations of it.

Chapter 10 implements several variations of the Visitor design pattern in a generic manner.

Chapter 11 implements several multimethod engines, solutions that foster various trade-offs.

The design themes cover many important situations that C++ programmers have to cope with on a regular basis. I personally consider object factories (Chapter 8) a cornerstone of virtually any quality polymorphic design. Also, smart pointers (Chapter 7) are an important component of many C++ applications, small and large. Generalized functors (Chapter 5) have an incredibly broad range of applications. Once you have generalized functors, many complicated design problems become very simple. The other, more specialized, generic components, such as Visitor (Chapter 10) or multimethods (Chapter 11), have important niche applications and stretch the boundaries of language support.

Acknowledgments

I would like to thank my parents for diligently taking care of the longest, toughest part of them all.

It should be stressed that this book, and much of my professional development, wouldn't have existed without Scott Meyers. Since we met at the C++ World Conference in 1998, Scott has constantly helped me do more and do better. Scott was the first person who enthusiastically encouraged me to develop my early ideas. He introduced me to John Vlissides, catalyzing another fruitful cooperation; lobbied Herb Sutter to accept me as a columnist for *C++ Report*; and introduced me to Addison-Wesley, practically forcing me into starting this book, at a time when I still had trouble understanding New York sales clerks. Ultimately, Scott helped me all the way through the book with reviews and advice, sharing with me all the pains of writing, and none of the benefits.

Many thanks to John Vlissides, who, with his sharp insights, convinced me of the problems with my solutions and suggested much better ones. Chapter 9 exists because John insisted that "things could be done better."

Thanks to P. J. Plauger and Marc Briand for encouraging me to write for the *C/C++ Users Journal*, at a time when I still believed that magazine columnists were inhabitants of another planet.

I am indebted to my editor, Debbie Lafferty, for her continuous support and sagacious advice.

My colleagues at RealNetworks, especially Boris Jerkunica and Jim Knaack, helped me very much by fostering an atmosphere of freedom, emulation, and excellence. I am grateful to them all for that.

I also owe much to all participants in the comp.lang.c++.moderated and comp.std.c++ Usenet newsgroups. These people greatly and generously contributed to my understanding of C++.

I would like to address thanks to the reviewers of early drafts of the manuscript: Mihail Antonescu, Bob Archer (my most thorough reviewer of all), Allen Broadman, Ionut Burete, Mirel Chirita, Steve Clamage, James O. Coplien, Doug Hazen, Kevlin Henney, John Hickin, Howard Hinnant, Sorin Jianu, Zoltan Kormos, James Kuyper, Lisa Lippincott, Jonathan H. Lundquist, Petru Marginean, Patrick McKillen, Florin Mihaila, Sorin Oprea,

John Potter, Adrian Rapiteanu, Monica Rapiteanu, Brian Stanton, Adrian Steflea, Herb Sutter, John Torjo, Florin Trofin, and Cristi Vlasceanu. They all have invested significant efforts in reading and providing input, without which this book wouldn't have been half of what it is.

Thanks to Greg Comeau for providing me with his top-notch C++ compiler for free.

Last but not least, I would like to thank all my family and friends for their continuous encouragement and support.

Part I

Techniques

1

Policy-Based Class Design

This chapter describes policies and policy classes, important class design techniques that enable the creation of flexible, highly reusable libraries—as Loki aims to be. In brief, policy-based class design fosters assembling a class with complex behavior out of many little classes (called *policies*), each of which takes care of only one behavioral or structural aspect. As the name suggests, a policy establishes an interface pertaining to a specific issue. You can implement policies in various ways as long as you respect the policy interface.

Because you can mix and match policies, you can achieve a combinatorial set of behaviors by using a small core of elementary components.

Policies are used in many chapters of this book. The generic SingletonHolder class template (Chapter 6) uses policies for managing lifetime and thread safety. SmartPtr (Chapter 7) is built almost entirely from policies. The double-dispatch engine in Chapter 11 uses policies for selecting various trade-offs. The generic Abstract Factory (Gamma et al. 1995) implementation in Chapter 9 uses a policy for choosing a creation method.

This chapter explains the problem that policies are intended to solve, provides details of policy-based class design, and gives advice on decomposing a class into policies.

1.1 The Multiplicity of Software Design

Software engineering, maybe more than any other engineering discipline, exhibits a rich multiplicity: You can do the same thing in many correct ways, and there are infinite nuances between right and wrong. Each path opens up a new world. Once you choose a solution, a host of possible variants appears, on and on at all levels—from the system architecture level down to the smallest coding detail. The design of a software system is a choice of solutions out of a combinatorial solution space.

Let's think of a simple, low-level design artifact: a smart pointer (Chapter 7). A smart pointer class can be single threaded or multithreaded, can use various ownership strategies, can make various trade-offs between safety and speed, and may or may not support automatic conversions to the underlying raw pointer type. All these features can be combined freely, and usually exactly one solution is best suited for a given area of your application.

The multiplicity of the design space constantly confuses apprentice designers. Given a software design problem, what's a good solution to it? Events? Objects? Observers?

3

Callbacks? Virtuals? Templates? Up to a certain scale and level of detail, many different solutions seem to work equally well.

The most important difference between an expert software architect and a beginner is *the
knowledge of what works and what doesn't*. For any given architectural problem, there are many
competing ways of solving it. However, they scale differently and have distinct sets of advantages and disadvantages, which may or may not be suitable for the problem at hand. A
solution that appears to be acceptable on the whiteboard might be unusable in practice.

Designing software systems is hard because it constantly asks you to *choose*. And in program design, just as in life, choice is hard.

Good, seasoned designers know what choices will lead to a good design. For a beginner, each design choice opens a door to the unknown. The experienced designer is like a
good chess player: She can see more moves ahead. This takes time to learn. Maybe this is
the reason why programming genius may show at an early age, whereas software design
genius tends to take more time to ripen.

In addition to being a puzzle for beginners, the combinatorial nature of design decisions
is a major source of trouble for library writers. To implement a useful library of designs, the
library designer must classify and accommodate many typical situations, yet still leave the
library open-ended so that the application programmer can tailor it to the specific needs of
a particular situation.

Indeed, how can one package flexible, sound design components in libraries? How can
one let the user configure these components? How does one fight the "evil multiplicity" of
design with a reasonably sized army of code? These are the questions that the remainder
of this chapter, and ultimately this whole book, tries to answer.

1.2 The Failure of the Do-It-All Interface

Implementing everything under the umbrella of a do-it-all interface is not a good solution,
for several reasons.

Some important negative consequences are intellectual overhead, sheer size, and inefficiency. Mammoth classes are unsuccessful because they incur a big learning overhead, tend
to be unnecessarily large, and lead to code that's much slower than the equivalent handcrafted version.

But maybe the most important problem of an overly rich interface is *loss of static type
safety*. One essential purpose of the architecture of a system is to enforce certain axioms "by
design"—for example, you cannot create two Singleton objects (see Chapter 6) or create objects of disjoint families (see Chapter 9). Ideally, a design should enforce most constraints
at compile time.

In a large, all-encompassing interface, it is very hard to enforce such constraints. Typically, once you have chosen a certain set of design constraints, only certain subsets of the
large interface remain semantically valid. A gap grows between *syntactically valid* and *semantically valid* uses of the library. The programmer can write an increasing number of constructs that are syntactically valid, but semantically illegal.

For example, consider the thread-safety aspect of implementing a Singleton object. If the
library fully encapsulates threading, then the user of a particular, nonportable threading

system cannot use the Singleton library. If the library gives access to the unprotected primitive functions, there is the risk that the programmer will break the design by writing code that's syntactically—but not semantically—valid.

What if the library implements different design choices as different, smaller classes? Each class would represent a specific canned design solution. In the smart pointer case, for example, you would expect a battery of implementations: `SingleThreadedSmartPtr`, `MultiThreadedSmartPtr`, `RefCountedSmartPtr`, `RefLinkedSmartPtr`, and so on.

The problem that emerges with this second approach is the combinatorial explosion of the various design choices. The four classes just mentioned lead necessarily to combinations such as `SingleThreadedRefCountedSmartPtr`. Adding a third design option such as conversion support leads to exponentially more combinations, which will eventually overwhelm both the implementer and the user of the library. Clearly this is not the way to go. Never use brute force in fighting an exponential.

Not only does such a library incur an immense intellectual overhead, but it also is extremely rigid. The slightest unpredicted customization—such as trying to initialize default-constructed smart pointers with a particular value—renders all the carefully crafted library classes useless.

Designs enforce constraints; consequently, design-targeted libraries must help user-crafted designs to enforce *their own* constraints, instead of enforcing *predefined* constraints. Canned design choices would be as uncomfortable in design-targeted libraries as magic constants would be in regular code. Of course, batteries of "most popular" or "recommended" canned solutions are welcome, as long as the client programmer can change them if needed.

These issues have led to an unfortunate state of the art in the library space: Low-level general-purpose and specialized libraries abound, while libraries that directly assist the design of an application—the higher-level structures—are practically nonexistent. This situation is paradoxical because any nontrivial application has a design, so a design-targeted library would apply to most applications.

Frameworks try to fill the gap here, but they tend to lock an application into a specific design rather than help the user to *choose* and *customize* a design. If programmers need to implement an original design, they have to start from first principles—classes, functions, and so on.

1.3 Multiple Inheritance to the Rescue?

A `TemporarySecretary` class inherits both the `Secretary` and the `Temporary` classes.[1] `TemporarySecretary` has the features of both a secretary and a temporary employee, and possibly some more features of its own. This leads to the idea that multiple inheritance might help with handling the combinatorial explosion of design choices through a small number of cleverly chosen base classes. In such a setting, the user would build a multithreaded, reference-counted smart pointer class by inheriting some `BaseSmartPtr` class and

---

[1]This example is drawn from an old argument that Bjarne Stroustrup made in favor of multiple inheritance, in the first edition of *The C++ Programming Language*. At that time, multiple inheritance had not yet been introduced in C++.

two classes: `MultiThreaded` and `RefCounted`. Any experienced class designer knows that such a naïve design does not work.

Analyzing the reasons why multiple inheritance fails to allow the creation of flexible designs provides interesting ideas for reaching a sound solution. The problems with assembling separate features by using multiple inheritance are as follows:

1. *Mechanics.* There is no boilerplate code to assemble the inherited components in a controlled manner. The only tool that combines `BaseSmartPtr`, `MultiThreaded`, and `RefCounted` is a language mechanism called *multiple inheritance.* The language applies simple superposition in combining the base classes and establishes a set of simple rules for accessing their members. This is unacceptable except for the simplest cases. Most of the time, you need to carefully orchestrate the workings of the inherited classes to obtain the desired behavior.
2. *Type information.* The base classes do not have enough type information to carry out their tasks. For example, imagine you try to implement deep copy for your smart pointer class by deriving from a `DeepCopy` base class. What interface would `DeepCopy` have? It must create objects of a type it doesn't know yet.
3. *State manipulation.* Various behavioral aspects implemented with base classes must manipulate the same state. This means that they must use virtual inheritance to inherit a base class that holds the state. This complicates the design and makes it more rigid because the premise was that user classes inherit library classes, not vice versa.

Although combinatorial in nature, multiple inheritance by itself cannot address the multiplicity of design choices.

1.4 The Benefit of Templates

Templates are a good candidate for coping with combinatorial behaviors because they generate code at compile time based on the types (and / or constant values) provided by the user.

Class templates are customizable in ways not supported by regular classes. If you want to implement a special case, you can specialize any member functions of a class template for a specific instantiation of the class template. For example, if the template is `SmartPtr<T>`, you can specialize any member function for, say, `SmartPtr<Widget>`. This gives you good granularity in customizing behavior.

Furthermore, for class templates you can use partial template specialization (as shown in Chapter 2). Partial template specialization gives you the ability to specialize a class template for only some of its arguments. For example, given the definition

```
template <class T, class U> class SmartPtr { ... };
```

you can specialize `SmartPtr<T, U>` for `Widget` and any other type using the following syntax:

```
template <class U> class SmartPtr<Widget, U> { ... };
```

The innate compile-time and combinatorial nature of templates makes them very attractive for creating design pieces. As soon as you try to implement such designs, you stumble upon several problems that are not self-evident:

1. *You cannot specialize structure.* Using templates alone, you cannot specialize the structure of a class (its data members). You can only specialize functions.
2. *Partial specialization of member functions does not scale.* You can specialize any member function of a class template with one template parameter, but you cannot specialize individual member functions for templates with multiple template parameters. For example:

```
template <class T> class Widget
{
    void Fun() { .. generic implementation ... }
};
// OK: specialization of a member function of Widget
template <> void Widget<char>::Fun()
{
    ... specialized implementation ...
}
template <class T, class U> class Gadget
{
    void Fun() { .. generic implementation ... }
};
// Error! Cannot partially specialize a member function of Gadget
template <class U> void Gadget<char, U>::Fun()
{
    ... specialized implementation ...
}
```

3. *The library writer cannot provide multiple default values.* At best, a class template implementer can provide a single default implementation for each member function. You cannot provide *several* defaults for a template member function.

Now compare the list of drawbacks of multiple inheritance with the list of drawbacks of templates. Interestingly, multiple inheritance and templates foster complementary trade-offs. Multiple inheritance has scarce mechanics; templates have rich mechanics. Multiple inheritance loses type information, which abounds in templates. Specialization of templates does not scale, but multiple inheritance scales quite nicely. You can provide only one default for a template member function, but you can write an unbounded number of base classes.

This analysis suggests that a combination of templates and multiple inheritance could engender a very flexible device, appropriate for creating libraries of design elements.

1.5 Policies and Policy Classes

Policies and policy classes help in implementing safe, efficient, and highly customizable design elements. A *policy* defines a class interface or a class template interface. The interface consists of one or all of the following: inner type definitions, member functions, and member variables.

Policies have much in common with traits (Alexandrescu 2000a) but differ in that they put less emphasis on type and more emphasis on behavior. Also, policies are reminiscent of the Strategy design pattern (Gamma et al. 1995), with the twist that policies are bound at compilation time.

For example, let's define a policy for creating objects. The **Creator** policy prescribes a class template of type T. This class template must expose a member function called `Create` that takes no arguments and returns a pointer to T. Semantically, each call to `Create` should return a pointer to a new object of type T. The exact mode in which the object is created is left to the latitude of the policy implementation.

Let's define some policy classes that implement the **Creator** policy. One possible way is to use the new operator. Another way is to use `malloc` and a call to the placement new operator (Meyers 1998b). Yet another way would be to create new objects by cloning a prototype object. Here are examples of all three methods:

```cpp
template <class T>
struct OpNewCreator
{
    static T* Create()
    {
        return new T;
    }
};

template <class T>
struct MallocCreator
{
    static T* Create()
    {
        void* buf = std::malloc(sizeof(T));
        if (!buf) return 0;
        return new(buf) T;
    }
};

template <class T>
struct PrototypeCreator
{
    PrototypeCreator(T* pObj = 0)
        :pPrototype_(pObj)
    {}
    T* Create()
    {
        return pPrototype_ ? pPrototype_->Clone() : 0;
    }
    T* GetPrototype() { return pPrototype_; }
    void SetPrototype(T* pObj) { pPrototype_ = pObj; }
private:
    T* pPrototype_;
};
```

For a given policy, there can be an unlimited number of implementations. The implementations of a policy are called *policy classes*.[2] Policy classes are not intended for stand-alone use; instead, they are inherited by, or contained within, other classes.

An important aspect is that, unlike classic interfaces (collections of pure virtual functions), policies' interfaces are loosely defined. Policies are syntax oriented, not signature oriented. In other words, Creator specifies which syntactic constructs should be valid for a conforming class, rather than which exact functions that class must implement. For example, the Creator policy does not specify that Create must be static or virtual—the only requirement is that the class template define a Create member function. Also, Creator says that Create *should* return a pointer to a new object (as opposed to *must*). Consequently, it is acceptable that in special cases, Create might return zero or throw an exception.

You can implement several policy classes for a given policy. They all must respect the interface as defined by the policy. The user then chooses which policy class to use in larger structures, as Part II of this book shows.

The three policy classes defined earlier have different implementations and even slightly different interfaces (for example, PrototypeCreator has two extra functions: GetPrototype and SetPrototype). However, they all define a function called Create with the required return type, so they conform to the Creator policy.

Let's see now how we can design a class that exploits the Creator policy. Such a class will either contain or inherit one of the three classes defined previously, as shown in the following:

```
// Library code
template <class CreationPolicy>
class WidgetManager : public CreationPolicy
{
    ...
};
```

The classes that use one or more policies are called *hosts* or *host classes*.[3] In the example above, WidgetManager is a host class with one policy. Hosts are responsible for assembling the structures and behaviors of their policies in a single complex unit.

When instantiating the WidgetManager template, the client passes the desired policy:

```
// Application code
typedef WidgetManager< OpNewCreator<Widget> > MyWidgetMgr;
```

Let's analyze the resulting context. Whenever an object of type MyWidgetMgr needs to create a Widget, it invokes Create() for its OpNewCreator<Widget> policy subobject. However, it is the user of WidgetManager who chooses the creation policy. Effectively, through its design, WidgetManager allows its users to configure a specific aspect of WidgetManager's functionality.

This is the gist of policy-based class design.

---

[2]This name is slightly inaccurate because, as you will see soon, policy implementations can be class *templates*.
[3]Although host classes are technically host class *templates*, let's stick to a unique definition. Both host classes and host class templates serve the same concept.

1.5.1 Implementing Policy Classes with Template Template Parameters

Often, as is the case above, the policy's template argument is redundant. It is awkward that the user must pass OpNewCreator's template argument explicitly. Typically, the host class already knows, or can easily deduce, the template argument of the policy class. In the example above, WidgetManager always manages objects of type Widget, so requiring the user to specify Widget again in the instantiation of OpNewCreator is redundant and potentially dangerous.

In this case, library code can use *template template parameters* for specifying policies, as shown in the following:

```
// Library code
template <template <class Created> class CreationPolicy>
class WidgetManager : public CreationPolicy<Widget>
{
    ...
};
```

In spite of appearances, the Created symbol does not contribute to the definition of WidgetManager. You cannot use Created inside WidgetManager—it is a formal argument for CreationPolicy (not WidgetManager) and can be simply omitted.

Application code now only needs to provide the name of the template in instantiating WidgetManager:

```
// Application code
typedef WidgetManager<OpNewCreator> MyWidgetMgr;
```

Using template template parameters with policy classes is not simply a matter of convenience; sometimes, it is essential that the host class have access to the template so that the host can instantiate it with a different type. For example, assume WidgetManager also needs to create objects of type Gadget using the same creation policy. Then the code would look like this:

```
// Library code
template <template <class> class CreationPolicy>
class WidgetManager : public CreationPolicy<Widget>
{
    ...
    void DoSomething()
    {
        Gadget* pW = CreationPolicy<Gadget>().Create();
        ...
    }
};
```

Does using policies give you an edge? At first sight, not a lot. For one thing, all implementations of the **Creator** policy are trivially simple. The author of WidgetManager could certainly have written the creation code inline and avoided the trouble of making WidgetManager a template.

But using policies gives great flexibility to `WidgetManager`. First, you can change policies *from the outside* as easily as changing a template argument when you instantiate `WidgetManager`. Second, you can provide your own policies that are specific to your concrete application. You can use `new`, `malloc`, prototypes, or a peculiar memory allocation library that only your system uses. *It is as if* `WidgetManager` *were a little code generation engine, and you configure the ways in which it generates code.*

To ease the lives of application developers, `WidgetManager`'s author might define a battery of often-used policies and, in addition, provide a default template argument for the policy that's most commonly used:

```
template <template <class> class CreationPolicy = OpNewCreator>
class WidgetManager ...
```

Note that policies are quite different from mere virtual functions. Virtual functions promise a similar effect: The implementer of a class defines higher-level functions in terms of primitive virtual functions and lets the user override the behavior of those primitives. As shown above, however, policies come with enriched type knowledge and static binding, which are essential ingredients for building designs. Aren't designs full of rules that dictate *before runtime* how types interact with each other and what you can and what you cannot do? Policies allow you to generate designs by combining simple choices in a type-safe manner. In addition, because the binding between a host class and its policies is done at compile time, the code is tight and efficient, comparable to its handcrafted equivalent.

Of course, policies' features also make them unsuitable for dynamic binding and binary interfaces, so in essence policies and classic interfaces do not compete.

1.5.2 Implementing Policy Classes with Template Member Functions

An alternative to using template template parameters is to use template member functions in conjunction with simple classes. That is, the policy implementation is a simple class (as opposed to a template class) but has one or more templated members.

For example, we can redefine the **Creator** policy to prescribe a regular (nontemplate) class that exposes a template function `Create<T>`. A conforming policy class looks like the following:

```
struct OpNewCreator
{
    template <class T>
    static T* Create()
    {
        return new T;
    }
};
```

This way of defining and implementing a policy has the advantage of being better supported by older compilers. On the other hand, policies defined this way might be harder to talk about, define, implement, and use.

1.6 Enriched Policies

The Creator policy prescribes only one member function, Create. However, Prototype-Creator defines two more functions: GetPrototype and SetPrototype. Let's analyze the resulting context.

Because WidgetManager inherits its policy class and because GetPrototype and Set-Prototype are public members of PrototypeCreator, the two functions propagate through WidgetManager and are directly accessible to clients.

However, WidgetManager asks only for the Create member function; that's all WidgetManager needs and uses for ensuring its own functionality. Users, however, can exploit the enriched interface.

A user who uses a prototype-based Creator policy class can write the following code:

```
typedef WidgetManager<PrototypeCreator>
    MyWidgetManager;
...
Widget* pPrototype = ...;
MyWidgetManager mgr;
mgr.SetPrototype(pPrototype);
... use mgr ...
```

If the user later decides to use a creation policy that does not support prototypes, the compiler pinpoints the spots where the prototype-specific interface was used. This is exactly what should be expected from a sound design.

The resulting context is very favorable. Clients who need enriched policies can benefit from that rich functionality, without affecting the basic functionality of the host class. Don't forget that *users*—and not the library—decide which policy class to use. Unlike regular multiple interfaces, policies give the user the ability to add functionality to a host class, in a typesafe manner.

1.7 Destructors of Policy Classes

There is an additional important detail about creating policy classes. Most often, the host class uses public inheritance to derive from its policies. For this reason, the user can automatically convert a host class pointer to a policy pointer and later delete the host class object through this pointer. Unless the policy class defines a virtual destructor, applying delete to a pointer to the policy class has undefined behavior,[4] as shown below.

```
typedef WidgetManager<PrototypeCreator>
    MyWidgetManager;
...
MyWidgetManager wm;
PrototypeCreator<Widget>* pCreator = &wm; // dubious, but legal
delete pCreator;  // compiles fine, but has undefined behavior
```

Defining a virtual destructor for a policy, however, works against its static nature and hurts performance. Many policies don't have any data members, but rather are purely be-

[4]In Chapter 4, Small-Object Allocation, you can find a discussion on exactly why this happens.

havioral by nature. The first virtual function added incurs some size overhead for the objects of that class, so the virtual destructor should be avoided.

A solution is to have the host class use protected or private inheritance when deriving from the policy class. However, this would disable enriched policies as well (Section 1.6).

The lightweight, effective solution that policies should use is to define a nonvirtual protected destructor:

```
template <class T>
struct OpNewCreator
{
    static T* Create()
    {
        return new T;
    }
protected:
    ~OpNewCreator() {}
};
```

Because the destructor is protected, only derived classes can destroy policy objects, so it's impossible for outsiders to apply delete to a pointer to a policy class. The destructor, however, is not virtual, so there is no size or speed overhead.

1.8 Optional Functionality Through Incomplete Instantiation

It gets even better. C++ contributes to the power of policies by providing an interesting feature. If a member function of a class template is never used, it is not even instantiated—the compiler does not look at it at all, except perhaps for syntax checking.[5]

This gives the host class a chance to specify and use optional features of a policy class. For example, let's define a SwitchPrototype member function for WidgetManager.

```
// Library code
template <template <class> class CreationPolicy>
class WidgetManager : public CreationPolicy<Widget>
{
    ...
    void SwitchPrototype(Widget* pNewPrototype)
    {
        CreationPolicy<Widget>& myPolicy = *this;
        delete myPolicy.GetPrototype();
        myPolicy.SetPrototype(pNewPrototype);
    }
};
```

The resulting context is very interesting:

- If the user instantiates WidgetManager with a Creator policy class that supports prototypes, she can use SwitchPrototype.

---

[5]According to the C++ standard, the degree of syntax checking for unused template functions is up to the implementation. The compiler does not do any semantic checking—for example, symbols are not looked up.

- If the user instantiates WidgetManager with a **Creator** policy class that does not support prototypes and tries to use SwitchPrototype, a compile-time error occurs.
- If the user instantiates WidgetManager with a **Creator** policy class that does not support prototypes and does not try to use SwitchPrototype, the program is valid.

This all means that WidgetManager can benefit from optional enriched interfaces but still work correctly with poorer interfaces—as long as you don't try to use certain member functions of WidgetManager.

The author of WidgetManager can define the **Creator** policy in the following manner:

> **Creator** prescribes a class template of one type T that exposes a member function Create. Create should return a pointer to a new object of type T. Optionally, the implementation can define two additional member functions—T* GetPrototype() and SetPrototype(T*)—having the semantics of getting and setting a prototype object used for creation. In this case, WidgetManager exposes the SwitchPrototype(T* pNewPrototype) member function, which deletes the current prototype and sets it to the incoming argument.

In conjunction with policy classes, incomplete instantiation brings remarkable freedom to you as a library designer. You can implement lean host classes that are able to use additional features and degrade graciously, allowing for Spartan, minimal policies.

1.9 Combining Policy Classes

The greatest usefulness of policies is apparent when you combine them. Typically, a highly configurable class uses several policies for various aspects of its workings. Then the library user selects the desired high-level behavior by combining several policy classes.

For example, consider designing a generic smart pointer class. (Chapter 7 builds a full implementation.) Say you identify two design choices that you should establish with policies: threading model and checking before dereferencing. Then you implement a SmartPtr class template that uses two policies, as shown:

```
template
<
    class T,
    template <class> class CheckingPolicy,
    template <class> class ThreadingModel
>
class SmartPtr;
```

SmartPtr has three template parameters: the pointee type and two policies. Inside SmartPtr, you orchestrate the two policies into a sound implementation. SmartPtr becomes a coherent shell that integrates several policies, rather than a rigid, canned implementation. By designing SmartPtr this way, you allow the user to configure SmartPtr with a simple typedef:

```
typedef SmartPtr<Widget, NoChecking, SingleThreaded>
    WidgetPtr;
```

Inside the same application, you can define and use several smart pointer classes:

```
typedef SmartPtr<Widget, EnforceNotNull, SingleThreaded>
    SafeWidgetPtr;
```

The two policies can be defined as follows:

Checking: The `CheckingPolicy<T>` class template must expose a `Check` member function, callable with an lvalue of type `T*`. `SmartPtr` calls `Check`, passing it the pointee object before dereferencing it.

ThreadingModel: The `ThreadingModel<T>` class template must expose an inner type called `Lock`, whose constructor accepts a `T&`. For the lifetime of a `Lock` object, operations on the `T` object are serialized.

For example, here is the implementation of the `NoChecking` and `EnforceNotNull` policy classes:

```
template <class T> struct NoChecking
{
    static void Check(T*) {}
};
template <class T> struct EnforceNotNull
{
    class NullPointerException : public std::exception { ... };
    static void Check(T* ptr)
    {
        if (!ptr) throw NullPointerException();
    }
};
```

By plugging in various checking policy classes, you can implement various behaviors. You can even initialize the pointer with a default value by accepting a reference to a pointer, as shown:

```
template <class T> struct EnsureNotNull
{
    static void Check(T*& ptr)
    {
        if (!ptr) ptr = GetDefaultValue();
    }
};
```

`SmartPtr` uses the **Checking** policy this way:

```
template
<
    class T,
    template <class> class CheckingPolicy,
    template <class> class ThreadingModel
>
class SmartPtr
    : public CheckingPolicy<T>
```

```
    , public ThreadingModel<SmartPtr>
{
    ...
    T* operator->()
    {
        typename ThreadingModel<SmartPtr>::Lock guard(*this);
        CheckingPolicy<T>::Check(pointee_);
        return pointee_;
    }
private:
    T* pointee_;
};
```

Notice the use of both the CheckingPolicy and ThreadingModel policy classes in the same function. Depending on the two template arguments, SmartPtr::operator-> behaves differently on two orthogonal dimensions. Such is the power of combining policies.

If you manage to decompose a class in orthogonal policies, you can cover a large spectrum of behaviors with a small amount of code.

1.10 Customizing Structure with Policy Classes

One of the limitations of templates, mentioned in Section 1.4, is that you cannot use templates to customize the structure of a class—only its behavior. Policy-based designs, however, do support structural customization in a natural manner.

Suppose that you want to support nonpointer representations for SmartPtr. For example, on certain platforms some pointers might be represented by a handle—an integral value that you pass to a system function to obtain the actual pointer. To solve this you might "indirect" the pointer access through a policy, say, a Structure policy. The Structure policy abstracts the pointer storage. Consequently, Structure should expose types called PointerType (the type of a pointer to the pointed-to object) and ReferenceType (the type of a reference to the pointed-to object) and functions such as GetPointer and SetPointer.

The fact that the pointer type is not hardcoded to T* has important advantages. For example, you can use SmartPtr with nonstandard pointer types (such as near and far pointers on segmented architectures), or you can easily implement clever solutions such as before and after functions (Stroustrup 2000a). The possibilities are extremely interesting.

The default storage of a smart pointer is a plain-vanilla pointer adorned with the Structure policy interface, as shown in the following code.

```
template <class T>
class DefaultSmartPtrStorage
{
public:
    typedef T* PointerType;
    typedef T& ReferenceType;
protected:
    PointerType GetPointer() { return ptr_; }
    void SetPointer(PointerType ptr)
```

```
      { ptr_ = ptr; }
   private:
      PointerType ptr_;
   };
```

The actual storage used is completely hidden behind Structure's interface. Now SmartPtr can use a Storage policy instead of aggregating a T*.

```
   template
   <
      class T,
      template <class> class CheckingPolicy,
      template <class> class ThreadingModel,
      template <class> class Storage = DefaultSmartPtrStorage
   >
   class SmartPtr;
```

Of course, SmartPtr must either derive from Storage<T> or aggregate a Storage<T> object in order to embed the needed structure.

1.11 Compatible and Incompatible Policies

Suppose you create two instantiations of SmartPtr: FastWidgetPtr, a pointer without checking, and SafeWidgetPtr, a pointer with checking before dereference. An interesting question is: Should you be able to assign FastWidgetPtr objects to SafeWidgetPtr objects? Should you be able to assign them the other way around? If you want to allow such conversions, how can you implement that?

Starting from the reasoning that SafeWidgetPtr is more restrictive than FastWidgetPtr, it is natural to accept the conversion from FastWidgetPtr to SafeWidgetPtr. This is because C++ already supports implicit conversions that increase restrictions—namely, from non-const to const types.

On the other hand, freely converting SafeWidgetPtr objects to FastWidgetPtr objects is dangerous. This is because in an application, the majority of code would use SafeWidgetPtr and only a small, speed-critical core would use FastWidgetPtr. Allowing only explicit, controlled conversions to FastWidgetPtr would help keep FastWidgetPtr's usage to a minimum.

The best, most scalable way to implement conversions between policies is to initialize and copy SmartPtr objects *policy by policy*, as shown below. (Let's simplify the code by getting back to only one policy—the Checking policy.)

```
   template
   <
      class T,
      template <class> class CheckingPolicy
   >
   class SmartPtr : public CheckingPolicy<T>
   {
      ...
      template
```

```
    <
        class T1,
        template <class> class CP1
    >
    SmartPtr(const SmartPtr<T1, CP1>& other)
        : pointee_(other.pointee_), CheckingPolicy<T>(other)
    { ... }
    template <class T1, template<class> class CP1>
    friend class SmartPtr;
};
```

SmartPtr implements a templated copy constructor, which accepts any other instantiation of SmartPtr. The code in bold initializes the components of SmartPtr with the components of the other SmartPtr<T1,CP1> received as arguments.

Here's how it works. (Follow the constructor code.) Assume you have a class ExtendedWidget, derived from Widget. If you initialize a SmartPtr<Widget,NoChecking> with a SmartPtr<ExtendedWidget, NoChecking>, the compiler attempts to initialize a Widget* with an ExtendedWidget* (which works), and a NoChecking with a SmartPtr <ExtendedWidget,NoChecking>. This might look suspicious, but don't forget that SmartPtr derives from its policy, so in essence the compiler will easily figure out that you initialize a NoChecking with a NoChecking. The whole initialization works.

Now for the interesting part. Say you initialize a SmartPtr<Widget, EnforceNotNull> with a SmartPtr<ExtendedWidget, NoChecking>. The ExtendedWidget* to Widget* conversion works just as before. Then the compiler tries to match SmartPtr<ExtendedWidget, NoChecking> to EnforceNotNull's constructors.

If EnforceNotNull implements a constructor that accepts a NoChecking object, then the compiler matches that constructor. If NoChecking implements a conversion operator to EnforceNotNull, that conversion is invoked. In any other case, the code fails to compile.

As you can see, you have two-sided flexibility in implementing conversions between policies. You can implement a conversion constructor on the left-hand side, or you can implement a conversion operator on the right-hand side.

The assignment operator looks like an equally tricky problem, but fortunately, Sutter (2000) describes a very nifty technique that allows you to implement the assignment operator in terms of the copy constructor. (It's so nifty, you *have* to read about it. You can see the technique at work in Loki's SmartPtr implementation.)

Although conversions from NoChecking to EnforceNotNull and even vice versa are quite sensible, some conversions don't make any sense at all. Imagine converting a reference-counted pointer to a pointer that supports another ownership strategy, such as destructive copy (*à la* std::auto_ptr). Such a conversion is semantically wrong. The definition of reference counting is that all pointers to the same object are known and tracked by a unique counter. As soon as you try to confine a pointer to another ownership policy, you break the invariant that makes reference counting work.

In conclusion, conversions that change the ownership policy should not be allowed implicitly and should be treated with maximum care. At best, you can change the ownership policy of a reference-counted pointer by explicitly calling a function. That function succeeds if and only if the reference count of the source pointer is 1.

1.12 Decomposing a Class into Policies

The hardest part of creating policy-based class design is to correctly decompose the functionality of a class in policies. The rule of thumb is to identify and name the design decisions that take part in a class's behavior. Anything that can be done in more than one way should be identified and migrated from the class to a policy. Don't forget: Design constraints buried in a class's design are as bad as magic constants buried in code.

For example, consider a `WidgetManager` class. If `WidgetManager` creates new `Widget` objects internally, creation should be deferred to a policy. If `WidgetManager` stores a collection of `Widget`s, it makes sense to make that collection a storage policy, unless there is a strong preference for a specific storage mechanism.

At an extreme, a host class is totally depleted of any intrinsic policy. It delegates all design decisions and constraints to policies. Such a host class is a shell over a collection of policies and deals only with assembling the policies into a coherent behavior.

The disadvantage of an overly generic host class is the abundance of template parameters. In practice, it is awkward to work with more than four to six template parameters. Still, they justify their presence if the host class offers complex, useful functionality.

Type definitions—`typedef` statements—are an essential tool in using classes that rely on policies. Using `typedef` is not merely a matter of convenience; it ensures ordered use and easy maintenance. For example, consider the following type definition:

```
typedef SmartPtr
<
    Widget,
    RefCounted,
    NoChecked
>
WidgetPtr;
```

It would be very tedious to use the lengthy specialization of `SmartPtr` instead of `WidgetPtr` in code. But the tediousness of writing code is nothing compared with the major problems in *understanding* and *maintaining* that code. As the design evolves, `WidgetPtr`'s definition might change—for example, to use a checking policy other than `NoChecked` in debug builds. It is essential that all the code use `WidgetPtr` instead of a hardcoded instantiation of `SmartPtr`. It's just like the difference between calling a function and writing the equivalent inline code: The inline code technically does the same thing but fails to build an abstraction behind it.

When you decompose a class in policies, it is very important to find an *orthogonal* decomposition. An orthogonal decomposition yields policies that are completely independent of each other. You can easily spot a nonorthogonal decomposition when various policies need to know about each other.

For example, think of an **Array** policy in a smart pointer. The **Array** policy is very simple—it dictates whether or not the smart pointer points to an array. The policy can be defined to have a member function `T& ElementAt(T* ptr, unsigned int index)`, plus a similar version for `const T`. The non-array policy simply does not define an `ElementAt` member function, so trying to use it would yield a compile-time error. The ElementAt function is an optional enriched behavior as defined in Section 1.6.

The implementations of two policy classes that implement the **Array** policy follow.

```
template <class T>
struct IsArray
{
    T& ElementAt(T* ptr, unsigned int index)
    {
        return ptr[index];
    }
    const T& ElementAt(T* ptr, unsigned int index) const
    {
        return ptr[index];
    }
};
template <class T> struct IsNotArray {};
```

The problem is that purpose of the Array policy—specifying whether or not the smart pointer points to an array—interacts unfavorably with another policy: destruction. You must destroy pointers to objects using the delete operator, and destroy pointers to arrays of objects using the delete[] operator.

Two policies that do not interact with each other are orthogonal. By this definition, the **Array** and the **Destroy** policies are not orthogonal.

If you still need to confine the qualities of being an array and of destruction to separate policies, you need to establish a way for the two policies to communicate. You must have the **Array** policy expose a Boolean constant in addition to a function, and pass that Boolean to the **Destroy** policy. This complicates and somewhat constrains the design of both the **Array** and the **Destroy** policies.

Nonorthogonal policies are an imperfection you should strive to avoid. They reduce compile-time type safety and complicate the design of both the host class and the policy classes.

If you must use nonorthogonal policies, you can minimize dependencies by passing a policy class as an argument to another policy class's template function. This way you can benefit from the flexibility specific to template-based interfaces. The downside remains that one policy must expose some of its implementation details to other policies. This decreases encapsulation.

1.13 Summary

Design is choice. Most often, the struggle is not that there is no way to solve a design problem, but that there are too many ways that apparently solve the problem. You must know which collection of solutions solves the problem in a satisfactory manner. The need to choose propagates from the largest architectural levels down to the smallest unit of code. Furthermore, choices can be combined, which confers on design an evil multiplicity.

To fight the multiplicity of design with a reasonably small amount of code, a writer of a design-oriented library needs to develop and use special techniques. These techniques are purposely conceived to support flexible code generation by combining a small number of primitive devices. The library itself provides a number of such devices. Furthermore, the library exposes the *specifications* from which these devices are built, so the client can build her own. This essentially makes a policy-based design open-ended. These devices are called *policies*, and the implementations thereof are called *policy classes*.

The mechanics of policies consist of a combination of templates with multiple inheritance. A class that uses policies—a *host* class—is a template with many template parameters (often, *template template parameters*), each parameter being a policy. The host class "indirects" parts of its functionality through its policies and acts as a receptacle that combines several policies in a coherent aggregate.

Classes designed around policies support enriched behavior and graceful degradation of functionality. A policy can provide supplemental functionality that propagates through the host class due to public inheritance. Furthermore, the host class can implement enriched functionality that uses the optional functionality of a policy. If the optional functionality is not present, the host class still compiles successfully, provided the enriched functionality is not used.

The power of policies comes from their ability to mix and match. A policy-based class can accommodate very many behaviors by combining the simpler behaviors that its policies implement. This effectively makes policies a good weapon for fighting against the evil multiplicity of design.

Using policy classes, you can customize not only behavior but also structure. This important feature takes policy-based design beyond the simple type genericity that's specific to container classes.

Policy-based classes support flexibility when it comes to conversions. If you use policy-by-policy copying, each policy can control which other policies it accepts, or converts to, by providing the appropriate conversion constructors, conversion operators, or both.

In breaking a class into policies, you should follow two important guidelines. One is to localize, name, and isolate design decisions in your class—things that are subject to a trade-off or could be sensibly implemented in various ways. The other guideline is to look for orthogonal policies, that is, policies that don't need to interact with each other and that can be changed independently.

2

Techniques

This chapter presents a host of C++ techniques that are used throughout the book. Because they are of help in various contexts, the techniques presented tend to be general and reusable, so you might find applications for them in other contexts. Some of the techniques, such as partial template specialization, are language features. Others, such as compile-time assertions, come with some support code.

In this chapter you will get acquainted with the following techniques and tools:

- Compile-time assertions
- Partial template specialization
- Local classes
- Mappings between types and values (the Int2Type and Type2Type class templates)
- The Select class template, a tool that chooses a type at compile time based on a Boolean condition
- Detecting convertibility and inheritance at compile time
- TypeInfo, a handy wrapper around std::type_info
- Traits, a collection of traits that apply to any C++ type

Taken in isolation, each technique and its support code might look trivial; the norm is five to ten lines of easy-to-understand code. However, the techniques have an important property: They are "nonterminal"; that is, you can combine them to generate higher-level idioms. Together, they form a strong foundation of services that helps in building powerful architectural structures.

The techniques come with examples, so don't expect the discussion to be dry. As you read through the rest of the book, you might want to return to this chapter for reference.

2.1 Compile-Time Assertions

As generic programming in C++ took off, the need for better static checking (and better, more customizable error messages) emerged.

Suppose, for instance, you are developing a function for safe casting. You want to cast from one type to another, while making sure that information is preserved; larger types must not be cast to smaller types.

```
template <class To, class From>
To safe_reinterpret_cast(From from)
{
    assert(sizeof(From) <= sizeof(To));
    return reinterpret_cast<To>(from);
}
```

You call this function using the same syntax as the native C++ casts:

```
int i = ...;
char* p = safe_reinterpret_cast<char*>(i);
```

You specify the To template argument explicitly, and the compiler deduces the From template argument from i's type. By asserting on the size comparison, you ensure that the destination type can hold all the bits of the source type. This way, the code above yields either an allegedly correct cast[1] or an assertion at runtime.

Obviously, it would be more desirable to detect such an error during compilation. For one thing, the cast might be on a seldom-executed branch of your program. As you port the application to a new compiler or platform, you cannot remember every potentially nonportable part and might leave the bug dormant until it crashes the program in front of your customer.

There is hope; the expression being evaluated is a compile-time constant, which means that you can have the compiler, instead of runtime code, check it. The idea is to pass the compiler a language construct that is legal for a nonzero expression and illegal for an expression that evaluates to zero. This way, if you pass an expression that evaluates to zero, the compiler will signal a compile-time error.

The simplest solution to compile-time assertions (Van Horn 1997), and one that works in C as well as in C++, relies on the fact that a zero-length array is illegal.

```
#define STATIC_CHECK(expr) { char unnamed[(expr) ? 1 : 0]; }
```

Now if you write

```
template <class To, class From>
To safe_reinterpret_cast(From from)
{
    STATIC_CHECK(sizeof(From) <= sizeof(To));
    return reinterpret_cast<To>(from);
}
...
void* somePointer = ...;
char c = safe_reinterpret_cast<char>(somePointer);
```

and if on your system pointers are larger than characters, the compiler complains that you are trying to create an array of length zero.

The problem with this approach is that the error message you receive is not terribly informative. "Cannot create array of size zero" does not suggest "Type char is too narrow to hold a pointer." It is very hard to provide customized error messages portably. Error

---

[1] On most machines, that is—with reinterpret_cast, you can never be sure.

messages have no rules that they must obey; it's all up to the compiler. For instance, if the error refers to an undefined variable, the name of that variable does not necessarily appear in the error message.

A better solution is to rely on a template with an informative name; with luck, the compiler will mention the name of that template in the error message.

```
template<bool> struct CompileTimeError;
template<> struct CompileTimeError<true> {};

#define STATIC_CHECK(expr) \
    (CompileTimeError<(expr) != 0>())
```

CompileTimeError is a template taking a nontype parameter (a Boolean constant). Compile-TimeError is defined only for the true value of the Boolean constant. If you try to instantiate CompileTimeError<false>, the compiler utters a message such as "Undefined specialization CompileTimeError<false>." This message is a slightly better hint that the error is intentional and not a compiler or a program bug.

Of course, there's a lot of room for improvement. What about customizing that error message? An idea is to pass an additional parameter to STATIC_CHECK and somehow make that parameter appear in the error message. The disadvantage that remains is that the custom error message you pass must be a legal C++ identifier (no spaces, cannot start with a digit, and so on). This line of thought leads to an improved CompileTimeError, as shown in the following code. Actually, the name CompileTimeError is no longer suggestive in the new context; as you'll see in a minute, CompileTimeChecker makes more sense.

```
template<bool> struct CompileTimeChecker
{
    CompileTimeChecker(...);
}
template<> struct CompileTimeChecker<false> { };
#define STATIC_CHECK(expr, msg) \
{\
        class ERROR_##msg; \
        (void)sizeof(::Loki::CompileTimeChecker<\
            (expr) !=0>((ERROR_##msg()))));\
}
```

Assume that sizeof(char) < sizeof(void*). (The standard does not guarantee that this is necessarily true.) Let's see what happens when you write the following:

```
template <class To, class From>
To safe_reinterpret_cast(From from)
{
    STATIC_CHECK(sizeof(From) <= sizeof(To),
        Destination_Type_Too_Narrow);
    return reinterpret_cast<To>(from);
}
...
void* somePointer = ...;
char c = safe_reinterpret_cast<char>(somePointer);
```

After macro preprocessing, the code of safe_reinterpret_cast expands to the following:

```
template <class To, class From>
To safe_reinterpret_cast(From from)
{
   {
      class ERROR_Destination_Type_Too_Narrow {};
      (void)sizeof(
         CompileTimeChecker<(sizeof(From) <= sizeof(To))>((
            ERROR_Destination_Type_Too_Narrow()))));
   }
   return reinterpret_cast<To>(from);
}
```

The code defines a *local class* called ERROR_Destination_Type_Too_Narrow that has an empty body. Then, it creates a temporary value of type CompileTimeChecker< (sizeof(From) <= sizeof(To))>, initialized with a temporary value of type ERROR_Destination_Type_Too_Narrow. Finally, sizeof gauges the size of the resulting temporary value.

Now here's the trick. The CompileTimeChecker<true> specialization has a constructor that accepts anything; it's an ellipsis function. This means that if the compile-time expression checked evaluates to true, the resulting program is valid. If the comparison between sizes evaluates to false, a compile-time error occurs: The compiler cannot find a conversion from an ERROR_Destination_Type_Too_Narrow to a CompileTimeChecker<false>. And the nicest thing of all is that a decent compiler outputs an error message such as "Error: Cannot convert ERROR_Destination_Type_Too_Narrow to CompileTimeChecker <false>."

Bingo!

2.2 Partial Template Specialization

Partial template specialization allows you to specialize a class template for subsets of that template's possible instantiations set.

Let's first recap total explicit template specialization. If you have a class template Widget,

```
template <class Window, class Controller>
class Widget
{
   ... generic implementation ...
};
```

then you can explicitly specialize the Widget class template as shown:

```
template <>
class Widget<ModalDialog, MyController>
{
   ... specialized implementation ...
};
```

ModalDialog and MyController are classes defined by your application.

After seeing the definition of Widget's specialization, the compiler uses the specialized implementation wherever you define an object of type Widget<ModalDialog, MyController> and uses the generic implementation if you use any other instantiation of Widget.

Sometimes, however, you might want to specialize Widget for *any* Window and MyController. Here is where partial template specialization comes into play.

```
// Partial specialization of Widget
template <class Window>
class Widget<Window, MyController>
{
    ... partially specialized implementation ...
};
```

Typically, in a partial specialization of a class template, you specify only some of the template arguments and leave the other ones generic. When you instantiate the class template in your program, the compiler tries to find the best match. The matching algorithm is very intricate and accurate, allowing you to partially specialize in innovative ways. For instance, assume you have a class template Button that accepts one template parameter. Then, even if you specialized Widget for any Window and a specific MyController, you can further partially specialize Widgets for *all* Button instantiations and MyController:

```
template <class ButtonArg>
class Widget<Button<ButtonArg>, MyController>
{
    ... further specialized implementation ...
};
```

As you can see, the capabilities of partial template specialization are pretty amazing. When you instantiate a template, the compiler does a *pattern matching* of existing partial and total specializations to find the best candidate; this gives you enormous flexibility.

Unfortunately, partial template specialization does not apply to functions—be they member or nonmember—which somewhat reduces the flexibility and the granularity of what you can do.

- Although you can *totally specialize* member functions of a class template, you cannot *partially specialize* member functions.
- You cannot partially specialize namespace-level (nonmember) template functions. The closest thing to partial specialization for namespace-level template functions is overloading. For practical purposes, this means that you have fine-grained specialization abilities only for the function parameters—not for the return value or for internally used types. For example,

```
template <class T, class U> T Fun(U obj); // primary template
template <class U> void Fun<void, U>(U obj); // illegal partial
//        specialization
template <class T> T Fun (Window obj); // legal (overloading)
```

This lack of granularity in partial specialization certainly makes life easier for compiler writers, but has bad effects for developers. Some of the tools presented later (such as Int2Type and Type2Type) specifically address this limitation of partial specialization.

This book uses partial template specialization copiously. Virtually the entire typelist facility (Chapter 3) is built using this feature.

2.3 Local Classes

Local classes are an interesting and little-known feature of C++. You can define classes right inside functions, as follows:

```
void Fun()
{
    class Local
    {
        ... member variables ...
        ... member function definitions ...
    };
    ... code using Local ...
}
```

There are some limitations—local classes cannot define static member variables and cannot access nonstatic local variables. What makes local classes truly interesting is that you can use them in template functions. Local classes defined inside template functions can use the template parameters of the enclosing function.

The template function MakeAdapter in the following code adapts one interface to another. MakeAdapter implements an interface on the fly with the help of a local class. The local class stores members of generic types.

```
class Interface
{
public:
    virtual void Fun() = 0;
    ...
};
template <class T, class P>
Interface* MakeAdapter(const T& obj, const P& arg)
{
    class Local : public Interface
    {
    public:
        Local(const T& obj, const P& arg)
            : obj_(obj), arg_(arg) {}
        virtual void Fun()
        {
            obj_.Call(arg_);
        }
    private:
        T obj_;
        P arg_;
    };
    return new Local(obj, arg);
}
```

It can be easily proven that any idiom that uses a local class can be implemented using a template class outside the function. In other words, local classes are not an idiom-enabling feature. On the other hand, local classes can simplify implementations and improve locality of symbols.

Local classes do have a unique feature, though: They are *final*. Outside users cannot derive from a class hidden in a function. Without local classes, you'd have to add an unnamed namespace in a separate translation unit.

Chapter 11 uses local classes to create trampoline functions.

2.4 Mapping Integral Constants to Types

A simple template, initially described in Alexandrescu (2000b), can be very helpful to many generic programming idioms. Here it is:

```
template <int v>
struct Int2Type
{
    enum { value = v };
};
```

`Int2Type` generates a distinct type for each distinct constant integral value passed. This is because different template instantiations are distinct types; thus, `Int2Type<0>` is different from `Int2Type<1>`, and so on. In addition, the value that generates the type is "saved" in the `enum` member `value`.

You can use `Int2Type` whenever you need to "typify" an integral constant quickly. This way you can select different functions, depending on the result of a compile-time calculation. Effectively, you achieve static dispatching on a constant integral value.

Typically, you use `Int2Type` when both of the following conditions are satisfied:

* You need to call one of several different functions, depending on a compile-time constant.
* You need to do this dispatch at compile time.

For dispatching at runtime, you can use simple `if-else` statements or the `switch` statement. The runtime cost is negligible in most cases. However, you often cannot do this. The `if-else` statement requires both branches to compile successfully, even when the condition tested by `if` is known at compile time. Confused? Read on.

Consider this situation: You design a generic container `NiftyContainer`, which is templated by the type contained:

```
template <class T> class NiftyContainer
{
    ...
};
```

Say `NiftyContainer` contains pointers to objects of type T. To duplicate an object contained in `NiftyContainer`, you want to call either its copy constructor (for nonpolymorphic types) or a `Clone()` virtual function (for polymorphic types). You get this information from the user in the form of a Boolean template parameter.

```cpp
template <typename T, bool isPolymorphic>
class NiftyContainer
{
    ...
    void DoSomething()
    {
        T* pSomeObj = ...;
        if (isPolymorphic)
        {
            T* pNewObj = pSomeObj->Clone();
            ... polymorphic algorithm ...
        }
        else
        {
            T* pNewObj = new T(*pSomeObj);
            ... nonpolymorphic algorithm ...
        }
    }
};
```

The problem is that the compiler won't let you get away with this code. For example, because the polymorphic algorithm uses `pObj->Clone()`, `NiftyContainer::DoSomething` does not compile for any type that doesn't define a member function `Clone()`. True, it is obvious at compile time which branch of the `if` statement executes. However, that doesn't matter to the compiler—it diligently tries to compile both branches, even if the optimizer will later eliminate the dead code. If you try to call `DoSomething` for `NiftyContainer<int,false>`, the compiler stops at the `pObj->Clone()` call and says, "Huh?"

It is also possible for the nonpolymorphic branch of the code to fail to compile. If T is a polymorphic type and the nonpolymorphic code branch attempts `new T(*pObj)`, the code might fail to compile. This might happen if T has disabled its copy constructor (by making it private), as a well-behaved polymorphic class should.

It would be nice if the compiler didn't bother about compiling code that's dead anyway, but that's not the case. So what would be a satisfactory solution?

As it turns out, there are a number of solutions, and `Int2Type` provides a particularly clean one. It can transform ad hoc the Boolean value `isPolymorphic` into two distinct types corresponding to `isPolymorphic`'s `true` and `false` values. Then you can use `Int2Type<isPolymorphic>` with simple overloading, and *voilà*!

```cpp
template <typename T, bool isPolymorphic>
class NiftyContainer
{
private:
    void DoSomething(T* pObj, Int2Type<true>)
    {
        T* pNewObj = pObj->Clone();
        ... polymorphic algorithm ...
```

```
        }
        void DoSomething(T* pObj, Int2Type<false>)
        {
            T* pNewObj = new T(*pObj);
            ... nonpolymorphic algorithm ...
        }
    public:
        void DoSomething(T* pObj)
        {
            DoSomething(pObj, Int2Type<isPolymorphic>());
        }
    };
```

Int2Type comes in very handy as a means to translate a value into a type. You then pass a temporary value of that type to an overloaded function. The overloads implement the two needed algorithms.

The trick works because the compiler does not compile template functions that are never used—it only checks their syntax. And, of course, you usually perform dispatch at compile time in template code.

You will see Int2Type at work in several places in Loki, notably in Chapter 11, Multimethods. There, the template class is a double-dispatch engine, and the bool template parameter provides the option of supporting symmetric dispatch or not.

2.5 Type-to-Type Mapping

As Section 2.2 mentions, partial specialization for template functions does not exist. At times, however, you might need to simulate similar functionality. Consider the following function.

```
        template <class T, class U>
        T* Create(const U& arg)
        {
            return new T(arg);
        }
```

Create makes a new object, passing an argument to its constructor.

Now say there is a rule in your application: Objects of type Widget are untouchable legacy code and must take two arguments upon construction, the second being a fixed value such as −1. Your own classes, derived from Widget, don't have this problem.

How can you specialize Create so that it treats Widget differently from all other types? An obvious solution is to make a separate CreateWidget function that copes with the particular case. Unfortunately, now you don't have a uniform interface for creating Widgets and objects derived from Widget. This renders Create unusable in any generic code.

You cannot partially specialize a function; that is, you can't write something like this:

```
        // Illegal code - don't try this at home
        template <class U>
        Widget* Create<Widget, U>(const U& arg)
```

```
    {
        return new Widget(arg, -1);
    }
```

In the absence of partial specialization of functions, the only tool available is, again, overloading. A solution would be to pass a dummy object of type T and rely on overloading:

```
    template <class T, class U>
    T* Create(const U& arg, T /* dummy */)
    {
        return new T(arg);
    }
    template <class U>
    Widget* Create(const U& arg, Widget /* dummy */)
    {
        return new Widget(arg, -1);
    }
```

Such a solution would incur the overhead of constructing an arbitrarily complex object that remains unused. We need a light vehicle for transporting the type information about T to Create. This is the role of Type2Type: It is a type's representative, a light identifier that you can pass to overloaded functions.

The definition of Type2Type is as follows.

```
    template <typename T>
    struct Type2Type
    {
        typedef T OriginalType;
    };
```

Type2Type is devoid of any value, but distinct types lead to distinct Type2Type instantiations, which is what we need.

Now you can write the following:

```
    // An implementation of Create relying on overloading
    //         and Type2Type
    template <class T, class U>
    T* Create(const U& arg, Type2Type<T>)
    {
        return new T(arg);
    }
    template <class U>
    Widget* Create(const U& arg, Type2Type<Widget>)
    {
        return new Widget(arg, -1);
    }
    // Use Create()
    String* pStr = Create("Hello", Type2Type<String>());
    Widget* pW = Create(100, Type2Type<Widget>());
```

The second parameter of Create serves only to select the appropriate overload. Now you can specialize Create for various instantiations of Type2Type, which you map to various types in your application.

2.6 Type Selection

Sometimes generic code needs to select one type or another, depending on a Boolean constant.

In the NiftyContainer example discussed in Section 2.4, you might want to use an std::vector as your back-end storage. Obviously, you cannot store polymorphic types by value, so you must store pointers. On the other hand, you might want to store nonpolymorphic types by value, because that is more efficient.

In your class template,

```
template <typename T, bool isPolymorphic>
class NiftyContainer
{
    ...
};
```

you need to store either a vector<T*> (if isPolymorphic is true) or a vector<T> (if isPolymorphic is false). In essence, you need a typedef ValueType that is either T* or T, depending on the value of isPolymorphic.

You can use a traits class template (Alexandrescu 2000a), as follows.

```
template <typename T, bool isPolymorphic>
struct NiftyContainerValueTraits
{
    typedef T* ValueType;
};
template <typename T>
struct NiftyContainerValueTraits<T, false>
{
    typedef T ValueType;
};
template <typename T, bool isPolymorphic>
class NiftyContainer
{
    ...
    typedef NiftyContainerValueTraits<T, isPolymorphic>
        Traits;
    typedef typename Traits::ValueType ValueType;
};
```

This way of doing things is unnecessarily clumsy. Moreover, it doesn't scale: For each type selection, you must define a new traits class template.

The library class template Select provided by Loki makes type selection available right on the spot. Its definition uses partial template specialization.

```
template <bool flag, typename T, typename U>
struct Select
{
    typedef T Result;
};
template <typename T, typename U>
struct Select<false, T, U>
{
    typedef U Result;
};
```

Here's how it works. If flag evaluates to true, the compiler uses the first (generic) definition and therefore Result evaluates to T. If flag is false, then the specialization enters into action and therefore Result evaluates to U.

Now you can define NiftyContainer::ValueType much more easily.

```
template <typename T, bool isPolymorphic>
class NiftyContainer
{
    ...
    typedef typename Select<isPolymorphic, T*, T>::Result
        ValueType;
    ...
};
```

2.7 Detecting Convertibility and Inheritance at Compile Time

When you're implementing template functions and classes, a question arises every so often: Given two arbitrary types T and U that you know nothing about, how can you detect whether or not U inherits from T? Discovering such relationships at compile time is key to implementing advanced optimizations in generic libraries. In a generic function, you can rely on an optimized algorithm if a class implements a certain interface. Discovering this at compile time means not having to use dynamic_cast, which is costly at runtime.

Detecting inheritance relies on a more general mechanism, that of detecting convertibility. The more general problem is, How can you detect whether an arbitrary type T supports automatic conversion to an arbitrary type U?

There is a solution to this problem, and it relies on sizeof. There is a surprising amount of power in sizeof: You can apply sizeof to any expression, no matter how complex, and sizeof returns its size without actually evaluating that expression at runtime. This means that sizeof is aware of overloading, template instantiation, conversion rules—*everything* that can take part in a C++ expression. In fact, sizeof conceals a complete facility for deducing the type of an expression; eventually, sizeof throws away the expression and returns only the size of its result.[2]

The idea of conversion detection relies on using sizeof in conjunction with overloaded

---

[2] There is a proposal for adding a typeof operator to C++, that is, an operator returning the type of an expression. Having typeof would make much template code easier to write and understand. Gnu C++ already implements typeof as an extension. Obviously, typeof and sizeof share the same back end, because sizeof has to figure out the type anyway.

functions. We provide two overloads of a function: One accepts the type to convert to (U), and the other accepts just about anything else. We call the overloaded function with a temporary of type T, the type whose convertibility to U we want to determine. If the function that accepts a U gets called, we know that T is convertible to U; if the fallback function gets called, then T is not convertible to U. To detect which function gets called, we arrange the two overloads to return types of different sizes, and then we discriminate with sizeof. The types themselves do not matter, as long as they have different sizes.

Let's first create two types of different sizes. (Apparently, char and long double do have different sizes, but that's not guaranteed by the standard.) A foolproof scheme would be the following:

```
typedef char Small;
class Big { char dummy[2]; };
```

By definition, sizeof(Small) is 1. The size of Big is unknown, but it's certainly greater than 1, which is the only guarantee we need.

Next, we need the two overloads. One accepts a U and returns, say, a Small:

```
Small Test(U);
```

How can we write a function that accepts "anything else"? A template is not a solution because the template would always qualify as the best match, thus hiding the conversion. We need a match that's "worse" than an automatic conversion—that is, a conversion that kicks in if and only if there's no automatic conversion. A quick look through the conversion rules applied for a function call yields the ellipsis match, which is the worst of all—the bottom of the list. That's exactly what the doctor prescribed.

```
Big Test(...);
```

(Passing a C++ object to a function with ellipses has undefined results, but this doesn't matter. Nothing actually calls the function. It's not even implemented. Recall that sizeof does not evaluate its argument.)

Now we need to apply sizeof to the call of Test, passing it a T:

```
const bool convExists = sizeof(Test(T())) == sizeof(Small);
```

That's it! The call of Test gets a default-constructed object—T()—and then sizeof extracts the size of the result of that expression. It can be either sizeof(Small) or sizeof(Big), depending on whether or not the compiler found a conversion.

There is one little problem. If T makes its default constructor private, the expression T() fails to compile and so does all of our scaffolding. Fortunately, there is a simple solution—just use a strawman function returning a T. (Remember, we're in the sizeof wonderland where no expression is actually evaluated.) In this case, the compiler is happy and so are we.

```
T MakeT(); // not implemented
const bool convExists = sizeof(Test(MakeT())) == sizeof(Small);
```

(By the way, isn't it nifty just how much you can do with functions, like MakeT and Test, that not only don't do anything but don't even really exist at all?)

Now that we have it working, let's package everything in a class template that hides all the details of type deduction and exposes only the result.

```cpp
template <class T, class U>
class Conversion
{
    typedef char Small;
    class Big { char dummy[2]; };
    static Small Test( const U& );
    static Big Test(...);
    static T MakeT();
public:
    enum { exists =
        sizeof(Test(MakeT())) == sizeof(Small) };
};
```

Now you can test the Conversion class template by writing

```cpp
int main()
{
    using namespace std;
    cout
        << Conversion<double, int>::exists << ' '
        << Conversion<char, char*>::exists << ' '
        << Conversion<size_t, vector<int> >::exists << ' ';
}
```

This little program prints "1 0 0." Note that although std::vector does implement a constructor taking a size_t, the conversion test returns 0 because that constructor is explicit.

We can implement one more constant inside Conversion: sameType, which is true if T and U represent the same type:

```cpp
template <class T, class U>
class Conversion
{
    ... as above ...
    enum { sameType = false };
};
```

We implement sameType through a partial specialization of Conversion:

```cpp
template <class T>
class Conversion<T, T>
{
public:
    enum { exists = 1, sameType = 1 };
};
```

Finally, we're back home. With the help of `Conversion`, it is now very easy to determine inheritance:

```
#define SUPERSUBCLASS(T, U) \
    (::Loki::Conversion<const U*, const T*>::exists && \
    !::Loki::Conversion<const T*, const void*>::sameType)
```

`SUPERSUBCLASS(T, U)` evaluates to `true` if `U` inherits from `T` publicly, or if `T` and `U` are actually the same type. `SUPERSUBCLASS` does its job by evaluating the convertibility from a `const U*` to a `const T*`. There are only three cases in which `const U*` converts implicitly to `const T*`:

1. `T` is the same type as `U`.
2. `T` is an unambiguous public base of `U`.
3. `T` is `void`.

The last case is eliminated by the second test. In practice it's useful to accept the first case (`T` is the same as `U`) as a degenerated case of "is-a" because for practical purposes you can often consider a class to be its own superclass. If you need a stricter test, you can write it this way:

```
#define SUPERSUBCLASS_STRICT(T, U) \
    (SUPERSUBCLASS(T, U) && \
    !::Loki::Conversion<const T*, const U*>::sameType)
```

Why does the code add all those `const` modifiers? The reason is that we don't want the conversion test to fail due to `const` issues. If template code applies `const` twice (to a type that's already `const`), the second `const` is ignored. In a nutshell, by using `const` in `SUPERSUBCLASS`, we're always on the safe side.

Why use `SUPERSUBCLASS` and not the cuter `BASE_OF` or `INHERITS`? For a very practical reason. Initially Loki used `INHERITS`. But with `INHERITS(T,U)` it was a constant struggle to say which way the test worked—did it tell whether `T` inherited `U` or vice versa? Arguably, `SUPERSUBCLASS(T, U)` makes it clearer which one is first and which one is second.

2.8 A Wrapper Around `type_info`

Standard C++ provides the `std::type_info` class, which gives you the ability to investigate object types at runtime. You typically use `type_info` in conjunction with the `typeid` operator. The `typeid` operator returns a reference to a `type_info` object:

```
void Fun(Base* pObj)
{
    // Compare the two type_info objects corresponding
    // to the type of *pObj and Derived
```

```
        if (typeid(*pObj) == typeid(Derived))
        {
            ... aha, pObj actually points to a Derived object ...
        }
        ...
    }
```

In addition to supporting the comparison operators `operator==` and `operator!=`, `type_info` provides two more functions:

- The `name` member function returns a textual representation of a type, in the form of `const char*`. There is no standardized way of mapping class names to strings, so you shouldn't expect `typeid(Widget)` to return "`Widget`". A conforming (but not necessarily award-winning) implementation can have `type_info::name` return the empty string for all types.
- The `before` member function introduces an ordering relationship for `type_info` objects. Using `type_info::before`, you can perform indexing on `type_info` objects.

Unfortunately, `type_info`'s useful capabilities are packaged in a way that makes them unnecessarily hard to exploit. The `type_info` class disables the copy constructor and assignment operator, which makes storing `type_info` objects impossible. However, you can store *pointers* to `type_info` objects. The objects returned by `typeid` have static storage, so you don't have to worry about lifetime issues. You do have to worry about *pointer identity*, though.

The standard does not guarantee that each invocation of, say, `typeid(int)` returns a reference to the same `type_info` object. Consequently, you cannot compare pointers to `type_info` objects. What you should do is to store pointers to `type_info` objects and compare them by applying `type_info::operator==` to the dereferenced pointers.

If you want to sort `type_info` objects, again you must actually store pointers to `type_info`, and this time you must use the `before` member function. Consequently, if you want to use STL's ordered containers with `type_info`, you must write a little functor and deal with pointers.

All this is clumsy enough to mandate a wrapper class around `type_info` that stores a pointer to a `type_info` object and provides

- All the member functions of `type_info`
- Value semantics (public copy constructor and assignment operator)
- Seamless comparisons by defining `operator<` and `operator==`

Loki defines the wrapper class `TypeInfo` which implements such a handy wrapper around `type_info`. The synopsis of `TypeInfo` follows.

```
    class TypeInfo
    {
    public:
        // Constructors/destructors
        TypeInfo(); // needed for containers
        TypeInfo(const std::type_info&);
```

```
        TypeInfo(const TypeInfo&);
        TypeInfo& operator=(const TypeInfo&);
        // Compatibility functions
        bool before(const TypeInfo&) const;
        const char* name() const;
    private:
        const std::type_info* pInfo_;
    };
    // Comparison operators
    bool operator==(const TypeInfo&, const TypeInfo&);
    bool operator!=(const TypeInfo&, const TypeInfo&);
    bool operator<(const TypeInfo&, const TypeInfo&);
    bool operator<=(const TypeInfo&, const TypeInfo&);
    bool operator>(const TypeInfo&, const TypeInfo&);
    bool operator>=(const TypeInfo&, const TypeInfo&);
```

Because of the conversion constructor that accepts a std::type_info as a parameter, you can directly compare objects of type TypeInfo and std::type_info, as shown:

```
    void Fun(Base* pObj)
    {
        TypeInfo info = typeid(Derived);
        ...
        if (typeid(*pObj) == info)
        {
            ... pObj actually points to a Derived object ...
        }
        ...
    }
```

The ability to copy and compare TypeInfo objects is important in many situations. The cloning factory in Chapter 8 and one double-dispatch engine in Chapter 11 put TypeInfo to good use.

2.9 NullType and EmptyType

Loki defines two very simple types: NullType and EmptyType. You can use them in type calculations to mark certain border cases.

NullType is a class that serves as a null marker for types:

```
    class NullType {};
```

You usually don't create objects of type NullType—its only use is to indicate "I am not an interesting type." Section 2.10 uses NullType for cases in which a type must be there syntactically but doesn't have a semantic sense. (For example: "To what type does an int point?") Also, the typelist facility in Chapter 3 uses NullType to mark the end of a typelist and to return "type not found" information.

The second helper type is EmptyType. As you would expect, EmptyType's definition is

```
    struct EmptyType {};
```

EmptyType is a legal type to inherit from, and you can pass around values of type Empty-Type. You can use this insipid type as a default ("don't care") type for a template. The type-list facility in Chapter 3 uses EmptyType in such a way.

2.10 Type Traits

Traits are a generic programming technique that allows compile-time decisions to be made based on types, much as you would make runtime decisions based on values (Alexandrescu 2000a). By adding the proverbial "extra level of indirection" that solves many software engineering problems, traits let you take type-related decisions outside the immediate context in which they are made. This makes the resulting code cleaner, more readable, and easier to maintain.

Usually you will write your own trait templates and classes as your generic code needs them. Certain traits, however, are applicable to any type. They can help generic programmers to tailor template code better to the capabilities of a type.

Suppose, for instance, that you implement a copying algorithm:

```
template <typename InIt, typename OutIt>
OutIt Copy(InIt first, InIt last, OutIt result)
{
    for (; first != last; ++first, ++result)
        *result = *first;
    return result;
}
```

In theory, you shouldn't have to implement such an algorithm, because it duplicates the functionality of std::copy. But you might need to specialize your copying routine for specific types.

Let's say you develop code for a multiprocessor machine that has a very fast BitBlast fundamental function, and you would like to take advantage of that fundamental whenever possible.

```
// Prototype of BitBlast in "SIMD_Fundamentals.h"
void BitBlast(const void* src, void* dest, size_t bytes);
```

BitBlast, of course, works only for copying fundamental types and plain old data structures. You cannot use BitBlast with types having a nontrivial copy constructor. You would like, then, to implement Copy so as to take advantage of BitBlast whenever possible, and fall back on a more general, conservative algorithm for elaborate types. This way, Copy operations on ranges of fundamental types will "automagically" run faster.

What you need here are two tests:

- Are InIt and OutIt regular pointers (as opposed to fancier iterator types)?
- Is the type to which InIt and OutIt point copyable with bitwise copy?

If you can find answers to these questions at compile time and if the answer to both questions is yes, you can use BitBlast. Otherwise, you must rely on the generic for loop.

Type traits help in solving such problems. The type traits in this chapter owe a lot to the type traits implementation found in the Boost C++ library (Boost).

2.10.1 Implementing Pointer Traits

Loki defines a class template TypeTraits that collects a host of generic type traits. Type-Traits uses template specialization internally and exposes the results.

The implementation of most type traits relies on total or partial template specialization (Section 2.2). For example, the following code determines whether a type T is a pointer:

```
template <typename T>
class TypeTraits
{
private:
   template <class U> struct PointerTraits
   {
      enum { result = false };
      typedef NullType PointeeType;
   };
   template <class U> struct PointerTraits<U*>
   {
      enum { result = true };
      typedef U PointeeType;
   };
public:
   typedef typename PointerTraits<T>::PointeeType PointeeType;
   typedef typename Select<isStdArith || isPointer || isMemberPointer,
      T, ReferredType&>::Result ParameterType;
   typedef typename UnConst<T>::Result NonConstType;
   ...
};
```

The first definition introduces the PointerTraits class template, which says, "T is not a pointer, and a pointee type doesn't apply." Recall from Section 2.9 that NullType is a placeholder type for "doesn't apply" cases.

The second definition (the line in bold) introduces a partial specialization of Pointer-Traits, a specialization that matches any pointer type. For pointers to anything, the specialization in bold qualifies as a better match than the generic template for any pointer type. Consequently, the specialization enters into action for a pointer, so result evaluates to true. In addition, PointeeType is defined appropriately.

You can now gain some insight into the std::vector::iterator implementation—is it a plain pointer or an elaborate type?

```
int main()
{
   const bool
      iterIsPtr = TypeTraits<vector<int>::iterator>::isPointer;
   cout << "vector<int>::iterator is " <<
      (iterIsPtr ? "fast" : "smart") << '\n';
}
```

Similarly, TypeTraits implements an isReference constant and a ReferencedType type definition. For a reference type T, ReferencedType is the type to which T refers; if T is a straight type, ReferencedType is T itself.

Detection of pointers to members (consult Chapter 5 for a description of pointers to members) is a bit different. The specialization needed is as follows:

```
template <typename T>
class TypeTraits
{
private:
    template <class U> struct PToMTraits
    {
        enum { result = false };
    };
    template <class U, class V>
    struct PToMTraits<U V::*>
    {
        enum { result = true };
    };
public:
    enum { isMemberPointer = PToMTraits<T>::result };
    ...
};
```

2.10.2 Detection of Fundamental Types

TypeTraits<T> implements an isStdFundamental compile-time constant that says whether or not T is a standard fundamental type. Standard fundamental types consist of the type void and all numeric types (which in turn are floating-point and integral types). Type-Traits defines constants that reveal the categories to which a given type belongs.

At the price of anticipating a bit, it should be said that the magic of *typelists* (Chapter 3) makes it easy to detect whether a type belongs to a known set of types. For now, all you should know is that the expression

```
TL::IndexOf<TYPELIST_nn(comma-separated list of types), T>::value
```

(where *nn* is the number of types in the list of types) returns the zero-based position of T in the list, or −1 if T does not figure in the list. For example, the expression

```
TL::IndexOf<TYPELIST_4(signed char, short int,
    int, long int), T>::value
```

is greater than or equal to zero if and only if T is a signed integral type.

Following is the definition of the part of TypeTraits dedicated to fundamental types.

```
template <typename T>
class TypeTraits
{
    ... as above ...
public:
    typedef TYPELIST_4(
            unsigned char, unsigned short int,
            unsigned int, unsigned long int)
        UnsignedInts;
    typedef TYPELIST_4(signed char, short int, int, long int)
        SignedInts;
```

```
        typedef TYPELIST_3(bool, char, wchar_t) OtherInts;
        typedef TYPELIST_3(float, double, long double) Floats;
        enum { isStdUnsignedInt =
            TL::IndexOf<UnsignedInts, T>::value >= 0 };
        enum { isStdSignedInt = TL::IndexOf<SignedInts, T>::value >= 0 };
        enum { isStdIntegral = isStdUnsignedInt || isStdSignedInt ||
            TL::IndexOf <OtherInts, T>::value >= 0 };
        enum { isStdFloat = TL::IndexOf<Floats, T>::value >= 0 };
        enum { isStdArith = isStdIntegral || isStdFloat };
        enum { isStdFundamental = isStdArith || Conversion<T,
            void>::sameType };
        ...
    };
```

Using typelists and `TL::IndexOf` gives you the ability to infer information quickly about types, without having to specialize a template many times. If you cannot resist the temptation to delve into the details of typelists and `TL::IndexOf`, take a peek at Chapter 3—but don't forget to return here.

The actual implementation of detection of fundamental types is more sophisticated, allowing for vendor-specific extension types (such as `int64` or `long long`).

2.10.3 Optimized Parameter Types

In template code, you sometimes need to answer the question: Given an arbitrary type T, what is the most efficient way of passing and accepting objects of type T as arguments to functions? In general, the most efficient way is to pass elaborate types by reference and scalar types by value. (Scalar types consist of the arithmetic types described earlier as well as enums, pointers, and pointers to members.) For elaborate types you avoid the overhead of an extra temporary (constructor-plus-destructor calls), and for scalar types you avoid the overhead of the indirection resulting from the reference.

A detail that must be carefully handled is that C++ does not allow references to references. Thus, if T is *already* a reference, you should not add one more reference to it.

A bit of analysis on the optimal parameter type for a function call engenders the following algorithm. Let's call the parameter type that we look for `ParameterType`.

> If T is a reference to some type, `ParameterType` is the same as T (unchanged). *Reason:* References to references are not allowed.
> Else:
> > If T is a scalar type (`int`, `float`, etc.), `ParameterType` is T. *Reason:* Fundamental types are best passed by value.
> > Else `ParameterType` is `const T&`. *Reason:* In general, non-fundamental types are best passed by reference.

One important achievement of this algorithm is that it avoids the reference-to-reference error, which might appear if you combined `bind2nd` with `mem_fun` standard library functions.

It is easy to implement `TypeTraits::ParameterType` using the techniques we already have in hand and the traits defined earlier—`ReferencedType` and `isFundamental`.

```
template <typename T>
class TypeTraits
{
    ... as above ...
public:
    typedef Select<isStdArith || isPointer || isMemberPointer,
            T, ReferencedType&>::Result
        ParameterType;
};
```

Unfortunately, this scheme fails to pass enumerated types (enums) by value.

The Functor class template defined in Chapter 5 uses TypeTraits::ParameterType.

2.10.4 *Stripping Qualifiers*

Given a type T, you can easily get to its constant sibling by simply typing const T. However, doing the opposite (stripping the const off a type) is slightly harder. Similarly, you sometimes might want to get rid of the volatile qualifier of a type.

Implementing a "const stripper" is easy, again by using partial template specialization:

```
template <typename T>
class TypeTraits
{
    ... as above ...
private:
    template <class U> struct UnConst
    {
        typedef U Result;
    };
    template <class U> struct UnConst<const U>
    {
        typedef U Result;
    };
public:
    typedef UnConst<T>::Result NonConstType;
};
```

2.10.5 *Using* TypeTraits

TypeTraits can help you do a lot of interesting things. For one thing, you can now implement the Copy routine to use BitBlast (the problem mentioned in Section 2.10) by simply assembling techniques presented in this chapter. You can use TypeTraits to figure out type information about the two iterators and the Int2Type template for dispatching the call either to BitBlast or to a classic copy routine.

```
enum CopyAlgoSelector { Conservative, Fast };

// Conservative routine-works for any type
template <typename InIt, typename OutIt>
OutIt CopyImpl(InIt first, InIt last, OutIt result,
    Int2Type<Conservative>)
```

```
    {
        for (; first != last; ++first, ++result)
            *result = *first;
        return result;
    }
    // Fast routine-works only for pointers to raw data
    template <typename InIt, typename OutIt>
    OutIt CopyImpl(InIt first, InIt last, OutIt result,
        Int2Type<Fast>)
    {
        const size_t n = last-first;
        BitBlast(first, result, n * sizeof(*first));
        return result + n;
    }
    template <typename InIt, typename OutIt>
    OutIt Copy(InIt first, InIt last, OutIt result)
    {
        typedef typename TypeTraits<InIt>::PointeeType SrcPointee;
        typedef typename TypeTraits<OutIt>::PointeeType DestPointee;
        enum { copyAlgo =
            TypeTraits<InIt>::isPointer &&
            TypeTraits<OutIt>::isPointer &&
            TypeTraits<SrcPointee>::isStdFundamental &&
            TypeTraits<DestPointee>::isStdFundamental &&
            TypeTraits<SrcPointee>::isStdFloat == TypeTraits<
                DestPointee>::isStdFloat &&
            sizeof(SrcPointee) == sizeof(DestPointee) ? Fast :
                Conservative };
        return CopyImpl(first, last, result, Int2Type<copyAlgo>());
    }
```

Although Copy itself doesn't do much, the interesting part is right in there. The enum value copyAlgo selects one implementation or the other. The logic is as follows: Use BitBlast if the two iterators are pointers, if both pointed-to types are fundamental, if you're not mixing floats and integers, and if the pointed-to types are of the same size. The last condition is an interesting twist. If you do this:

```
    int* p1 = ...;
    int* p2 = ...;
    unsigned int* p3 = ...;
    Copy(p1, p2, p3);
```

then Copy calls the fast routine, as it should, although the source and destination types are different.

The drawback of Copy is that it doesn't accelerate everything that could be accelerated. For example, you might have a plain C-like struct containing nothing but fundamental data—a so-called *plain old data,* or POD, structure. The standard allows bitwise copying of POD structures, but Copy cannot detect "PODness," so it will call the slow routine. Here you have to rely, again, on classic traits in addition to TypeTraits. For instance:

```
template <typename T> struct SupportsBitwiseCopy
{
    typedef typename TypeTraits<T>::NonConstType NonConstType;

    enum { result = TypeTraits<NonConstType>::isStdFundamental };
};
template <typename InIt, typename OutIt>
OutIt Copy(InIt first, InIt last, OutIt result,
    Int2Type<true>)
{
    typedef typename TypeTraits<typename TypeTraits<
        InIt>::PointeeType>::UnqualifiedType SrcPointee;
    typedef typename TypeTraits<typename Typetraits<
        OutIt>::PointeeType>::UnqualifiedType DestPointee;

    enum { useBitBlast = ... ? Fast : Conservative };
        TypeTraits<InIt>::isPointer &&
        TypeTraits<OutIt>::isPointer &&
        SupportsBitwiseCopy<SrcPointee>::result &&
        SupportsBitwiseCopy<DestPointee>::result &&
        Conversion<SrcPointee, DestPointee>::sameType || (
            TypeTraits<SrcPointee>::isStdFundamental &&
            TypeTraits<DestPointee>::isStdFundamental &&
            TypeTraits<SrcPointee>::isStdFloat ==
                TypeTraits<DestPointee>::isStdFloat &&
        sizeof(SrcPointee) == sizeof(DestPointee)) };
        return CopyImpl(first, last, result, Int2Type<useBitBlast>());
}
```

Now, to unleash `BitBlast` for your POD types of interest, you need only specialize `SupportsBitwiseCopy` and put a true in there:

```
template<> struct SupportsBitwiseCopy<MyType>
{
    enum { result = true };
};
```

Table 2.1 defines the complete set of traits implemented by Loki.

2.11 Summary

A number of techniques form the building blocks of the components presented in this book. Most of the techniques are related to template code.

- *Compile-time assertions* (Section 2.1) help libraries to generate meaningful error messages in templated code.
- *Partial template specialization* (Section 2.2) allows you to specialize a template, not for a specific, fixed set of parameters, but for a family of parameters that match a pattern.
- *Local classes* (Section 2.3) let you do interesting things, especially inside template functions.
- *Mapping integral constants to types* (Section 2.4) eases the compile-time dispatch based on numeric values (notably Boolean conditions).

Table 2.1: TypeTraits<T> Members

Name	Kind	Comments
isPointer	Boolean constant	True if T is a pointer.
PointeeType	Type	Evaluates to the type to which T points, if T is a pointer. Otherwise, evaluates to NullType.
isReference	Boolean constant	True if T is a reference.
ReferencedType	Type	If T is a reference, evaluates to the type to which T refers. Otherwise, evaluates to the type T itself.
ParameterType	Type	The type that's most appropriate as a parameter of a non-mutating function. Can be either T or const T&.
isConst	Boolean constant	True if T is a const-qualified type.
NonConstType	Type	Removes the const qualifier, if any, from type T.
isVolatile	Boolean constant	True if T is a volatile-qualified type.
NonVolatileType	Type	Removes the volatile qualifier, if any, from type T.
NonQualifiedType	Type	Removes both the const and volatile qualifiers, if any, from type T.
isStdUnsignedInt	Boolean constant	True if T is one of the four unsigned integral types (unsigned char, unsigned short int, unsigned int, or unsigned long int).
isStdSignedInt	Boolean constant	True if T is one of the four signed integral types (signed char, short int, int, or long int).
isStdIntegral	Boolean constant	True if T is a standard integral type.
isStdFloat	Boolean constant	True if T is a standard floating-point type (float, double, or long double).
isStdArith	Boolean constant	True if T is a standard arithmetic type (integral or floating point).
isStdFundamental	Boolean constant	True if T is a fundamental type (arithmetic or void).

- *Type-to-type mapping* (Section 2.5) allows you to substitute function overloading for function template partial specialization, a feature missing in C++.
- *Type selection* (Section 2.6) allows you to select types based on Boolean conditions.
- *Detecting convertibility and inheritance at compile time* (Section 2.7) gives you the ability to figure out whether two arbitrary types are convertible to each other, are aliases of the same type, or inherit one from the other.
- *TypeInfo* (Section 2.8) implements a wrapper around std::type_info, featuring value semantics and ordering comparisons.
- *The NullType and EmptyType classes* (Section 2.9) function as placeholder types in template metaprogramming.
- *The TypeTraits template* (Section 2.10) offers a host of general-purpose traits that you can use to tailor code to specific categories of types.

3

Typelists

Typelists are a C++ tool for manipulating collections of types. They offer for types all the fundamental operations that lists of values support.

Some design patterns specify and manipulate collections of types, either related by inheritance or not. Notable examples are Abstract Factory and Visitor (Gamma et al. 1995). If you use traditional coding techniques, you can only manipulate collections of types by sheer repetition. This repetition leads to a subtle form of code bloating. Most people don't think it could get any better than that. However, typelists let you automate tasks that you usually confine to your editor's macro capability. Typelists bring power from another planet to C++, enabling it to support new, interesting idioms.

This chapter is dedicated to presenting a complete typelist facility for C++, together with a couple of examples of their use. After reading this chapter, you will

- Understand the typelist concept
- Understand how typelists can be created and processed
- Be able to manipulate typelists effectively
- Know the main uses of typelists and the programming idioms they enable and support

Chapters 9, 10, and 11 use typelists as an enabling technology.

3.1 The Need for Typelists

Sometimes you must repeat the same code for a number of types, and templates cannot be of help. Consider, for instance, implementing an Abstract Factory (Gamma et al. 1995). Here you define one virtual function for each type in a collection of types known at design time:

```
class WidgetFactory
{
public:
    virtual Window* CreateWindow() = 0;
    virtual Button* CreateButton() = 0;
    virtual ScrollBar* CreateScrollBar() = 0;
};
```

If you want to generalize the concept of Abstract Factory and put it into a library, you have to make it possible for the user to create factories of arbitrary collections of types—not just Window, Button, and ScrollBar. Templates don't support this feature out of the box.

Although at first Abstract Factory may not seem to provide much opportunity for abstraction and generalization, there are a few things that make the investigation worthwhile:

1. If you cannot take a stab at generalizing the fundamental concept, you won't be given a chance to generalize the concrete instances of that concept. This is a crucial principle. If the essence escapes generalization, you continue to struggle with the concrete artifacts of that essence. In the Abstract Factory case, although the abstract base class is quite simple, you can get a nasty amount of code duplication when implementing various concrete factories.

2. You cannot easily manipulate the member functions of WidgetFactory (see the previous code). A collection of virtual function signatures is essentially impossible to handle in a generic way. For instance, consider this:

    ```
    template <class T>
    T* MakeRedWidget(WidgetFactory& factory)
    {
        T* pW = factory.CreateT(); // huh???
        pW->SetColor(RED);
        return pW;
    }
    ```

    You need to call CreateWindow, CreateButton, or CreateScrollBar, depending on T being a Window, Button, or ScrollBar, respectively. C++ doesn't allow you to do this kind of text substitution.

3. Last, but not least, good libraries have the nice side effect of putting aside endless debates about naming conventions (createWindow, create_window, or CreateWindow?) and little tweaks like that. They introduce a preferred, standardized way of doing things. Abstracting, well, Abstract Factory would have this nice side effect.

Let's put together a wish list. For addressing item 1, it would be nice if we could create a WidgetFactory by passing a parameter list to an AbstractFactory template:

```
typedef AbstractFactory<Window, Button, ScrollBar> WidgetFactory;
```

For addressing item 2, we need a template-like invocation for various CreateXxx functions, such as Create<Window>(), Create<Button>(), and so on. Then we can invoke it from generic code:

```
template <class T>
T* MakeRedWidget(WidgetFactory& factory)
{
    T* pW = factory.Create<T>(); // aha!
    pW->SetColor(RED);
    return pW;
}
```

However, we cannot fulfill these needs. First, the `typedef` for `WidgetFactory` above is not possible because templates cannot have a variable number of parameters. Second, the template syntax `Create<Xxx>()` is not legal because virtual functions cannot be templates.

By this point, you should see what good abstraction and reuse opportunities we have, and how badly we are constrained in exploiting these opportunities due to language limitations.

Typelists make it possible to create generic Abstract Factories and much more.

3.2 Defining Typelists

For a variety of reasons, C++ is a language that leads its users sometimes to say, "These are the smartest five lines of code I ever wrote." Maybe it is its semantic richness or the ever-exciting (and surprising?) way its features interact. In line with this tradition, typelists are fundamentally very simple:

```
template <class T, class U>
struct Typelist
{
    typedef T Head;
    typedef U Tail;
};
namespace TL
{
    ...typelist algorithms ...
}
```

Everything related to typelists, except the definition of `Typelist` itself, lives in the TL namespace. In turn, TL is inside the `Loki` namespace, as is all of Loki's code. To simplify examples, this chapter omits mentioning the TL namespace. You'll have to remember it when using the `Typelist.h` header. (If you forget, the compiler will remind you.)

`Typelist` holds two types. They are accessible through the `Head` and `Tail` inner names. That's it! We don't need typelists that hold three or more elements, because we already have them. For instance, here's a typelist of three elements holding the three char variants of C++:

```
typedef Typelist<char, Typelist<signed char, unsigned char> >
    CharList;
```

(Notice the annoying, but required, space between the two > tokens at the end.)

Typelists are devoid of any value: Their bodies are empty, they don't hold any state, and they don't define any functionality. At runtime, typelists don't carry any value at all. Their only *raison d'être* is to carry type information. It follows that any typelist processing must necessarily occur at compile time, not at runtime. Typelists are not meant to be instantiated, although there's no harm in doing that. Thus, whenever this book talks about "a typelist," it really is referring to a typelist type, not a typelist value. Typelist values are not interesting; only their types are of use. (Section 3.13.2 shows how to use typelists to create collections of values.)

The property of templates used here is that a template parameter can be any type, including another instantiation of the same template. This is an old, well-known property of templates, often used to implement ad hoc matrices as vector< vector<double> >. Because Typelist accepts two parameters, we can always extend a given Typelist by replacing one of the parameters with another Typelist, *ad infinitum*.

There is a little problem, though. We can express typelists of two types or more, but we're unable to express typelists containing zero or one type. What's needed is a *null list type*, and the NullType class described in Chapter 2 is exactly suited for such uses.

We establish the convention that every typelist must end with a NullType. NullType serves as a useful termination marker, much like the \0 that helps traditional C string functions. Now we can define a typelist of only one element:

```
// See Chapter 2 for the definition of NullType
typedef Typelist<int, NullType> OneTypeOnly;
```

The typelist containing the three char variants becomes

```
typedef Typelist<char, Typelist<signed char,
    Typelist<unsigned char, NullType> > > AllCharTypes;
```

Therefore, we have obtained an open-ended Typelist template that can, by compounding a basic cell, hold any number of types.

Let's see now how we can manipulate typelists. (Again, this means Typelist types, not Typelist objects.) Prepare for an interesting journey. From here on we delve into the underground of C++, a world with strange, new rules—the world of compile-time programming.

3.3 Linearizing Typelist Creation

Right off the bat, typelists are just too LISP-ish to be easy to use. LISP-style constructs are great for LISP programmers, but they don't dovetail nicely with C++ (to say nothing about the spaces between >s that you have to take care of). For instance, here's a typelist of integral types:

```
typedef Typelist<signed char,
    Typelist<short int,
        Typelist<int, Typelist<long int, NullType> > > >
    SignedIntegrals;
```

Typelists might be a cool concept, but they definitely need nicer packaging.

In order to linearize typelist creation, the typelist library (see Loki's file Typelist.h) defines a plethora of macros that transform the recursion into simple enumeration, at the expense of tedious repetition. This is not a problem, however. The repetition is done only once, in the library code, and it scales typelists to a large library-defined number (50). The macros look like this:

```
#define TYPELIST_1(T1) Typelist<T1, NullType>
#define TYPELIST_2(T1, T2) Typelist<T1, TYPELIST_1(T2) >
#define TYPELIST_3(T1, T2, T3) Typelist<T1, TYPELIST_2(T2, T3) >
#define TYPELIST_4(T1, T2, T3, T4) \
```

```
    Typelist<T1, TYPELIST_3(T2, T3, T4) >
    ...
    #define TYPELIST_50(...) ...
```

Each macro uses the previous one, which makes it easy for the library user to extend the upper limit, should this necessity emerge.

Now the earlier type definition of SignedIntegrals can be expressed in a much more pleasant way:

```
    typedef TYPELIST_4(signed char, short int, int, long int)
        SignedIntegrals;
```

Linearizing typelist creation is only the beginning. Typelist manipulation is still very clumsy. For instance, accessing the last element in SignedIntegrals requires using Signed-Integrals::Tail::Tail::Head. It's not yet clear how we can manipulate typelists generically. It's time, then, to define some fundamental operations for typelists by thinking of the primitive operations available to lists of values.

3.4 Calculating Length

Here's a simple operation. Given a typelist TList, obtain a compile-time constant that evaluates its length. The constant ought to be a compile-time one because typelists are static constructs, so we'd expect all calculations related to typelists to be performed at compile time.

The idea underlying most typelist manipulations is to exploit recursive templates, which are templates that use instantiations of themselves as part of their definition. While doing this, they pass a different template argument list. The recursion obtained this way is stopped with an explicit specialization for a border case.

The code that computes a typelist's length is, again, quite concise:

```
    template <class TList> struct Length;
    template <> struct Length<NullType>
    {
        enum { value = 0 };
    };
    template <class T, class U>
    struct Length< Typelist<T, U> >
    {
        enum { value = 1 + Length<U>::value };
    };
```

This is the C++ way of saying, "The length of a null typelist is 0. The length of any other typelist is 1 plus the length of the tail of that typelist."

The implementation of Length uses *partial template specialization* (see Chapter 2) to distinguish between NullType and a non-empty typelist. The first specialization of Length is totally specialized and matches only NullType. The second, partial, specialization of Length matches any Typelist<T, U>, including compound typelists, that is, those in which U is in turn a Typelist<V, W>.

The second specialization performs the computation by recursion. It defines `value` as 1 (which counts the head T) plus the length of the tail of the typelist. When the tail becomes `NullType`, the first definition is matched, the recursion is stopped, and so is the length calculation, which comes back nicely with the result. Suppose, for example, that you want to define a C-style array that collects pointers to `std::type_info` objects for all signed integrals. Using `Length`, you can write

```
std::type_info* intsRtti[Length<SignedIntegrals>::value];
```

You allocate four elements for `intsRtti` through a compile-time calculation.[1]

3.5 Intermezzo

You can find early examples of template metaprograms in Veldhuizen (1995). Czarnecki and Eisenecker (2000) discuss this problem in depth and provide a full collection of compile-time simulations for C++ statements.

The conception and implementation of `Length` resembles a classic recursion example given in computer science classes: the algorithm that computes the length of a singly linked list structure. (There are two major differences, though: The algorithm for `Length` is performed at compile time, and it operates on types, not on values.)

This naturally leads to the following question: Couldn't we develop a version of `Length` that's iterative, instead of recursive? After all, iteration is more natural to C++ than recursion. Getting an answer to this question will guide us in implementing the other `Typelist` facilities.

The answer is no, and for interesting reasons.

Our tools for compile-time programming in C++ are templates, compile-time integer calculations, and type definitions (`typedefs`). Let's see in what ways each of these tools serves us.

Templates—more specifically, template specialization—provide the equivalent of `if` statements at compile time. As seen earlier in the implementation of `Length`, template specialization enables differentiation between typelists and other types.

Integer calculations allow you to make true value computations, to jump from types to values. However, there is a peculiarity: All compile-time values are *immutable*. After you've defined an integral constant, say an enumerated value, you cannot change it (that is, assign another value to it).

Type definitions (`typedefs`) can be seen as introducing named type constants. Again, after definition, they are frozen—you cannot later redefine a `typedef`'d symbol to hold another type.

These two peculiarities of compile-time calculation make it fundamentally incompatible with iteration. Iteration is about holding an iterator and changing it until some condition is met. Because we don't have mutable entities in the compile-time world, we cannot do any iteration at all. Therefore, although C++ is mostly an imperative language, any compile-time computation must rely on techniques that definitely are reminiscent of pure functional languages—languages that cannot mutate values. Be prepared to recurse heavily.

---

[1]You can also initialize the array without code repetition. Doing this is left as an exercise for the reader.

3.6 Indexed Access

Having access by index to the elements of a typelist would certainly be a desirable feature. It would linearize typelist access, making it easier to manipulate typelists comfortably. Of course, just like all other entities we manipulate in our static world, the index must be a compile-time value.

The declaration of a template for an indexed operation would look like this:

```
template <class TList, unsigned int index> struct TypeAt;
```

Let's define the algorithm. Keep in mind that we cannot use mutable, modifiable values.

TypeAt
Inputs: Typelist TList, index i
Output: Inner type Result

If TList is non-null and i is zero, then Result is the head of TList.
Else
    If TList is non-null and index i is nonzero, then Result is obtained by applying
        TypeAt to the tail of TList and i-1.
    Else there is an out-of-bound access that translates into a compile-time error.

Here's the incarnation of the TypeAt algorithm:

```
template <class Head, class Tail> struct TypeAt;
struct TypeAt<Typelist<Head, Tail>, 0>
{
    typedef Head Result;
};
template <class Head, class Tail, unsigned int i>
struct TypeAt<Typelist<Head, Tail>, i>
{
    typedef typename TypeAt<Tail, i - 1>::Result Result;
};
```

If you try an out-of-bound access, the compiler will complain that there's no specialization defined for TypeAt<NullType,*x*>, where *x* is the amount by which you bypass the list size. This message could be a bit more informative, but it's not bad, either.

Loki (file Typelist.h) also defines a variant of TypeAt, called TypeAtNonStrict. TypeAtNonStrict implements the same functionality as TypeAt, with the difference that an out-of-bound access is more forgiving, yielding a user-chosen default type as the result instead of a compile-time error. The generalized callback implementation described in Chapter 5 uses TypeAtNonStrict.

Indexed access in typelists takes linear time according to the size of the typelist. For lists of values, this method is inefficient (for this reason, std::list does not define an operator[]). However, in the case of typelists, the time is consumed during compilation, and compile time is in a sense "free."[2]

---

[2]Actually, this is not quite true for large projects. It is possible, at least in theory, that heavy typelist manipulation could slow down compilation time considerably. Anyway, a program that contains very large typelists is

3.7 Searching Typelists

How would you search a typelist for a given type? Let's try to implement an IndexOf algorithm that computes the index of a type in a typelist. If the type is not found, the result will be an invalid value, say -1. The algorithm is a classic linear search implemented recursively.

> **IndexOf**
> *Inputs:* Typelist TList, type T
> *Output:* Inner compile-time constant value
>
> If TList is NullType, then value is -1.
> Else
>   If the head of TList is T, then value is 0.
>   Else
>   Compute the result of IndexOf applied to TList's tail and T into a temporary value temp.
>   If temp is -1, then value is -1.
>   Else value is 1 plus temp.

IndexOf is a relatively simple algorithm. Special care is given to propagate the "not found" value (-1) to the result. We need three specializations—one for each branch in the algorithm. The last branch (value's computation from temp) is a numeric calculation that we carry with the conditional operator ?:. Here's the implementation:

```cpp
template <class TList, class T> struct IndexOf;

template <class T>
struct IndexOf<NullType, T>
{
    enum { value = -1 };
};

template <class T, class Tail>
struct IndexOf<Typelist<T, Tail>, T>
{
    enum { value = 0 };
};

template <class Head, class Tail, class T>
struct IndexOf<Typelist<Head, Tail>, T>
{
private:
    enum { temp = IndexOf<Tail, T>::value };
public:
    enum { value = temp == -1 ? -1 : 1 + temp };
};
```

---

either runtime speed-hungry—in which case you are willing to accept slower compilations—or too coupled, in which case a design review would be in order.

3.8 Appending to Typelists

We need a means to append a type or a typelist to a typelist. Because modifying a typelist is not possible, as discussed previously, we will "return by value" by creating a brand new typelist that contains the result.

Append
Inputs: Typelist TList, type or typelist T
Output: Inner type definition Result

If TList is NullType and T is NullType, then Result is NullType.
Else
   If TList is NullType and T is a single (nontypelist) type, then Result is a typelist having T as its only element.
   Else
      If TList is NullType and T is a typelist, Result is T itself.
      Else if TList is non-null, then Result is a typelist having TList::Head as its head and the result of appending T to TList::Tail as its tail.

This algorithm maps naturally to the following code:

```
template <class TList, class T> struct Append;

template <> struct Append<NullType, NullType>
{
    typedef NullType Result;
};

template <class T> struct Append<NullType, T>
{
    typedef TYPELIST_1(T) Result;
};

template <class Head, class Tail>
struct Append<NullType, Typelist<Head, Tail> >
{
    typedef Typelist<Head, Tail> Result;
};

template <class Head, class Tail, class T>
struct Append<Typelist<Head, Tail>, T>
{
    typedef Typelist<Head,
        typename Append<Tail, T>::Result>
      Result;
};
```

Note, again, how the last partially specialized version of Append instantiates the Append template recursively, passing it the tail of the list and the type to append.

Now we have a unified Append operation for single types and typelists. For instance, the statement

```
typedef Append<SignedIntegrals,
       TYPELIST_3(float, double, long double)>::Result
   SignedTypes;
```

defines a list containing all signed numeric types in C++.

3.9 Erasing a Type from a Typelist

Now for the opposite operation— erasing a type from a typelist—we have two options: Erase only the first occurrence, or erase all occurrences of a given type.

Let's think of removing only the first occurrence.

> **Erase**
> *Input:* Typelist TList, type T
> *Output:* Inner type definition Result
>
> If TList is NullType, then Result is NullType.
> Else
>   If T is the same as TList::Head, then Result is TList::Tail.
>   Else Result is a typelist having TList::Head as its head and the result of applying
>   Erase to TList::Tail and T as its tail.

Here's how this algorithm maps to C++.

```
template <class TList, class T> struct Erase;

template <class T>                            // Specialization 1
struct Erase<NullType, T>
{
    typedef NullType Result;
};

template <class T, class Tail>                // Specialization 2
struct Erase<Typelist<T, Tail>, T>
{
    typedef Tail Result;
};

template <class Head, class Tail, class T> // Specialization 3
struct Erase<Typelist<Head, Tail>, T>
{
    typedef Typelist<Head,
        typename Erase<Tail, T>::Result>
      Result;
};
```

As in the case of TypeAt, there is no default version of the template. This means you can instantiate Erase only with certain types. For instance, Erase<double,int> yields a compile-time error because there's no match for it. Erase needs its first parameter to be a typelist.

Using our `SignedTypes` definition, we can now say the following:

```
// SomeSignedTypes contains the equivalent of
// TYPELIST_6(signed char, short int, int, long int,
// double, long double)
typedef Erase<SignedTypes, float>::Result SomeSignedTypes;
```

Let's tap into the recursive erase algorithm. The `EraseAll` template erases all occurrences of a type in a typelist. The implementation is similar to `Erase`'s, with one difference. When detecting a type to erase, the algorithm doesn't stop. `EraseAll` continues looking for and removing matches down the tail of the list by recursively applying itself:

```
template <class TList, class T> struct EraseAll;

template <class T>
struct EraseAll<NullType, T>
{
    typedef NullType Result;
};

template <class T, class Tail>
struct EraseAll<Typelist<T, Tail>, T>
{
    // Go all the way down the list removing the type
    typedef typename EraseAll<Tail, T>::Result Result;
};

template <class Head, class Tail, class T>
struct EraseAll<Typelist<Head, Tail>, T>
{
    // Go all the way down the list removing the type
    typedef Typelist<Head,
        typename EraseAll<Tail, T>::Result>
        Result;
};
```

3.10 Erasing Duplicates

An important operation on typelists is to erase duplicate values.

The need is to transform a typelist so that each type appears only once. For example, from this:

```
TYPELIST_6(Widget, Button, Widget, TextField, ScrollBar, Button)
```

we need to obtain this:

```
TYPELIST_4(Widget, Button, TextField, ScrollBar)
```

This processing is a bit more complex, but, as you might guess, we can use `Erase` to help.

NoDuplicates
Input: Typelist `TList`
Output: Inner type definition `Result`

If TList is NullType, then Result is NullType.
Else
    Apply NoDuplicates to TList::Tail, obtaining a temporary typelist L1.
    Apply Erase to L1 and TList::Head. Obtain L2 as the result.
    Result is a typelist whose head is TList::Head and whose tail is L2.

Here's how this algorithm translates to code:

```
template <class TList> struct NoDuplicates;

template <> struct NoDuplicates<NullType>
{
    typedef NullType Result;
};

template <class Head, class Tail>
struct NoDuplicates< Typelist<Head, Tail> >
{
private:
    typedef typename NoDuplicates<Tail>::Result L1;
    typedef typename Erase<L1, Head>::Result L2;
public:
    typedef Typelist<Head, L2> Result;
};
```

Why was Erase enough when EraseAll would have seemed appropriate? We want to remove all duplicates for a type, right? The answer is that Erase is applied *after* the recursion to NoDuplicates. This means we erase a type from a list that already has no duplicates, so at most one instance of the type to be erased will appear. Recursive programming is quite interesting.

3.11 Replacing an Element in a Typelist

Sometimes a replacement is needed instead of a removal. As you'll see in Section 3.12, replacing a type with another is an important building block for more advanced idioms.

We need to replace type T with type U in a typelist TList.

    Replace
    Inputs: Typelist TList, type T (to replace), and type U (to replace with)
    Output: Inner type definition Result

    If TList is NullType, then Result is NullType.
    Else
        If the head of the typelist TList is T, then Result is a typelist with U as its head and TList::Tail as its tail.
        Else Result is a typelist with TList::Head as its head and the result of applying Replace to TList, T, and U as its tail.

After you figure out the correct recursive algorithm, the code writes itself:

```
template <class TList, class T, class U> struct Replace;

template <class T, class U>
struct Replace<NullType, T, U>
{
    typedef NullType Result;
};

template <class T, class Tail, class U>
struct Replace<Typelist<T, Tail>, T, U>
{
    typedef Typelist<U, Tail> Result;
};

template <class Head, class Tail, class T, class U>
struct Replace<Typelist<Head, Tail>, T, U>
{
    typedef Typelist<Head,
            typename Replace<Tail, T, U>::Result>
        Result;
};
```

We easily obtain the ReplaceAll algorithm by changing the second specialization for one that recursively applies the algorithm to Tail.

3.12 Partially Ordering Typelists

Suppose we want to order a typelist by inheritance relationship. We'd like, for instance, derived types to appear before base types. For example, say we have a class hierarchy like the one in Figure 3.1:

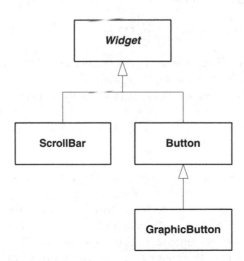

Figure 3.1: A simple class hierarchy

If we have this typelist:

```
TYPELIST_4(Widget, ScrollBar, Button, GraphicButton)
```

the challenge is to transform it into

```
TYPELIST_4(ScrollBar, GraphicButton, Button, Widget)
```

That is, we need to bring the most derived types to the front and leave the order of sibling types unaltered.

This seems like an exercise of intellectual value only, but there are important practical applications for it. Scanning a typelist ordered with the most derived types first ensures a bottom-up traversal of a class hierarchy. The double-dispatch engine in Chapter 11 applies this important property for figuring out information about types.

When ordering a collection, we need an ordering function. We already have a compile-time means to detect inheritance relationships, described in detail in Chapter 2. Recall that we have a handy macro, SUPERSUBCLASS(T,U), which evaluates to true if U is derived from T. We just have to combine the inheritance detection mechanism with typelists.

We cannot use a full-fledged sorting algorithm here because we don't have a total ordering relationship; we don't have the equivalent of operator< for classes. Two sibling classes cannot be ordered by SUPERSUBCLASS(T,U). We will therefore use a custom algorithm that will bring derived classes to the front and will let other classes remain in the same relative positions.

DerivedToFront
Input: Typelist TList
Output: Inner type definition Result

If TList is NullType, then Result is NullType.
Else
    Find the most derived type from TList::Head in TList::Tail. Save that type via a typedef to a type called TheMostDerived.
    Replace TheMostDerived in TList::Tail with TList::Head, obtaining L as the result.
    Build the result as a typelist having TheMostDerived as its head and DerivedToFront<L>::Result as its tail.

When this algorithm is applied to a typelist, derived types will migrate to the top of the typelist, and base types will be pushed to the bottom.

There is a piece missing here—the algorithm that finds the most derived type of a given type in a typelist. Because SUPERSUBCLASS yields a compile-time Boolean value, we'll find the little Select class template (also presented in Chapter 2) to be useful. Recall that Select is a template that selects one of two types based on a compile-time Boolean constant.

The `MostDerived` algorithm accepts a typelist and a type `Base` and returns the most derived type from `Base` in the typelist (or possibly `Base` itself, if no derived type is found). It looks like this:

MostDerived
Input: Typelist TList, type T
Output: Inner type definition Result

If `TList` is `NullType`, the result is T.
Else
    Apply `MostDerived` to `TList::Tail` and T. Obtain `Candidate`.
    If `TList::Head` is derived from `Candidate`, the result is `TList::Head`.
    Else, the result is `Candidate`.

The implementation of `MostDerived` is as follows:

```
template <class TList, class T> struct MostDerived;

template <class T>
struct MostDerived<NullType, T>
{
    typedef T Result;
};

template <class Head, class Tail, class T>
struct MostDerived<Typelist<Head, Tail>, T>
{
private:
    typedef typename MostDerived<Tail, T>::Result Candidate;
public:
    typedef typename Select<
        SUPERSUBCLASS(Candidate, Head),
            Head, Candidate>::Result Result;
};
```

The `DerivedToFront` algorithm uses `MostDerived` as a primitive. Here is Derived-ToFront's implementation:

```
template <class T> struct DerivedToFront;

template <>
struct DerivedToFront<NullType>
{
    typedef NullType Result;
};

template <class Head, class Tail>
struct DerivedToFront< Typelist<Head, Tail> >
{
private:
    typedef typename MostDerived<Tail, Head>::Result
```

```
        TheMostDerived;
    typedef typename Replace<Tail,
        TheMostDerived, Head>::Result Temp;
    typedef typename DerivedToFront<Temp>::Result L;
public:
    typedef Typelist<TheMostDerived, L> Result;
};
```

This complex typelist manipulation is of considerable strength. The DerivedToFront transformation effectively automates type processing that otherwise can be performed only with much discipline and attention. Automatic maintenance of parallel class hierarchies, anyone?

3.13 Class Generation with Typelists

If, until now, you found typelists intriguing, interesting, or just ugly, you haven't seen anything yet. This section is dedicated to defining fundamental constructs for code generation with typelists. That is, we don't write code anymore; instead, we put the compiler to work generating code for us. These constructs use one of the most powerful constructs of C++, a feature unmatched by any other language—*template template parameters.*

So far, typelist manipulation has not yielded actual code; the processing has produced only typelists, types, or compile-time numeric constants (as was the case with Length). Let's tap into generating some real code, that is, stuff that leaves traces in the compiled code.

Typelist objects have no use as they are; they are devoid of any runtime state or functionality. An important need in programming with typelists is to generate classes from typelists. Application programmers sometimes need to fill a class with code—be it virtual function signatures, data declarations, or function implementations—in ways directed by a typelist. We will try to automate such processes with typelists.

Because C++ lacks compile-time iteration or recursive macros, the task of adding some code for each type in a typelist is difficult. You can use partial template specialization in ways resembling the algorithms described earlier, but implementing this solution in user code is clumsy and complicated. Loki should be of help with this task.

3.13.1 Generating Scattered Hierarchies

A powerful utility template provided by Loki makes it easy to build classes by applying each type in a typelist to a basic template, provided by the user. This way, the clumsy process of distributing types in the typelist to user code is encapsulated in the library; the user need only define a simple template of one parameter.

The library class template is called GenScatterHierarchy. Although it has a simple definition, GenScatterHierarchy has amazing horsepower under its hood, as you'll see soon. For now, let's look at its definition.[3]

```
template <class TList, template <class> class Unit>
class GenScatterHierarchy;

// GenScatterHierarchy specialization: Typelist to Unit
```

---

[3]This is one of those situations in which presenting the idea before its potential applications (as opposed to a problem-solution sequence) is more appropriate.

```
template <class Head, class Tail, template <class> class Unit>
class GenScatterHierarchy<Typelist<Head, Tail>, Unit>
    : public GenScatterHierarchy<Head, Unit>
    , public GenScatterHierarchy<Tail, Unit>
{
public:
    typedef typename Typelist<Head, Tail> TList;
    typedef typename GenScatterHierarchy<Head, Unit> LeftBase;
    typedef typename GenScatterHierarchy<Tail, Unit> RightBase;
};

// Pass an atomic type (non-typelist) to Unit
template <class AtomicType, template <class> class Unit>
class GenScatterHierarchy : public Unit<AtomicType>
{
    typedef typename Unit<AtomicType> LeftBase;
};

// Do nothing for NullType
template <template <class> class Unit>
class GenScatterHierarchy<NullType, Unit>
{
};
```

Template template parameters work much as you would expect (see also Chapter 1). You pass a template class Unit to GenScatterHierarchy as its second argument. Internally, GenScatterHierarchy uses its template template parameter Unit just as it would have used any regular template class with one template parameter. The power comes from your ability—as the user of GenScatterHierarchy—to pass it a template written by you.

What does GenScatterHierarchy do? If its first template argument is an atomic type (as opposed to a typelist), GenScatterHierarchy passes that type to Unit, and inherits from the resulting class Unit<T>. If GenScatterHierarchy's first template argument is a typelist TList, GenScatterHierarchy recurses to GenScatterHierarchy<TList::Head, Unit> and GenScatterHierarchy<TList::Tail, Unit>, and inherits both. GenScatterHierarchy-<NullType, Unit> is an empty class.[4]

Ultimately, an instantiation of GenScatterHierarchy ends up inheriting Unit instantiated with *every type in the typelist*. For instance, consider this code:

```
template <class T>
struct Holder
{
    T value_;
};

typedef GenScatterHierarchy<
    TYPELIST_3(int, string, Widget),
    Holder>
  WidgetInfo;
```

---

[4]The actual Loki implementation of GenScatterHierarchy includes a slight refinement that caters for repeated types in the passed-in typelist.

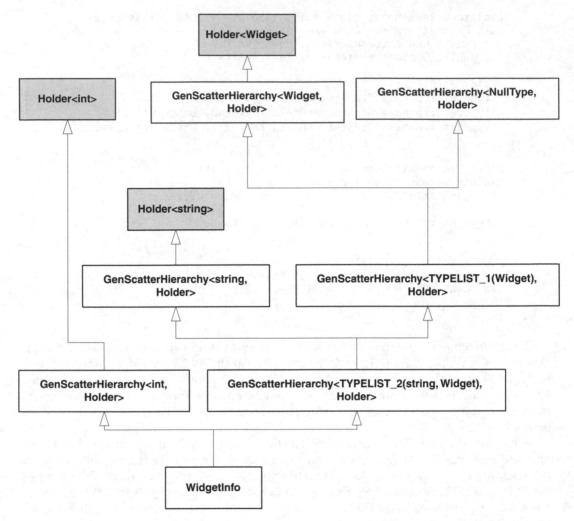

Figure 3.2: The inheritance structure of `WidgetInfo`

Figure 3.2. shows the inheritance hierarchy generated by `WidgetInfo`. We call the class hierarchy in Figure 3.2 *scattered,* because the types in the typelist are scattered in distinct root classes. This is the gist of `GenScatteredHierarchy`: It generates a class hierarchy for you by repeatedly instantiating a class template that you provide as a model. Then it collects all such generated classes in a single leaf class—in our case, `WidgetInfo`.

As an effect of inheriting `Holder<int>`, `Holder<string>`, and `Holder<Widget>`, `WidgetInfo` has one member variable `value_` for each type in the typelist. Figure 3.3 shows a likely binary layout of a `WidgetInfo` object. The layout assumes that empty classes such as `GenScatterHierarchy<NullType,Holder>` are optimized away and do not occupy any storage in the compound object.

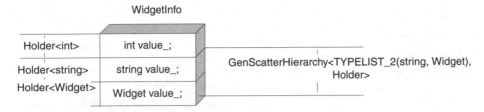

Figure 3.3: Memory layout for `WidgetInfo`

You can do interesting things with `WidgetInfo` objects. You can, for instance, access the `string` stored in a `WidgetInfo` object by writing

```
WidgetInfo obj;
string name = (static_cast<Holder<string>&>(obj)).value_;
```

The explicit cast is necessary to disambiguate the member variable name `value_`. Otherwise, the compiler is confused as to which `value_` member you are referring to.

This cast is quite ugly, so let's try to make `GenScatterHierarchy` easier to use by providing some handy access functions. For instance, a nice member function would access a member by its type. This is quite easy.

```
// Refer to HierarchyGenerators.h for FieldTraits' definition
template <class T, class H>
typename Private::FieldTraits<H>::Rebind<T>::Result&
Field(H& obj)
{
    return obj;
}
```

`Field` relies on implicit derived-to-base conversion. If you call `Field<Widget>(obj)` (`obj` being of type `WidgetInfo`), the compiler figures out that `Holder<Widget>` is a base class of `WidgetInfo` and simply returns a reference to that part of the compound object.

Why is `Field` a namespace-level function and not a member function? Well, such highly generic programming must play very carefully with names. Imagine, for instance, that `Unit` itself defines a symbol with the name `Field`. Had `GenScatterHierarchy` itself defined a member function `Field`, it would have masked `Unit`'s `Field` member. This would be a major source of annoyance to the user.

There is one more major source of annoyance with `Field`: You cannot use it when you have duplicate types in your typelists. Consider this slightly modified definition of `WidgetInfo`:

```
typedef GenScatterHierarchy<
    TYPELIST_4(int, int, string, Widget),
    Value>
WidgetInfo;
```

Now `WidgetInfo` has two `value_` members of type `int`. If you try to call `Field<int>` for a `WidgetInfo` object, the compiler complains about an ambiguity. There is no easy way to

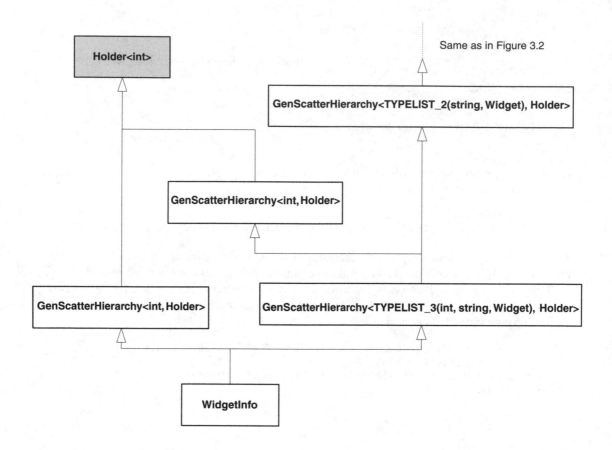

Figure 3.4: WidgetInfo inherits Holder<int> twice

solve the ambiguity, because the WidgetInfo ends up inheriting Holder<int> twice through different paths, as shown in Figure 3.4.

We need a means of selecting fields in an instantiation of GenScatterHierarchy by *positional index*, not by type name. If you could refer to each of the two fields of type int by its position in the typelist (that is, as Field<0>(obj) and Field<1>(obj)), you would get rid of the ambiguity.

Let's implement an index-based field access function. We have to dispatch at compile time between the field index zero, which accesses the head of the typelist, and nonzero, which accesses the tail of the typelist. Dispatching is easy with the help of the little Int2Type template defined in Chapter 2. Recall that Int2Type simply transforms each distinct constant integral into a distinct type. Also, we use Type2Type to transport the result type appropriately, as shown below.

```
    template <class H, typename R>
    inline R& FieldHelper(H& obj, Type2Type<R>, Int2Type<0>)
    {
        typename H::LeftBase& subobj = obj;
        return subobj;
    }
    template <class H, typename R, int i>
    inline R& FieldHelper(H& obj, Type2Type<R> tt, Int2Type<i>)
    {
        typename H::RightBase& subobj = obj;
        return FieldHelper(subobj, tt, Int2Type<i - 1>());
    }
    //Refer to HierarchyGenerators.h for FieldTraits' definition
    template <int i, class H>
    typename Private::FieldTraits<H>::At<i>::Result&
    Field(H& obj)
    {
        typedef typename Private::FieldTraits<H>::At<i>::Result
            Result;
        return FieldHelper(obj, Type2Type<Result>(), Int2type<i>());
    }
```

It takes a while to figure out how to write such an implementation, but fortunately explaining it is quite easy. Two overloaded functions called FieldHelper do the actual job. The first one accepts a parameter of type Int2Type<0>, and the second is a template that accepts Int2Type<*any integer*>. Consequently, the first overload returns the value corresponding to the Unit<T1>&, and the other returns the type at the specified index in the typelist. Field uses a helper template FieldTraits to figure out what type it must return. Field passes that type to FieldHelper through Type2Type.

The second overload of FieldHelper recurses to FieldHelper, passing it the right-hand base of GenScatterHierarchy and Int2Type<index - 1>. This happens because field N in a typelist is field N - 1 in the tail of that typelist, for any positive N. (And indeed, the N = 0 case is handled by the first overload of FieldHelper.)

For a streamlined interface, we need two additional Field functions: the const versions of the two Field functions defined above. They are similar to their non-const counterparts, except that they accept and return references to const types.

Field makes GenScatterHierarchy very easy to use. Now we can write

```
    WidgetInfo obj;
    ...
    int x = Field<0>(obj).value_; // first int
    int y = Field<1>(obj).value_; // second int
```

The GenScatterHierarchy template is very suitable for generating elaborate classes from typelists by compounding a simple template. You can use GenScatterHierarchy to generate virtual functions for each type in a typelist. Chapter 9, Abstract Factory, uses GenScatterHierarchy to generate abstract creation functions starting from a typelist. Chapter 9 also shows how to implement hierarchies generated by GenScatterHierarchy.

3.13.2 Generating Tuples

Sometimes you might need to generate a small structure with unnamed fields, known in some languages (such as ML) as a *tuple*. A tuple facility in C++ was first introduced by Jakko Järvi (1999a) and then refined by Järvi and Powell (1999b).

What are tuples? Consider the following example.

```
template <class T>
struct Holder
{
    T value_;
};

typedef GenScatterHierarchy<
    TYPELIST_3(int, int, int),
    Holder>
Point3D;
```

Working with `Point3D` is a bit clumsy, because you have to write `.value_` after any field access function. What you need here is to generate a structure the same way `GenScatterHierarchy` does, but with the `Field` access functions returning references to the `value_` members directly. That is, `Field<n>` should not return a `Holder<int>&`, but an `int&` instead.

Loki defines a `Tuple` template class that is implemented similarly to `GenScatterHierarchy` but that provides direct field access. `Tuple` works as follows:

```
typedef Tuple<TYPELIST_3(int, int, int)>
    Point3D;
Point3D pt;
Field<0>(pt) = 0;
Field<1>(pt) = 100;
Field<2>(pt) = 300;
```

Tuples are useful for creating small anonymous structures that don't have member functions. For example, you can use tuples for returning multiple values from a function:

```
Tuple<TYPELIST_3(int, int, int)>
GetWindowPlacement(Window&);
```

The fictitious function `GetWindowPlacement` allows users to get the coordinates of a window and its position in the window stack using a single function call. The library implementer does not have to provide a distinct structure for tuples of three integers.

You can see other tuple-related functions offered by Loki by looking in the file `Tuple.h`.

3.13.3 Generating Linear Hierarchies

Consider the following simple template that defines an event handler interface. It only defines an `OnEvent` member function.

```
template <class T>
class EventHandler
{
public:
   virtual void OnEvent(const T&, int eventId) = 0;
   virtual ~EventHandler() {}
};
```

To be politically correct, EventHandler also defines a virtual destructor, which is not germane to our discussion, but necessary nonetheless (see Chapter 4 on why).

We can use GenScatterHierarchy to distribute EventHandler to each type in a typelist:

```
typedef GenScatterHierarchy
<
   TYPELIST_3(Window, Button, ScrollBar),
   EventHandler
>
WidgetEventHandler;
```

The disadvantage of GenScatterHierarchy is that it uses multiple inheritance. If you care about optimizing size, GenScatterHierarchy might be inconvenient, because Widget-EventHandler contains three pointers to virtual tables,[5] one for each EventHandler instantiation. If sizeof(EventHandler) is 4 bytes, then sizeof(WidgetEventHandler) will likely be 12 bytes, and it grows as you add types to the typelist. The most space-efficient configuration is to have all virtual functions declared right inside WidgetEventHandler, but this dismisses any code generation opportunities.

A nice configuration that decomposes WidgetEventHandler into one class per virtual function is a linear inheritance hierarchy, as shown in Figure 3.5. By using single inheritance, WidgetEventHandler would have only one vtable pointer, thus maximizing space efficiency.

How can we provide a mechanism that automatically generates a hierarchy like this? A recursive template similar to GenScatterHierarchy can be of help here. There is a difference, though. The user-provided class template must now accept *two* template parameters. One of them is the current type in the typelist, as in GenScatterHierarchy. The other one is the base from which the instantiation derives. The second template parameter is needed because, as shown in Figure 3.5, the user-defined code now participates in the *middle* of the class hierarchy, not only at its roots (as was the case with GenScatterHierarchy).

Let's write a recursive template GenLinearHierarchy. It bears a similarity to Gen-ScatterHierarchy, the difference being the way it handles the inheritance relationship and the user-provided template unit.

```
template
<
   class TList,
   template <class AtomicType, class Base> class Unit,
```

---

[5]An implementation does not need to use virtual tables, but most implementations do. For a description of virtual tables, refer to Lippman (1994).

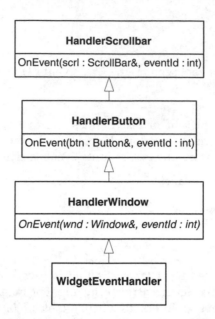

Figure 3.5: A size-optimized structure for `WidgetEventHandler`

```
    class Root = EmptyType // For EmptyType, consult Chapter 2
>
class GenLinearHierarchy;

template
<
    class T1,
    class T2,
    template <class, class> class Unit,
    class Root
>
class GenLinearHierarchy<Typelist<T1, T2>, Unit, Root>
    : public Unit< T1, GenLinearHierarchy<T2, Unit, Root> >
{
};

template
<
    class T,
    template <class, class> class Unit,
    class Root
>
class GenLinearHierarchy<TYPELIST_1(T), Unit, Root>
    : public Unit<T, Root>
{
};
```

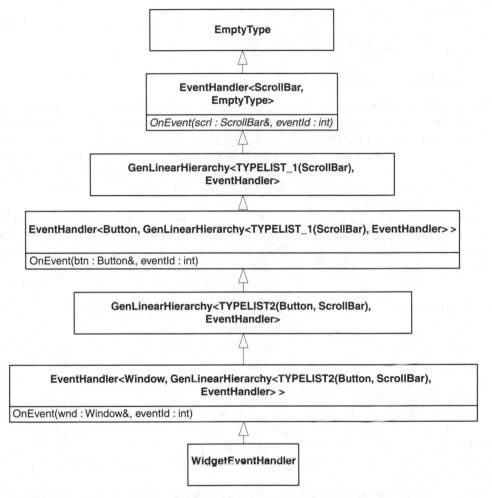

Figure 3.6: The class hierarchy generated by `GenLinearHierarchy`

This code is slightly more complicated than `GenScatterHierarchy`'s, but the structure of a hierarchy generated by `GenLinearHierarchy` is simpler. Let's verify the adage that an image is worth 1,024 words by looking at Figure 3.6, which shows the hierarchy generated by the following code.

```
template <class T, class Base>
class EventHandler : public Base
{
public:
    virtual void OnEvent(T& obj, int eventId);
};
```

```
typedef GenLinearHierarchy
<
    TYPELIST_3(Window, Button, ScrollBar),
    EventHandler
>
WidgetEventHandler;
```

In conjunction with `EventHandler`, `GenLinearHierarchy` defines a linear, rope-shaped, single-inheritance class hierarchy. Each other node in the hierarchy defines one pure virtual function, as prescribed by `EventHandler`. Consequently, `MyEventHandler` defines three virtual functions, as needed. `GenLinearHierarchy` adds a requirement to its template template parameter: `Unit` (in our example, `EventHandler`) must accept a second template argument, and inherit from it. In compensation, `GenLinearHierarchy` does the laborious task of generating the class hierarchy.

`GenScatterHierarchy` and `GenLinearHierarchy` work great in tandem. In most cases, you would generate an interface with `GenScatterHierarchy` and implement it with `GenLinearHierarchy`. Chapters 9 and 10 demonstrate concrete uses of these two hierarchy generators.

3.14 Summary

Typelists are an important generic programming technique. They add new capabilities for library writers: expressing and manipulating arbitrarily large collections of types, generating data structures and code from such collections, and more.

At compile time, typelists offer most of the primitive functions that lists of values typically implement: add, erase, search, access, replace, erase duplicates, and even sorting by inheritance relationship. The code that implements typelist manipulation is confined to a pure functional style because there are no compile-time mutable values—a type or compile-time constant, once defined, cannot be changed. For this reason, most typelist processing relies on recursive templates and pattern matching through partial template specialization.

Typelists are useful when you have to write the same code—either declarative or imperative—for a collection of types. They enable you to abstract and generalize entities that escape all other generic programming techniques. For this reason, typelists are the enabling means for genuinely new idioms and library implementations, as you will see in Chapters 9 and 10.

Loki provides two powerful primitives for automatic generation of class hierarchies from typelists: `GenScatterHierarchy` and `GenLinearHierarchy`. They generate two basic class structures: scattered (Figure 3.2) and linear (Figure 3.6). The linear class hierarchy structure is the more size efficient one. A scattered class hierarchy has a useful property: All instantiations of the user-defined template (passed as an argument to `GenScatterHierarchy`) are roots of the final class, as Figure 3.2 shows.

3.15 Typelist Quick Facts

- *Header file:* Typelist.h.
- All typelist utilities reside in namespace Loki::TL.
- Class template Typelist<Head, Tail> is defined.
- Typelist creation: Macros TYPELIST_1 to TYPELIST_50 are defined. They accept the number of parameters stated in their name.
- The upper limit of macros (50) can be extended by the user. For instance:

```
#define TYPELIST_51(T1, repeat here up to T51) \
    Typelist<T1, TYPELIST_50(T2, repeat here up to T51) >
```

- By convention, typelists are proper—they always have a simple type (nontypelist) as the first element (the head). The tail can only be a typelist or NullType.
- The header defines a collection of primitives that operate on typelists. By convention, all the primitives return the result in a nested (inner) public type definition called Result. If the result of the primitive is a value, then its name is value.
- The primitives are described in Table 3.1.
- Synopsis of class template GenScatterHierarchy:

```
template <class TList, template <class> class Unit>
class GenScatterHierarchy;
```

- GenScatterHierarchy generates a hierarchy that instantiates Unit with each type in the typelist TList. An instantiation of GenScatterHierarchy directly or indirectly inherits Unit<T> for each T in TList.
- The structure of a hierarchy generated by GenScatterHierarchy is depicted in Figure 3.2.
- Synopsis of class template GenLinearHierarchy:

```
template <class TList, template <class, class> class Unit>
class GenLinearHierarchy;
```

- GenLinearHierarchy generates a linear hierarchy, depicted in Figure 3.6.
- GenLinearHierarchy instantiates Unit by passing each type in the typelist TList as Unit's first template argument. *Important:* Unit must derive publicly from its second template parameter.
- The overloaded Field functions provide by-type and by-index access to the nodes of the hierarchies.
- Field<Type>(obj) returns a reference to the Unit instantiation that corresponds to the specified type Type.
- Field<index>(obj) returns a reference to the Unit instantiation that corresponds to the type found in the typelist at the position specified by the integral constant index.

Table 3.1: Compile-Time Algorithms Operating on Typelists

Primitive Name	Description
Length<TList>	Computes the length of TList.
TypeAt<TList, idx>	Returns the type at a given position (zero-based) in TList. If the index is greater than or equal to the length of TList, a compile-time error occurs.
TypeAtNonStrict<TList, idx>	Returns the type at a given position (zero-based) in a typelist. If the index is greater than or equal to the length of TList, Null Type is returned.
IndexOf<TList, T>	Returns the index of the first occurrence of type T in typelist TList. If the type is not found, the result is –1.
Append<TList, T>	Appends a type or a typelist to TList.
Erase<TList, T>	Erases the first occurrence, if any, of T in TList.
EraseAll<TList, T>	Erases all occurrences, if any, of T in TList.
NoDuplicates<TList>	Eliminates all the duplicates from TList.
Replace<TList, T, U>	Replaces the first occurrence, if any, of T in TList with U.
ReplaceAll<TList, T, U>	Replaces all occurrences, if any, of T in TList with U.
MostDerived<TList, T>	Returns the most derived type from T in TList. If no such type is found, T is returned.
DerivedToFront<TList>	Brings the most derived types to the front of TList.

4

Small-Object Allocation

This chapter discusses the design and the implementation of a fast allocator for small objects. If you use this allocator, the extra cost of dynamically allocated objects compared with stack-allocated objects often becomes negligible.

In various places, Loki uses very small objects—as small as a few bytes. Chapter 5 (Generalized Functors) and Chapter 7 (Smart Pointers) use small objects heavily. For various reasons, polymorphic behavior being the most important, these small objects cannot be stored on the stack and must live on the free store.

C++ provides the operators new and delete as the primary means of using the free store. The problem is, these operators are general purpose and perform badly for allocating small objects. To give an idea of just how bad "badly" is when it comes to small objects, some standard free store allocators may perform up to an order of magnitude slower, and also eat up twice as much memory, as the allocator that is the subject of this chapter.

"Early optimization is the root of all evils," Knuth said, but on the other hand, "belated pessimization is the leaf of no good," according to Len Lattanzi. A pessimization of one order of magnitude in the runtime of a core object like a functor, a smart pointer, or a string can easily make the difference between success and failure of a whole project. The benefit of cheap and fast dynamic allocation for small objects can be enormous because it allows you to apply advanced techniques without worrying about significant loss in performance. This provides a lot of incentive for looking into optimizing free store allocation for small objects.

Many C++ experts, such as Sutter (2000) and Meyers (1998a), mention the usefulness of writing your own specialized memory allocator. Meyers, after describing an implementation, leaves some details "in the form of the dreaded exercise for the reader," and Sutter sends you to "your favorite advanced C++ or general-purpose programming textbook." The book you're now reading doesn't pretend to become your favorite; however, this chapter does go down to the metal and implement a standard C++ custom allocator in every detail.

After reading this chapter, you will understand the subtle, interesting issues associated with tuning memory allocators. You will also know how to use Loki's heavy-duty small-object allocator, the workhorse of smart pointers and generalized functors.

4.1 The Default Free Store Allocator

For occult reasons, the default allocator is notoriously slow. A possible reason is that it is usually implemented as a thin wrapper around the C heap allocator (`malloc`/`realloc`/`free`). The C heap allocator is not focused on optimizing small chunk allocations. C programs usually make ordered, conservative use of dynamic memory. They don't naturally foster idioms and techniques that lead to numerous allocations and deallocations of small chunks of memory. Instead, C programs usually allocate medium- to large-sized objects (hundreds to thousands of bytes). Consequently, this is the behavior for which `malloc`/`free` is optimized.

In addition to being slow, the genericity of the default C++ allocator makes it very space inefficient for small objects. The default allocator manages a pool of memory, and such management often requires some extra memory. Usually, the bookkeeping memory amounts to a few extra bytes (4 to 32) for each block allocated with `new`. If you allocate 1024-byte blocks, the per-block space overhead is insignificant (0.4% to 3%). If you allocate 8-byte objects, the per-object overhead becomes 50% to 400%, a figure big enough to make you worry if you allocate many such small objects.

In C++, dynamic allocation is very important. Runtime polymorphism is most often associated with dynamic allocation. Strategies such as "the pimpl idiom" (Sutter 2000) prescribe replacing stack allocation with free store allocation.

Therefore, the poor performance of the default allocator makes it a bump on the road toward efficient C++ programs. Seasoned C++ programmers instinctively avoid constructs that foster using free store allocation because they know its costs from experience. Not only is the default allocator a concrete problem, but it also might become a psychological barrier.

4.2 The Workings of a Memory Allocator

Studying memory usage trends of programs is a very interesting activity, as proven by Knuth's seminal work (Knuth 1998). Knuth established many fundamental memory allocation strategies, and even more were invented later.

How does a memory allocator work? A memory allocator manages a pool of raw bytes and is able to allocate chunks of arbitrary size from that pool. The bookkeeping structure can be a simple control block having a structure like the following:

```
struct MemControlBlock
{
    std::size_t size_;
    bool available_;
};
```

The memory managed by a `MemControlBlock` object lies right after it and has `size_` bytes. After the chunk of memory, there is another `MemControlBlock`, and so on.

When the program starts, there is only one `MemControlBlock` at the beginning of the pool, managing the entire memory as a big chunk. This is the root control block, which will never move from its original location. Figure 4.1 shows the memory layout for a 1MB memory pool at startup.

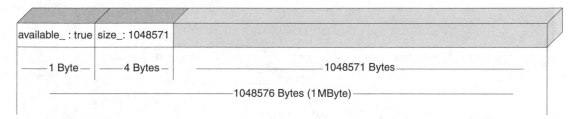

Figure 4.1: The memory map at program startup

For each allocation request, a linear search of memory blocks finds a suitable block for the requested size. Its size must be equal to or larger than the size requested. It is amazing just how many strategies for fitting requests with available blocks exist, and how oddly they perform. You can go for first fit, best fit, worst fit, or even a random fit. Interestingly, worst fit is sometimes better than best fit—how's that for an oxymoron?

Each deallocation incurs, again, a linear search for figuring out the memory block that precedes the block being deallocated, and an adjustment of its size.

As you can see, this strategy is not terribly time efficient. However, the overhead in size is quite small—only one size_t plus a bool per memory block. In most concrete cases, you can even give up a bit in size_ and store available_ there, thus squeezing MemControl Block to the ultimate:

```
// Platform- and compiler-dependent code
struct MemControlBlock
{
    std::size_t size_ : 31;
    bool available_ : 1;
};
```

If you store pointers to the previous and next MemControlBlock in each MemControl- Block, you can achieve constant-time deallocation. This is because a block that's freed can access the adjacent blocks directly and adjust them accordingly. The necessary memory control block structure is

```
struct MemControlBlock
{
    bool available_ ;
    MemControlBlock* prev_;
    MemControlBlock* next_;
};
```

Figure 4.2 shows the layout of a memory pool fostering such a doubly linked list of blocks. As you can see, the size_ member variable is not needed anymore because you can compute the size as this->next_ - this. Still, you have the overhead of two point- ers and a bool for each allocated memory block. (Again, you can do some system- dependent tricks to pack that bool together with one of the pointers.)

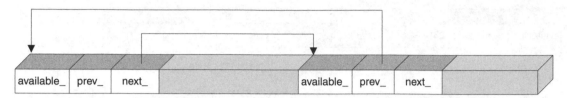

Figure 4.2: An allocator with constant-time deallocations

Still, allocations take linear time. There are many neat techniques for mitigating that, each fostering a different set of trade-offs. Interestingly, there's no perfect memory allocation strategy; each of them has a memory use trend that makes it perform worse than others.

We don't need to optimize general allocators. Let's focus on specialized allocators—allocators that deal best with small objects.

4.3 A Small-Object Allocator

The small-object allocator described in this chapter sports a four-layer structure, shown in Figure 4.3. The upper layers use functionality provided by the lower layers. At the bottom is a Chunk type. Each object of type Chunk contains and manages a chunk of memory consisting of an integral number of fixed-size blocks. Chunk contains logic that allows you to allocate and deallocate memory blocks. When there are no more blocks available in the chunk, the allocation function fails by returning zero.

The next layer features the FixedAllocator class. A FixedAllocator object uses Chunk as a building block. FixedAllocator's primary purpose is to satisfy memory requests that go beyond a Chunk's capacity. FixedAllocator does this by aggregating an array of Chunks. Whenever a request for memory comes and all existing Chunks are occupied, FixedAllocator creates a new Chunk and appends it to the array. Then it satisfies the request by forwarding the request to that new Chunk.

SmallObjAllocator provides general allocation and deallocation functions. A Small-ObjAllocator holds several FixedAllocator objects, each specialized for allocating objects of one size. Depending on the number of bytes requested, SmallObjAllocator dispatches memory allocation requests to one of its FixedAllocators or to the default ::operator new if the size requested is too large.

Finally, SmallObject wraps FixedAllocator to offer encapsulated allocation services for C++ classes. SmallObject overloads operator new and operator delete and passes the allocation/deallocation requests to a SmallObjAllocator object. This way, you make your objects benefit from specialized allocation by simply deriving them from SmallObject.

You can also use SmallObjAllocator and FixedAllocator directly. (Chunk is too primitive and unsafe, so it is defined in the private section of FixedAllocator.) Most of the time, however, client code will simply derive from the SmallObject base class to take advantage of efficient allocation. That's quite an easy-to-use interface.

SmallObject	Object-level services Transparent – you derive your classes only from SmallObject
SmallObjAllocator	Able to allocate small objects of various sizes Configurable parameters
FixedAllocator	Allocates only objects of one given size
Chunk	Allocates objects of one given size Has a fixed upper limit of number of objects allocated

Figure 4.3: The layered structure of the small-object allocator

4.4 Chunks

Each object of type Chunk contains and manages a chunk of memory containing a fixed amount of blocks. At construction time, you configure the block size and the number of blocks.

A Chunk contains logic that allows you to allocate and deallocate memory blocks from that chunk of memory. When there are no more blocks available in the chunk, the allocation function returns zero.

The definition of Chunk is as follows:

```
// Nothing is private - Chunk is a Plain Old Data (POD) structure
// structure defined inside FixedAllocator
// and manipulated only by it
struct Chunk
{
    void Init(std::size_t blockSize, unsigned char blocks);
    void* Allocate(std::size_t blockSize);
    void Deallocate(void* p, std::size_t blockSize);
    void Release();
    unsigned char* pData_;
    unsigned char
        firstAvailableBlock_,
        blocksAvailable_;
};
```

In addition to a pointer to the managed memory itself, a chunk stores the following integral values:

- firstAvailableBlock_, which holds the index of the first block available in this chunk
- blocksAvailable_, the number of blocks available in this chunk

The interface of Chunk is very simple. Init initializes a Chunk object, and Release releases the allocated memory. The Allocate function allocates a block, and Deallocate deallocates a block. You have to pass a size to Allocate and Deallocate because Chunk does not hold it. This is because the block size is known at a superior level. Chunk would waste space and time if it redundantly kept a blockSize_ member. Don't forget we are at the very bottom here—everything matters. Again for efficiency reasons, Chunk does not define constructors, destructor, or assignment operator. Defining proper copy semantics at this level hurts efficiency at upper levels, where we store Chunk objects in a vector.

The Chunk structure reveals important trade-offs. Because blocksAvailable_ and first-AvailableBlock_ are of type unsigned char, it follows that you cannot have a chunk that contains more than 255 blocks (on a machine with 8-bit characters). As you will soon see, this decision is not bad at all and saves us a lot of headaches.

Now for the interesting part. A block can be either used or unused. We can store whatever we want in an unused block, so we take advantage of this. The first byte of an unused block holds the index of the next unused block. Because we hold the first available index in firstAvailableBlock_, we have a full-fledged singly linked list of unused blocks without using any extra memory.

At initialization, a chunk looks like Figure 4.4. The code that initializes a Chunk object looks like this:

```
void Chunk::Init(std::size_t blockSize, unsigned char blocks)
{
    pData_ = new unsigned char[blockSize * blocks];
    firstAvailableBlock_ = 0;
    blocksAvailable_ = blocks;
    unsigned char i = 0;
    unsigned char* p = pData_;
    for (; i != blocks; p += blockSize)
    {
        *p = ++i;
    }
}
```

This singly linked list melted inside the data structure is an essential goodie. It offers a fast, efficient way of finding available blocks inside a chunk—without any extra cost in size. Allocating and deallocating a block inside a Chunk takes constant time, which is exclusively thanks to the embedded singly linked list.

Now you see why the number of blocks is limited to a value that fits in an unsigned char. Suppose we used a larger type instead, such as unsigned short (which is 2 bytes on many machines). We would now have two problems—a little one and a big one.

- We cannot allocate blocks smaller than sizeof(unsigned short), which is awkward because we're building a *small*-object allocator. This is the little problem.
- We run into alignment issues. Imagine you build an allocator for 5-byte blocks. In this case, casting a pointer that points to such a 5-byte block to unsigned int engenders undefined behavior. This is the big problem.

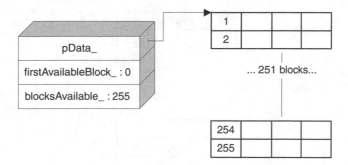

Figure 4.4: A chunk of 255 blocks of 4 bytes each

The solution is simple: We use unsigned char as the type of the "stealth index." A character type has size 1 by definition and does not have any alignment problem because even the pointer to the raw memory points to unsigned char.

This setting imposes a limitation on the maximum number of blocks in a chunk. We cannot have more than UCHAR_MAX blocks in a chunk (255 on most systems). This is acceptable even if the size of the block is really small, such as 1 to 4 bytes. For larger blocks, the limitation doesn't make a difference because we don't want to allocate chunks that are too big anyway.

The allocation function fetches the block indexed by firstAvailableBlock_ and adjusts firstAvailableBlock_ to refer to the next available block—typical list stuff.

```
void* Chunk::Allocate(std::size_t blockSize)
{
    if (!blocksAvailable_) return 0;
    unsigned char* pResult =
        pData_ + (firstAvailableBlock_ * blockSize);
    // Update firstAvailableBlock_ to point to the next block
    firstAvailableBlock_ = *pResult;
    --blocksAvailable_;
    return pResult;
}
```

The cost of Chunk::Allocate is one comparison, one indexed access, two dereference operations, an assignment, and a decrement—quite a small cost. Most important, there are no searches. We're in pretty good shape so far. Figure 4.5 shows the layout of a Chunk object after the first allocation.

The deallocation function does exactly the opposite: It passes the block back to the free blocks list and increments blocksAvailable_. Don't forget that because Chunk is agnostic regarding the block size, you must pass the size as a parameter to Deallocate.

```
void Chunk::Deallocate(void* p, std::size_t blockSize)
{
    assert(p >= pData_);
```

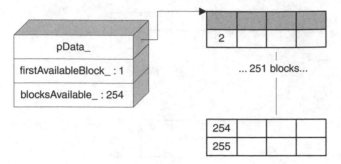

Figure 4.5: A Chunk object after the one allocation. The allocated memory is shown in gray.

```
unsigned char* toRelease = static_cast<unsigned char*>(p);
// Alignment check
assert((toRelease - pData_) % blockSize == 0);
*toRelease = firstAvailableBlock_;
firstAvailableBlock_ = static_cast<unsigned char>(
    (toRelease - pData_) / blockSize);
// Truncation check
assert(firstAvailableBlock_ ==
    (toRelease - pData_) / blockSize);
++blocksAvailable_;
}
```

The deallocation function is lean, but it does a lot of assertions (which still don't catch all error conditions). Chunk respects the grand C and C++ tradition in memory allocation: Prepare for the worst if you pass the wrong pointer to Chunk::Deallocate.

4.5 The Fixed-Size Allocator

The next layer of our small-object allocator consists of FixedAllocator. FixedAllocator knows how to allocate and deallocate blocks of a fixed size but is not limited to a chunk's size. Its capacity is limited only by available memory.

To achieve this, FixedAllocator aggregates a vector of Chunk objects. Whenever an allocation request occurs, FixedAllocator looks for a Chunk that can accommodate the request. If all Chunks are filled up, FixedAllocator appends a new Chunk. Here is the relevant part of the definition of FixedAllocator:

```
class FixedAllocator
{
   ...
private:
   std::size_t blockSize_;
   unsigned char numBlocks_;
   typedef std::vector<Chunk> Chunks;
   Chunks chunks_;
```

```
        Chunk* allocChunk_;
        Chunk* deallocChunk_;
    };
```

To achieve a speedy lookup, FixedAllocator does not iterate through chunks_ looking for a space for each allocation. Instead, it holds a pointer to the last chunk that was used for an allocation (allocChunk_). Whenever an allocation request comes, FixedAllocator:: Allocate first checks allocChunk_ for available space. If allocChunk_ has a slot available, the allocation request is satisfied—presto—using allocChunk_. If not, a linear search occurs (and, possibly, a new Chunk is appended to the chunks_ vector). In any case, allocChunk_ is updated to point to that found or added chunk. This way we increase the likelihood of a fast allocation next time. Here's the code that implements this algorithm:

```
    void* FixedAllocator::Allocate()
    {
        if (allocChunk_ == 0 ||
            allocChunk_->blocksAvailable_ == 0)
        {
            // No available memory in this chunk
            // Try to find one
            Chunks::iterator i = chunks_.begin();
            for (;; ++i)
            {
                if (i == chunks_.end())
                {
                    // All filled up-add a new chunk
                    chunks_.reserve(chunks_.size()+1);
                    Chunk newChunk;
                    newChunk.Init(blockSize_, numBlocks_);
                    chunks_.push_back(newChunk);
                    allocChunk_ = &chunks_.back();
                    deallocChunk_ = &chunks_.back();
                    break;
                }
                if (i->blocksAvailable_ > 0)
                {
                    // Found a chunk
                    allocChunk_ = &*i;
                    break;
                }
            }
        }
        assert(allocChunk_ != 0);
        assert(allocChunk_->blocksAvailable_ > 0);
        return allocChunk_->Allocate(blockSize_);
    }
```

Using this strategy, FixedAllocator satisfies most of the allocations in constant time, with occasional slowdowns caused by finding and adding a new block. Some memory allocation trends make this scheme work inefficiently; however, they tend not to appear often in practice. Don't forget that every allocator has an Achilles' heel.

Memory deallocation is more problematic, because at deallocation time there's a piece of information missing—all we have is a pointer to deallocate, and we don't know to what Chunk that pointer belongs. We could walk through chunks_ and check whether the given pointer falls in between pData_ and pData_ + blockSize_ * numBlocks_. If that's the case, then we pass the pointer to that Chunk's Deallocate member function. The problem is, this takes time. Although allocations are fast, deallocations take linear time. We need an additional device that speeds up deallocations.

We could use a supplemental *cache* memory for freed blocks. When user code frees a block using FixedAllocator::Deallocate(p), the FixedAllocator does not pass p back to the corresponding Chunk; instead, it adds p to an internal memory—a cache that holds available blocks. When a new allocation request comes, FixedAllocator first looks up the cache. If the cache is not empty, FixedAllocator fetches the last available pointer from cache and returns it right away. This is a very fast operation. Only when the cache is depleted does FixedAllocator need to go the standard route by forwarding the allocation request to a Chunk. This is a promising strategy, but it works badly with certain allocation and deallocation trends that are common to small-object use.

There are four main trends in allocating small objects:

- *Bulk allocation.* Many small objects are allocated at the same time. For example, this is the case when you initialize a collection of pointers to small objects.
- *Deallocation in same order.* Many small objects are deallocated in the same order as they were allocated. This happens when most STL containers are destroyed.[1]
- *Deallocation in reverse order.* Many small objects are deallocated in the reverse order of their allocation. This trend occurs naturally in C++ programs as you call functions that manipulate small objects. Function arguments and temporary stack variables follow this trend.
- *Butterfly allocation and deallocation.* Objects are created and destroyed without following a certain order. This happens as your program is running and has occasional need for small objects.

A caching strategy serves the butterfly trend very well because it can sustain quick allocations and deallocations if they arrive randomly. However, for bulk allocation and deallocation, caching is not of help. Worse, caching slows down deallocations because clearing the cache memory takes its own time.[2]

A better strategy is to rely on the same concept as with allocation. The member variable FixedAllocator::deallocChunk_ points to the last Chunk object that was used for a deallocation. Whenever a deallocation occurs, deallocChunk_ is checked first. Then, if it's the wrong chunk, Deallocate performs a linear search, satisfies the request, and updates deallocChunk_.

---

[1]Standard C++ does not define the order of destruction of objects within a standard container. Therefore, each implementer has to make a choice. Usually, containers are destroyed through a simple forward iteration. However, some implementers go for the more "natural" order by destroying objects in reverse order. The rationale is that in C++ objects are destroyed in reverse order of their creation.

[2]I could not come up with a reasonable caching scheme that works equally well for same-order deallocation and reverse-order deallocation. Caching hurts either one or the other. Because both trends are likely to occur in real programs, caching is not a good choice.

Two important tweaks increase the speed of Deallocate for the allocation trends enumerated earlier. First, the Deallocate function searches the appropriate Chunk starting from deallocChunk_'s vicinity. That is, chunks_ is searched starting from deallocChunk_ and going up and down with two iterators. This greatly improves the speed of bulk deallocations in any order (normal or reversed). During a bulk allocation, Allocate adds chunks in order. During deallocation, either deallocChunk_ hits right away or the correct chunk is fetched in the next step.

The second tweak is the avoidance of borderline conditions. Say both allocChunk_ and deallocChunk_ point to the last Chunk in the vector, and there is no space left in the current set of chunks. Now imagine the following code is run:

```
for (...)
{
    // Some smart pointers use the small-object
    // allocator internally (see Chapter 7)
    SmartPtr p;
    ... use p ....
}
```

Each pass through the loop creates and destroys a SmartPtr object. At creation time, because there's no more memory, FixedAllocator::Allocate creates a new Chunk and appends it to the chunks_ vector. At destruction time, FixedAllocator::Deallocate detects an empty block and frees it. This costly cycle gets repeated for each iteration of the for loop.

This inefficiency is unacceptable. Therefore, during deallocation, a chunk is freed only when there are *two* empty chunks. If there's only one empty chunk, it is efficiently swapped to the end of the chunks_ vector. Thus, we avoid costly vector<Chunk>::erase operations by always deleting the last element.

Of course, some situations defeat this simple heuristic. If you allocate a vector of SmartPtrs of appropriate size in a loop, you are back to the same problem. However, such situations tend to appear more rarely. Besides, as mentioned in the introduction of this chapter, *any* allocator may perform worse than others under specific circumstances.

The deallocation strategy chosen also fits the butterfly allocation trend acceptably. Even if not allocating data in an ordered manner, programs tend to foster a certain *locality;* that is, they access a small amount of data at a time. The allocChunk_ and deallocChunk_ pointers deal nicely with such memory use because they act as a cache for the latest allocations and deallocations.

In conclusion, we now have a FixedAllocator class that can satisfy fixed-memory allocation requests in an acceptably fast and memory-efficient manner. FixedAllocator is optimized for typical trends in small-object allocation.

4.6 The SmallObjAllocator Class

The third layer in our allocator architecture consists of SmallObjAllocator, a class capable of allocating objects of any size. SmallObjAllocator does so by aggregating several FixedAllocator objects. When SmallObjAllocator receives an allocation request, it

either forwards it to the best matching FixedAllocator object or passes it to the default
::operator new.

The following is a synopsis of SmallObjAllocator. Explanations follow the code.

```
class SmallObjAllocator
{
public:
    SmallObjAllocator(
        std::size_t chunkSize,
        std::size_t maxObjectSize);
    void* Allocate(std::size_t numBytes);
    void Deallocate(void* p, std::size_t size);
    ...
private:
    std::vector<FixedAllocator> pool_;
    ...
};
```

The constructor takes two parameters that configure SmallObjAllocator. The chunk-
Size parameter is the default chunk size (the length in bytes of each Chunk object),
and maxObjectSize is the maximum size of objects that must be considered to be "small."
SmallObjAllocator forwards requests for blocks larger than maxObjectSize directly to
::operator new.

Oddly enough, Deallocate takes the size to deallocate as an argument. Deallocations
are much faster this way. Otherwise, SmallObjAllocator::Deallocate would have to
search through all FixedAllocators in pool_ to find the one to which the pointer belongs.
This is too expensive, so SmallObjAllocator requires you to pass the size of the block to
deallocate. As you'll see in the next section, this task is graciously handled by the compiler
itself.

What's the mapping between the block size of FixedAllocator and pool_? In other
words, given a size, what's the FixedAllocator that handles allocations and deallocations
for blocks of that size?

A simple and efficient idea is to have pool_[i] handle objects of size i. You
initialize pool_ to have a size of maxObjectSize, and then initialize each Fixed-
Allocator accordingly. When an allocation request of size numBytes comes, SmallObj-
Allocator forwards it either to pool_[numBytes]—a constant-time operation—or to
::operator new.

However, this solution is not as clever as it seems. "Efficient" is not always "effective."
The problem is, you might need allocators only for certain sizes, depending on your application. For instance, maybe you create only objects of size 4 and 64—nothing else. In this
case, you allocate 64 or more entries for pool_ although you use only 2.

Alignment and padding issues further contribute to wasting space in pool_. For instance, many compilers pad all user-defined types up to a multiple of a number (2, 4, or
more). If the compiler pads all structures to a multiple of 4, for instance, you can count on
using only 25% of pool_—the rest is wasted.

A better approach is to sacrifice a bit of lookup speed for the sake of memory conservation.[3] We store FixedAllocators only for sizes that are requested at least once. This way pool_ can accommodate various object sizes without growing too much. To improve lookup speed, pool_ is kept sorted by block size.

To improve lookup speed, we can rely on the same strategy as in FixedAllocator. SmallObjAllocator keeps a pointer to the last FixedAllocator used for allocation and a pointer to the last FixedAllocator used for deallocation. The following is the complete set of member variables in SmallObjAllocator.

```
class SmallObjAllocator
{
    ...
private:
    std::vector<FixedAllocator> pool_;
    FixedAllocator* pLastAlloc_;
    FixedAllocator* pLastDealloc_;
};
```

When an allocation request arrives, pLastAlloc_ is checked first. If it is not of the correct size, SmallObjAllocator::Allocate performs a binary search in pool_. Deallocation requests are handled in a similar way. The only difference is that Small-ObjAllocator::Allocate can end up inserting a new FixedAllocator object in pool_.

As discussed with FixedAllocator, this simple caching scheme favors bulk allocations and deallocations, which take place in constant time.

4.7 A Hat Trick

The last layer of our architecture consists of SmallObject, the base class that conveniently wraps the functionality provided by SmallObjAllocator.

SmallObject overloads operator new and operator delete. This way, whenever you create an object derived from SmallObject, the overloads enter into action and route the request to the fixed allocator object.

The definition of SmallObject is quite simple, if a bit intriguing.

```
class SmallObject
{
public:
    static void* operator new(std::size_t size);
    static void operator delete(void* p, std::size_t size);
    virtual ~SmallObject() {}
};
```

SmallObject looks perfectly kosher, except for a little detail. Many C++ books, such as Sutter (2000), explain that if you want to overload the default operator delete in a class, operator delete must take a pointer to void as its only argument.

[3] Actually, on modern systems, you can count on an increase in speed when you use less memory. This is due to the big difference in speed between the main memory (large and slow) and the cache memory (small and fast).

C++ offers a kind of a loophole that is of great interest to us. (Recall that we designed SmallObjAllocator to take the size of the block to be freed as an argument.) In standard C++ you can overload the default operator delete in two ways—either as

```
void operator delete(void* p);
```

or as

```
void operator delete(void* p, std::size_t size);
```

This issue is thoroughly explained in Sutter (2000), page 144.

If you use the first form, you choose to ignore the size of the memory block to deallocate. But we badly need that block size so that we can pass it to SmallObjAlloc. Therefore, SmallObject uses the second form of overloading operator delete.

How does the compiler provide the object size automagically? It seems as if the compiler is adding all by itself a per-object memory overhead that we have tried to avoid all through this chapter.

No, there is no overhead at all. Consider the following code:

```
class Base
{
    int a_[100];
public:
    virtual ~Base() {}
};
class Derived : public Base
{
    int b_[200];
public:
    virtual ~Derived() {}
};
...
Base* p = new Derived;
delete p;
```

Base and Derived have different sizes. To avoid the overhead of storing the size of the actual object to which p points, the compiler does a hat trick: It generates code that figures out the size on the fly. Four possible techniques of achieving that are listed here. (Wearing a compiler writer hat from time to time is fun—you suddenly can do little miracles inaccessible to programmers.)

1. Pass a Boolean flag to the destructor meaning "Call/don't call operator delete after destroying the object." Base's destructor is virtual, so, in our example, delete p will reach the right object, Derived. At that time, the size of the object is known statically—it's sizeof(Derived)—and the compiler simply passes this constant to operator delete.

2. Have the destructor return the size of the object. You can arrange (you're the compiler writer, remember?) that each destructor, after destroying the object, returns

sizeof(Class). Again, this scheme works because the destructor of the base class is virtual. After invoking the destructor, the runtime calls operator delete, passing it the "result" of the destructor.

3.   Implement a hidden virtual member function that gets the size of an object, say _Size(). In this case, the runtime calls that function, stores the result, destroys the object, and invokes operator delete. This implementation might look inefficient, but its advantage is that the compiler can use _Size() for other purposes as well.

4.   Store the size directly somewhere in the virtual function table (vtable) of each class. This solution is both flexible and efficient, but less easy to implement.

(Compiler writer hat off.) As you see, the compiler makes quite an effort in passing the appropriate size to your operator delete. Why, then, ignore it and perform a costly search each time you deallocate an object?

It all dovetails so nicely. SmallObjAllocator needs the size of the block to deallocate. The compiler provides it, and SmallObject forwards it to FixedAllocator.

Most of the solutions listed assume you defined a virtual destructor for Base, which explains again why it is so important to make all of your polymorphic classes' destructors virtual. If you fail to do this, deleteing a pointer to a base class that actually points to an object of a derived class engenders undefined behavior. The allocator discussed herein will assert in debug mode and crash your program in NDEBUG mode. Anybody would agree that this behavior fits comfortably into the realm of "undefined."

To protect you from having to remember all this (and from wasting nights debugging if you don't), SmallObject defines a virtual destructor. Any class that you derive from SmallObject will inherit its virtual destructor. This brings us to the implementation of SmallObject.

We need a unique SmallObjAllocator object for the whole application. That SmallObj-Allocator must be properly constructed and properly destroyed, which is a thorny issue on its own. Fortunately, Loki solves this problem thoroughly with its SingletonHolder template, described in Chapter 6. (Referring you to subsequent chapters is a pity, but it would be even more pitiful to waste this reuse opportunity.) For now, just think of SingletonHolder as a device that offers you advanced management of a unique instance of a class. If that class is X, you instantiate SingletonHolder<X>. Then, to access the unique instance of that class, you call SingletonHolder<X>::Instance(). The Singleton design pattern is described in Gamma et al. (1995).

Using SingletonHolder renders SmallObject's implementation extremely simple:

```
typedef SingletonHolder<SmallObjAllocator> MyAlloc;
void* SmallObject::operator new(std::size_t size)
{
    return MyAlloc::Instance().Allocate(size);
}
void SmallObject::operator delete(void* p, std::size_t size)
{
    MyAlloc::Instance().Deallocate(p, size);
}
```

4.8 Simple, Complicated, Yet Simple in the End

The implementation of SmallObject turned out to be quite simple. However, it cannot remain that simple because of multithreading issues. The unique SmallObjAllocator is shared by all instances of SmallObject. If these instances belong to different threads, we end up sharing the SmallObjAllocator between multiple threads. As discussed in the appendix, in this case we must take special measures. It seems as if we must go back to all layers' implementations, figure out the critical operations, and add locking appropriately.

However, although it's true that multithreading complicates things a bit, it's not *that* complicated because Loki already defines high-level object synchronization mechanisms. Following the principle that the best step toward reuse is to use, let's include Loki's Threads.h and make the following changes to SmallObject (changes are shown in bold):

```
template <template <class T> class ThreadingModel>
class SmallObject : public ThreadingModel<SmallObject>
{
    ... as before ...
};
```

The definitions of operator new and operator delete also undergo a bit of surgery:

```
template <template <class T> class ThreadingModel>
void* SmallObject<ThreadingModel>::operator new(std::size_t size)
{
    typename ThreadingModel <SmallObject>::Lock lock;
    return MyAlloc::Instance().Allocate(size);
}

template <template <class T> class ThreadingModel>
void SmallObject<ThreadingModel>::operator delete(void* p, std::size_t size)
{
    typename ThreadingModel<SmallObject>::Lock lock;
    return MyAlloc::Instance().Deallocate(p, size);
}
```

That's it! We don't have to modify any of the previous layers—their functionality will be properly guarded by locking at the highest level.

Using the Singleton management and the multithreading features of Loki right inside Loki is witness to the power of reuse. Each of these two domains—global variables' lifetimes and multithreading—has its own complications. Trying to handle them all in SmallObject starting from first principles would have been overwhelmingly difficult—just try to get peace of mind for implementing FixedAllocator's intricate caching while facing the spectrum of multiple threads spuriously initializing the same object. . .

4.9 Administrivia

This section discusses how to use the `SmallObj.h` file in your applications.

To use `SmallObject`, you must provide appropriate parameters to `SmallObj-Allocator`'s constructor: the chunk size and the maximum size of a small object. How is a small object defined? What is the size under which an object can be considered small?

To find an answer to this question, let's go back to the purpose of building a small-object allocator. We wanted to mitigate the inefficiencies in size and time introduced by the default allocator.

The size overhead imposed by the default allocator varies largely. After all, the default allocator can use similar strategies to the ones discussed in this chapter. For most generic allocators, however, you can expect a per-object overhead that varies between 4 and 32 bytes per object in typical desktop machines. For an allocator with 16 bytes of overhead per object, an object of 64 bytes wastes 25% of memory; thus, a 64-byte object should be considered small.

On the other hand, if `SmallObjAllocator` handles objects that are too large, you end up allocating much more memory than needed (don't forget that `FixedAllocator` tends to keep one chunk allocated even after you have freed all small objects).

Loki gives you a choice and tries to provide appropriate defaults. The `SmallObj.h` file uses three preprocessor symbols, described in Table 4.1. You should compile all the source files in a given project with the same preprocessor symbols defined (or don't define them at all and rely on the defaults). If you don't do this, nothing lethal happens; you just end up creating more `FixedAllocators` tuned to different sizes.

The defaults are targeted toward a desktop machine with a reasonable amount of physical memory. If you `#define` either `MAX_SMALL_OBJECT_SIZE` or `DEFAULT_CHUNK_SIZE` to be zero, then `SmallObj.h` uses conditional compilation to generate code that simply uses the default `::operator new` and `::operator delete`, without incurring any overhead at all. The interface of the objects defined remains the same, but their functions are inline stubs that forward to the default free store allocator.

The class template `SmallObject` used to have one parameter. To support different chunk sizes and object sizes, `SmallObject` gets two more template parameters. They default to `DEFAULT_CHUNK_SIZE` and `MAX_SMALL_OBJECT_SIZE`, respectively.

```
template
<
    template <class T>
        class ThreadingModel = DEFAULT_THREADING,
    std::size_t chunkSize = DEFAULT_CHUNK_SIZE,
    std::size_t maxSmallObjectSize = MAX_SMALL_OBJECT_SIZE
>
class SmallObject;
```

If you just say `SmallObject<>`, you get a class that can work with your default threading model, garnished with the default choices concerning memory management.

Table 4.1: Preprocessor Symbols Used by `SmallObj.h`

Symbol	Meaning	Default Value
DEFAULT_CHUNK_SIZE	The default size (in bytes) of a memory chunk.	4096
MAX_SMALL_OBJECT_SIZE	The maximum value that is handled by `SmallObjAllocator`.	64
DEFAULT_THREADING	The default threading model used by the application. A multithreaded application should define this symbol to `ClassLevelLockable`.	Inherited from `Threads.h`

4.10 Summary

Some C++ idioms make heavy use of small objects allocated on the free store. This is because in C++, runtime polymorphism goes hand in hand with dynamic allocation and pointer/reference semantics. However, the default free store allocator (accessible through the global `::operator new` and `::operator delete`) is often optimized for allocating large objects, not small ones. This renders the default free store allocator unsuitable for allocating small objects because it is often slow and brings non-negligible per-object memory overhead.

The solution is to rely on small-object allocators—specialized allocators that are tuned for dealing with small memory blocks (tens to hundreds of bytes). Small-object allocators use larger chunks of memory and organize them in ingenious ways to reduce space and time penalties. The C++ runtime support helps by providing the size of the block to be released. This information can be grabbed by simply using a less-known overloaded form of `operator delete`.

Is Loki's small-object allocator the fastest possible? Definitely not. Loki's allocator operates only within the confines of standard C++. As you saw throughout this chapter, issues such as alignment must be treated very conservatively, and being conservative spells being less than optimal. However, Loki is a reasonably fast, simple, and robust allocator that has the advantage of portability.

4.11 Small-Object Allocator Quick Facts

- The allocator implemented by Loki has a four-layered architecture. The first layer consists of a private type Chunk, which deals with organizing memory chunks in equally sized blocks. The second layer is `FixedAllocator`, which uses a variable-length vector of chunks to satisfy memory allocation to the extent of the available memory in the system. In the third layer, `SmallObjAllocator` uses multiple `FixedAllocator` objects to provide allocations of any object size. Small objects are allocated using a `FixedAllocator`, and requests for large objects are forwarded to `::operator new`.

Finally, the fourth layer consists of `SmallObject`, a class template that wraps a `Small-ObjAllocator` object.

- `SmallObject` class template synopsis:

```
template
<
    template <class T>
        class ThreadingModel = DEFAULT_THREADING,
    std::size_t chunkSize = DEFAULT_CHUNK_SIZE,
    std::size_t maxSmallObjectSize = MAX_SMALL_OBJECT_SIZE
>
class SmallObject
{
public:
    static void* operator new(std::size_t size);
    static void operator delete(void* p, std::size_t size);
    virtual ~SmallObject() {}
};
```

- You can benefit from a small-object allocator by deriving from an instantiation of `SmallObject`. You can instantiate the `SmallObject` class template with the default parameters (`SmallObject<>`) or tweak its threading model or its memory allocation parameters.
- If you create objects with new in multiple threads, you must use a multithreaded model as the `ThreadingModel` parameter. Refer to the appendix for information concerning `ThreadingModel`.
- The default value of `DEFAULT_CHUNK_SIZE` is 4096.
- The default value of `MAX_SMALL_OBJECT_SIZE` is 64.
- You can #**define** `DEFAULT_CHUNK_SIZE` or `MAX_SMALL_OBJECT_SIZE`, or both, to override the default values. After expansion, the macros must expand to constants of type (convertible to) `std::size_t`.
- If you #define either `DEFAULT_CHUNK_SIZE` or `MAX_SMALL_OBJECT_SIZE` to zero, then the `SmallAlloc.h` file uses conditional compilation to generate code that forwards directly to the free store allocator. The interface remains the same. This is useful if you need to compare how your program behaves with and without specialized memory allocation.

Part II

Components

5

Generalized Functors

This chapter describes generalized functors, a powerful abstraction that allows decoupled interobject communication. Generalized functors are especially useful in designs that need requests to be stored in objects. The design pattern that describes encapsulated requests, and that generalized functors follow, is Command (Gamma et al. 1995).

In brief, a generalized functor is *any processing invocation that C++ allows, encapsulated as a typesafe first-class object*. In a more detailed definition, a generalized functor

- *Encapsulates* any processing invocation because it accepts pointers to simple functions, pointers to member functions, functors, and even other generalized functors—together with some or all of their respective arguments.
- Is *typesafe* because it never matches the wrong argument types to the wrong functions.
- Is an *object with value semantics* because it fully supports copying, assignment, and pass by value. A generalized functor can be copied freely and does not expose virtual member functions.

Generalized functors allow you to store processing requests as values, pass them as parameters, and invoke them apart from the point of their creation. They are a much-modernized version of pointers to functions. The essential differences between pointers to functions and generalized functors are that the latter can store state and invoke member functions.

After reading this chapter, you will

- Understand the Command design pattern and how generalized functors relate to it
- Know when the Command pattern and generalized functors are useful
- Grasp the mechanics of various functional entities in C++ and how to encapsulate them under a uniform interface
- Know how to store a processing request and some or all of its parameters in an object, pass it around, and invoke it freely
- Know how to chain multiple such delayed calls and have them performed in sequence
- Know how to use the powerful Functor class template that implements the described functionality

5.1 The Command Design Pattern

According to the Gang of Four (GoF) book (Gamma et al. 1995), the Command pattern's intent is to *encapsulate a request in an object.* A Command object is a piece of work that is stored away from its actual executor. The general structure of the Command pattern is presented in Figure 5.1.

The pattern's main piece is the Command class itself. Its most important purpose is to reduce the dependency between two parts of a system—the invoker and the receiver.

A typical sequence of actions is as follows:

1. The application (client) creates a ConcreteCommand object, passing it enough information to carry on a task. The dotted line in Figure 5.1 illustrates the fact that the Client influences ConcreteCommand's state.
2. The application passes the Command interface of the ConcreteCommand object to the invoker. The invoker stores this interface.
3. Later, the invoker decides it's time to execute the action and fires Command's Execute virtual member function. The virtual call mechanism dispatches the call to the ConcreteCommand object, which takes care of the details. ConcreteCommand reaches the Receiver object (the one that is to do the job) and uses that object to perform the actual processing, such as calling its Action member function. Alternatively, the ConcreteCommand object might carry the processing all by itself. In this case, the receiver in Figure 5.1 disappears.

The invoker can invoke Execute at its leisure. Most important, at runtime you can plug various actions into the invoker by replacing the Command object that the invoker holds.

Two things are worth noting here. First, the invoker is not aware of how the work is done. This is not a new concept—to use a sorting algorithm, you don't need to know its implementation. But what's particular to Command is that the invoker doesn't even know *what* kind of processing the Command object is supposed to do. (By contrast, you certainly would expect the sorting algorithm to have a certain effect.) The invoker only calls for Execute for the Command interface it holds when certain circumstances occur. On the other side, the receiver itself is not necessarily aware that its Action member function was called by an invoker or otherwise.

The Command object thus ensures an important separation between the invoker and the receiver: They might be completely invisible to each other, yet communicate via Commands. Usually, an Application object decides the wiring between invokers and receivers. This means that you can use different invokers for a given set of receivers, and that you can plug different receivers into a given invoker—all without their knowing anything about each other.

Second, let's look at the Command pattern from a timing perspective. In usual programming tasks, when you want to perform an action, you assemble an object, a member function of it, and the arguments to that member function into a call. For example:

```
window.Resize(0, 0, 200, 100); // Resize the window
```

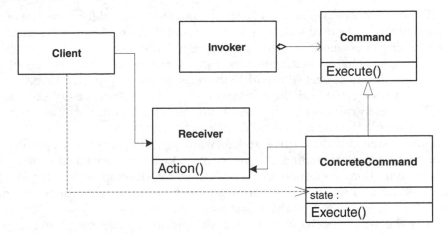

Figure 5.1: The Command design pattern

The moment of initiating such a call is conceptually indistinguishable from the moment of gathering the elements of that call (the object, the procedure, and the arguments). In the Command pattern, however, the invoker has the elements of the call, yet postpones the call itself indefinitely. The Command pattern enables delayed calls as in the following example:

```
Command resizeCmd(
    window,           // Object
    &Window::Resize,  // Member function
    0, 0, 200, 100);  // Arguments
// Later on...
resizeCmd.Execute();  // Resize the window
```

(We will dwell on the slightly less-known C++ construct &Window::Resize a bit later.) In the Command pattern, the moment of *gathering* the environment necessary to perform a processing is different from the moment of *performing* the processing. Between the two moments, the program stores and passes around the processing request as an object. Had this timing-related desire not existed, there would have been no Command pattern. From this standpoint, the very existence of the Command object is a consequence of the timing issue: Because you need to perform processing later, there has to be an object that holds the request until then.

These points lead to two important aspects of the Command pattern:

- *Interface separation.* The invoker is isolated from the receiver.
- *Time separation.* Command stores a ready-to-go processing request that's to be started later.

The notion of environment is also important. The *environment* of a point of execution is the set of entities (variables and functions) that are visible from that point of execution. When the processing is actually started, the necessary environment must be available or else the processing cannot take place. A `ConcreteCommand` object might store part of its necessary environment as its own state and access part of it during `Execute`. The more environment a `ConcreteCommand` stores, the more independence it has.

From an implementation standpoint, two kinds of concrete `Command` classes can be identified. Some simply delegate the work to the receiver. All they do is call a member function for a `Receiver` object. We call them *forwarding commands*. Others do tasks that are more complex. They might call member functions of other objects, but they also embed logic that's beyond simple forwarding. Let's call them *active commands*.

Separating commands into active and forwarding is important for establishing the scope of a generic implementation. Active commands cannot be canned—the code they contain is by definition application-specific—but we can develop helpers for forwarding commands. Because forwarding commands act much like pointers to functions and their C++ colleagues, functors, we call them *generalized functors*.

The aim of the rest of this chapter is to obtain a `Functor` class template that encapsulates any object, any member function of that object, and any set of arguments pertaining to that member function. Once executed, the `Functor` animates all these little things to obtain a function call.

A `Functor` object can be of tremendous help to a design that uses the Command pattern. In hand-coded implementations, the Command pattern doesn't scale well. You must write lots of small concrete `Command` classes (one for each action in the application: `CmdAddUser`, `CmdDeleteUser`, `CmdModifyUser`, and so on), each having a trivial `Execute` member function that just calls a specific member function of some object. A generic `Functor` class that can forward a call to any member function of any object would be of great help to such a design.

Some particular active commands are also worth implementing in `Functor`, such as the sequencing of multiple actions. `Functor` should be able to assemble multiple actions and execute them in order. The GoF book mentions such a useful object, `Macro-Command`.

5.2 Command in the Real World

A popular example associated with the Command pattern is tied to windowing environments. Good object-oriented GUI frameworks have used one form or another of the Command pattern for years.

Windowing-system writers need a generic way to transmit user actions (such as mouse clicks and keystrokes) to the application. When the user clicks a button, selects a menu option, or the like, the windowing system must notify the underlying application logic. From the windowing system's standpoint, the Options command under the Tools menu does not hold any special meaning. If it did, the application would have been locked into a very rigid framework. An effective way to decouple the windowing system from the application is to use `Command` objects for passing user actions. `Commands` serve as generic vehicles that transport actions from the windows to the application logic.

In the windowing example, the invokers are user interface elements (such as buttons, checkboxes, menu items, and widgets), and the receiver is the object responsible for reacting to user interface commands (for example, a dialog or the application itself).

Command objects constitute the *lingua franca* that the user interface and the application use. As discussed in the previous section, Command offers double-ended flexibility. First, you can plug in new kinds of user interface elements without changing the application logic. Such a program is known as *skinnable* because you can add new "skins" without changing the design of the product itself. Skins do not encompass any architecture—they only provide slots for Commands and knowledge to fire them appropriately. Second, you can easily reuse the same user interface elements across different applications.

5.3 C++ Callable Entities

To put together a generic implementation for forwarding commands, let's try to get Command-specific notions closer to terms familiar to C++ programming.

A forwarding command is a callback on steroids, a *generalized callback.* A callback is a pointer to a function that can be passed around and called at any time, as illustrated in the following example.

```
void Foo();
void Bar();

int main()
{
    // Define a pointer to a function that takes no
    // parameters and returns void.
    // Initialize that pointer with the address of Foo
    void (*pF)() = &Foo;
    Foo();                  // Call Foo directly
    Bar();                  // Call Bar directly
    (*pF)();                // Call Foo via pF
    void (*pF2)() = pF;     // Create a copy of pF
    pF = &Bar;              // Change pF to point to Bar
    (*pF)();                // Now call Bar via pF
    (*pF2)();               // Call Foo via pF2
}
```

There is an essential difference between calling Foo and calling (*pF).[1] The difference is that in the latter case you can copy and change pointers to functions. You can take a pointer to a function, store it somewhere, and call it when the right time comes—hence, the similarity with forwarding Commands, which are essentially a piece of work that is stored away from its actual executor and processed later.

In fact, callbacks are the C way of using the Command pattern in many windowing systems. X Windows, for instance, stores such a callback in each menu item and in each widget. The widget calls the callback when the user does something (like clicking on the widget). The widget does not know what the callback actually does.

In addition to simple callbacks, C++ defines many more entities that support the function-call operator. Let's enumerate all the things that support operator() in C++.

---

[1] The compiler offers a syntactic shortcut: (*pF)() is equivalent to pF(). However, (*pF)() is more suggestive of what actually happens—pF is dereferenced, and the function-call operator () is applied to the dereferenced pointer.

- C-like functions
- C-like pointers to functions
- References to functions (which essentially act like const pointers to functions)
- Functors, that is, objects that define an operator()
- The result of applying operator.* or operator->* having a pointer to a member function in the right-hand side of the expression

You can add a pair of parentheses to the right of any of the enumerated items, put an appropriate list of arguments inside, and get some processing done. No other objects in C++ allow this except the ones just listed.

The objects that support operator() are known as *callable entities.* The goal of this chapter is to implement a set of forwarding commands that store and can forward a call to any callable entity.[2] The Functor class template will encapsulate the forwarding commands and provide a uniform interface.

The implementation must handle the three essential cases: simple function calls, functor calls (including Functor calls; that is, you should be able to forward calls from one Functor to another), and member function calls. You might think to define an abstract base class and create a subclass for each case. All this sounds like straightforward C++. As you launch your favorite editor and start to type, however, an abundant crop of problems appears.

5.4 The Functor Class Template Skeleton

For Functor's implementation, we're certainly looking at the handle-body idiom (Coplien 1992). As Chapter 7 discusses in detail, in C++ a bald pointer to a polymorphic type does not strictly have first-class semantics because of the ownership issue. To lift the burden of lifetime management from Functor's clients, it's best to provide Functor with value semantics (well-defined copying and assignment). Functor does have a polymorphic implementation, but that's hidden inside it. We name the implementation base class FunctorImpl.

Let's now make an important observation. Command::Execute in the Command pattern should become a user-defined operator() in C++. There is a sound argument in favor of using operator() here: For C++ programmers, the function-call operator has the exact meaning of "execute," or "do your stuff." But there's a much more interesting argument for this: syntactic uniformity. A forwarding Functor not only delegates to a callable entity, but also *is* a callable entity itself. This renders a Functor able to hold other Functors. So from now on Functor constitutes part of the callable entities set; this will allow us to treat things in a more uniform manner in the future.

The problems start to crop up as soon as we try to define the Functor wrapper. The first shot might look like the following:

```
class Functor
{
```

---

[2]Note the avoidance of the notion of type here. We could have simply said, "Objects of types that support operator() are callable entities." But, incredible as it seems, in C++ there are things to which you can apply operator() although they don't have a type, as you will soon see.

```
public:
    void operator()();
    // other member functions
private:
    // implementation goes here
};
```

The first issue is the return type of `operator()`. Should it be `void`? In certain cases, you would like to return something else, such as a `bool` or a `std::string`. There's no reason to disallow parameterized return values.

Templates are intended to solve this kind of problem, so, without further ado:

```
template <typename ResultType>
class Functor
{
public:
    ResultType operator()();
    // other member functions
private:
    // implementation
};
```

This looks acceptable, although now we don't have one `Functor`; we have a family of `Functor`s. This is quite sensible because `Functor`s that return strings are functionally different from `Functor`s that return integers.

Now for the second issue: Shouldn't `Functor`'s `operator()` accept arguments too? You might want to pass to the `Functor` some information that was not available at `Functor`'s construction time. For example, if mouse clicks on a window are passed via a `Functor`, the caller should pass position information (available exactly and only at call time) to the `Functor` object when calling its `operator()`.

Moreover, in the generic world, parameters can be of any number, and each of them can have any type. There is no ground for limiting either the types that can be passed or their number.

The conclusion that stems from these facts is that each `Functor` is defined by its return type and its arguments' types. The language support needed here sounds a bit scary: variable template parameters combined with variable function-call parameters.

Unfortunately, such language support is very scarce. Variable template parameters simply don't exist. There are variable-argument functions in C++ (as there are in C), but although they do a decent job for C if you're *really* careful, they don't get along as well with C++. Variable arguments are supported via the dreaded ellipsis (*à la* `printf` or `scanf`). Calling `printf` or `scanf` without matching the format specification with the number and types of the arguments is a common and dangerous mistake illustrating the shortcomings of ellipsis functions. The variable-parameter mechanism is unsafe, is low level, and does not fit the C++ object model. To make a long story short, once you use ellipses, you're left in a world with no type safety, no object semantics (using full-fledged objects with ellipses engenders undefined behavior), and no support for reference types. Even the number of arguments is not accessible to the called function. Indeed, where there are ellipses, there's not much C++ left.

The alternative is to limit the number of arguments a `Functor` can take to an arbitrary (yet reasonably large) number. Choosing something in an arbitrary way is one of the most unpleasant tasks a programmer has to do. However, the choice can be made based on experimental grounds. Libraries (especially older ones) commonly use up to 12 parameters for their functions. Let's limit the number of arguments to 15. We cast this embarrassing arbitrary decision in stone and don't think about it again.

Even after making this decision, life is not a lot easier. C++ does not allow templates with the same name and different numbers of parameters. That is, the following code is invalid:

```
// Functor with no arguments
template <typename ResultType>
class Functor
{
    ...
};


// Functor with one argument
template <typename ResultType, typename Parm1>
class Functor
{
    ...
};
```

Naming the template classes Functor1, Functor2, and so on, would be a hassle.

Chapter 3 defines typelists, a general facility for dealing with collections of types. Functor's parameter types do form a collection of types, so typelists fit here nicely. The definition of Functor with typelists looks like this:

```
// Functor with any number and types of arguments
template <typename ResultType, class TList>
class Functor
{
    ...
};
```

A possible instantiation is as follows:

```
// Define a Functor that accepts an int and a double and
// returns a double
Functor<double, TYPELIST_2(int, double)> myFunctor;
```

An appealing advantage of this approach is that we can reuse all the goodies defined by the typelist facility instead of developing similar ones for Functor.

As you will soon see, typelists, although helpful, still require the Functor implementation to do painstaking repetition to encompass any number of arguments. From now on, let's focus on a maximum of 2 arguments. The included Functor.h file scales up to 15 arguments, as established.

The polymorphic class `FunctorImpl`, wrapped by `Functor`, has the same template parameters as `Functor`:[3]

```
template <typename R, class TList>
class FunctorImpl;
```

`FunctorImpl` defines a polymorphic interface that abstracts a function call. For each number of parameters, we define a `FunctorImpl` partial specialization (see Chapter 2). Each specialization defines a pure virtual `operator()` for the appropriate number and types of parameters, as shown in the following:

```
template <typename R>
class FunctorImpl<R, NullType>
{
public:
   virtual R operator()() = 0;
   virtual FunctorImpl* Clone() const = 0;
   virtual ~FunctorImpl() {}
};

template <typename R, typename P1>
class FunctorImpl<R, TYPELIST_1(P1)>
{
public:
   virtual R operator()(P1) = 0;
   virtual FunctorImpl* Clone() const = 0;
   virtual ~FunctorImpl() {}
};

template <typename R, typename P1, typename P2>
class FunctorImpl<R, TYPELIST_2(P1, P2)>
{
public:
   virtual R operator()(P1, P2) = 0;
   virtual FunctorImpl* Clone() const = 0;
   virtual ~FunctorImpl() {}
};
```

The `FunctorImpl` classes are partial specializations of the primary `FunctorImpl` template. Chapter 2 describes the partial template specialization feature in detail. In our situation, partial template specialization allows us to define different versions of `FunctorImpl`, depending on the number of elements in the typelist.

In addition to `operator()`, `FunctorImpl` defines two scaffolding member functions—`Clone` and a virtual destructor. The purpose of `Clone` is the creation of a polymorphic copy of the `FunctorImpl` object. (Refer to Chapter 8 for details on polymorphic cloning.) The virtual destructor allows us to destroy objects derived from `FunctorImpl` by invoking `delete`

---

[3]Using `typename` or `class` for specifying a template parameter makes no difference. This book, by convention, uses `typename` for template parameters that can be primitive types (such as `int`), and `class` for template parameters that must be user-defined types.

on a pointer to a `FunctorImpl`. Chapter 4 provides an extensive discussion of why this do-nothing destructor is vital.

Functor follows a classic handle-body implementation, as shown here.

```
template <typename R, class TList>
class Functor
{
public:
    Functor();
    Functor(const Functor&);
    Functor& operator=(const Functor&);
    explicit Functor(std::auto_ptr<Impl> spImpl);
    ...
private:
    // Handy type definition for the body type
    typedef FunctorImpl<R, TList> Impl;
    std::auto_ptr<Impl> spImpl_;
};
```

Functor holds a smart pointer to `FunctorImpl<R, TList>`, which is its corresponding body type, as a private member. The smart pointer chosen is the standard `std::auto_ptr`.

The previous code also illustrates the presence of some Functor artifacts that prove its value semantics. These artifacts are the default constructor, the copy constructor, and the assignment operator. An explicit destructor is not needed, because `auto_ptr` cleans up resources automatically.

Functor also defines an "extension constructor" that accepts an `auto_ptr` to `FunctorImpl`. The extension constructor allows you to define classes derived from `FunctorImpl` and to initialize Functor directly with pointers to those classes.

Why does the extension constructor take as its argument an `auto_ptr` and not a simple pointer? Constructing from `auto_ptr` is a clear statement to the outside world that Functor takes ownership of the `FunctorImpl` object. Users of Functor will actually have to type `auto_ptr` whenever they invoke this constructor; we assume that if they type `auto_ptr`, they know what `auto_ptr` is about.[4]

5.5 Implementing the Forwarding `Functor::operator()`

Functor needs an `operator()` that forwards to `FunctorImpl::operator()`. We can use the same approach as with `FunctorImpl` itself: Provide a bunch of Functor partial specializations, one for each parameter count. However, this approach is not appropriate here.

---

[4]Of course, this is not necessarily true. However, it's better than just silently choosing one option (here, copying versus taking ownership). Good C++ libraries sport this interesting feature: Whenever something ambiguous may appear, they allow the user to disambiguate it by writing some explicit code. At the other end of the spectrum are libraries that misuse silent C++ features (especially conversions and pointer ownership). They allow the user to type less, but at the cost of making dubious assumptions and decisions on the user's behalf.

Functor defines a considerable amount of code, and it would be wasteful to duplicate it all only for the sake of operator().

But first, let's define the parameter types. Typelists are of great help here:

```
template <typename R, class TList>
class Functor
{
    typedef TList ParmList;
    typedef typename TypeAtNonStrict<TList, 0, EmptyType>::Result
        Parm1;
    typedef typename TypeAtNonStrict<TList, 1, EmptyType>::Result
        Parm2;
    ... as above ...
};
```

TypeAtNonStrict is a template that accesses the type at a given position in a typelist. If no type is found, the result (i.e., the inner class TypeAtNonStrict<...>::Result) evaluates to the third template argument of TypeAtNonStrict. We chose EmptyType as that third argument. EmptyType is, as its name hints, a class that holds nothing between its brackets. (Refer to Chapter 3 for details on TypeAtNonStrict and to Chapter 2 for a description of EmptyType.) In conclusion, ParmN will be either the Nth type in the typelist, or EmptyType if the typelist has fewer than N elements.

To implement operator(), let's rely on an interesting trick. We define *all* versions of operator()—for any number of parameters—inside Functor's definition, as follows.

```
template <typename R, class TList>
class Functor
{
    ... as above ...
public:
    R operator()()
    {
        return (*spImpl_)();
    }
    R operator()(Parm1 p1)
    {
        return (*spImpl_)(p1); `
    }
    R operator()(Parm1 p1, Parm2 p2)
    {
        return (*spImpl_)(p1, p2);
    }
};
```

Where's the trick? For a given Functor instantiation, only one operator() is correct. All others constitute compile-time errors. You would expect Functor not to compile at all. This is because each FunctorImpl specialization defines only one operator(), not a bunch of them as Functor does. The trick relies on the fact that C++ does not instantiate member functions for templates until they are *actually used*. Until you call the wrong operator(), the compiler doesn't complain. If you try to call an overload of operator() that doesn't make sense, the compiler tries to generate the body of operator() and discovers the mismatch. Here's an example.

```
// Define a Functor that accepts an int and a double and
// returns a double.
Functor<double, TYPELIST_2(int, double)> myFunctor;
// Invoke it.
// operator()(int, double) is generated.
double result = myFunctor(4, 5.6);
// Wrong invocation.
double result = myFunctor(); // error!
// operator()() is invalid because
// FunctorImpl<double, TYPELIST_2(int, double)>
// does not define one.
```

Because of this neat trick, we don't have to specialize Functor partially for zero, one, two, and so forth parameters—specializations that would have led to much code duplication. We just define all versions and let the compiler generate only the ones that are used.

Now that the necessary scaffolding is in place, we're ready to start defining concrete classes derived from FunctorImpl.

5.6 Handling Functors

Let's start with handling functors. Functors are loosely defined as instances of classes that define operator(), just as Functor itself does (that is, Functor is a functor). Consequently, Functor's constructor that accepts a functor object will be a template parameterized with the type of that functor.

```
template <typename R, class TList>
class Functor
{
    ... as above ...
public:
    template <class Fun>
    Functor(const Fun& fun);
};
```

To implement this constructor we need a simple class template FunctorHandler derived from FunctorImpl<R,TList>. That class stores an object of type Fun and forwards operator() to it. We resort to the same trick as in the previous section for implementing operator() properly.

To avoid defining too many template parameters for FunctorHandler, we make the Functor instantiation itself a template parameter. This single parameter collects all the others because it provides inner typedefs.

```
template <class ParentFunctor,  typename Fun>
class FunctorHandler
    : public FunctorImpl
        <
            typename ParentFunctor::ResultType,
```

```
                    typename ParentFunctor::ParmList
        >
    {
    public:
        typedef typename ParentFunctor::ResultType ResultType;

        FunctorHandler(const Fun& fun) : fun_(fun) {}
        FunctorHandler* Clone() const
        { return new FunctorHandler(*this); }

        ResultType operator()()
        {
            return fun_();
        }
        ResultType operator()(typename ParentFunctor::Parm1 p1)
        {
            return fun_(p1);
        }
        ResultType operator()(typename ParentFunctor::Parm1 p1,
            typename ParentFunctor::Parm2 p2)
        {
            return fun_(p1, p2);
        }
    private:
        Fun fun_;
    };
```

FunctorHandler looks much like Functor itself: It forwards requests to a stored member variable. The main difference is that the functor is stored by value, not by pointer. This is because, in general, functors are meant to be this way—nonpolymorphic types with regular copy semantics.

Notice the use of the inner types ParentFunctor::ResultType, ParentFunctor::Parm1, and ParentFunctor::Parm2 where needed. FunctorHandler implements a simple constructor, the cloning function, and multiple operator() versions. The compiler picks up the appropriate one. If you use an illegal overload of operator(), a compile-time error occurs, as it should.

There is nothing special about FunctorHandler's implementation. This doesn't mean it didn't require a lot of thought. You will see in the next section just how much genericity this little class template brings us.

Given FunctorHandler's declaration, it's easy to write the templated constructor of Functor declared earlier in this section.

```
    template <typename R, class TList>
    template <typename Fun>
    Functor<R, TList>::Functor(const Fun& fun)
        : spImpl_(new FunctorHandler<Functor, Fun>(fun));
    {
    }
```

There's no copyediting error here. The two template parameter sets are necessary: The template <typename R, class TList> stands for the class template Functor, and template

<typename Fun> stands for the parameter that the constructor itself takes. In standardese, this type of code is known as an "out-of-class member template definition."

The body of the constructor initializes the spImpl_ member to point to a new object of type FunctorHandler, instantiated and initialized with the proper arguments.

There's something worth mentioning here, something that's germane to understanding the Functor implementation we're building. Note that upon entering this constructor of Functor, we have full type knowledge via the template parameter Fun. Upon exiting the constructor, the type information is lost as far as Functor is concerned, because all that Functor knows is spImpl_, which points to the base class FunctorImpl. This apparent loss of type information is interesting: The constructor knows the type and acts like a factory that transforms it in polymorphic behavior. The type information is preserved in the dynamic type of the pointer to FunctorImpl.

Although we haven't written much code (just a bunch of one-line functions), we're ready for a test drive. Here it is:

```
// Assume Functor.h includes the Functor implementation
#include "Functor.h"
#include <iostream>
// The using directive is acceptable for a small C++ program
using namespace std;

// Define a test functor
struct TestFunctor
{
    void operator()(int i, double d)
    {
        cout << "TestFunctor::operator()(" << i
            << ", " << d << ") called.\n";
    }
};

int main()
{
    TestFunctor f;
    Functor<void, TYPELIST_2(int, double)> cmd(f);
    cmd(4, 4.5);
}
```

This little program will reliably print

```
TestFunctor::operator()(4, 4.5) called.
```

This means we've achieved our goal. We can now proceed to the next step.

5.7 Build One, Get One Free

Reading the previous section, you may have asked yourself, Why didn't we start with implementing support for pointers to regular functions, which seems to be the simplest case? Why did we jump directly to functors, templates, and so on? The answer is simple: By now, support for regular functions *is already implemented.* Let's modify the test program a bit:

```
#include "Functor.h"
#include <iostream>
using namespace std;

// Define a test function
void TestFunction(int i, double d)
{
    cout << "TestFunction(" << i
        << ", " << d << ") called." << endl;
}

int main()
{
    Functor<void, TYPELIST_2(int, double)> cmd(
        TestFunction);
    // will print: "TestFunction(4, 4.5) called."
    cmd(4, 4.5);
}
```

The explanation for this nice surprise comes from the workings of template parameter deduction. When the compiler sees a Functor constructed from TestFunction, it has no choice but to try the templated constructor. The compiler will then instantiate the template constructor with the template argument void (&)(int, double), which is the type of TestFunction. The constructor instantiates FunctorHandler<Functor<...>, void (&)(int, double)>. Consequently, the type of fun_ in FunctorHandler is void (&)(int, double) as well. When you invoke FunctorHandler<...>::operator(), it forwards to fun_(), which is legal syntax for invoking a function through a reference to function. Thus, FunctorHandler supports pointers to functions out of the box because of two things: the syntactic similarity between pointers to functions and functors and the type inference mechanism that C++ uses.

There is a problem, though. (It couldn't be perfect, could it?) If you overload Test-Function—or any function that you pass to Functor<...>—you have to help a bit with some disambiguation. The reason is that if TestFunction is overloaded, the type of the symbol TestFunction is no longer defined. To illustrate this, let's add an overloaded version of TestFunction just before main:

```
// Declare an overloaded test function
// (no definition necessary)
void TestFunction(int);
```

Suddenly the compiler complains it cannot figure out which overload of TestFunction it should use. Because there are two functions called TestFunction, this name alone no longer suffices for identification.

In essence, in the presence of overloading, there are two ways to identify a specific function: by using initialization (or an assignment) and by using a cast. Let's illustrate both methods:

```
// as above, TestFunction is overloaded
int main()
{
    // Typedef used for convenience
    typedef void (*TpFun)(int, double);
```

```
        // Method 1: use an initialization
        TpFun pF = TestFunction;
        Functor<void, TYPELIST_2(int, double)> cmd1 (pF);
        cmd1(4, 4.5);
        // Method 2: use a cast
        Functor<void, TYPELIST_2(int, double)> cmd2(
            static_cast<TpFun>(TestFunction)); // Ok
        cmd2(4, 4.5);
    }
```

Both the initialization and the static cast let the compiler know that you're actually interested in the TestFunction that takes an int and a double and returns void.

5.8 Argument and Return Type Conversions

In an ideal world, we would like conversions to work for Functor just as they work for regular function calls. That is, we'd like to see this running:

```
        #include <string>
        #include <iostream>
        #include "Functor.h"
        using namespace std;

        // Ignore arguments-not of interest
        // in this example
        const char* TestFunction(double, double)
        {
            static const char buffer[] = "Hello, world!";
            // It's safe to return a pointer to a static buffer
            return buffer;
        }

        int main()
        {
            Functor<string, TYPELIST_2(int, int)> cmd(TestFunction);
            // Should print "world!"
            cout << cmd(10, 10).substr(7);
        }
```

Although the actual TestFunction has a slightly different signature (it takes two doubles and returns a const char *), it still should be bindable to a Functor<string, TYPELIST_2(int, int)>. We expect this to happen because int can be implicitly converted to double, and const char * is implicitly convertible to string. If Functor does not accept the same conversions that C++ accepts, Functor would be unnecessarily rigid.

To satisfy this new requirement, we don't have to write any new code. The previous example compiles and runs as expected with our current codebase. Why? The answer is found, again, in the way we defined FunctorHandler.

Let's see what happens with the code in the example after all the dust of template instantiation has settled. The function

```
string Functor<...>::operator()(int i, int j)
```

forwards to the virtual function

```
string FunctorHandler<...>::operator()(int i, int j)
```

whose implementation ultimately calls

```
return fun_(i, j);
```

where `fun_` has type `const char* (*)(double, double)` and evaluates to `TestFunction`.

When the compiler encounters the call to `fun_`, it compiles it normally, just as if you had written it by hand. "Normally" here means that conversion rules apply as usual. The compiler then generates code to convert `i` and `j` to `double`, and the result to `std::string`.

The generality and flexibility of `FunctorHandler` illustrate the power of code generation. The syntactic replacement of template arguments for their respective parameters is typical of generic programming. Template processing predates compiling, allowing you to operate at source-code level. In object-oriented programming, in contrast, the power comes from late (after compilation) binding of names to values. Thus, object-oriented programming fosters reuse in the form of binary components, whereas generic programming fosters reuse at the source-code level. Because source code is inherently more information rich and higher level than binary code, generic programming allows richer constructs. This richness, however, comes at the expense of lowered runtime dynamism. You cannot do with STL what you can do with CORBA, and vice versa. The two techniques complement each other.

We are now able to handle functors of all kinds and regular functions using the same small codebase. As a bonus, we have implicit conversion for arguments and for the return value.

5.9 Handling Pointers to Member Functions

Although not very common in day-to-day programming activities, *pointers to member functions* can sometimes be of help. They act much like pointers to functions, but when you want to invoke them, you must pass an object (in addition to the arguments). The following example depicts the syntax and the semantics of pointers to member functions.

```
#include <iostream>
using namespace std;

class Parrot
{
```

```
public:
    void Eat()
    {
        cout << "Tsk, knick, tsk...\n";
    }
    void Speak()
    {
        cout << "Oh Captain, my Captain!\n";
    }
};

int main()
{
    // Define a type: pointer to a member function of
    // Parrot, taking no arguments and
    // returning void.
    typedef void (Parrot::* TpMemFun)();

    // Create an object of that type
    // and initialize it with the address of
    // Parrot::Eat.
    TpMemFun pActivity = &Parrot::Eat;
    // Create a Parrot...
    Parrot geronimo;
    // ...and a pointer to it
    Parrot* pGeronimo = &geronimo;

    // Invoke the member function stored in Activity
    // via an object. Notice the use of operator.*
    (geronimo.*pActivity)();

    // Same, via pointer. Now we use operator->*
    (pGeronimo->*pActivity)();
    // Change the activity
    pActivity = &Parrot::Speak;

    // Wake up, Geronimo!
    (geronimo.*pActivity)();
}
```

A closer look at pointers to member functions and their two related operators—.*
and ->*—reveals strange features. There is no C++ type for the result of geronimo.*p-
Activity and pGeronimo->*pActivity. Both are binary operators all right, and they
return something to which you can apply the function-call operator immediately, but
that "something" does not have a type.[5] You cannot store the result of operator.*
or operator->* in any way, although there is an entity that holds the fusion between
your object and the pointer to a member function. This fusion seems to be very unstable.
It appears from chaos just as you invoke operator.* or operator->*, exists just long
enough to apply operator(), and then goes back to chaos. There's nothing else you can do
with it.

---

[5] The standard says, "If the result of .* or ->* is a function, then that result can be used only as the operand
for the function call operator ()."

In C++, where every object has a type, the result of `operator->*` or `operator.*` is a unique exception. It's even trickier than the ambiguity of pointers to functions introduced by overloading (discussed in the previous section). There we had too many types to choose from, but we could disambiguate the choice; here, we don't have any type to start with. For this reason, pointers to member functions and the two related operators are a curiously half-baked concept in C++. And by the way, you cannot have references to member functions (although you can have references to regular functions).

Some C++ compiler vendors define a new type and allow you to store the result of `operator.*` by using a syntax like this:

```
// __closure is a language extension
// defined by some vendors
void (__closure:: * geronimosWork)() =
    geronimo.*pActivity;
// Invoke whatever Geronimo is doomed to do
geronimosWork();
```

There's nothing about `Parrot` in the type of `geronimosWork`. This means that later, you can bind `geronimosWork` to something that's not `geronimo`, and even to something that's not a `Parrot`. All you have to commit to is the return type and the arguments of the pointer to a member function. In fact, this language extension is a kind of `Functor` class, but restricted to objects and member functions only (it does not allow regular functions or functors).

Let's implement support for bound pointers to member functions in `Functor`. The experience with functors and functions suggests that it's good to keep things generic and not to jump too early into specificity. In the implementation of `MemFunHandler`, the object type (`Parrot` in the previous example) is a template parameter. Furthermore, let's make the pointer to a member function a template parameter as well. By doing this, we get automatic conversions for free, as happened with the implementation of `FunctorHandler`.

Here's the implementation of `MemFunHandler`. It incarnates the ideas just discussed, plus the ones already exploited in `FunctorHandler`.

```
template <class ParentFunctor, typename PointerToObj,
    typename PointerToMemFn>
class MemFunHandler
    : public FunctorImpl
        <
            typename ParentFunctor::ResultType,
            typename ParentFunctor::ParmList
        >
{
public:
    typedef typename ParentFunctor::ResultType ResultType;
    MemFunHandler(const PointerToObj& pObj, PointerToMemFn pMemFn)
    : pObj_(pObj), pMemFn_(pMemFn) {}

    MemFunHandler* Clone() const
    { return new MemFunHandler(*this); }
```

```
    ResultType operator()()
    {
        return ((*pObj_).*pMemFn_)();
    }

    ResultType operator()(typename ParentFunctor::Parm1 p1)
    {
        return ((*pObj_).*pMemFn_)(p1);
    }

    ResultType operator()(typename ParentFunctor::Parm1 p1,
        typename ParentFunctor::Parm2 p2)
    {
        return ((*pObj_).*pMemFn_)(p1, p2);
    }

private:
    PointerToObj pObj_;
    PointerToMemFn pMemFn_;
};
```

Why is MemFunHandler parameterized with the type of the pointer (PointerToObj) and not with the type of the object itself? A more straightforward implementation would have looked like this:

```
template <class ParentFunctor, typename Obj,
    typename PointerToMemFn>
class MemFunHandler
    : public FunctorImpl
        <
            typename ParentFunctor::ResultType,
            typename ParentFunctor::ParmList
        >
{
private:
    Obj* pObj_;
    PointerToMemFn pMemFn_;
public:
    MemFunHandler(Obj* pObj, PointerToMemFn pMemFn)
    : pObj_(pObj), pMemFn_(pMemFn) {}
    ...
};
```

This code would have been easier to understand. However, the first implementation is more generic. The second implementation hardwires the pointer-to-object type in its implementation. It stores a *bare, bald, unadorned* pointer to Obj. Can this be a problem?

Yes it is, if you want to use smart pointers with MemFunHandler. Aha! The first implementation supports smart pointers; the second does not. The first implementation can store any type that *acts* as a pointer to an object; the second is hardwired to store and use only simple pointers. Moreover, the second version does not work for pointers to const. Such is the negative effect of hardwiring types.

Now that we have MemFunHandler in place, we also need to add a constructor to Functor itself. The new constructor takes a pointer to object and a pointer to member function and creates the appropriate MemFunHandler instantiation.

```
template <class PtrObj, typename MemFn>
Functor(const PtrObj& p, MemFn memFn)
: spImpl_(new MemFunHandler<Functor, PtrObj, MemFn>(p, memFn))
{}
```

Let's put in place a test run for the newly implemented feature. Parrot gets reused.

```
#include "Functor.h"
#include <iostream>
using namespace std;

class Parrot
{
public:
   void Eat()
   {
      cout << "Tsk, knick, tsk...\n";
   }
   void Speak()
   {
      cout << "Oh Captain, my Captain!\n";
   }
};

int main()
{
   Parrot geronimo;
   // Define two Functors
   Functor<void>
      cmd1(&geronimo, &Parrot::Eat),
      cmd2(&geronimo, &Parrot::Speak);
   // alternatively, Functor can have void as
   // its default R parameter
   // Invoke each of them
   cmd1();
   cmd2();
}
```

Because MemFunHandler took the precaution of being as generic as possible, automatic conversions come for free—just as they did for FunctorHandler.

5.10 Binding

We could stop here. By now, we have everything in place—Functor supports all the C++ callable entities defined in the beginning of the discussion, and in a nice manner. However, as Pygmalion might have remarked, sometimes the actual outcome of work is impossible to predict when you start doing it.

As soon as Functor is ready, new ideas come to mind. For instance, we'd like to be able to convert from a type of Functor to another. One such conversion is *binding*: Given a Functor that takes two integers, you want to bind one integer to some fixed value and let only the other one vary. Binding yields a Functor that takes only one integer, because the other one is fixed and therefore known, as illustrated in the following example.

```
void f()
{
    // Define a Functor of two arguments
    Functor<void, TYPELIST_2(int, int)> cmd1(something);
    // Bind the first argument to 10
    Functor<void, TYPELIST_1(int)> cmd2(BindFirst(cmd1, 10));
    // Same as cmd1(10, 20)
    cmd2(20);
    // Further bind the first (and only) argument
    // of cmd2 to 30
    Functor<void> cmd3(BindFirst(cmd2, 30));
    // Same as cmd1(10, 30)
    cmd3();
}
```

Binding is a powerful feature. You can store not only callable entities but also part (or all) of their arguments. This greatly increases the expressive power of Functor because it allows packaging of functions and arguments without requiring glue code.

For instance, think of implementing redo support in a text editor. When the user types an "a," you execute the member function Document::InsertChar('a'). Then you append a canned Functor that contains the pointer to Document, the member function InsertChar, and the actual character. When the user selects Redo, all you have to do is fire that Functor and you're finished. Section 5.14 provides further discussion of undo and redo.

Binding is powerful from another, more profound, standpoint. Think of a Functor as a computation, and of its arguments as the *environment* necessary to perform that computation. So far, Functor delays the computation by storing pointers to functions and pointers to methods. However, Functor stores only the computation and nothing about the environment of that computation. Binding allows Functor to store *part of the environment* together with the computation and to reduce progressively the environment necessary at invocation time.

Before jumping into the implementation, let's recap the requirement. For an instantiation Functor<R, TList>, we want to bind the first argument (TList::Head) to a fixed value. Therefore, the return type is Functor<R, TList::Tail>.

This being said, implementing the BinderFirst class template is a breeze. We have to pay special attention only to the fact that there are two instantiations of Functor involved: the incoming Functor and the outgoing Functor. The incoming Functor type is passed as the Incoming parameter. The outgoing Functor type is computed.

```
template <class Incoming>
class BinderFirst
    : public FunctorImpl<typename Incoming::ResultType,
        typename Incoming::ParmList::Tail>
{
    typedef Functor<typename Incoming::ResultType,
        Incoming::ParmList::Tail> Outgoing;
    typedef typename Incoming::Parm1 Bound;
    typedef typename Incoming::ResultType ResultType;

public:
    BinderFirst(const Incoming& fun, Bound bound)
    : fun_(fun), bound_(bound)
    {
    }
```

```
    BinderFirst* Clone() const
    { return new BinderFirst(*this); }

        ResultType operator()()
        {
            return fun_(bound_);
        }
        ResultType operator()(typename Outgoing::Parm1 p1)
        {
            return fun_(bound_, p1);
        }
        ResultType operator()(typename Outgoing::Parm1 p1,
            typename Outgoing::Parm2 p2)
        {
            return fun_(bound_, p1, p2);
        }
    private:
        Incoming fun_;
        Bound bound_;
    };
```

The class template BinderFirst works in conjunction with the template function Bind-First. The merit of BindFirst is that it automatically deduces its template parameters from the types of the actual arguments that you pass it.

```
    // See Functor.h for the definition of BinderFirstTraits
    template <class Fctor>
    typename Private::BinderFirstTraits<Fctor>::BoundFunctorType
    BindFirst(
        const Fctor& fun,
        typename Fctor::Parm1 bound)
    {
        typedef typename
            Private::BinderFirstTraits<Fctor>::BoundFunctorType
                Outgoing;
        return Outgoing(std::auto_ptr<typename Outgoing::Impl>(
            new BinderFirst<Fctor>(fun, bound)));
    }
```

Binding dovetails nicely with automatic conversion, conferring incredible flexibility on Functor. The following example combines binding with automatic conversions.

```
    const char* Fun(int i, int j)
    {
        cout << "Fun(" << i << ", " << j << ") called\n";
        return "0";
    }

    int main()
    {
        Functor<const char*, TYPELIST_2(char, int)> f1(Fun);
        Functor<std::string, TYPELIST_1(double)> f2(
            BindFirst(f1, 10));
        // Prints: Fun(10, 15) called
        f2(15);
    }
```

5.11 Chaining Requests

The GoF book (Gamma et al. 1995) gives an example of a MacroCommand class, a command that holds a linear collection (such as a list or a vector) of Commands. When a MacroCommand is executed, it executes in sequence each of the commands that it holds.

This feature can be very useful. For instance, let's refer to the undo/redo example again. One "do" operation might be accompanied by multiple "undo" operations. For example, inserting a character may automatically scroll the text window (some editors do this to ensure better text visibility). On undoing that operation, you'd like the window to "unscroll" back to where it was. (Most editors don't unscroll correctly. What a nuisance.) To unscroll, you need to store multiple Commands in a single Functor object and execute them as a single unit. The Document::InsertChar member function pushes a Macro-Command onto the undo stack. The MacroCommand would be composed of Document::Delete-Char and Window::Scroll. The latter member function would be bound to an argument that holds the old position. (Again, binding comes in very handy.)

Loki defines a class Chainer and the helper function Chain. Chain's declaration looks like this:

```
template <class Fun1, class Fun2>
Fun2 Chain(
    const Fun1& fun1,
    const Fun2& fun2);
```

Chainer's class implementation is trivial—it stores the two functors, and Chainer::operator() calls them in sequence. You can chain multiple functors by issuing repeated calls to Chain.

Let's have Chain conclude the support for macro commands. One thing about "nice to have" features is that the list can go on forever. However, there's plenty of room to grow. Neither BindFirst nor Chain incurred any change to Functor, which is proof that you can build similar facilities on your own.

5.12 Real-World Issues I: The Cost of Forwarding Functions

The Functor class template is conceptually finished. Now we concentrate on optimizing it so that it works as efficiently as possible.[6]

Let's focus on one of Functor's operator() overloads, which forwards the call to the smart pointer.

```
// inside Functor<R, TList>
R operator()(Parm1 p1, Parm2 p2)
{
    return (*spImpl_)(p1, p2);
}
```

---

[6]Usually, premature optimization is not recommended. One reason is that programmers are not good at estimating which parts of the program should be optimized and (most important) which should not. However, library writers are in a different situation. They don't know whether or not their library will be used in a critical part of some application, so they should take their best shot at optimizing.

Each time you call `operator()`, an unnecessary copy is performed for each argument. If `Parm1` and `Parm2` are expensive to copy, you might have a performance problem.

Oddly enough, even if `Functor`'s `operator()` is inline, the compiler is not allowed to optimize the extra copies away. Item 46 in Sutter (2000) describes this late language change, made just before standardization. What's called *eliding of copy construction* was banned for forwarding functions. The only situation in which a compiler can elide a copy constructor is for the returned value, which cannot be optimized by hand.

Are references an easy fix for our problem? Let's try this:

```
// inside Functor<R, TList>
R operator()(Parm1& p1, Parm2& p2)
{
    return (*spImpl_)(p1, p2);
}
```

All looks fine, and it might actually work, until you try something like this:

```
void testFunction(std::string&, int);
Functor<void, TYPELIST_2(std::string&, int)> cmd(testFunction);
...
string s;
cmd(s, 5); //error!
```

The compiler will choke on the last line, uttering something like "References to references are not allowed." (Actually, the message may be slightly more cryptic.) The fact is, such an instantiation would render `Parm1` as a reference to `std::string`, and consequently `p1` would be a reference to a reference to `std::string`. References to references are illegal.[7]

Fortunately, Chapter 2 provides a tool that addresses exactly this kind of problem. Chapter 2 features a class template `TypeTraits<T>` that defines a bunch of types related to the type `T`. Examples of such related types are the non-`const` type (if `T` is a const type), the pointed-to type (if `T` is a pointer), and many others. The type that can be safely and efficiently passed as a parameter to a function is `ParameterType`. The following table illustrates the link between the type you pass to `TypeTraits` and the inner type definition `ParameterType`. Consider `U` to be a plain type, such as a class or a primitive type.

T	TypeTraits<T>::ParameterType
U	U if U is primitive; otherwise, const U &
const U	U if U is primitive; otherwise, const U &
U &	U &
const U &	const U &

---

[7] This problem appears with the standard binders, too. Bjarne Stroustrup has submitted a defect report to the Standards Committee. His proposal for a fix is to allow references to references and simply to treat them as references. At the time of this writing, the report was available at http://anubis.dkuug.dk/jtc1/sc22/wg21/docs/cwg_active.html#106.

If you substitute the types in the right column for the arguments in the forwarding function, it will work correctly for any case—and without any copy overhead:

```
// Inside Functor<R, TList>
R operator()(
    typename TypeTraits<Parm1>::ParameterType p1,
    typename TypeTraits<Parm2>::ParameterType p2)
{
    return (*spImpl_)(p1, p2);
}
```

What's even nicer is that references work great in conjunction with inline functions. The optimizer generates optimal code easier because all it has to do is short-circuit the references.

5.13 Real-World Issues II: Heap Allocation

Let's concentrate now on the cost of constructing and copying Functors. We have implemented correct copy semantics, but at a cost: heap allocation. Every Functor holds a (smart) pointer to an object allocated with new. When a Functor is copied, a deep copy is performed by using FunctorImpl::Clone.

This is especially bothersome when you think of the size of the objects we're using. Most of the time, Functor will be used with pointers to functions and with pairs of pointers to objects and pointers to member functions. On typical 32-bit systems, these objects occupy 4 and 20 bytes, respectively (4 for the pointer to an object and 16 for the pointer to a member function[8]). When binding is used, the size of the concrete functor object increases roughly with the size of the bound argument (it may actually increase slightly more because of padding).

Chapter 4 introduces an efficient small-object allocator. FunctorImpl and its derivatives are perfect candidates for taking advantage of that custom allocator. Recall from Chapter 4 that one way to use the small-object allocator is to derive your class from the SmallObject class template.

Using SmallObject is very simple. We need, however, to add a template parameter to Functor and FunctorImpl that reflects the threading model used by the memory allocator. This is not troublesome, because most of the time you'll use the default argument. In the following code, changes are shown in bold:

```
template
<
    class R,
    class TL,
    template <class T>
        class ThreadingModel = DEFAULT_THREADING
>
```

---

[8] You might expect a pointer to a member function to occupy 4 bytes, just as pointers to functions do. However, pointers to methods are actually little tagged unions. They deal with multiple virtual inheritance and virtual/nonvirtual functions.

```
class FunctorImpl : public SmallObject<ThreadingModel>
{
public:
   ... as above ...
};
```

That's all it takes for FunctorImpl to take full advantage of the custom allocator. Similarly, Functor itself adds a third template parameter:

```
template
<
   class R,
   class TL,
   template <class T>
      class ThreadingModel = DEFAULT_THREADING
>
class Functor
{
   ...
private:
   // Pass ThreadingModel to FunctorImpl
   std::auto_ptr<FunctorImpl<R, TL, ThreadingModel> > pImpl_;
};
```

Now if you want to use Functor with the default threading model, you don't have to specify its third template argument. Only if your application needs Functors that support two or more different threading models will you need to specify ThreadingModel explicitly.

5.14 Implementing Undo and Redo with Functor

The GoF book (Gamma et al. 1995) recommends that undo be implemented as an additional Unexecute member function of the Command class. The problem is, you cannot express Unexecute in a generic way because the relation between doing something and undoing something is unpredictable. The Unexecute solution is appealing when you have a concrete Command class for each operation in your application, but the Functor-based approach favors using a single class that can be bound to different objects and member function calls.

Al Stevens' article in *Dr. Dobb's Journal* (Stevens 1998) is of great help in studying generic implementations of undo and redo. He has built a generic undo/redo library that you certainly should check out before rolling your own, with Functor or not.

It's all about data structures. The basic idea in undo and redo is that you have to keep an undo stack and a redo stack. As the user "does" something, such as typing a character, you push a *different* Functor on the undo stack. This means the Document::InsertChar member function is responsible for pushing the action that appropriately undoes the insertion (such as Document::DeleteChar). This puts the burden on the member function that *does* the stuff and frees the Functor from knowing how to undo itself.

Optionally, you may want to push on the redo stack a Functor consisting of the

Document and a pointer to the Document::InsertChar member function, all bound to the actual character type. Some editors allow "retyping": After you type something and select Redo, that block of typing is repeated. The binding we built for Functor greatly helps with storing a call to Document::InsertChar for a given character, all encapsulated in a single Functor. Also, not only should the last character typed be repeated—that wouldn't be much of a feature—but the whole sequence of typing after the last nontyping action should be repeated. Chaining Functors enters into action here: As long as the user types, you append to the same Functor. This way you can treat later multiple keystrokes as a single action.

Document::InsertChar essentially pushes a Functor onto the undo stack. When the user selects Undo, that Functor will be executed and pushed onto the redo stack.

As you see, binding arguments and composition allows us to treat Functors in a very uniform way: No matter what kind of call there is, it's ultimately packed in a Functor. This considerably eases the task of implementing undo and redo.

5.15 Summary

Using good libraries in C++ is (or at least ought to be) a lot easier than writing them. On the other hand, writing libraries is a lot of fun. Looking back at all the implementation details, there are a few lessons to keep in mind when writing generic code:

- When it comes to types, templatize and postpone. Be generic. FunctorHandler and MemFunHandler gain a lot from postponing type knowledge by using templates. Pointers to functions came for free. Considering what it offers, the codebase is remarkably small. All this comes from using templates and letting the compiler infer types as much as possible.
- Encourage first-class semantics. It would have been an incredible headache to operate only with FunctorImpl pointers. Imagine yourself implementing binding and chaining.

Clever techniques should be applied for the benefit of simplicity. After all this discussion on templates, inheritance, binding, and memory, we distill a simple, easy-to-use, well-articulated library.

In a nutshell, Functor is a delayed call to a function, a functor, or a member function. It stores the callee and exposes operator() for invoking it. Let's highlight some quick facts about it.

5.16 Functor Quick Facts

- Functor is a template that allows the expression of calls with up to 15 arguments. The first parameter is the return type, and the second is a typelist containing the parameter types. The third template parameter establishes the threading model of the allocator used with Functor. Refer to Chapter 3 for details on typelists, the appendix for details on threading models, and Chapter 4 for details on small-object allocation.

- You initialize a Functor with a function, a functor, another Functor, or a pointer to an object and a pointer to a method, as exemplified in the following code:

```
void Function(int);

struct SomeFunctor
{
    void operator()(int);
};

struct SomeClass
{
    void MemberFunction(int);
};

void example()
{
    // Initialize with a function
    Functor<void, TYPELIST_1(int)> cmd1(Function);
    // Initialize with a functor
    SomeFunctor fn;
    Functor<void, TYPELIST_1(int)> cmd2(fn);
    // Initialize with a pointer to object
    // and a pointer to member function
    SomeClass myObject;
    Functor<void, TYPELIST_1(int)> cmd3(&myObject,
        &SomeClass::MemberFunction);
    // Initialize a Functor with another
    // (copying)
    Functor<void, TYPELIST_1(int)> cmd4(cmd3);
}
```

- You also can initialize Functor with a std::auto_ptr< FunctorImpl<R,TList> >. This enables user-defined extensions.
- Functor supports automatic conversions for arguments and return values. For instance, in the previous example, Function, SomeFunctor::operator(), and SomeClass:: MemberFunction might take a double, instead of an int, as an argument.
- Manual disambiguation is needed in the presence of overloading.
- Functor fully supports first-class semantics: copying, assigning to, and passing by value. Functor is not polymorphic and is not intended to be derived from. If you want to extend Functor, derive from FunctorImpl.
- Functor supports argument binding. A call to BindFirst binds the first argument to a fixed value. The result is a Functor parameterized with the rest of the arguments. Example:

```
void f()
{
    // Define a Functor of three arguments
    Functor<void, TYPELIST_3(int, int, double)> cmd1(
        someEntity);
    // Bind the first argument to 10
```

```
        Functor<void, TYPELIST_2(int, double)> cmd2(
            BindFirst(cmd1, 10));
        // Same as cmd1(10, 20, 5.6)
        cmd2(20, 5.6);
    }
```

- Multiple Functors can be chained in a single Functor object by using the Chain function.

```
    void f()
    {
        Functor<> cmd1(something);
        Functor<> cmd2(somethingElse);
        // Chain cmd1 and cmd2
        // as the container
        Functor<> cmd3(Chain(cmd1, cmd2));
        // Equivalent to cmd1(); cmd2();
        cmd3();
    }
```

- The cost of using Functor is one indirection (call via pointer) for simple Functor objects. For each binding, there is an extra virtual call cost. For chaining, there is an extra virtual call cost. Parameters are not copied, except when conversion is necessary.
- FunctorImpl uses the small-object allocator defined in Chapter 4.

6

Implementing Singletons

The Singleton design pattern (Gamma et al. 1995) is unique in that it's a strange combination: its description is simple, yet its implementation issues are complicated. This is proven by the abundance of Singleton discussions and implementations in books and magazine articles (e.g., Vlissides 1996, 1998). Singleton's description in the GoF book is as simple as it gets: "Ensure a class only has one instance, and provide a global point of access to it."

A singleton is an improved global variable. The improvement that Singleton brings is that you cannot create a secondary object of the singleton's type. Therefore, you should use Singleton when you model types that conceptually have a unique instance in the application, such as Keyboard, Display, PrintManager, and SystemClock. Being able to instantiate these types more than once is unnatural at best, and often dangerous.

Providing a global point of access has a subtle implication—from a client's standpoint, the Singleton object *owns itself*. There is no special client step for creating the singleton. Consequently, the Singleton object is responsible for creating and destroying itself. Managing a singleton's lifetime causes the most implementation headaches.

This chapter discusses the most important issues associated with designing and implementing various Singleton variants in C++:

- The features that set apart a singleton from a simple global object
- The basic C++ idioms supporting singletons
- Better enforcement of a singleton's uniqueness
- Destroying the singleton and detecting postdestruction access
- Implementing solutions for advanced lifetime management of the Singleton object
- Multithreading issues

We will develop techniques that address each issue. In the end, we will use these techniques for implementing a generic SingletonHolder class template.

There is no "best" implementation of the Singleton design pattern. Various Singleton implementations, including nonportable ones, are most appropriate depending on the problem at hand. This chapter's approach is to develop a family of implementations on a generic skeleton, following a policy-based design (see Chapter 1). SingletonHolder also provides hooks for extensions and customizations.

By the end of this chapter, we will have developed a `SingletonHolder` class template that can generate many different types of singletons. `SingletonHolder` gives you fine-grained control over how the Singleton object is allocated, when it is destroyed, whether it is thread safe, and what happens if a client attempts to use it after it's been destroyed. The `SingletonHolder` class template provides Singleton-specific services and functionality over any user-defined type.

6.1 Static Data + Static Functions != Singleton

At first glance, it seems that the need for Singleton can be easily obviated by using static member functions and static member variables:

```cpp
class Font { ... };
class PrinterPort { ... };
class PrintJob { ... };

class MyOnlyPrinter
{
public:
   static void AddPrintJob(PrintJob& newJob)
   {
      if (printQueue_.empty() && printingPort_.available())
      {
         printingPort_.send(newJob.Data());
      }
      else
      {
         printQueue_.push(newJob);
      }
   }
private:
   // All data is static
   static std::queue<PrintJob> printQueue_;
   static PrinterPort printingPort_;
   static Font defaultFont_;
};

PrintJob somePrintJob("MyDocument.txt");
MyOnlyPrinter::AddPrintJob(somePrintJob);
```

However, this solution[1] has a number of disadvantages in some situations. The main problem is that *static functions cannot be virtual,* which makes it difficult to change behavior without opening `MyOnlyPrinter`'s code.

A subtler problem of this approach is that it makes initialization and cleanup difficult. There is no central point of initialization and cleanup for `MyOnlyPrinter`'s data. Initialization and cleanup can be nontrivial tasks—for instance, `defaultFont_` can depend on the speed of `printingPort_`.

Singleton implementations therefore concentrate on creating and managing a unique object while not allowing the creation of another one.

---

[1] This code actually illustrates another pattern, the Monostate pattern (Ball and Crawford 1998).

6.2 The Basic C++ Idioms Supporting Singletons

Most often, singletons are implemented in C++ by using some variation of the following idiom:

```cpp
// Header file Singleton.h
class Singleton
{
public:
    static Singleton* Instance() // Unique point of access
    {
        if (!pInstance_)
            pInstance_ = new Singleton;
        return pInstance_;
    }
    ... operations ...
private:
    Singleton(); // Prevent clients from creating a new Singleton
    Singleton(const Singleton&); // Prevent clients from creating
                            // a copy of the Singleton
    static Singleton* pInstance_; // The one and only instance
};

// Implementation file Singleton.cpp
Singleton* Singleton::pInstance_ = 0;
```

Because all the constructors are private, user code cannot create Singletons. However, Singleton's own member functions—and Instance in particular—*are* allowed to create objects. Therefore, the uniqueness of the Singleton object is enforced at compile time. This is the essence of implementing the Singleton design pattern in C++.

If it's never used (no call to Instance occurs), the Singleton object is not created. The cost of this optimization is the (usually negligible) test incurred at the beginning of Instance. The advantage of the build-on-first-request solution becomes significant if Singleton is expensive to create and seldom used.

An ill-fated temptation is to simplify things by replacing the pointer pInstance_ in the previous example with a full Singleton object.

```cpp
// Header file Singleton.h
class Singleton
{
public:
    static Singleton* Instance() // Unique point of access
    {
        return &instance_;
    }
    int DoSomething();
private:
    static Singleton instance_;

};
// Implementation file Singleton.cpp
Singleton Singleton::instance_;
```

This is not a good solution. Although `instance_` is a static member of `Singleton` (just as `pInstance_` was in the previous example), there is an important difference between the two versions. `instance_` is initialized *dynamically* (by calling `Singleton`'s constructor at run-time), whereas `pInstance_` benefits from *static initialization* (it is a type without a constructor initialized with a compile-time constant).

The compiler performs static initialization before the very first assembly statement of the program gets executed. (Usually, static initializers are right in the file containing the executable program, so loading is initializing.) On the other hand, C++ does not define the order of initialization for dynamically initialized namespace-level objects found in different translation units, which is a major source of trouble. (A *translation unit* is, roughly speaking, a compilable C++ source file.) Consider this code:

```
// SomeFile.cpp
#include "Singleton.h"
int global = Singleton::Instance()->DoSomething();
```

Depending on the order of initialization that the compiler chooses for `instance_` and `global`, the call to `Singleton::Instance` may return an object that has not been constructed yet. This means that you cannot count on `instance_` being initialized if other external objects are using it.

6.3 Enforcing the Singleton's Uniqueness

A few language-related techniques are of help in enforcing the singleton's uniqueness. We've already used a couple of them: The *default constructor* and the *copy constructor* are private. The latter measure disables code such as this:

```
Singleton sneaky(*Singleton::Instance()); // error!
// Cannot make 'sneaky' a copy of the (Singleton) object
//    returned by Instance
```

If you don't define the copy constructor, the compiler does its best to be of help and defines a public one for you (Meyers 1998a). Declaring an explicit copy constructor disables automatic generation, and placing that constructor in the `private` section yields a compile-time error on `sneaky`'s definition.

Another slight improvement is to have `Instance` return a reference instead of a pointer. The problem with having `Instance` return a pointer is that callers might be tempted to `delete` it. To minimize the chances of that happening, it's safer to return a reference:

```
// inside class Singleton
static Singleton& Instance();
```

Another member function silently generated by the compiler is the assignment operator. Uniqueness is not directly related to assignment, but one obvious consequence of uniqueness is that you cannot assign one object to another because there aren't two objects to start with. For a `Singleton` object, any assignment is a self-assignment, which doesn't make much sense anyway; thus, it is worthwhile to disable the assignment operator (by making it private and never implementing it).

The last coat of the armor is to make the destructor private. This measure prevents clients that hold a pointer to the Singleton object from deleting it accidentally.

After the enumerated measures are added, Singleton's interface looks like the following.

```
class Singleton
{
    static Singleton& Instance();
    ... operations ...
private:
    Singleton();
    Singleton(const Singleton&);
    Singleton& operator=(const Singleton&);
    ~Singleton();
};
```

6.4 Destroying the Singleton

As discussed, Singleton is created on demand, when Instance is first called. The first call to Instance defines the construction moment but leaves the destruction problem open: When should the singleton destroy its instance? The GoF book doesn't discuss this issue, but, as John Vlissides's book *Pattern Hatching* (1998) witnesses, the problem is thorny.

Actually, if Singleton is not deleted, that's not a memory leak. Memory leaks appear when you allocate accumulating data and lose all references to it. This is not the case here: Nothing is accumulating, and we hold knowledge about the allocated memory until the end of the application. Furthermore, all modern operating systems take care of completely deallocating a process's memory upon termination. (For an interesting discussion on what is and is not a memory leak, refer to Item 10 in *Effective C++* [Meyers 1998a].)

However, there *is* a leak, and a more insidious one: a *resource leak*. Singleton's constructor may acquire an unbound set of resources: network connections, handles to OS-wide mutexes and other interprocess communication means, references to out-of-process CORBA or COM objects, and so on.

The only correct way to avoid resource leaks is to delete the Singleton object during the application's shutdown. The issue is that we have to choose the moment carefully so that no one tries to access the singleton after its destruction.

The simplest solution for destroying the singleton is to rely on language mechanisms. For example, the following code shows a different approach to implementing a singleton. Instead of using dynamic allocation and a static pointer, the Instance function relies on a *local static variable*.

```
Singleton& Singleton::Instance()
{
    static Singleton obj;
    return obj;
}
```

This simple and elegant implementation was first published by Scott Meyers (Meyers 1996a, Item 26); therefore, we'll refer to it as the *Meyers singleton*.

The Meyers singleton relies on some compiler magic. A function-static object is initialized when the control flow is first passing its definition. Don't confuse static variables that are initialized at runtime with primitive static variables initialized with compile-time constants. For example:

```
int Fun()
{
    static int x = 100;
    return ++x;
}
```

In this case, x is initialized before any code in the program is executed, most likely at load time. For all that Fun can tell when first called, x has been 100 since time immemorial. In contrast, when the initializer is not a compile-time constant, or the static variable is an object with a constructor, the variable is initialized at runtime during the first pass through its definition.

In addition, the compiler generates code so that after initialization, the runtime support registers the variable for destruction. A pseudo-C++ representation of the generated code may look like the following code. (The variables starting with two underscores should be thought of as hidden, that is, variables generated and managed only by the compiler.)

```
Singleton& Singleton::Instance()
{
    // Functions generated by the compiler
    extern void __ConstructSingleton(void* memory);
    extern void __DestroySingleton();
    // Variables generated by the compiler
    static bool __initialized = false;
    // Buffer that holds the singleton
    // (We assume it is properly aligned)
    static char __buffer[sizeof(Singleton)];
    if (!__initialized)
    {
        // First call, construct object
        // Will invoke Singleton::Singleton
        // In the __buffer memory
        __ConstructSingleton(__buffer);
        // register destruction
        atexit(__DestroySingleton);
        __initialized = true;
    }
    return *reinterpret_cast<Singleton *>(__buffer);
}
```

The core is the call to the atexit function. The atexit function, provided by the standard C library, allows you to register functions to be automatically called during a program's exit, in a last in, first out (LIFO) order. (By definition, destruction of objects in C++ is done in a LIFO manner: Objects created first are destroyed last. Of course, objects you manage yourself with new and delete don't obey this rule.) The signature of atexit is

```
// Takes a pointer to function
// Returns 0 if successful, or
// a nonzero value if an error occurs
int atexit(void (*pFun)());
```

The compiler generates the function __DestroySingleton—whose execution destroys the Singleton object seated in __buffer's memory—and passes the address of that function to atexit.

How does atexit work? Each call to atexit pushes its parameter on a private stack maintained by the C runtime library. During the application's exit sequence, the runtime support calls the functions registered with atexit.

We'll see in a short while that atexit has important—and sometimes unfortunate—links with implementing the Singleton design pattern in C++. Like it or not, it's going to be with us until the end of this chapter. No matter what solution for destroying singletons we try, it has to play nice with atexit or else we break programmers' expectations.

The Meyers singleton provides the simplest means of destroying the singleton during an application's exit sequence. It works fine in most cases. We will study its problems and provide some improvements and alternate implementations for special cases.

Finally, the simplest—albeit inelegant—solution is the "leaky" Singleton that never destroys itself and lets the operating system take care of cleanup.

6.5 The Dead Reference Problem

To make the discussion concrete, let's refer to an example that will be used throughout the rest of this chapter to validate various implementations. The example has the same traits as the Singleton pattern itself: It's easy to express and understand, but hard to implement.

Say we have an application that uses three singletons: Keyboard, Display, and Log. The first two model their physical counterparts. Log is intended for error reporting. Its incarnation can be a text file, a secondary console, or even a scrolling marquee on the LCD display of an embedded system.

We assume that Log's construction implies a certain amount of overhead, so it is best to instantiate it only if an error occurs. This way, in an error-free session, the program doesn't create Log at all.

The program reports to Log any error in instantiating Keyboard or Display. Log also collects errors in destroying Keyboard or Display.

Assuming we implement these three singletons as Meyers singletons, the program is incorrect. For example, assume that after Keyboard is constructed successfully, Display fails to initialize. Display's constructor creates Log, the error is logged, and it's likely the application is about to exit. At exit time, the language rule enters into action: The runtime support destroys local static objects in the reverse order of their creation. Therefore, Log is destroyed *before* Keyboard. If for some reason Keyboard fails to shut down and tries to report an error to Log, Log::Instance unwittingly returns a reference to the "shell" of a destroyed Log object. The program steps into the shady realm of undefined behavior. This is the dead-reference problem.

The order of construction and destruction of Keyboard, Log, and Display is not known beforehand. The need is to have Keyboard and Display follow the C++ rule (last created is first destroyed) but also to exempt Log from this rule. No matter when it was created, Log must be always destroyed after *both* Keyboard and Display so that it can collect errors from the destruction of either of these.

If an application uses multiple interacting singletons, we cannot provide an automated way to control their lifetime. A reasonable singleton should at least perform dead-reference *detection*. We can achieve this by tracking destruction with a static Boolean member variable destroyed_. Initially, destroyed_ is false. Singleton's destructor sets destroyed_ to true.

Before jumping to the implementation, it's time for an overhaul. In addition to creating and returning a reference to the Singleton object, Singleton::Instance now has an additional responsibility—detecting the dead reference. Let's apply the design guideline that says, One function, one responsibility. We therefore define three distinct member functions: Create, which effectively creates the Singleton object; OnDeadReference, which performs error handling; and the well-known Instance, which gives access to the unique Singleton object. Of these, only Instance is public.

Let's implement a Singleton that performs dead-reference detection. First, we add a static bool member variable called destroyed_ to the Singleton class. Its role is to detect the dead reference. Then we change the destructor of Singleton to set pInstance_ to zero and destroyed_ to true. Here's the new class and the OnDeadReference function:

```cpp
// Singleton.h
class Singleton
{
public:
    static Singleton& Instance()
    {
        if (!pInstance_)
        {
            // Check for dead reference
            if (destroyed_)
            {
                OnDeadReference();
            }
            else
            {
                // First call—initialize
                Create();
            }
        }
        return *pInstance_;
    }
private:
    // Create a new Singleton and store a
    // pointer to it in pInstance_
    static void Create()
    {
        // Task: initialize pInstance_
        static Singleton theInstance;
        pInstance_ = &theInstance;
    }
    // Gets called if dead reference detected
    static void OnDeadReference()
    {
        throw std::runtime_error("Dead Reference Detected");
    }
    virtual ~Singleton()
    {
        pInstance_ = 0;
```

```
        destroyed_ = true;
    }
    // Data
    static Singleton* pInstance_;
    static bool destroyed_;
    ... disabled constructors/destructor/operator= ...
};

// Singleton.cpp
Singleton* Singleton::pInstance_ = 0;
bool Singleton::destroyed_ = false;
```

It works! As soon as the application exits, Singleton's destructor gets called. The destructor sets pInstance_ to zero and destroyed_ to true. If some longer-living object tries to access the singleton afterward, the control flow reaches OnDeadReference, which throws an exception of type runtime_error. This solution is inexpensive, simple, and effective.

6.6 Addressing the Dead Reference Problem (I): The Phoenix Singleton

If we apply the solution in the previous section to the KDL (Keyboard, Display, Log) problem, the result is unsatisfactory. If Display's destructor needs to report an error after Log has been destroyed, Log::Instance throws an exception. We got rid of undefined behavior; now we have to deal with unsatisfactory behavior.

We need Log to be available at any time, no matter when it was initially constructed. At an extreme, we'd even prefer to create Log again (although it's been destroyed) so that we can use it for error reporting at *any* time. This is the idea behind the Phoenix Singleton design pattern.

Just as the legendary Phoenix bird rises repeatedly from its own ashes, the Phoenix singleton is able to rise again after it has been destroyed. A single instance of the Singleton object at any given moment is still guaranteed (no two singletons ever exist simultaneously), yet the instance can be created again if the dead reference is detected. With the Phoenix Singleton pattern, we can solve the KDL problem easily: Keyboard and Display can remain "regular" singletons, while Log becomes a Phoenix singleton.

The implementation of the Phoenix Singleton with a static variable is simple. When we detect the dead reference, we create a new Singleton object in the shell of the old one. (C++ guarantees this is possible. Static objects' memory lasts for the duration of the program.) We also register this new object's destruction with atexit. We don't have to change Instance; the only change is in the OnDeadReference primitive.

```
class Singleton
{
    ... as before ...
    static void KillPhoenixSingleton(); // Added
};

void Singleton::OnDeadReference()
{
```

```
    // Obtain the shell of the destroyed singleton
    Create();
    // Now pInstance_ points to the "ashes" of the singleton
    // - the raw memory that the singleton was seated in.
    // Create a new singleton at that address
    new(pInstance_) Singleton;
    // Queue this new object's destruction
    atexit(KillPhoenixSingleton);
    // Reset destroyed_ because we're back in business
    destroyed_ = false;
}

void Singleton::KillPhoenixSingleton()
{
    // Make all ashes again
    // - call the destructor by hand.
    // It will set pInstance_ to zero and destroyed_ to true
    pInstance_->~Singleton();
}
```

The new operator that `OnDeadReference` uses is called the *placement new operator*. The placement new operator does not allocate memory; it only constructs a new object at the address passed—in our case, pInstance_. For an interesting discussion about the placement new operator, you may want to consult Meyers (1998b).

The `Singleton` above added a new member function, `KillPhoenixSingleton`. Now that we use new to resurrect the Phoenix singleton, the compiler magic will no longer destroy it, as it does with static variables. We built it by hand, so we must destroy it by hand, which is what `atexit(KillPhoenixSingleton)` ensures.

Let's analyze the flow of events. During the application exit sequence, `Singleton`'s destructor is called. The destructor resets the pointer to zero and sets `destroyed_` to `true`. Now assume some global object tries to access `Singleton` again. `Instance` calls `OnDead-Reference`. `OnDeadReference` reanimates `Singleton` and queues a call to `KillPhoenix-Singleton`, and `Instance` successfully returns a reference to a valid `Singleton` object. From now on, the cycle may repeat.

The Phoenix Singleton class ensures that global objects and other singletons can get a valid instance of it, at any time. This is a strong enough guarantee to make the Phoenix singleton an appealing solution for robust, all-terrain objects, like the `Log` in our problem. If we make `Log` a Phoenix singleton, the program will work correctly, no matter what the sequence of failures is.

6.6.1 Problems with `atexit`

If you compared the code given in the previous section with Loki's actual code, you would notice a difference: The call to `atexit` is surrounded by an `#ifdef` preprocessor directive:

```
#ifdef ATEXIT_FIXED
    // Queue this new object's destructor
    atexit(KillPhoenixSingleton);
#endif
```

If you don't #define `ATEXIT_FIXED`, the newly created Phoenix singleton will not be destroyed, and it will leak, which is exactly what we are striving to avoid.

This measure has to do with an unfortunate omission in the C++ standard. The standard fails to describe what happens when you register functions with `atexit` during a call made as the effect of another `atexit` registration.

To illustrate this problem, let's write a short test program:

```
#include <cstdlib>
void Bar()
{
    ...
}
void Foo()
{
    std::atexit(Bar);
}
int main()
{
    std::atexit(Foo);
}
```

This little program registers `Foo` with `atexit`. `Foo` calls `atexit(Bar)`, a case in which the behavior is not covered by the two standards. Because `atexit` and destruction of static variables go hand in hand, once the application exit sequence has started, we're left on shaky ground. Both the C and C++ standards are self-contradictory. They say that `Bar` will be called before `Foo` because `Bar` was registered last, but at the time it's registered, it's too late for `Bar` to be first because `Foo` is already being called.

Does this problem sound too academic? Let's put it another way: At the time of this writing, on three widely used compilers, the behavior ranges from incorrect (resource leaks) to application crashes.[2]

Compilers will take some time to catch up with the solution to this problem. As of this moment, the macro is in there. On some compilers, if you create a Phoenix singleton the second time, it will eventually leak. Depending on what your compiler's documentation says, you may want to #define `ATEXIT_FIXED` prior to including the `Singleton.h` header file.

6.7 Addressing the Dead Reference Problem (II): Singletons with Longevity

The Phoenix singleton is satisfactory in many contexts but has a couple of disadvantages. The Phoenix singleton breaks the normal lifetime cycle of a singleton, which may

---

[2] I have had a newsgroup (comp.std.c++) and e-mail discussion with Steve Clamage, chairman of the ANSI/ISO C++ Standards Committee, regarding the state of affairs with `atexit`. He was well aware of the problem and had already submitted a defect report for both C9X and C++. The submittal can be found at http://anubis.dkuug.dk/jtc1/sc22/wg21/docs/lwg-issues.html#3. Fortunately, the current proposed resolution favors the Singleton implementation discussed in this chapter: Even for functions called during exit processing, `atexit` still behaves in a stack manner, which is what is wanted. At the time of this writing, the resolution is approved and ready to be committed to the standard.

confuse some clients. If the singleton keeps state, that state is lost after a destruction-creation cycle. The implementer of a concrete singleton that uses the Phoenix strategy must pay extra attention to keeping state between the moment of destruction and the moment of reconstruction.

This is annoying especially because in situations such as the KDL example, you *do* know what the order should be: No matter what, if Log gets created, it must be destroyed after both Keyboard and Display. In other words, in this case we need Log to die after Keyboard and Display. We need an easy way to control the lifetime of various singletons. If we can do that, we can solve the KDL problem by assigning Log a longer lifetime than both Display and Keyboard.

But wait, there's more: This problem applies not only to singletons but also to global objects in general. The concept emerging here is that of *longevity control* and is independent of the concept of a singleton: The greater longevity an *object* has, the later it will be destroyed. It doesn't matter whether the object is a singleton or some global dynamically allocated object. We need to write code like this:

```
// This is a Singleton class
class SomeSingleton { ... };
// This is a regular class
class SomeClass { ... };

SomeClass* pGlobalObject(new SomeClass);

int main()
{
   SetLongevity(&SomeSingleton().Instance(), 5);
   // Ensure pGlobalObject will be deleted
   // after SomeSingleton's instance
   SetLongevity(pGlobalObject, 6);
   ...
}
```

The function SetLongevity takes a pointer to an object of *any* type and an integral value (the longevity).

```
// Takes a pointer to an object allocated with new and
// the longevity of that object
template <typename T>
void SetLongevity(T* pDynObject, unsigned int longevity);
```

SetLongevity ensures that pDynObject will outlive all objects that have lesser longevity. When the application exits, all objects registered with SetLongevity are deleted in increasing order of their longevity.

You cannot apply SetLongevity to objects whose lifetimes are controlled by the compiler, such as regular global objects, static objects, and automatic objects. The compiler already generates code for destroying them, and calling SetLongevity for those objects would destroy them twice. (That never helps.) SetLongevity is intended for objects allocated with new only. Moreover, by calling SetLongevity for an object, you commit to not calling delete for that object.

An alternative would be to create a dependency manager, an object that controls dependencies between other objects. DependencyManager would expose a generic function SetDependency as shown:

```cpp
class DependencyManager
{
public:
    template <typename T, typename U>
    void SetDependency(T* dependent, U& target);
    ...
};
```

DependencyManager's destructor would destroy the objects in an ordered manner, destroying dependents before their targets.

The DependencyManager-based solution has a major drawback—both objects must be in existence. This means that if you try to establish a dependency between Keyboard and Log, for example, you must create the Log object—even if you are not going to need it at all.

In an attempt to avoid this problem, you might establish the Keyboard-Log dependency inside Log's constructor. This, however, tightens the coupling between Keyboard and Log to an unacceptable degree: Keyboard depends on Log's class definition (because Keyboard uses the Log), and Log depends on Keyboard's class definition (because Log sets the dependency). This is a *circular dependency,* and, as discussed in detail in Chapter 10, circular dependencies should be avoided.

Let's get back then to the longevity paradigm. Because SetLongevity has to play nice with atexit, we must carefully define the interaction between these two functions. For example, let's define the exact sequence of destructor calls for the following program.

```cpp
class SomeClass { ... };

int main()
{
    // Create an object and assign a longevity to it
    SomeClass* pObj1 = new SomeClass;
    SetLongevity(pObj1, 5);
    // Create a static object whose lifetime
    // follows C++ rules
    static SomeClass obj2;
    // Create another object and assign a greater
    // longevity to it
    SomeClass* pObj3 = new SomeClass;
    SetLongevity(pObj3, 6);
    // How will these objects be destroyed?
}
```

main defines a mixed bag of objects with longevity and objects that obey C++ rules. Defining a reasonable destruction order for these three objects is hard because, aside from using `atexit`, we don't have any means of manipulating the hidden stack maintained by the runtime support.

A careful constraints analysis leads to the following design decisions.

- Each call to `SetLongevity` issues a call to `atexit`.
- Destruction of objects with lesser longevity takes place before destruction of objects with greater longevity.
- Destruction of objects with the same longevity follows the C++ rule: last built, first destroyed.

In the example program, the rules lead to the following guaranteed order of destruction: `*pObj1, obj2, *pObj3`. The first call to `SetLongevity` will issue a call to `atexit` for destroying `*pObj3`, and the second call will correspondingly issue a call to `atexit` for destroying `*pObj1`.

`SetLongevity` gives developers a great deal of power for managing objects' lifetimes, and it has well-defined and reasonable ways of interacting with the built-in C++ rules related to object lifetime. Note, however, that, like many other powerful tools, it can be dangerous. The rule of thumb in using it is as follows: Any object that uses an object with longevity must have a shorter longevity than the used object.

6.8 Implementing Singletons with Longevity

Once `SetLongevity`'s specification is complete, the implementation is not that complicated. `SetLongevity` maintains a hidden *priority queue,* separate from the inaccessible `atexit` stack. In turn, `SetLongevity` calls `atexit`, always passing it the same pointer to a function. This function pops one element off the priority queue and deletes it. It's that simple.

The core is the priority queue data structure. The longevity value passed to `SetLongevity` establishes the priorities. For a given longevity, the queue behaves like a stack. Destruction of objects with the same longevity follows the last in, first out rule. In spite of its name, we cannot use the standard `std::priority_queue` class because it does not guarantee the ordering of the elements having the same priority.

The elements that the data structure holds are pointers to the type `LifetimeTracker`. Its interface consists of a virtual destructor and a comparison operator. Derived classes must override the destructor. (You will see in a minute what `Compare` is good for.)

```
namespace Private
{
    class LifetimeTracker
    {
    public:
        LifetimeTracker(unsigned int x) : longevity_(x) {}
        virtual ~LifetimeTracker() = 0;
        friend inline bool Compare(
            unsigned int longevity,
            const LifetimeTracker* p)
        { return p->longevity_ < longevity; }
    private:
        unsigned int longevity_;
    };
```

```
        // Definition required
        inline LifetimeTracker::~LifetimeTracker() {}
    }
```

The priority queue data structure is a simple dynamically allocated array of pointers to `LifetimeTracker`:

```
namespace Private
{
    typedef LifetimeTracker** TrackerArray;
    extern TrackerArray pTrackerArray;
    extern unsigned int elements;
}
```

There is only one instance of the `TrackerArray` type. Consequently, `pTrackerArray` is exposed to all the Singleton problems just discussed. We are caught in an interesting chicken-and-egg problem: `SetLongevity` must be available at any time, yet it has to manage private storage. To deal with this problem, `SetLongevity` carefully manipulates `pTrackerArray` with the low-level functions in the `std::malloc` family (`malloc`, `realloc`, and `free`).[3] This way, we transfer the chicken-and-egg problem to the C heap allocator, which fortunately is guaranteed to work correctly for the whole lifetime of the application. This being said, `SetLongevity`'s implementation is simple: It creates a concrete tracker object, adds it to the priority queue, and registers a call to `atexit`.

The following code makes an important step toward generalization. It introduces a functor that takes care of *destroying* the tracked object. The rationale is that you don't always use `delete` to deallocate an object; it can be an object allocated on an alternate heap, and so on. By default, the destroyer is a pointer to a function that calls `delete`. The default function is called `Delete` and is templated with the type of the object to be deleted.

```
        namespace Private
        {
        //Helper destroyer function
        template <typename T>
        struct Deleter
        {
            static void Delete(T* pObj)
            { delete pObj; }
        };

        // Concrete lifetime tracker for objects of type T
        template <typename T, typename Destroyer>
        class ConcreteLifetimeTracker : public LifetimeTracker
        {
        public:
                ConcreteLifetimeTracker(T* p,
                    unsigned int longevity,
                    Destroyer d)
                    :LifetimeTracker(longevity)
```

---

[3]Actually, `SetLongevity` uses `std::realloc` only. The `realloc` function can replace both `malloc` and `free`: If you call it with a null pointer, it behaves like `std::malloc`; if you call it with a zero size, it behaves like `std::free`. Basically, `std::realloc` is a one-stop shop for `malloc`-based allocation.

```
            ,pTracked_(p)
            ,destroyer_(d)
            {}
            ~ConcreteLifetimeTracker()
            {
                destroyer_(pTracked_);
            }
        private:
            T* pTracked_;
            Destroyer destroyer_;
        };
        void AtExitFn(); // Declaration needed below
    }

    template <typename T, typename Destroyer>
    void SetLongevity(T* pDynObject, unsigned int longevity,
        Destroyer d = Private::Deleter<T>::Delete)
    {
        TrackerArray pNewArray = static_cast<TrackerArray>(
                std::realloc(pTrackerArray, sizeof(*pTrackerArray) *
            (elements + 1)));
        if (!pNewArray) throw std::bad_alloc();
        pTrackerArray = pNewArray;
        LifetimeTracker* p = new ConcreteLifetimeTracker<T, Destroyer>(
            pDynObject, longevity, d);
        TrackerArray pos = std::upper_bound(
            pTrackerArray, pTrackerArray + elements, longevity, Compare);
        std::copy_backward(pos, pTrackerArray + elements,
            pTrackerArray + elements + 1);
        *pos = p;
        ++elements;
        std::atexit(AtExitFn);
    }
    }
```

It takes a while to get used to things like std::upper_bound and std::copy_backward, but indeed they make nontrivial code easy to write and read. The function above inserts a newly created pointer to ConcreteLifetimeTracker in the sorted array pointed to by pTrackerArray, keeps it ordered, and handles errors and exceptions.

Now the purpose of LifetimeTracker::Compare is clear. The array to which pTrackerArray points is sorted by longevity. Objects with longer longevity are toward the beginning of the array. Objects of the same longevity appear in the order in which they were inserted. SetLongevity ensures all this.

The AtExitFn function pops the object with the smallest longevity (that is, the one at the end of the array) and deletes it. Deleting the pointer to LifetimeTracker invokes ConcreteLifetimeTracker's destructor, which in turn deletes the tracked object.

```
        static void AtExitFn()
        {
            assert(elements > 0 && pTrackerArray != 0);
            // Pick the element at the top of the stack
            LifetimeTracker* pTop = pTrackerArray[elements - 1];
```

```
            // Remove that object off the stack
            // Don't check errors-realloc with less memory
            // can't fail
            pTrackerArray = static_cast<TrackerArray>(std::realloc(
                pTrackerArray, sizeof(*pTrackerArray) * --elements));
            // Destroy the element
            delete pTop;
        }
```

Writing AtExitFn requires a bit of care. AtExitFn must pop the top element off the stack and delete it. In its destructor, the element deletes the managed object. The trick is, AtExitFn must pop the stack *before* deleting the top object because destroying some object may create another one, thus pushing another element onto the stack. Although this looks quite unlikely, it's exactly what happens when Keyboard's destructor tries to use the Log.

The code conveniently hides the data structures and AtExitFn in the Private namespace. The clients see only the tip of the iceberg—the SetLongevity function.

Singletons with longevity can use SetLongevity in the following manner:

```
        class Log
        {
        public:
            static void Create()
            {
                // Create the instance
                pInstance_ = new log;
                // This line added
                SetLongevity(pInstance_, longevity_);
            }
            // Rest of implementation omitted
            // Log::Instance remains as defined earlier
        private:
            // Define a fixed value for the longevity
            static const unsigned int longevity_ = 2;
            static Log* pInstance_;
        };
```

If you implement Keyboard and Display in a similar fashion, but define longevity_ to be 1, the Log will be guaranteed to be alive at the time when both Keyboard and Display are destroyed. This solves the KDL problem—or does it? What if your application uses multiple threads?

6.9 Living in a Multithreaded World

Singleton has to deal with threads, too. Suppose we have an application that has just started, and two threads access the following Singleton:

```
        Singleton& Singleton::Instance()
        {
            if (!pInstance_)                         // 1
            {
```

```
    pInstance_ = new Singleton;    // 2
  }
  return *pInstance_;              // 3
}
```

The first thread enters Instance and tests the if condition. Because it's the very first access, pInstance_ is null, and the thread reaches the line marked // 2 and is ready to invoke the new operator. It might just happen that the OS scheduler unwittingly interrupts the first thread at this point and passes control to the other thread.

The second thread enters the stage, invokes Singleton::Instance(), and finds a null pInstance_ as well because the first thread hasn't yet had a chance to modify it. So far, the first thread has managed only to *test* pInstance_. Now say the second thread manages to call the new operator, assigns pInstance_ in peace, and gets away with it.

Unfortunately, as the first thread becomes conscious again, it remembers it was just about to execute line 2, so it reassigns pInstance_ and gets away with it, too. When the dust settles, there are two Singleton objects instead of one, and one of them will leak for sure. Each thread holds a distinct instance of Singleton, and the application is surely slipping toward chaos. And that's only one possible situation—what if multiple threads scramble to access the singleton? (Imagine yourself debugging this.)

Experienced multithreaded programmers will recognize a classic race condition here. It is to be expected that the Singleton design pattern meets threads. A singleton object is a shared global resource, and all shared global resources are always suspect for race conditions and threading issues.

6.9.1 The Double-Checked Locking Pattern

A thorough discussion of multithreaded singletons was first presented by Douglas Schmidt (1996). The same article describes a very nifty solution, called the Double-Checked Locking pattern, devised by Doug Schmidt and Tim Harrison.

The obvious solution works but is not appealing:

```
Singleton& Singleton::Instance()
{
  // mutex_ is a mutex object
  // Lock manages the mutex
  Lock guard(mutex_);
  if (!pInstance_)
  {
    pInstance_ = new Singleton;
  }
  return *pInstance_;
}
```

Class Lock is a classic mutex handler (refer to the appendix for details on mutexes). Lock's constructor locks the mutex, and its destructor unlocks the mutex. While mutex_ is locked, other threads that try to lock the same mutex are waiting.

We got rid of the race condition: While a thread assigns to pInstance_, all others stop in guard's constructor. When another thread locks the lock, it will find pInstance_ already initialized, and everything works smoothly.

However, a correct solution is not always an appealing one. The inconvenience is its lack of efficiency. Each call to `Instance` incurs locking and unlocking the synchronization object, although the race condition occurs only, so to say, once in a lifetime. These operations are usually very costly, much more costly than the simple `if (!pInstance_)` test. (On today's systems, the times taken by a test-and-branch and a critical-section lock differ typically by a couple of orders of magnitude.)

A would-be solution that attempts to avoid the overhead is presented in the following code:

```
Singleton& Singleton::Instance()
{
   if (!pInstance_)
   {
      Lock guard(mutex_);
      pInstance_ = new Singleton;
   }
   return *pInstance_;
}
```

Now the overhead is gone, but the race condition is back. The first thread passes the `if` test, but just when it is about to enter the synchronized portion of code, the OS scheduler interrupts it and passes control to the other thread. The second thread passes the `if` test itself (and to no one's surprise, finds a null pointer), enters the synchronized portion, and completes it. When the first thread is reactivated, it also enters the synchronized portion, but it's just too late—again, two `Singleton` objects are constructed.

This seems like one of those brainteasers with no solution, but in fact there is a very simple and elegant one. It's called the Double-Checked Locking pattern.

The idea is simple: Check the condition, enter the synchronized code, and then check the condition again. By this time, *rien ne va plus*—the pointer is either initialized or null all right. The code that will help you to understand and savor the Double-Checked pattern follows. Indeed, there *is* beauty in computer engineering.

```
Singleton& Singleton::Instance()
{
   if (!pInstance_)              // 1
   {                            // 2
      Guard myGuard(mutex_);    // 3
      if (!pInstance_)          // 4
      {
         pInstance_ = new Singleton;
      }
   }
   return *pInstance_;
}
```

Assume the flow of execution of a thread enters the twilight zone (commented line 2). Here several threads may enter at once. However, in the synchronized section only one thread makes it at a time. On line 3, there's no twilight anymore. All is clear: The pointer has been either fully initialized or not at all. The first thread that enters initializes the variable, and all others fail the test on line 4 and do not create anything.

The first test is quick and coarse. If the `Singleton` object is available, you get it. If not, further investigation is necessary. The second test is slow and accurate: It tells whether `Singleton` was indeed initialized or the thread is responsible for initializing it. This is the Double-Checked Locking pattern. Now we have the best of both worlds: Most of the time the access to the singleton is as fast as it gets. During construction, however, no race conditions occur. Awesome. But . . .

Very experienced multithreaded programmers know that even the Double-Checked Locking pattern, although correct on paper, is not always correct in practice. In certain symmetric multiprocessor environments (the ones featuring the so-called relaxed memory model), the writes are committed to the main memory in bursts, rather than one by one. The bursts occur in increasing order of addresses, not in chronological order. Due to this rearranging of writes, the memory as seen by one processor at a time might look as if the operations are not performed in the correct order by another processor. Concretely, the assignment to `pInstance_` performed by a processor might occur *before* the Singleton object has been fully initialized! Thus, sadly, the Double-Checked Locking pattern is known to be defective for such systems.

In conclusion, you should check your compiler documentation before implementing the Double-Checked Locking pattern. (This makes it the Triple-Checked Locking pattern.) Usually the platform offers alternative, nonportable concurrency-solving primitives, such as memory barriers, which ensure ordered access to memory. At least, put a `volatile` qualifier next to `pInstance_`. A reasonable compiler should generate correct, nonspeculative code around `volatile` objects.

6.10 Putting It All Together

This chapter has wandered around various possible implementations of Singleton, commenting on their relative strengths and weaknesses. The discussion doesn't lead to a unique implementation because the problem at hand is what dictates the best Singleton implementation.

The `SingletonHolder` class template defined by Loki is a Singleton container that assists you in using the Singleton design pattern. Following a policy-based design (see Chapter 1), `SingletonHolder` is a specialized container for a user-defined Singleton object. When using `SingletonHolder`, you pick the features needed, and maybe provide some code of your own. In extreme cases, you might still need to start all over again—which is okay, as long as those are indeed extreme cases.

This chapter visited quite a few issues that are mostly independent of each other. How, then, can Singleton implement so many cases without utter code bloating? The key is to decompose Singleton carefully into policies, as discussed in Chapter 1. By decomposing `SingletonHolder` into several policies, we can implement *all* the cases discussed previously in a small number of lines of code. By using template instantiation, you select the features needed and don't pay anything for the unneeded ones. This is important: The implementation of Singleton put together here is not the do-it-all class. Only the features used are ultimately included in the generated code. Plus, the implementation leaves room for tweaks and extensions.

6.10.1 Decomposing `SingletonHolder` into Policies

Let's start by delimiting what policies we can distinguish for the implementations discussed. We identified creation issues, lifetime issues, and threading issues. These are the three most important aspects of Singleton development. The three corresponding polices therefore are as follows:

1. *Creation.* You can create a singleton in various ways. Typically, the **Creation** policy invokes the `new` operator to create an object. Isolating creation as a policy is essential because it enables you to create polymorphic objects.
2. *Lifetime.* We identified the following lifetime policies:
   a. Following C++ rules—last created, first destroyed
   b. Recurring (Phoenix singleton)
   c. User controlled (singleton with longevity)
   d. Infinite (the "leaking" singleton, an object that's never destroyed)
3. *ThreadingModel.* Whether singleton is single threaded, is standard multithreaded (with a mutex and the Double-Checked Locking pattern), or uses a nonportable threading model.

All Singleton implementations must take the same precautions for enforcing uniqueness. These are not policies, because changing them would break the definition of Singleton.

6.10.2 Defining Requirements for `SingletonHolder`'s Policies

Let's define the necessary requirements that `SingletonHolder` imposes on its policies.

The **Creation** policy must create and destroy objects, so it must expose two corresponding functions. Therefore, assuming `Creator<T>` is a class compliant with the **Creation** policy, `Creator<T>` must support the following calls:

```
T* pObj = Creator<T>::Create();
Creator<T>::Destroy(pObj);
```

Notice that `Create` and `Destroy` must be two `static` members of `Creator`. Singleton does not hold a `Creator` object—this would perpetuate the Singleton lifetime issues.

The **Lifetime** policy essentially must schedule the destruction of the Singleton object created by the **Creation** policy. In essence, **Lifetime** policy's functionality boils down to its ability to destroy the Singleton object at a specific time during the lifetime of the application. In addition, **Lifetime** decides the action to be taken if the application violates the lifetime rules of the Singleton object. Hence:

- If you need the singleton to be destroyed according to C++ rules, then **Lifetime** uses a mechanism similar to `atexit`.
- For the Phoenix singleton, **Lifetime** still uses an `atexit`-like mechanism but accepts the re-creation of the Singleton object.
- For a singleton with longevity, **Lifetime** issues a call to `SetLongevity`, described in Sections 6.7 and 6.8.
- For infinite lifetime, **Lifetime** does not take any action.

In conclusion, the **Lifetime** policy prescribes two functions: `ScheduleDestruction`, which takes care of setting the appropriate time for destruction, and `OnDeadReference`, which establishes the behavior in case of dead-reference detection.

If `Lifetime<T>` is a class that implements the **Lifetime** policy, the following expressions make sense:

```
void (*pDestructionFunction)();
...
Lifetime<T>::ScheduleDestruction(pDestructionFunction);
Lifetime<T>::OnDeadReference();
```

The `ScheduleDestruction` member function accepts a pointer to the actual function that performs the destruction. This way, we can compound the **Lifetime** policy with the **Creation** policy. Don't forget that **Lifetime** is not concerned with the destruction method, which is **Creation**'s charter; the only preoccupation of **Lifetime** is timing—that is, *when* the destruction will occur.

`OnDeadReference` throws an exception in all cases except for the Phoenix singleton, a case in which it does nothing.

The **ThreadingModel** policy is the one described in the appendix. `SingletonHolder` does not support object-level locking, only class-level locking. This is because you have only one object anyway.

6.10.3 Assembling `SingletonHolder`

Now let's begin defining the `SingletonHolder` class template. As discussed in Chapter 1, each policy mandates one template parameter. In addition to it, we prepend a template parameter (T) that's the type for which we provide singleton behavior. The `SingletonHolder` class template is not itself a Singleton. `SingletonHolder` provides only singleton behavior and management over an existing class.

```
template
<
    class T,
    template <class> class CreationPolicy = CreateUsingNew,
    template <class> class LifetimePolicy = DefaultLifetime,
    template <class> class ThreadingModel = SingleThreaded
>
class SingletonHolder
{
public:
    static T& Instance();
private:
    // Helpers
    static void DestroySingleton();
    // Protection
    SingletonHolder();

    ...
    // Data
    typedef ThreadingModel<T>::VolatileType InstanceType;
    static InstanceType* pInstance_;
```

```
      static bool destroyed_;
   };
```

The type of the instance variable is not T* as you would expect. Instead, it's Threading-Model<T>::VolatileType*. The ThreadingModel<T>::VolatileType type definition expands either to T or to volatile T, depending on the actual threading model. The volatile qualifier applied to a type tells the compiler that values of that type might be changed by multiple threads. Knowing this, the compiler avoids some optimizations (such as keeping values in its internal registers) that would make multithreaded code run erratically. A safe decision would be then to define pInstance_ to be type volatile T*: It works with multi-threaded code (subject to your checking your compiler's documentation) and doesn't hurt in single-threaded code.

On the other hand, in a single-threaded model, you *do* want to take advantage of those optimizations, so T* would be the best type for pInstance_. That's why the actual type of pInstance_ is decided by the ThreadingModel policy. If ThreadingModel is a single-threaded policy, it simply defines VolatileType as follows:

```
template <class T> class SingleThreaded
{
   ...
public:
   typedef T VolatileType;
};
```

A multithreaded policy would have a definition that qualifies T with volatile. See the appendix for more details on threading models.

Let's now define the Instance member function, which wires together the three policies.

```
template <...>
T& SingletonHolder<...>::Instance()
{
   if (!pInstance_)
   {
      typename ThreadingModel<T>::Lock guard;
      if (!pInstance_)
      {
         if (destroyed_)
         {
            LifetimePolicy<T>::OnDeadReference();
            destroyed_ = false;
         }
         pInstance_ = CreationPolicy<T>::Create();
         LifetimePolicy<T>::ScheduleDestruction(&DestroySingleton);
      }
   }
   return *pInstance_;
}
```

Instance is the one and only public function exposed by SingletonHolder. Instance implements a shell over CreationPolicy, LifetimePolicy, and ThreadingModel. The

ThreadingModel<T> policy class exposes an inner class Lock. For the lifetime of a Lock object, all other threads trying to create objects of type Lock will block. (Refer to the appendix.)

DestroySingleton simply destroys the Singleton object, cleans up the allocated memory, and sets destroyed_ to true. SingletonHolder never calls DestroySingleton; it only passes its address to LifetimePolicy<T>::ScheduleDestruction.

```
template <...>
void SingletonHolder<...>::DestroySingleton()
{
    assert(!destroyed_);
    CreationPolicy<T>::Destroy(pInstance_);
    pInstance_ = 0;
    destroyed_ = true;
}
```

SingletonHolder passes pInstance_ and the address of DestroySingleton to LifetimePolicy<T>. The intent is to give LifetimePolicy enough information to implement the known behaviors: C++ rules, recurring (Phoenix singleton), user controlled (singleton with longevity), and infinite. Here's how:

- *Per C++ rules.* LifetimePolicy<T>::ScheduleDestruction calls atexit, passing it the address of DestroySingleton. OnDeadReference throws a std::logic_error exception.
- *Recurring.* Same as above, except that OnDeadReference does not throw an exception. SingletonHolder's flow of execution continues and will re-create the object.
- *User controlled.* LifetimePolicy<T>::ScheduleDestruction calls SetLongevity(GetLongevity(pInstance)).
- *Infinite.* LifetimePolicy<T>::ScheduleDestruction has an empty implementation.

SingletonHolder handles the dead-reference problem as the responsibility of LifetimePolicy. It's very simple: If SingletonHolder::Instance detects a dead reference, it calls LifetimePolicy::OnDeadReference. If OnDeadReference returns, Instance continues with re-creating a new instance. In conclusion, OnDeadReference should throw an exception or terminate the program if you do not want Phoenix Singleton behavior. For a Phoenix singleton, OnDeadReference does nothing.

Well, that is the whole SingletonHolder implementation. Of course, now much work gets delegated to the three policies.

6.10.4 Stock Policy Implementations

Decomposition into policies is hard. After you do that, the policies are easy to implement. Let's collect the policy classes that implement the common types of singletons. Table 6.1 shows the predefined policy classes for SingletonHolder. The policy classes in bold are the default template parameters.

Table 6.1: Predefined Policies for SingletonHolder

Policy	Predefined Class Template	Comment
Creation	**CreateUsingNew**	Creates an object by using the new operator and the default constructor.
	CreateUsingMalloc	Creates an object by using std::malloc and its default constructor.
	CreateStatic	Creates an object in static memory.
Lifetime	**DefaultLifetime**	Manages the object's lifetime by obeying C++ rules. Uses atexit to get the job done.
	PhoenixSingleton	Same as DefaultLifetime but allows re-creation of the Singleton object.
	SingletonWithLongevity	Assigns longevity to the Singleton object. Assumes the existence of a namespace-level function GetLongevity that, called with pInstance_, returns the longevity of the Singleton object.
	NoDestroy	Does not destroy the Singleton object.
ThreadingModel	**SingleThreaded**	See the appendix for details about threading models.
	ClassLevelLockable	

What remains is only to figure out how to use and extend this small yet mighty SingletonHolder template.

6.11 Working with SingletonHolder

The SingletonHolder class template does not provide application-specific functionality. It merely provides Singleton-specific services over another class—T in the code in this chapter. We call T the *client class.*

The client class must take all the precautionary measures against unattended construction and destruction: The default constructor, the copy constructor, the assignment operator, the destructor, and the address-of operator should be made private.

If you take these protective measures, you also have to grant friendship to the Creator policy class that you use. These protective measures and the friend declaration are all the changes needed for a class to work with SingletonHolder. Note that these changes are optional and constitute a trade-off between the inconvenience of touching existing code and the risk of spurious instances.

The design decisions concerning a specific Singleton implementation usually are reflected in a type definition like the following one. Just as you would pass flags and options when calling some function, so you pass flags to the type definition selecting the desired behavior.

```
class A { ... };
typedef SingletonHolder<A, CreateUsingNew> SingleA;
// from here on you use SingleA::Instance()
```

Providing a singleton that returns an object of a derived class is as simple as changing the Creator policy class:

```
class A { ... };
class Derived : public A { ... };

template <class T> struct MyCreator : public CreateUsingNew<T>
{
    static T* Create()
    {
        return new Derived;
    }
};

typedef SingletonHolder<A, MyCreator> SingleA;
```

Similarly, you can provide parameters to the constructor or use a different allocation strategy. You can tweak Singleton along each policy. This way you can largely customize Singleton, while still benefiting from default behavior when you want to.

The SingletonWithLongevity policy class relies on you to define a namespace-level function GetLongevity. The definition would look something like this:

```
inline unsigned int GetLongevity(A*) { return 5; }
```

This is needed only if you use SingletonWithLongevity in the type definition of SingleA.

The intricate KDL problem has driven our tentative implementations. Here's the KDL problem solved by making use of the Singleton class template. Of course, these definitions go to their appropriate header files.

```
class KeyboardImpl { ... };
class DisplayImpl { ... };
class LogImpl { ... };
    ...
```

```
inline unsigned int GetLongevity(KeyboardImpl*) { return 1; }
inline unsigned int GetLongevity(DisplayImpl*) { return 1; }
// The log has greater longevity
inline unsigned int GetLongevity(LogImpl*) { return 2; }

typedef SingletonHolder<KeyboardImpl, CreateUsingNew,
   SingletonWithLongevity> Keyboard;
typedef SingletonHolder<DisplayImpl, CreateUsingNew,
   SingletonWithLongevity> Display;
typedef SingletonHolder<LogImpl, CreateUsingNew,
   SingletonWithLongevity> Log;
```

It's a rather easy-to-grasp and self-documenting solution, given the complexity of the problem.

6.12 Summary

The introduction to this chapter describes the most popular C++ implementations of Singleton. It's relatively easy to protect Singleton against multiple instantiations because there is good language support in this area. The most complicated problem is managing a singleton's lifetime, especially its destruction.

Detecting postdestruction access is easy and inexpensive. This dead-reference detection ought to be part of any Singleton implementation.

We discussed four main variations on the theme: the compiler-controlled singleton, the Phoenix singleton, the singleton with longevity, and the "leaking" singleton. Each of these has different strengths and weaknesses.

There are serious threading issues surrounding the Singleton design pattern. The Double-Checked Locking pattern is of great help in implementing thread-safe singletons.

In the end, we collected and classified the variations, which helped us in defining policies and decomposing Singleton along these policies. We identified three policies with Singleton: Creation, Lifetime, and ThreadingModel. We harnessed the policies in a class template SingletonHolder with four template parameters (the client type plus one parameter for each policy) that cover all the combinations among these design choices.

6.13 SingletonHolder Class Template Quick Facts

*   SingletonHolder's declaration is as follows:

```
template <
   class T,
   template <class> class CreationPolicy = CreateUsingNew,
   template <class> class LifetimePolicy = DefaultLifetime,
   template <class> class ThreadingModel = SingleThreaded
>
class SingletonHolder;
```

- You instantiate `SingletonHolder` by passing it your class as the first template parameter. You select design variations by combining the other three parameters. Example:

```
class MyClass { ... };
typedef SingletonHolder<MyClass, CreateStatic>
    MySingleClass;
```

- You must define the default constructor, or you must use a creator other than the stock implementations of the **Creator** policy.
- The canned implementations of the three policies are described in Table 6.1. You can add your own policy classes as long as you respect the requirements.

7

Smart Pointers

Smart pointers have been the subject of hecatombs of code written and rivers of ink consumed by programmers and writers around the world. Perhaps the most popular, intricate, and powerful C++ idiom, smart pointers are interesting in that they combine many syntactic and semantic issues. This chapter discusses smart pointers, from their simplest aspects to their most complex ones and from the most obvious errors in implementing them to the subtlest ones—some of which also happen to be the most gruesome.

In brief, smart pointers are C++ objects that simulate simple pointers by implementing operator-> and the unary operator*. In addition to sporting pointer syntax and semantics, smart pointers often perform useful tasks—such as memory management or locking—under the covers, thus freeing the application from carefully managing the lifetime of pointed-to objects.

This chapter not only discusses smart pointers but also implements a SmartPtr class template. SmartPtr is designed around policies (see Chapter 1), and the result is a smart pointer that has the exact levels of safety, efficiency, and ease of use that you want.

After reading this chapter, you will be an expert in smart pointer issues such as the following:

* The advantages and disadvantages of smart pointers
* Ownership management strategies
* Implicit conversions
* Tests and comparisons
* Multithreading issues

This chapter implements a generic SmartPtr class template. Each section presents one implementation issue in isolation. At the end, the implementation puts all the pieces together. In addition to understanding the design rationale of SmartPtr, you will know how to use, tweak, and extend it.

7.1 Smart Pointers 101

So what's a smart pointer? A smart pointer is a C++ class that mimics a regular pointer in syntax and some semantics, but it does more. Because smart pointers to different types of objects tend to have a lot of code in common, almost all good-quality smart pointers in existence are templated by the pointee type, as you can see in the following code:

```
template <class T>
class SmartPtr
{
public:
    explicit SmartPtr(T* pointee) : pointee_(pointee) {...}
    SmartPtr& operator=(const SmartPtr& other);
    ~SmartPtr();
    T& operator*() const
    {
        ...
        return *pointee_;
    }
    T* operator->() const
    {
        ...
        return pointee_;
    }
private:
    T* pointee_;
    ...
};
```

SmartPtr<T> aggregates a pointer to T in its member variable pointee_. That's what most smart pointers do. In some cases, a smart pointer might aggregate some handles to data and compute the pointer on the fly.

The two operators give SmartPtr pointer-like syntax and semantics. That is, you can write

```
class Widget
{
public:
    void Fun();
};

SmartPtr<Widget> sp(new Widget);
sp->Fun();
(*sp).Fun();
```

Aside from the definition of sp, nothing reveals it as not being a pointer. This is the mantra of smart pointers: You can replace pointer definitions with smart pointer definitions without incurring major changes to your application's code. You thus get extra goodies with ease. Minimizing code changes is very appealing and vital for getting large applications to use smart pointers. As you will soon see, however, smart pointers are not a free lunch.

7.2 The Deal

But what's the deal with smart pointers? you might ask. What do you gain by replacing simple pointers with smart pointers? The explanation is simple. Smart pointers have value semantics, whereas some simple pointers do not.

An object with value semantics is an object that you can *copy* and *assign to.* A plain `int` is the perfect example of a first-class object. You can create, copy, and change integer values freely. A pointer that you use to iterate in a buffer also has value semantics—you initialize it to point to the beginning of the buffer, and you bump it until you reach the end. Along the way, you can copy its value to other variables to hold temporary results.

With pointers that hold values allocated with `new`, however, the story is very different. Once you have written

```
Widget* p = new Widget;
```

the variable p not only points to, but also *owns,* the memory allocated for the `Widget` object. This is because later you must issue `delete p` to ensure that the `Widget` object is destroyed and its memory is released. If in the line after the line just shown you write

```
p = 0; // assign something else to p
```

you lose ownership of the object previously pointed to by p, and you have no chance at all to get a grip on it again. You have a resource leak, and resource leaks never help.

Furthermore, when you copy p into another variable, the compiler does not automatically manage the ownership of the memory to which the pointer points. All you get is two raw pointers pointing to the same object, and you have to track them even more carefully because double deletions are even more catastrophic than no deletion. Consequently, pointers to allocated objects do *not* have value semantics—you cannot copy and assign to them at will.

Smart pointers can be of great help in this area. Most smart pointers offer *ownership management* in addition to pointer-like behavior. Smart pointers can figure out how ownership evolves, and their destructors can release the memory according to a well-defined strategy. Many smart pointers hold enough information to take full initiative in releasing the pointed-to object.

Smart pointers may manage ownership in various ways, each appropriate to a category of problems. Some smart pointers transfer ownership automatically: After you copy a smart pointer to an object, the source smart pointer becomes null, and the destination points to (and holds ownership of) the object. This is the behavior implemented by the standard-provided `std::auto_ptr`. Other smart pointers implement reference counting: They track the total count of smart pointers that point to the same object, and when this count goes down to zero, they `delete` the pointed-to object. Finally, some others duplicate their pointed-to object whenever you copy them.

In short, in the smart pointers' world, ownership is an important topic. By providing ownership management, smart pointers are able to support integrity guarantees and full value semantics. Because ownership has much to do with constructing, copying, and destroying smart pointers, it's easy to figure out that these are the most vital functions of a smart pointer.

The following few sections discuss various aspects of smart pointer design and implementation. The goal is to render smart pointers as close to raw pointers as possible, but not closer. It's a contradictory goal: After all, if your smart pointers behave *exactly* like dumb pointers, they *are* dumb pointers.

In implementing compatibility between smart pointers and raw pointers, there is a thin line between nicely filling compatibility checklists and paving the way to chaos. You will find that adding seemingly worthwhile features might expose the clients to costly risks. Much of the craft of implementing good smart pointers consists of carefully balancing their set of features.

7.3 Storage of Smart Pointers

To start, let's ask a fundamental question about smart pointers. Is pointee_'s type necessarily T*? If not, what else could it be? In generic programming, you should always ask yourself questions like these. Each type that's hardcoded in a piece of generic code decreases the genericity of the code. Hardcoded types are to generic code what magic constants are to regular code.

In several situations, it is worthwhile to allow customizing the pointee type. One situation is when you deal with nonstandard pointer modifiers. In the 16-bit Intel 80x86 days, you could qualify pointers with modifiers like __near, __far, and __huge. Other segmented memory architectures use similar modifiers.

Another situation is when you want to layer smart pointers. What if you have a Legacy-SmartPtr<T> smart pointer implemented by someone else, and you want to enhance it? Would you derive from it? That's a risky decision. It's better to wrap the legacy smart pointer into a smart pointer of your own. This is possible because the inner smart pointer supports pointer syntax. From the outer smart pointer's viewpoint, the pointee type is not T* but LegacySmartPtr<T>.

There are interesting applications of smart pointer layering, mainly because of the mechanics of operator->. When you apply operator-> to a type that's not a built-in pointer, the compiler does an interesting thing. After looking up and applying the user-defined operator-> to that type, it applies operator-> again to the result. The compiler keeps doing this recursively until it reaches a native pointer, and only then proceeds with member access. It follows that a smart pointer's operator-> does not have to return a pointer. It can return an object that in turn implements operator->, without changing the use syntax.

This leads to a very interesting idiom: pre- and postfunction calls (Stroustrup 2000). If you return an object of type PointerType by value from operator->, the sequence of execution is as follows:

1. Constructor of PointerType
2. PointerType::operator-> called; likely returns a pointer to an object of type PointeeType
3. Member access for PointeeType—likely a function call
4. Destructor of PointerType

In a nutshell, you have a nifty way of implementing locked function calls. This idiom has broad uses with multithreading and locked resource access. You can have PointerType's constructor lock the resource, and then you can access the resource; finally, PointerType's destructor unlocks the resource.

The generalization doesn't stop here. The syntax-oriented "pointer" part might sometimes pale in comparison with the powerful resource management techniques that are included in smart pointers. It follows that, in rare cases, smart pointers could drop the pointer syntax. An object that does not define `operator->` and `operator*` violates the definition of a smart pointer, but there are objects that do deserve smart pointer–like treatment, although they are not, strictly speaking, smart pointers.

Look at real-world APIs and applications. Many operating systems foster *handles* as accessors to certain internal resources, such as windows, mutexes, or devices. Handles are intentionally obfuscated pointers; one of their purposes is to prevent their users from manipulating critical operating system resources directly. Most of the time, handles are integral values that are indices in a hidden table of pointers. The table provides the additional level of indirection that protects the inner system from the application programmers. Although they don't provide an `operator->`, handles resemble pointers in semantics and in the way they are managed.

For such a smart resource, it does not make sense to provide `operator->` or `operator*`. However, you do take advantage of all the resource management techniques that are specific to smart pointers.

To generalize the type universe of smart pointers, we distinguish three potentially distinct types in a smart pointer:

- *The storage type.* This is the type of `pointee_`. By "default"—in regular smart pointers— it is a raw pointer.
- *The pointer type.* This is the type returned by `operator->`. It can be different from the storage type if you want to return a proxy object instead of just a pointer. (You will find an example of using proxy objects later in this chapter.)
- *The reference type.* This is the type returned by `operator*`.

It would be useful if `SmartPtr` supported this generalization in a flexible way. Thus, the three types mentioned here ought to be abstracted in a policy called **Storage**.

In conclusion, smart pointers can, and should, generalize their pointee type. To do this, `SmartPtr` abstracts three types in a **Storage** policy: the stored type, the pointer type, and the reference type. Not all types necessarily make sense for a given `SmartPtr` instantiation. Therefore, in rare cases (handles), a policy might disable access to `operator->` or `operator*` or both.

7.4 Smart Pointer Member Functions

Many existing smart pointer implementations allow operations through member functions, such as `Get` for accessing the pointee object, `Set` for changing it, and `Release` for taking over ownership. This is the obvious and natural way of encapsulating `SmartPtr`'s functionality.

However, experience has proven that member functions are not very suitable for smart pointers. The reason is that the interaction between member function calls for the smart pointer and for the *pointed-to* object can be extremely confusing.

Suppose, for instance, that you have a `Printer` class with member functions such as `Acquire` and `Release`. With `Acquire` you take ownership of the printer so that no other application prints to it, and with `Release` you relinquish ownership. As you use a smart pointer to `Printer`, you may notice a strange syntactical closeness to things that are very far apart semantically.

```
SmartPtr<Printer> spRes = ...;
spRes->Acquire(); // acquire the printer
... print a document ...
spRes->Release(); // release the printer
spRes.Release();  // release the pointer to the printer
```

The user of `SmartPtr` now has access to two totally different worlds: the world of the pointed-to object members and the world of the smart pointer members. A matter of a dot or an arrow thinly separates the two worlds.

On the face of it, C++ does force you routinely to observe certain slight differences in syntax. A Pascal programmer learning C++ might even feel that the slight syntactic difference between & and && is an abomination. Yet C++ programmers don't even blink at it. They are trained by habit to distinguish such syntax matters easily.

However, smart pointer member functions defeat training by habit. Raw pointers don't have member functions, so C++ programmers' eyes are not habituated to detect and distinguish dot calls from arrow calls. The compiler does a good job at that: If you use a dot after a raw pointer, the compiler will yield an error. Therefore, it is easy to imagine, and experience proves, that even seasoned C++ programmers find it extremely disturbing that both `sp.Release()` and `sp->Release()` compile flag-free but do very different things. The cure is simple: A smart pointer should not use member functions. `SmartPtr` uses only nonmember functions. These functions become friends of the smart pointer class.

Overloaded functions can be just as confusing as member functions of smart pointers, but there is an important difference. C++ programmers already use overloaded functions. Overloading is an important part of the C++ language and is used routinely in library and application development. This means that C++ programmers *do* pay attention to differences in function call syntax—such as `Release(*sp)` versus `Release(sp)`—in writing and reviewing code.

The only functions that necessarily remain members of `SmartPtr` are the constructors, the destructor, `operator=`, `operator->`, and unary `operator*`. All other operations of `SmartPtr` are provided through named nonmember functions.

For reasons of clarity, `SmartPtr` does not have any named member functions. The only functions that access the pointee object are `GetImpl`, `GetImplRef`, `Reset`, and `Release`, which are defined at the namespace level.

```
template <class T> T* GetImpl(SmartPtr<T>& sp);
template <class T> T*& GetImplRef(SmartPtr<T>& sp);
template <class T> void Reset(SmartPtr<T>& sp, T* source);
template <class T> void Release(SmartPtr<T>& sp, T*& destination);
```

- `GetImpl` returns the pointer object stored by `SmartPtr`.
- `GetImplRef` returns *a reference* to the pointer object stored by `SmartPtr`. `GetImplRef` allows you to change the underlying pointer, so it requires extreme care in use.
- `Reset` resets the underlying pointer to another value, releasing the previous one.
- `Release` releases ownership of the smart pointer, giving its user the responsibility of managing the pointee object's lifetime.

The actual declarations of these four functions in Loki are slightly more elaborate. They don't assume that the type of the pointer object stored by SmartPtr is T*. As discussed in Section 7.3, the Storage policy defines the storage type. Most of the time, it's a straight pointer, except in exotic implementations of Storage, when it might be a handle or an elaborate type.

7.5 Ownership-Handling Strategies

Ownership handling is often the most important *raison d'être* of smart pointers. Usually, from their clients' viewpoint, smart pointers own the objects to which they point. A smart pointer is a first-class value that takes care of deleting the pointed-to object under the covers. The client can intervene in the pointee object's lifetime by issuing calls to helper management functions.

For implementing self-ownership, smart pointers must carefully track the pointee object, especially during copying, assignment, and destruction. Such tracking brings some overhead in space, time, or both. An application should settle on the strategy that best fits the problem at hand and does not cost too much.

The following subsections discuss the most popular ownership management strategies and how SmartPtr implements them.

7.5.1 Deep Copy

The simplest strategy applicable is to copy the pointee object whenever you copy the smart pointer. If you ensure this, there is only one smart pointer for each pointee object. Therefore, the smart pointer's destructor can safely delete the pointee object. Figure 7.1 depicts the state of affairs if you use smart pointers with deep copy.

At first glance, the deep copy strategy sounds rather dull. It seems as if the smart pointer does not add any value over regular C++ value semantics. Why would you make the effort of using a smart pointer, when simple pass by value of the pointee object works just as well?

The answer is *support for polymorphism*. Smart pointers are vehicles for transporting polymorphic objects safely. You hold a smart pointer to a base class, which might actually point to a derived class. When you copy the smart pointer, you want to copy its polymorphic behavior, too. It's interesting that you don't exactly know what behavior and state you are dealing with, but you certainly need to duplicate that behavior and state.

Because deep copy most often deals with polymorphic objects, the following naive implementation of the copy constructor is wrong:

```
template <class T>
class SmartPtr
{
public:
    SmartPtr(const SmartPtr& other)
    : pointee_(new T(*other.pointee_))
    {
    }
    ...
};
```

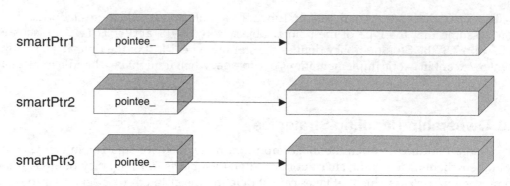

Figure 7.1: Memory layout for smart pointers with deep copy

Say you copy an object of type SmartPtr<Widget>. If other points to an instance of a class ExtendedWidget that derives from Widget, the copy constructor above copies only the Widget part of the ExtendedWidget object. This phenomenon is known as *slicing*—only the Widget "slice" of the object of the presumably larger type ExtendedWidget gets copied. Slicing is most often undesirable. It is a pity that C++ allows slicing so easily—a simple call by value slices objects without any warning.

Chapter 8 discusses cloning in depth. As shown there, the classic way of obtaining a polymorphic clone for a hierarchy is to define a virtual Clone function and implement it as follows:

```
class AbstractBase
{
    ...
    virtual AbstractBase* Clone() = 0;
};


class Concrete : public AbstractBase
{
    ...
    virtual AbstractBase* Clone()
    {
        return new Concrete(*this);
    }
};
```

The Clone implementation must follow the same pattern in all derived classes; in spite of its repetitive structure, there is no reasonable way to automate defining the Clone member function (beyond macros, that is).

A generic smart pointer cannot count on knowing the exact name of the cloning member function—maybe it's clone, or maybe MakeCopy. Therefore, the most flexible approach is to parameterize SmartPtr with a policy that addresses cloning.

7.5.2 Copy on Write

Copy on write (COW, as it is fondly called by its fans) is an optimization technique that avoids unnecessary object copying. The idea that underlies COW is to clone the pointee object at the first attempt of modification; until then, several pointers can share the same object.

Smart pointers, however, are not the best place to implement COW, because smart pointers cannot differentiate between calls to const and non-const member functions of the pointee object. Here is an example:

```
template <class T>
class SmartPtr
{
public:
   T* operator->() { return pointee_; }
   ...
};

class Foo
{
public:
   void ConstFun() const;
   void NonConstFun();
};


...
SmartPtr<Foo> sp;
sp->ConstFun(); // invokes operator->, then ConstFun
sp->NonConstFun(); // invokes operator >, then NonConstFun
```

The same operator-> gets invoked for both functions called; therefore, the smart pointer does not have any clue whether to make the COW or not. Function invocations for the pointee object happen somewhere beyond the reach of the smart pointer. (Section 7.11 explains how const interacts with smart pointers and the objects they point to.)

In conclusion, COW is effective mostly as an implementation optimization for full-featured classes. Smart pointers are at too low a level to implement COW semantics effectively. Of course, smart pointers can be good building blocks in implementing COW for a class.

The SmartPtr implementation in this chapter does not provide support for COW.

7.5.3 Reference Counting

Reference counting is the most popular ownership strategy used with smart pointers. Reference counting tracks the number of smart pointers that point to the same object. When that number goes to zero, the pointee object is deleted. This strategy works very well if you don't break certain rules—for instance, you should not keep dumb pointers and smart pointers to the same object.

The actual counter must be shared among smart pointer objects, leading to the structure

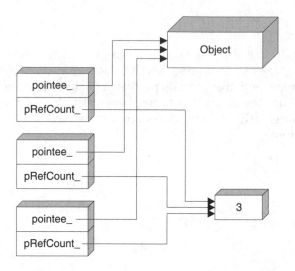

Figure 7.2: Three reference-counted smart pointers pointing to the same object

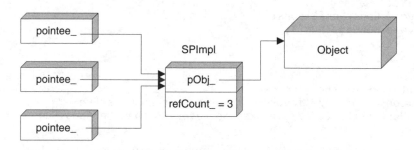

Figure 7.3: An alternate structure of reference-counted pointers

depicted in Figure 7.2. Each smart pointer holds a pointer to the reference counter (pRef-Count_ in Figure 7.2) in addition to the pointer to the object itself. This usually doubles the size of the smart pointer, which may or may not be an acceptable amount of overhead, depending on your needs and constraints.

There is another, subtler overhead issue. Reference-counted smart pointers must store the reference counter on the free store. The problem is that in many implementations, the default C++ free store allocator is remarkably slow and wasteful of space when it comes to allocating small objects, as discussed in Chapter 4. (Obviously, the reference count, typically occupying 4 bytes, does qualify as a small object.) The overhead in speed stems from slow algorithms in finding available chunks of memory, and the overhead in size is incurred by the bookkeeping information that the allocator holds for each chunk.

The relative size overhead can be partially mitigated by holding the pointer and the reference count together, as in Figure 7.3. The structure in Figure 7.3 reduces the size of the smart pointer to that of a pointer, but at the expense of access speed: The pointee object is

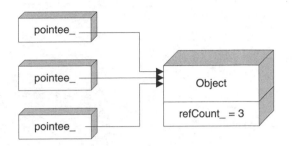

Figure 7.4: Intrusive reference counting

an extra level of indirection away. This is a considerable drawback because you typically use a smart pointer several times, whereas you obviously construct and destroy it only once.

The most efficient solution is to hold the reference counter in the pointee object itself, as shown in Figure 7.4. This way SmartPtr is just the size of a pointer, and there is no extra overhead at all. This technique is known as *intrusive reference counting*, because the reference count is an "intruder" in the pointee—it semantically belongs to the smart pointer. The name also gives a hint about the Achilles' heel of the technique: You must design up front or modify the pointee class to support reference counting.

A generic smart pointer should use intrusive reference counting where available and implement a nonintrusive reference counting scheme as an acceptable alternative. For implementing nonintrusive reference counting, the small-object allocator presented in Chapter 4 can help a great deal. The SmartPtr implementation using nonintrusive reference counting leverages the small-object allocator, thus slashing the performance overhead caused by the reference counter.

7.5.4 Reference Linking

Reference linking relies on the observation that you don't really need the actual count of smart pointer objects pointing to one pointee object; you only need to detect when that count goes down to zero. This leads to the idea of keeping an "ownership list," as shown in Figure 7.5.[1]

All SmartPtr objects that point to a given pointee form a doubly linked list. When you create a new SmartPtr from an existing SmartPtr, the new object is appended to the list; SmartPtr's destructor takes care of removing the destroyed object from the list. When the list becomes empty, the pointee object is deleted.

The doubly linked list structure fits reference linking like a glove. You cannot use a singly linked list because removals from such a list take linear time. You cannot use a vector because the SmartPtr objects are not contiguous (and removals from vectors take linear time anyway). You need a structure sporting constant-time append, constant-time remove, and constant-time empty detection. This bill is fit precisely and exclusively by doubly linked lists.

---

[1]Risto Lankinen described the reference-linking mechanism on the Usenet in November 1995.

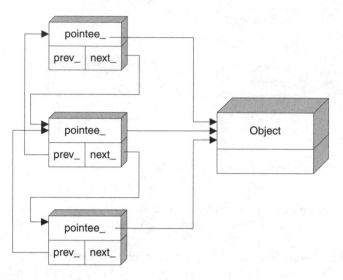

Figure 7.5: Reference linking in action

In a reference-linking implementation, each SmartPtr object holds two extra pointers—one to the next element and one to the previous element.

The advantage of reference linking over reference counting is that the former does not use extra free store, which makes it more reliable: Creating a reference-linked smart pointer cannot fail. The disadvantage is that reference linking needs more memory for its book-keeping (three pointers versus only one pointer plus one integer). Also, reference counting should be a bit speedier—when you copy smart pointers, only an indirection and an increment are needed. The list management is slightly more elaborate. In conclusion, you should use reference linking only when the free store is scarce. Otherwise, prefer reference counting.

To wrap up the discussion on reference count management strategies, let's note a significant disadvantage that they have. Reference management—be it counting or linking—is a victim of the resource leak known as *cyclic reference*. Imagine an object A holds a smart pointer to an object B. Also, object B holds a smart pointer to A. These two objects form a cyclic reference; even though you don't use any of them anymore, they use each other. The reference management strategy cannot detect such cyclic references, and the two objects remain allocated forever. The cycles can span multiple objects, closing circles that often reveal unexpected dependencies that are very hard to debug.

In spite of this, reference management is a robust, speedy ownership-handling strategy. If used with precaution, reference management makes application development significantly easier.

7.5.5 Destructive Copy

Destructive copy does exactly what you think it does: During copying, it destroys the object being copied. In the case of smart pointers, destructive copy destroys the source smart pointer by taking its pointee object and passing it to the destination smart pointer. The `std::auto_ptr` class template features destructive copy.

In addition to being suggestive about the action taken, "destructive" also vividly describes the dangers associated with this strategy. Misusing destructive copy may have destructive effects on your program data, your program correctness, and your brain cells.

Smart pointers may use destructive copy to ensure that at any time there is only one smart pointer pointing to a given object. During the copying or assignment of one smart pointer to another, the "living" pointer is passed to the destination of the copy, and the source's `pointee_` becomes zero. The following code illustrates a copy constructor and an assignment operator of a simple `SmartPtr` featuring destructive copy.

```
template <class T>
class SmartPtr
{
public:
    SmartPtr(SmartPtr& src)
    {
        pointee_ = src.pointee_;
        src.pointee_ = 0;
    }
    SmartPtr& operator=(SmartPtr& src)
    {
        if (this != &src)
        {
            delete pointee_;
            pointee_ - src.pointee_;
            src.pointee_ = 0;
        }
        return *this;
    }
    ...
};
```

C++ etiquette calls for the right-hand side of the copy constructor and the assignment operator to be a reference to a `const` object. Classes that foster destructive copy break this convention for obvious reasons. Because etiquette exists for a reason, you should expect negative consequences if you break it. Indeed, here they are:

```
void Display(SmartPtr<Something> sp);
...
SmartPtr<Something> sp(new Something);
Display(sp);  // sinks sp
```

Although `Display` means no harm to its argument (accepts it by value), it acts like a maelstrom of smart pointers: It sinks any smart pointer passed to it. After `Display(sp)` is called, sp holds the null pointer.

Because they do not support value semantics, smart pointers with destructive copy cannot be stored in standard containers and in general must be handled with almost as much care as raw pointers.

The ability to store smart pointers in a container is very important. Containers of raw pointers make manual ownership management tricky, so many containers of pointers can use smart pointers to good advantage. Smart pointers with destructive copy, however, do not mix with containers.

On the bright side, smart pointers with destructive copy have significant advantages:

- They incur almost no overhead.
- They are good at enforcing ownership transfer semantics. In this case, you use the "maelstrom effect" described earlier to your advantage: You make it clear that your function takes over the passed-in pointer.
- They are good as return values from functions. If the smart pointer implementation uses a certain trick,[2] you can return smart pointers with destructive copy from functions. This way, you can be sure that the pointee object gets destroyed if the caller doesn't use the return value.
- They are excellent as stack variables in functions that have multiple return paths. You don't have to remember to delete the pointee object manually—the smart pointer takes care of this for you.

The destructive copy strategy is used by the standard-provided `std::auto_ptr`. This brings destructive copy another important advantage:

- Smart pointers with destructive copy semantics are the only smart pointers that the standard provides, which means that many programmers will get used to their behavior sooner or later.

For these reasons, the `SmartPtr` implementation should provide optional support for destructive copy semantics.

Smart pointers use various ownership semantics, each having its own trade-offs. The most important techniques are deep copy, reference counting, reference linking, and destructive copy. `SmartPtr` implements all these strategies through an **Ownership** policy, allowing its users to choose the one that best fits an application's needs. The default strategy is reference counting.

7.6 The Address-of Operator

In striving to make smart pointers as indistinguishable as possible from their native counterparts, designers stumbled upon an obscure operator that is on the list of overloadable operators: unary `operator&`, the *address-of operator*.[3]

An implementer of smart pointers might choose to overload the address-of operator like this:

```
template <class T>
class SmartPtr
{
public:
```

---

[2] Invented by Greg Colvin and Bill Gibbons for `std::auto_ptr`.
[3] *Unary* `operator&` is to differentiate it from binary `operator&`, which is the bitwise AND operator.

```
    T** operator&()
    {
        return &pointee_;
    }
    ...
};
```

After all, if a smart pointer is to simulate a pointer, then its address must be substitutable for the address of a regular pointer. This overload makes code like the following possible:

```
void Fun(Widget** pWidget);
...
SmartPtr<Widget> spWidget(...);
Fun(&spWidget); // okay, invokes operator& and obtains a
                // pointer to pointer to Widget
```

It seems very desirable to have such an accurate compatibility between smart pointers and dumb pointers, but overloading the unary operator& is one of those clever tricks that can do more harm than good. There are two reasons why overloading unary operator& is not a very good idea.

One reason is that exposing the address of the pointed-to object implies giving up any automatic ownership management. When a client freely accesses the address of the raw pointer, any helper structures that the smart pointer holds, such as reference counts, become invalid for all purposes. While the client deals directly with the address of the raw pointer, the smart pointer is completely unconscious.

The second reason, a more pragmatic one, is that overloading unary operator& makes the smart pointer unusable with STL containers. Actually, overloading unary operator& for a type pretty much makes generic programming impossible for that type, because the address of an object is too fundamental a property to play with naively. Most generic code assumes that applying & to an object of type T returns an object of type T*—you see, address-of is a fundamental concept. If you defy this concept, generic code behaves strangely either at compile time or—worse—at runtime.

Thus, it is not recommended that unary operator& be overloaded for smart pointers or for any objects in general. SmartPtr does not overload unary operator&.

7.7 Implicit Conversion to Raw Pointer Types

Consider this code:

```
void Fun(Something* p);
...
SmartPtr<Something> sp(new Something);
Fun(sp); // OK or error?
```

Should this code compile or not? Following the "maximum compatibility" line of thought, the answer is yes.

Technically, it is very simple to render the previous code compilable by introducing a user-defined conversion:

```
template <class T>
class SmartPtr
{
public:
    operator T*() // user-defined conversion to T*
    {
        return pointee_;
    }
    ...
};
```

However, this is not the end of the story.

User-defined conversions in C++ have an interesting history. Back in the 1980s, when user-defined conversions were introduced, most programmers considered them a great invention. User-defined conversions promised a more unified type system, expressive semantics, and the ability to define new types that were indistinguishable from built-in ones. With time, however, user-defined conversions revealed themselves as awkward and potentially dangerous. They might become dangerous especially when they expose handles to internal data (Meyers 1998a, Item 29), which is precisely the case with the operator T* in the previous code. That's why you should think carefully before allowing automatic conversions for the smart pointers you design.

One potential danger comes inherently from giving the user unattended access to the raw pointer that the smart pointer wraps. Passing the raw pointer around defeats the inner workings of the smart pointer. Once unleashed from the confines of its wrapper, the raw pointer can easily become a threat to program sanity again, just as it was before smart pointers were introduced.

Another danger is that user-defined conversions pop up unexpectedly, even when you don't need them. Consider the following code:

```
SmartPtr<Something> sp;
...
// A gross semantic error
// However, it goes undetected at compile time
delete sp;
```

The compiler matches operator delete with the user-defined conversion to T*. At runtime, operator T* is called, and delete is applied to its result. This is certainly not what you want to do to a smart pointer, because it is supposed to manage ownership itself. An extra unwitting delete call throws out the window all the careful ownership management that the smart pointer performs under the covers.

There are quite a few ways to prevent the delete call from compiling. Some of them are very ingenious (Meyers 1996). One that's very effective and easy to implement is to make the call to delete intentionally *ambiguous.* You can achieve this by providing *two* automatic conversions to types that are susceptible to a call to delete. One type is T* itself, and the other can be void*.

```
template <class T>
class SmartPtr
{
public:
   operator T*() // User-defined conversion to T*
   {
      return pointee_;
   }
   operator void*() // Added conversion to void*
   {
      return pointee_;
   }
   ...
};
```

A call to delete against such a smart pointer object is ambiguous. The compiler cannot decide which conversion to apply, and the trick above exploits this indecision to good advantage.

Don't forget that disabling the delete operator was only a part of the issue. Whether to provide an automatic conversion to a raw pointer remains an important decision in implementing a smart pointer. It's too dangerous just to let it in, yet too convenient to rule it out. The final SmartPtr implementation will give you a choice about that.

However, forbidding implicit conversion does not necessarily eliminate all access to the raw pointer; it is often necessary to gain such access. Therefore, all smart pointers do provide *explicit* access to their wrapped pointer via a call to a function:

```
void Fun(Something* p);
...
SmartPtr<Something> sp;
Fun(GetImpl(sp)); // OK, explicit conversion always allowed
```

It's not a matter of whether you can get to the wrapped pointer; it's how easy it is. This may seem like a minor difference, but it's actually very important. An implicit conversion happens without the programmer or the maintainer noticing or even knowing it. An explicit conversion—as is the call to GetImpl—passes through the mind, the understanding, and the fingers of the programmer and remains written in the code for everybody to see it.

Implicit conversion from the smart pointer type to the raw pointer type is desirable, but sometimes dangerous. SmartPtr provides this implicit conversion as a choice. The default is on the safe side—no implicit conversions. Explicit access is always available through the GetImpl function.

7.8 Equality and Inequality

C++ teaches its users that any clever trick such as the one presented in the previous section (intentional ambiguity) establishes a new context, which in turn may have unexpected ripples.

Consider tests for equality and inequality of smart pointers. A smart pointer should support the same comparison syntax that raw pointers support. Programmers expect the following tests to compile and run as they do for a raw pointer.

```
SmartPtr<Something> sp1, sp2;
Something* p;
...
if (sp1)     // Test 1: direct test for non-null pointer
  ...
if (!sp1)      // Test 2: direct test for null pointer
  ...
if (sp1 == 0)   // Test 3: explicit test for null pointer
  ...
if (sp1 == sp2) // Test 4: comparison of two smart pointers
  ...
if (sp1 == p)   // Test 5: comparison with a raw pointer
  ...
```

There are more tests than depicted here if you consider symmetry and operator!=. If we solve the equality tests, we can easily define the corresponding symmetric and inequality tests.

There is an unfortunate interference between the solution to the previous issue (preventing delete from compiling) and a possible solution to this issue. With one user-defined conversion to the raw pointer type, most of the test expressions (except test 4) compile successfully and run as expected. The downside is that you can accidentally call the delete operator against the smart pointer. With two user-defined conversions (intentional ambiguity), you detect wrongful delete calls, but none of these tests compiles anymore—they have become ambiguous too.

An additional user-defined conversion to bool helps, but this, to nobody's surprise, introduces new trouble. Given this smart pointer:

```
template <class T>
class SmartPtr
{
public:
   operator bool() const
   {
      return pointee_ != 0;
   }
   ...
};
```

the four tests compile, but so do the following nonsensical operations:

```
SmartPtr<Apple> sp1;
SmartPtr<Orange> sp2; // Orange is unrelated to Apple
if (sp1 == sp2)       // Converts both pointers to bool
                      // and compares results
  ...
if (sp1 != sp2)       // Ditto
  ...
```

```
    bool b = sp1;           // The conversion allows this, too
    if (sp1 * 5 == 200)     // Ouch! SmartPtr behaves like an integral
                            // type!
    ...
```

As you can see, it's either not at all or too much: Once you add a user-defined conversion to bool, you allow SmartPtr to act as a bool in many more situations than you actually wanted. For all practical purposes, defining an operator bool for a smart pointer is not a smart solution.

A true, complete, rock-solid solution to this dilemma is to go all the way and overload each and every operator separately. This way any operation that makes sense for the bare pointer makes sense for the smart pointer, and nothing else. Here is the code that implements this idea.

```
template <class T>
class SmartPtr
{
public:
    bool operator!() const // Enables "if (!sp) ..."
    {
        return pointee_ == 0;
    }
    inline friend bool operator==(const SmartPtr& lhs,
        const T* rhs)
    {
        return lhs.pointee_ == rhs;
    }
    inline friend bool operator==(const T* lhs,
        const SmartPtr& rhs)
    {
        return lhs == rhs.pointee_;
    }
    inline friend bool operator!=(const SmartPtr& lhs,
        const T* rhs)
    {
        return lhs.pointee_ != rhs;
    }
    inline friend bool operator!=(const T* lhs,
        const SmartPtr& rhs)
    {
        return lhs != rhs.pointee_;
    }
    ...
};
```

Yes, it's a pain, but this approach solves the problems with almost all comparisons, including the tests against the literal zero. What the forwarding operators in this code do is to pass operators that client code applies to the smart pointer on to the raw pointer that the smart pointer wraps. No simulation can be more realistic than that.

We still haven't solved the problem completely. If you provide an automatic conversion to the pointee type, there still is the risk of ambiguities. Suppose you have a class `Base` and a class `Derived` that inherits `Base`. Then the following code makes practical sense yet is ill formed due to ambiguity.

```
SmartPtr<Base> sp;
Derived* p;
...
if (sp == p) {} // error! Ambiguity between:
                //  '(Base*)sp == (Base*)p'
                // and 'operator==(sp, (Base*)p)'
```

Indeed, smart pointer development is not for the faint of heart.

We're not out of bullets, though. In addition to the definitions of `operator==` and `operator!=`, we can add *templated* versions of them, as you can see in the following code:

```
template <class T>
class SmartPtr
{
public:
   ... as above ...
   template <class U>
   inline friend bool operator==(const SmartPtr& lhs,
      const U* rhs)
   {
      return lhs.pointee_ == rhs;
   }
   template <class U>
   inline friend bool operator==(const U* lhs,
      const SmartPtr& rhs)
   {
      return lhs == rhs.pointee_;
   }
   ... similarly defined operator!= ...
};
```

The templated operators are "greedy" in the sense that they match comparisons with any pointer type whatsoever, thus consuming the ambiguity.

If that's the case, why should we keep the nontemplated operators—the ones that take the pointee type? They never get a chance to match, because the template matches any pointer type, including the pointee type itself.

The rule that "never" actually means "almost never" applies here, too. In the test `if (sp == 0)`, the compiler tries the following matches.

- *The templated operators.* They don't match because the type of literal zero is not a pointer type. A literal zero can be implicitly converted to a pointer type, but template matching does not include conversions.
- *The nontemplated operators.* After eliminating the templated operators, the compiler tries the nontemplated ones. One of these operators kicks in through an implicit conversion from the literal zero to the pointee type. Had the nontemplated operators not existed, the test would have been an error.

In conclusion, we need *both* the nontemplated and the templated comparison operators.

Let's see now what happens if we compare two SmartPtrs instantiated with different types.

```
SmartPtr<Apple> sp1;
SmartPtr<Orange> sp2;
if (sp1 == sp2)
    ...
```

The compiler chokes on the comparison because of an ambiguity: Each of the two SmartPtr instantiations defines an operator==, and the compiler does not know which one to choose. We can dodge this problem by defining an "ambiguity buster" as shown:

```
template <class T>
class SmartPtr
{
public:
    // Ambiguity buster
    template <class U>
    bool operator==(const SmartPtr<U>& rhs) const
    {
        return pointee_ == rhs.pointee_;
    }
    // Similarly for operator!=
    ...
};
```

This newly added operator is a member that specializes exclusively in comparing SmartPtr<...> objects. The beauty of this ambiguity buster is that it makes smart pointer comparisons act like raw pointer comparisons. If you compare two smart pointers to Apple and Orange, the code will be essentially equivalent to comparing two raw pointers to Apple and Orange. If the comparison makes sense, then the code compiles; otherwise, it's a compile-time error.

```
SmartPtr<Apple> sp1;
SmartPtr<Orange> sp2;
if (sp1 == sp2)    // Semantically equivalent to
                   // sp1.pointee_ == sp2.pointee_
    ...
```

There is one unsatisfied syntactic artifact left, namely, the direct test if (sp). Here life becomes really interesting. The if statement applies only to expressions of arithmetic and pointer type. Consequently, to allow if (sp) to compile, we must define an automatic conversion to either an arithmetic or a pointer type.

A conversion to arithmetic type is not recommended, as the earlier experience with operator bool witnesses. A pointer is not an arithmetic type, period. A conversion to a pointer type makes a lot more sense, and here the problem branches.

If you want to provide automatic conversions to the pointee type (see previous section), then you have two choices: Either you risk unattended calls to operator delete, or you forgo the if (sp) test. The tiebreaker is between the lack of convenience and a risky life. The winner is safety, so you cannot write if (sp). Instead, you can choose between if(sp != 0) and the more baroque if(!!sp). End of story.

If you don't want to provide automatic conversions to the pointee type, there is an interesting trick you can use to make if (sp) possible. Inside the SmartPtr class template, define an inner class Tester and define a conversion to Tester*, as shown in the following code:

```
template <class T>
class SmartPtr
{
   class Tester
   {
      void operator delete(void*);
   };
public:
   operator Tester*() const
   {
      if (!pointee_) return 0;
      static Tester test;
      return &test;
   }
   ...
};
```

Now if you write if (sp), operator Tester* enters into action. This operator returns a null value if and only if pointee_ is null. Tester itself disables operator delete, so if somebody calls delete sp, a compile-time error occurs. Interestingly, Tester's definition itself lies in the private part of SmartPtr, so the client code cannot do anything else with it.

SmartPtr addresses the issue of tests for equality and inequality as follows:

• Define operator== and operator!= in two flavors (templated and nontemplated).
• Define operator!.
• If you allow automatic conversion to the pointee type, then define an additional conversion to void* to ambiguate a call to the delete operator intentionally; otherwise, define a private inner class Tester that declares a private operator delete, and define a conversion to Tester* for SmartPtr that returns a null pointer if and only if the pointee_ is null.

7.9 Ordering Comparisons

The ordering comparison operators are operator<, operator<=, operator>, and operator>=. You can implement them all in terms of operator<.

Whether to allow ordering of smart pointers is an interesting question in and of itself and relates to the dual nature of pointers, which consistently confuses programmers. Pointers are two concepts in one: iterators and monikers. The iterative nature of pointers allows you to walk through an array of objects using a pointer. Pointer arithmetic, including comparisons, supports this iterative nature of pointers. At the same time, pointers are monikers—inexpensive object representatives that can travel quickly and access the objects in a snap. The dereferencing operators * and -> support the moniker concept.

The two natures of pointers can be confusing at times, especially when you need only one of them. For operating with a vector, you might use both iteration and dereferencing, whereas for walking through a linked list or for manipulating individual objects, you use only dereferencing.

Ordering comparisons for pointers is defined only when the pointers belong to the same contiguous memory. In other words, you can use ordering comparisons only for pointers that point to elements in the same array.

Defining ordering comparisons for smart pointers boils down to this question: Do smart pointers to the objects in the same array make sense? On the face of it, the answer is no. Smart pointers' main feature is to manage object ownership, and objects with separate ownership do not usually belong to the same array. Therefore, it would be dangerous to allow users to make nonsensical comparisons.

If you really need ordering comparisons, you can always use explicit access to the raw pointer. The issue here is, again, to find the safest and most expressive behavior for most situations.

The previous section concludes that an implicit conversion to a raw pointer type is optional. If SmartPtr's client chooses to allow implicit conversion, the following code compiles:

```
SmartPtr<Something> sp1, sp2;
if (sp1 < sp2) // Converts sp1 and sp2 to raw pointer type,
               // then performs the comparison
...
```

This means that if we want to disable ordering comparisons, we must be proactive, disabling them explicitly. A way of doing this is to declare them and never define them, which means that any use will trigger a link-time error.

```
template <class T>
class SmartPtr
{ ... };

template <class T, class U>
bool operator<(const SmartPtr<T>&, const U&); // Not defined
template <class T, class U>
bool operator<(const T&, const SmartPtr<U>&); // Not defined
```

However, it is wiser to define all other operators in terms of operator<, as opposed to leaving them undefined. This way, if SmartPtr's users think it's best to introduce smart pointer ordering, they need only define operator<.

```
// Ambiguity buster
template <class T, class U>
bool operator<(const SmartPtr<T>& lhs, const SmartPtr<U>& rhs)
{
    return lhs < GetImpl(rhs);
```

```
}
// All other operators
template <class T, class U>
bool operator>(SmartPtr<T>& lhs, const U& rhs)
{
    return rhs < lhs;
}
... similarly for the other operators ...
```

Note the presence, again, of an ambiguity buster. Now if some library user thinks that SmartPtr<Widget> should be ordered, the following code is the ticket:

```
inline bool operator<(const SmartPtr<Widget>& lhs,
    const Widget* rhs)
{
    return GetImpl(lhs) < rhs;
}

inline bool operator<(const Widget* lhs,
    const SmartPtr<Widget>& rhs)
{
    return lhs < GetImpl(rhs);
}
```

It's a pity that the user must define two operators instead of one, but it's so much better than defining eight.

This would conclude the issue of ordering, were it not for an interesting detail. Sometimes it is very useful to have an ordering of arbitrarily located objects, not just objects belonging to the same array. For example, you might need to store supplementary per-object information, and you need to access that information quickly. A map ordered by the address of objects is very effective for such a task.

Standard C++ helps in implementing such designs. Although pointer comparison for arbitrarily located objects is undefined, the standard guarantees that std::less yields meaningful results for any two pointers of the same type. Because the standard associative containers use std::less as the default ordering relationship, you can safely use maps that have pointers as keys.

SmartPtr should support this idiom, too; therefore, SmartPtr specializes std::less. The specialization simply forwards the call to std::less for regular pointers:

```
namespace std
{
    template <class T>
    struct less<SmartPtr<T> >
        : public binary_function<SmartPtr<T>, SmartPtr<T>, bool>
    {
        bool operator()(const SmartPtr<T>& lhs,
            const SmartPtr<T>& rhs) const
        {
            return less<T*>()(GetImpl(lhs), GetImpl(rhs));
        }
    };
}
```

In summary, `SmartPtr` does not define ordering operators by default. It declares—without implementing—two generic `operator<`s and implements all other ordering operators in terms of `operator<`. The user can define either specialized or generic versions of `operator<`.

`SmartPtr` specializes `std::less` to provide an ordering of arbitrary smart pointer objects.

7.10 Checking and Error Reporting

Applications need various degrees of safety from smart pointers. Some programs are computation-intensive and must be optimized for speed, whereas some others (actually, most) are input/output intensive, which allows better runtime checking without degrading performance.

Most often, right inside an application, you might need both models: low safety/high speed in some critical areas, and high safety/lower speed elsewhere.

We can divide checking issues with smart pointers into two categories: initialization checking and checking before dereference.

7.10.1 Initialization Checking

Should a smart pointer accept the null (zero) value?

It is easy to implement a guarantee that a smart pointer cannot be null, and it may be very useful in practice. It means that any smart pointer is always valid (unless you fiddle with the raw pointer by using `GetImplRef`). The implementation is easy with the help of a constructor that throws an exception if passed a null pointer.

```
template <class T>
class SmartPtr
{
public:
    SmartPtr(T* p) : pointee_(p)
    {
        if (!p) throw NullPointerException();
    }
    ...
};
```

On the other hand, the null value is a convenient "not a valid pointer" placeholder and can often be useful.

Whether to allow null values affects the default constructor, too. If the smart pointer doesn't allow null values, then how would the default constructor initialize the raw pointer? The default constructor could be lacking, but that would make smart pointers harder to deal with. For example, what should you do when you have a `SmartPtr` member variable but don't have an appropriate initializer for it at construction time? In conclusion, customizing initialization involves providing an appropriate default value.

7.10.2 Checking Before Dereference

Checking before dereference is important because dereferencing the null pointer engenders undefined behavior. For many applications, undefined behavior is not acceptable, so checking the pointer for validity before dereference is the way to go. Checks before dereference belong to SmartPtr's operator-> and unary operator*.

In contrast to the initialization check, the check before dereference can become a major performance bottleneck in your application, because typical applications use (dereference) smart pointers much more often than they create smart pointer objects. Therefore, you should keep a balance between safety and speed. A good rule of thumb is to start with rigorously checked pointers and remove checks from selected smart pointers as profiling demonstrates a need for it.

Can initialization checking and checking before dereference be conceptually separated? No, because there are links between them. If you enforce strict checking upon initialization, then checking before dereference becomes redundant because the pointer is always valid.

This little efficiency victory brought by encapsulation is, however, amended by the loophole provided by GetImplRef which allows arbitrary replacement of the underlying raw pointer.

7.10.3 Error Reporting

The only sensible choice for reporting an error is to throw an exception.

You can do something in the sense of avoiding errors. For example, if a pointer is null upon dereference, you can initialize it on the fly. This is a valid and valuable strategy called *lazy initialization*—you construct the value only when you first need it.

If you want to check things only during debugging, you can use the standard assert or similar, more sophisticated macros. The compiler ignores the tests in release mode, so, assuming you remove all null pointer errors during debugging, you reap the advantages of both checking and speed.

SmartPtr migrates checking to a dedicated Checking policy. This policy implements checking functions (which can optionally provide lazy initialization) and the error reporting strategy.

7.11 Smart Pointers to const and const Smart Pointers

Raw pointers allow two kinds of constness: the constness of the pointed-to object and that of the pointer itself. The following is an illustration of these two attributes:

```
const Something* pc = new Something; // points to const object
pc->ConstMemberFunction(); // ok
pc->NonConstMemberFunction(); // error
delete pc; // ok (surprisingly)⁴
Something* const cp = new Something; // const pointer
cp->NonConstMemberFunction(); // ok
cp = new Something; // error, can't assign to const pointer
const Something* const cpc = new Something; // const, points to const
cpc->ConstMemberFunction(); // ok
```

---

[4]Every once in a while, the question "Why can you apply the delete operator to pointers to const?" starts a fierce debate in the comp.std.c++ newsgroup. The fact is, for better or worse, the language allows it.

```
cpc->NonConstMemberFunction(); // error
cpc = new Something; // error, can't assign to const pointer
```

The corresponding uses of SmartPtr look like this:

```
// Smart pointer to const object
SmartPtr<const Something> spc(new Something);
// const smart pointer
const SmartPtr<Something> scp(new Something);
// const smart pointer to const object
const SmartPtr<const Something> scpc(new Something);
```

The SmartPtr class template can detect the constness of the pointed-to object either through partial specialization or by using the TypeTraits template defined in Chapter 2. The latter method is preferable because it does not incur source-code duplication as partial specialization does.

SmartPtr imitates the semantics of pointers to const objects, const pointers, and the combinations thereof.

7.12 Arrays

In most cases, instead of dealing with heap-allocated arrays and using new[] and delete[], you're better off with std::vector. The standard-provided std::vector class template provides everything that dynamically allocated arrays provide, plus much more. The extra overhead incurred is negligible in most cases.

However, "most cases" is not "always." There are many situations in which you don't need and don't want a full-fledged vector; a dynamically allocated array is exactly what you need. It is awkward in these cases to be unable to exploit smart pointer capabilities. There is a certain gap between the sophisticated std::vector and dynamically allocated arrays. Smart pointers could close that gap by providing array semantics if the user needs them.

From the viewpoint of a smart pointer to an array, the only important issue is to call delete[] pointee_ in its destructor instead of delete pointee_. This issue is already tackled by the Ownership policy.

A secondary issue is providing indexed access, by overloading operator[] for smart pointers. This is technically feasible; in fact, a preliminary version of SmartPtr did provide a separate policy for optional array semantics. However, only in very rare cases do smart pointers point to arrays. In those cases, there already is a way of providing indexed accessing if you use GetImpl:

```
SmartPtr<Widget> sp = ...;
// Access the sixth element pointed to by sp
Widget& obj = GetImpl(sp)[5];
```

It seems like a bad decision to strive to provide extra syntactic convenience at the expense of introducing a new policy.

SmartPtr supports customized destruction via the Ownership policy. You can therefore arrange array-specific destruction via delete[]. However, SmartPtr does not provide pointer arithmetic.

7.13 Smart Pointers and Multithreading

Most often, smart pointers help with sharing objects. Multithreading issues affect object sharing. Therefore, multithreading issues affect smart pointers.

The interaction between smart pointers and multithreading takes place at two levels. One is the pointee object level, and the other is the bookkeeping data level.

7.13.1 Multithreading at the Pointee Object Level

If multiple threads access the same object and if you access that object through a smart pointer, it can be desirable to lock the object during a function call made through operator->. This is possible by having the smart pointer return a proxy object instead of a raw pointer. The proxy object's constructor locks the pointee object, and its destructor unlocks it. The technique is illustrated in Stroustrup (2000). Some code that illustrates this approach is provided here.

First, let's consider a class Widget that has two locking primitives: Lock and Unlock. After a call to Lock, you can access the object safely. Any other threads calling Lock will block. When you call Unlock, you let other threads lock the object.

```
class Widget
{
    ...
    void Lock();
    void Unlock();
};
```

Next, we define a class template LockingProxy. Its role is to lock an object (using the Lock/Unlock convention) for the duration of LockingProxy's lifetime.

```
template <class T>
class LockingProxy
{
public:
    LockingProxy(T* pObj) : pointee_ (pObj)
    { pointee_->Lock(); }
    ~LockingProxy()
    { pointee_->Unlock(); }
    T* operator->() const
    { return pointee_; }
private:
    LockingProxy& operator=(const LockingProxy&);
    T* pointee_;
};
```

In addition to the constructor and destructor, LockingProxy defines an operator-> that returns a pointer to the pointee object.

Although LockingProxy looks somewhat like a smart pointer, there is one more layer to it—the SmartPtr class template itself.

```
template <class T>
class SmartPtr
{
    ...
    LockingProxy<T> operator->() const
    { return LockingProxy<T>(pointee_); }
private:
    T* pointee_;
};
```

Recall from Section 7.3, which explains the mechanics of operator->, that the compiler can apply operator-> multiple times to one -> expression, until it reaches a native pointer. Now imagine you issue the following call (assuming Widget defines a function DoSomething):

```
SmartPtr<Widget> sp = ...;
sp->DoSomething();
```

Here's the trick: SmartPtr's operator-> returns a temporary LockingProxy<T> object. The compiler keeps applying operator->. LockingProxy<T>'s operator-> returns a Widget*. The compiler uses this pointer to Widget to issue the call to DoSomething. During the call, the temporary object LockingProxy<T> is alive and locks the object, which means that the object is safely locked. As soon as the call to DoSomething returns, the temporary Locking-Proxy<T> object is destroyed, so the Widget object is unlocked.

Automatic locking is a good application of smart pointer layering. You can layer smart pointers this way by changing the Storage policy.

7.13.2 Multithreading at the Bookkeeping Data Level

Sometimes smart pointers manipulate data in addition to the pointee object. As you read in Section 7.5, reference-counted smart pointers share some data—namely the reference count—under the covers. If you copy a reference-counted smart pointer from one thread to another, you end up having two smart pointers pointing to the same reference counter. Of course, they also point to the same pointee object, but that's accessible to the user, who can lock it. In contrast, the reference count is not accessible to the user, so managing it is entirely the responsibility of the smart pointer.

Not only reference-counted pointers are exposed to multithreading-related dangers. Reference-linked smart pointers (Section 7.5.4) internally hold pointers to each other, which are shared data as well. Reference linking leads to communities of smart pointers, not all of which necessarily belong to the same thread. Therefore, every time you copy, assign, and destroy a reference-linked smart pointer, you must issue appropriate locking; otherwise, the doubly linked list might get corrupted.

In conclusion, multithreading issues ultimately affect smart pointers' implementation. Let's see how to address the multithreading issue in reference counting and reference linking.

7.13.2.1 Multithreaded Reference Counting

If you copy a smart pointer between threads, you end up incrementing the reference count from different threads at unpredictable times.

As the appendix explains, incrementing a value is not an atomic operation. For incrementing and decrementing integral values in a multithreaded environment, you must use the type `ThreadingModel<T>::IntType` and the `AtomicIncrement` and `AtomicDecrement` functions.

Here things become a bit tricky. Better said, they become tricky if you want to separate reference counting from threading.

Policy-based class design prescribes that you decompose a class into elementary behavioral elements and confine each of them to a separate template parameter. In an ideal world, `SmartPtr` would specify an **Ownership** policy and a **ThreadingModel** policy and would use them both for a correct implementation.

In the case of multithreaded reference counting, however, things are much too tied together. For example, the counter must be of type `ThreadingModel<T>::IntType`. Then, instead of using `operator++` and `operator--`, you must use `AtomicIncrement` and `AtomicDecrement`. Threading and reference counting melt together; it is unjustifiably hard to separate them.

The best thing to do is to incorporate multithreading in the **Ownership** policy. Then you can have two implementations: `RefCounting` and `RefCountingMT`.

7.13.2.2 Multithreaded Reference Linking

Consider the destructor of a reference-linked smart pointer. It likely looks like this:

```
template <class T>
class SmartPtr
{
public:
   ~SmartPtr()
   {
      if (prev_ == this)
      {
         delete pointee_;
      }
      else
      {
         prev_->next_ = next_;
         next_->prev_ = prev_;
      }
   }
   ...
private:
   T* pointee_;
   SmartPtr* prev_;
```

```
        SmartPtr* next_;
    };
```

The code in the destructor performs a classic doubly linked list deletion. To make implementation simpler and faster, the list is circular—the last node points to the first node. This way we don't have to test prev_ and next_ against zero for any smart pointer. A circular list with only one element has prev_ and next_ equal to this.

If multiple threads destroy smart pointers that are linked to each other, clearly the destructor must be atomic (uninterruptible by other threads). Otherwise, another thread can interrupt the destructor of a SmartPtr, for instance, between updating prev_->next_ and updating next_->prev_. That thread will then operate on a corrupt list.

Similar reasoning applies to SmartPtr's copy constructor and the assignment operator. These functions must be atomic because they manipulate the ownership list.

Interestingly enough, we cannot apply object-level locking semantics here. The appendix divides locking strategies into *class-level* and *object-level* strategies. A class-level locking operation locks all objects in a given class during that operation. An object-level locking operation locks only the object that's subject to that operation. The former technique leads to less memory being occupied (only one mutex per class) but is exposed to performance bottlenecks. The latter is heavier (one mutex per object) but might be speedier.

We cannot apply object-level locking to smart pointers because an operation manipulates up to three objects: the current object that's being added or removed, the previous object, and the next object in the ownership list.

If we want to introduce object-level locking, the starting observation is that there must be one mutex per pointee object—because there's one list per pointee object. We can dynamically allocate a mutex for each object, but this nullifies the main advantage of reference linking over reference counting. Reference linking was more appealing exactly because it didn't use the free store.

Alternatively, we can use an intrusive approach: The pointee object holds the mutex, and the smart pointer manipulates that mutex. But the existence of a sound, effective alternative—reference-counted smart pointers—removes the incentive to provide this feature.

In summary, smart pointers that use reference counting or reference linking are affected by multithreading issues. Thread-safe reference counting needs integer atomic operations. Thread-safe reference linking needs mutexes. SmartPtr provides only thread-safe reference counting.

7.14 Putting It All Together

Not much to go! Here comes the fun part. So far we have treated each issue in isolation. It's now time to collect all the decisions into a unique SmartPtr implementation.

The strategy we'll use is the one described in Chapter 1: policy-based class design. Each design aspect that doesn't have a unique solution migrates to a policy. The SmartPtr class template accepts each policy as a separate template parameter. SmartPtr inherits all these template parameters, allowing the corresponding policies to store state.

Let's recap the previous sections by enumerating the variation points of SmartPtr. Each variation point translates into a policy.

- *Storage* policy *(Section 7.3)*. By default, the stored type is T* (T is the first template parameter of SmartPtr), the pointer type is again T*, and the reference type is T&. The means of destroying the pointee object is the delete operator.
- *Ownership* policy *(Section 7.5)*. Popular implementations are deep copy, reference counting, reference linking, and destructive copy. Note that **Ownership** is not concerned with the mechanics of destruction itself; this is **Storage**'s task. **Ownership** controls the *moment* of destruction.
- *Conversion* policy *(Section 7.7)*. Some applications need automatic conversion to the underlying raw pointer type; others do not.
- *Checking* policy *(Section 7.10)*. This policy controls whether an initializer for SmartPtr is valid and whether a SmartPtr is valid for dereferencing.

Other issues are not worth dedicating separate policies to them or have an optimal solution:

- The address-of operator (Section 7.6) is best not overloaded.
- Equality and inequality tests are handled with the tricks shown in Section 7.8.
- Ordering comparisons (Section 7.9) are left unimplemented; however, Loki specializes std::less for SmartPtr objects. The user may define an operator<, and Loki helps by defining all other ordering comparisons in terms of operator<.
- Loki defines const-correct implementations for the SmartPtr object, the pointee object, or both.
- There is no special support for arrays, but one of the canned **Storage** implementations can dispose of arrays by using operator delete[].

The presentation of the design issues surrounding smart pointers made these issues easier to understand and more manageable because each issue was discussed in isolation. It would be very helpful, then, if the implementation could decompose and treat issues in isolation instead of fighting with all the complexity at once.

Divide et Impera—this old principle coined by Julius Caesar can be of help even today with smart pointers. (I'd bet money he didn't predict that.) We break the problem into small component classes, called *policies*. Each policy class deals with exactly one issue. SmartPtr inherits all these classes, thus inheriting all their features. It's that simple—yet incredibly flexible, as you will soon see. Each policy is also a template parameter, which means you can mix and match existing stock policy classes or build your own.

The pointed-to type comes first, followed by each of the policies. Here is the resulting declaration of SmartPtr:

```
template
<
    typename T,
    template <class> class OwnershipPolicy = RefCounted,
    class ConversionPolicy = DisallowConversion,
    template <class> class CheckingPolicy = AssertCheck,
    template <class> class StoragePolicy = DefaultSPStorage
>
class SmartPtr;
```

The order in which the policies appear in SmartPtr's declaration puts the ones that you customize most often at the top.

The following four subsections discuss the requirements of the four policies we have defined. A rule for all policies is that they must have value semantics; that is, they must define a proper copy constructor and assignment operator.

7.14.1 The Storage Policy

The Storage policy abstracts the structure of the smart pointer. It provides type definitions and stores the actual pointee_ object.

If StorageImpl is an implementation of the Storage policy and storageImpl is an object of type StorageImpl<T>, then the constructs in Table 7.1 apply.

Here is the default Storage policy implementation:

```
template <class T>
class DefaultSPStorage
{
protected:
    typedef T* StoredType;     //the type of the pointee_ object
    typedef T* PointerType;    //type returned by operator->
    typedef T& ReferenceType;  //type returned by operator*
public:
    DefaultSPStorage() : pointee_(Default())
{}
    DefaultSPStorage(const StoredType& p): pointee_(p) {}
    PointerType operator->() const { return pointee_; }
    ReferenceType operator*() const { return *pointee_; }
    friend inline PointerType GetImpl(const DefaultSPStorage& sp)
    { return sp.pointee_; }
    friend inline const StoredType& GetImplRef(
        const DefaultSPStorage& sp)
    { return sp.pointee_; }
    friend inline StoredType& GetImplRef(DefaultSPStorage& sp)
    { return sp.pointee_; }
protected:
    void Destroy()
    { delete pointee_; }
    static StoredType Default()
    { return 0; }
private:
    StoredType pointee_;
};
```

In addition to DefaultSPStorage, other sensible policies to define are:

- ArrayStorage, which uses operator delete[] inside Destroy
- LockedStorage, which uses layering to provide a smart pointer that locks data while dereferenced (see Section 7.13.1)
- HeapStorage, which uses an explicit destructor call followed by std::free to release the data

Table 7.1: Storage Policy Constructs

Expression	Semantics
`StorageImpl<T>::StoredType`	The type actually stored by the implementation. Default: T*.
`StorageImpl<T>::PointerType`	The pointer type defined by the implementation. This is the type returned by `SmartPtr`'s `operator->`. Default: T*. Can be different from `StorageImpl<T>::StoredType` when you're using smart pointer layering (see Sections 7.3 and 7.13.1).
`StorageImpl<T>::ReferenceType`	The reference type. This is the type returned by `SmartPtr`'s `operator*`. Default: T&.
`GetImpl(storageImpl)`	Returns an object of type `StorageImpl<T>::StoredType`.
`GetImplRef(storageImpl)`	Returns an object of type `StorageImpl<T>::StoredType&`, qualified with `const` if `storageImpl` is const.
`storageImpl.operator->()`	Returns an object of type `StorageImpl<T>::PointerType`. Used by `SmartPtr`'s own `operator->`.
`storageImpl.operator*()`	Returns an object of type `StorageImpl<T>::ReferenceType`. Used by `SmartPtr`'s own `operator*`.
`StorageImpl<T>::StoredType p;` `p = storageImpl.Default();`	Returns the default value (usually zero).
`storageImpl.Destroy()`	Destroys the pointee object.

7.14.2 The Ownership Policy

The Ownership policy must support intrusive as well as nonintrusive reference counting. Therefore, it uses explicit function calls rather than constructor/destructor techniques, as Koenig (1996) does. The reason is that you can call member functions at any time, whereas constructors and destructors are called automatically and only at specific times.

The Ownership policy implementation takes one template parameter, which is the corresponding pointer type. `SmartPtr` passes `StoragePolicy<T>::PointerType` to `OwnershipPolicy`. Note that `OwnershipPolicy`'s template parameter is a pointer type, not an object type.

If `OwnershipImpl` is an implementation of Ownership and `ownershipImpl` is an object of type `OwnershipImpl<P>`, then the constructs in Table 7.2 apply.

Table 7.2: Ownership Policy Constructs

Expression	Semantics

`P val1;`
`P val2 = OwnershipImpl.`
`  Clone(val1);`
	Clones an object. It can modify the source value if `OwnershipImpl` uses destructive copy.

`const P val1;`
`P val2 = ownershipImpl.`
`  Clone(val1);`
	Clones an object.

`P val;`
`bool unique = ownershipImpl.`
`Release(val);`
	Releases ownership of an object. Returns true if the last reference to the object was released.

`bool dc = OwnershipImpl<P>` `  ::destructiveCopy;`	States whether `OwnershipImpl` uses destructive copy. If that's the case, `SmartPtr` uses the Colvin/Gibbons trick (Meyers 1999) used in `std::auto_ptr`.

An implementation of Ownership that supports reference counting is shown in the following:

```
template <class P>
class RefCounted
{
    unsigned int* pCount_;
protected:
    RefCounted() : pCount_(new unsigned int(1)) {}
    P Clone(const P & val)
    {
        ++*pCount_;
        return val;
    }
    bool Release(const P&)
    {
        if (!--*pCount_)
        {
            delete pCount_;
            return true;
        }
        return false;
    }
    enum { destructiveCopy = false }; // see below
};
```

Implementing a policy for other schemes of reference counting is very easy. Let's write an **Ownership** policy implementation for COM objects. COM objects have two functions: AddRef and Release. Upon the last Release call, the object destroys itself. You need only direct Clone to AddRef and Release to COM's Release:

```
template <class P>
class COMRefCounted
{
public:
    static P Clone(const P& val)
    {
        val->AddRef();
        return val;
    }
    static bool Release(const P& val)
    {
        val->Release();
        return false;
    }
    enum { destructiveCopy = false }; // see below
};
```

Loki defines the following **Ownership** implementations:

- DeepCopy, described in Section 7.5.1. DeepCopy assumes that pointee class implements a member function Clone.
- RefCounted, described in Section 7.5.3 and in this section.
- RefCountedMT, a multithreaded version of RefCounted.
- COMRefCounted, a variant of intrusive reference counting described in this section.
- RefLinked, described in Section 7.5.4.
- DestructiveCopy, described in Section 7.5.5.
- NoCopy, which does not define Clone, thus disabling any form of copying.

7.14.3 *The* Conversion *Policy*

Conversion is a simple policy: It defines a Boolean compile-time constant that says whether or not SmartPtr allows implicit conversion to the underlying pointer type.

If ConversionImpl is an implementation of **Conversion**, then the construct in Table 7.3 applies.

The underlying pointer type of SmartPtr is dictated by its **Storage** policy and is StorageImpl<T>::StorageType.

As you would expect, Loki defines precisely two **Conversion** implementations:

- AllowConversion
- DisallowConversion

Table 7.3: Conversion Policy Construct

Expression	Semantics
`bool allowConv =` `  ConversionImpl<P>::allow;`	If `allow` is `true`, `SmartPtr` allows implicit conversion to its underlying pointer type.

Table 7.4: Checking Policy Constructs

Expression	Semantics
`S value;` `checkingImpl.OnDefault(value);`	`SmartPtr` calls `OnDefault` in the default constructor call. If `CheckingImpl` does not define this function, it disables the default constructor at compile time.
`S value;` `checkingImpl.OnInit(value);`	`SmartPtr` calls `OnInit` upon a constructor call.

`S value;`
`checkingImpl.OnDereference`
`  (value);`
	`SmartPtr` calls `OnDereference` before returning from `operator->` and `operator*`.

`const S value;`
`checkingImpl.OnDereference`
`  (value);`
	`SmartPtr` calls `OnDereference` before returning from the const versions of `operator->` and `operator*`.

7.14.4 The Checking Policy

As discussed in Section 7.10, there are two main places to check a `SmartPtr` object for consistency: during initialization and before dereference. The checks themselves might use `assert`, exceptions, or lazy initialization or not do anything at all.

The Checking policy operates on the `StoredType` of the Storage policy, not on the `PointerType`. (See Section 7.14.1 for the definition of Storage.)

If `S` is the stored type as defined by the Storage policy implementation, and if `CheckingImpl` is an implementation of Checking, and if `checkingImpl` is an object of type `CheckingImpl<S>`, then the constructs in Table 7.4 apply.

Loki defines the following implementations of Checking:

*   `AssertCheck`, which uses `assert` for checking the value before dereferencing.
*   `AssertCheckStrict`, which uses `assert` for checking the value upon initialization.
*   `RejectNullStatic`, which does not define `OnDefault`. Consequently, any use of Smart-Ptr's default constructor yields a compile-time error.

- `RejectNull`, which throws an exception if you try to dereference a null pointer.
- `RejectNullStrict`, which does not accept null pointers as initializers (again, by throwing an exception).
- `NoCheck`, which handles errors in the grand C and C++ tradition—that is, it does no checking at all.

7.15 Summary

Congratulations! You have just read one of the longest, wildest chapters of this book—an effort that we hope has paid off. Now you know a lot of things about smart pointers and are equipped with a pretty comprehensive and configurable `SmartPtr` class template.

Smart pointers imitate built-in pointers in syntax and semantics. In addition, they perform a host of tasks that built-in pointers cannot. These tasks might include ownership management and checking against invalid values.

Smart pointer concepts go beyond actual pointer behavior; they can be generalized into smart resources, such as monikers (handles that don't have pointer syntax, yet resemble pointer behavior in the way they enable resource access).

Because they nicely automate things that are very hard to manage by hand, smart pointers are an essential ingredient of successful, robust applications. As small as they are, they can make the difference between a successful project and a failure—or, more often, between a correct program and one that leaks resources like a sieve.

That's why a smart pointer implementer should invest as much attention and effort in this task as possible; the investment is likely to pay in the long term. Similarly, smart pointer users should understand the conventions that smart pointers establish and use them in accordance with those conventions.

The presented implementation of smart pointers focuses on decomposing the areas of functionality into independent policies that the main class template `SmartPtr` mixes and matches. This is possible because each policy implements a well-defined interface.

7.16 `SmartPtr` Quick Facts

- `SmartPtr` declaration:

```
template
<
    typename T,
    template <class> class OwnershipPolicy = RefCounted,
    class ConversionPolicy = DisallowConversion,
    template <class> class CheckingPolicy = AssertCheck,
    template <class> class StoragePolicy = DefaultSPStorage
>
class SmartPtr;
```

- `T` is the type to which `SmartPtr` points. `T` can be a primitive type or a user-defined type. The `void` type is allowed.
- For the remaining class template parameters (`OwnershipPolicy`, `ConversionPolicy`, `CheckingPolicy`, and `StoragePolicy`), you can implement your own policies or choose from the defaults mentioned in Sections 7.14.1 through 7.14.4.

- `OwnershipPolicy` controls the ownership management strategy. You can select from the predefined classes `DeepCopy`, `RefCounted`, `RefCountedMT`, `COMRefCounted`, `RefLinked`, `DestructiveCopy`, and `NoCopy`, described in Section 7.14.2.
- `ConversionPolicy` controls whether implicit conversion to the pointee type is allowed. The default is to forbid implicit conversion. Either way, you can still access the pointee object by calling `GetImpl`. You can use the `AllowConversion` and `Disallow-Conversion` implementations (Section 7.14.3).
- `CheckingPolicy` defines the error checking strategy. The defaults provided are `Assert-Check`, `AssertCheckStrict`, `RejectNullStatic`, `RejectNull`, `RejectNullStrict`, and `NoCheck` (Section 7.14.4).
- `StoragePolicy` defines the details of how the pointee object is stored and accessed. The default is `DefaultSPStorage`, which, when instantiated with a type `T`, defines the reference type as `T&`, the stored type as `T*`, and the type returned from `operator->` as `T*` again. Other storage types defined by Loki are `ArrayStorage`, `LockedStorage`, and `HeapStorage` (Section 7.14.1).

8

Object Factories

Object-oriented programs use inheritance and virtual functions to achieve powerful abstractions and good modularity. By postponing until runtime the decision regarding which specific function will be called, polymorphism promotes binary code reuse and extensibility. The runtime system automatically dispatches virtual member functions to the appropriate derived object, allowing you to implement complex behavior in terms of polymorphic primitives.

You can find this kind of paragraph in any book teaching object-oriented techniques. The reason it is repeated here is to contrast the nice state of affairs in "steady mode" with the unpleasant "initialization mode" situation in which you must *create* objects in a polymorphic way.

In the steady state, you already hold pointers or references to polymorphic objects, and you can invoke member functions against them. Their dynamic type is well known (although the caller might not know it). However, there are cases when you need to have the same flexibility in creating objects—subject to the paradox of "virtual constructors." You need virtual constructors when the information about the object to be created is inherently dynamic and cannot be used directly with C++ constructs.

Most often, polymorphic objects are created on the free store by using the new operator:

```
class Base { ... };
class Derived : public Base { ... };
class AnotherDerived : public Base { ... };
...
// Create a Derived object and assign it to a pointer to Base
Base* pB = new Derived;
```

The issue here is the actual Derived type name appearing in the invocation of the new operator. In a way, Derived here is much like the magic numeric constants we are advised not to use. If you want to create an object of the type AnotherDerived, you have to go to the actual statement and replace Derived with AnotherDerived. You cannot make the new operator act more dynamically: You must pass it a type, and that type must be exactly known at compile time.

This marks a fundamental difference between creating objects and invoking virtual member functions in C++. Virtual member functions are fluid, dynamic—you can change their behavior without changing the call site. In contrast, each object creation is a stumbling block of statically bound, rigid code. One of the effects is that invoking virtual functions binds the caller to the interface only (the base class). Object orientation tries to break dependency on the actual concrete type. However, at least in C++, object creation binds the caller to the most derived, concrete class.

Actually, it makes a lot of conceptual sense that things are this way: Even in everyday life, creating something is very different from dealing with it. You are supposed, then, to know exactly what you want to do when you embark on the creation of an object. However, sometimes

- You want to leave this exact knowledge up to another entity. For instance, instead of invoking new directly, you might call a virtual function Create of some higher-level object, thus allowing clients to change behavior through polymorphism.
- You do have the type knowledge, but not in a form that's expressible in C++. For instance, you might have a string containing "Derived", so you actually know you have to create an object of type Derived, but you cannot pass a string containing a type name to new instead of a type name.

These two issues are the fundamental problems addressed by object factories, which we'll discuss in detail in this chapter. The topics of this chapter include the following:

- Examples of situations in which object factories are needed
- Why virtual constructors are inherently hard to implement in C++
- How to create objects by substituting values for types
- An implementation of a generic object factory

By the end of this chapter, we'll put together a generic object factory. You can customize the generic factory to a large degree—by the type of product, the creation method, and the product identification method. You can combine the factory thus created with other components described in this book, such as Singleton (Chapter 6)—for creating an application-wide object factory—and Functor (Chapter 5)—for tweaking factory behavior. We'll also introduce a clone factory, which can duplicate objects of any type.

8.1 The Need for Object Factories

There are two basic cases in which object factories are needed. The first occurs when a library needs not only to manipulate user-defined objects, but also to create them. For example, imagine you develop a framework for multiwindow document editors. Because you want the framework to be easily extensible, you provide an abstract class Document from which users can derive classes such as TextDocument and HTMLDocument. Another framework component may be a DocumentManager class that keeps the list of all open documents.

A good rule to introduce is that each document that exists in the application should be known by the DocumentManager. Therefore, creating a new document is tightly coupled with adding it to DocumentManager's list of documents. When two operations are so coupled, it is best to put them in the same function and never perform them separately:

```
class DocumentManager
{
    ...
public:
    Document* NewDocument();
    virtual Document* CreateDocument() = 0;
private:
    std::list<Document*> listOfDocs_;
};

Document* DocumentManager::NewDocument()
{
    Document* pDoc = CreateDocument();
    listOfDocs_.push_back(pDoc);
    ...
    return pDoc;
}
```

The CreateDocument member function replaces a call to new. NewDocument cannot use the new operator because the concrete document to be created is not known by the time DocumentManager is written. In order to use the framework, programmers will derive from DocumentManager and override the virtual member function CreateDocument (which is likely to be pure). The GoF book (Gamma et al. 1995) calls CreateDocument a *factory method*.

Because the derived class knows exactly the type of document to be created, it can invoke the new operator directly. This way, you can remove the type knowledge from the framework and have the framework operate on the base class Document only. The override is very simple and consists essentially of a call to new; for example:

```
Document* GraphicDocumentManager::CreateDocument()
{
    return new GraphicDocument;
}
```

Alternatively, an application built with this framework might support creation of multiple document types (for instance, bitmapped graphics and vectorized graphics). In that case, the overridden CreateDocument function might display a dialog to the user asking for the specific type of document to be created.

Thinking of opening a document previously saved on disk in the framework just outlined brings us to the second—and more complicated—case in which an object factory may be needed. When you save an object to a file, you must save its actual type in the form of a string, an integral value, an identifier of some sort. Thus, although the type information exists, its *form* does not allow you to create C++ objects.

The general concept underlying this situation is the creation of objects whose type information is genuinely postponed to runtime: entered by the end user, read from a persistent storage or network connection, or the like. Here the binding of types to values is pushed even further than in the case of polymorphism: When using polymorphism, the entity manipulating an object does not know its exact type; however, the object itself is of a well-determined type. When reading objects from some storage, the type comes "alone" at runtime. You must transform type information into an object. Finally, you must read the object from the storage, which is easy once an empty object is created, by invoking a virtual function.

Creating objects from "pure" type information, and consequently adapting *dynamic* information to *static* C++ types, is an important issue in building object factories. Let's focus on it in the next section.

8.2 Object Factories in C++: Classes and Objects

To come up with a solution, we need a good grasp of the problem. This section tries to answer the following questions: Why are C++ constructors so rigid? Why don't we have flexible means to create objects in the language itself?

Interestingly, seeking an answer to this question takes us directly to fundamental decisions about C++'s type system. To find out why a statement such as

```
Base* pB = new Derived;
```

is so rigid, we must answer two related questions: What is a class, and what is an object? This is because the culprit in the given statement is `Derived`, which is a class name, and we'd like it to be a value, that is, an object.

In C++, classes and objects are different beasts. Classes are what the programmer creates, and objects are what the program creates. You cannot create a new class at runtime, and you cannot create an object at compile time. Classes don't have first-class status: You cannot copy a class, store it in a variable, or return it from a function.

In contrast, there are languages in which classes *are* objects. In those languages, some objects with certain properties are simply considered classes by convention. Consequently, in those languages, you *can* create new classes at runtime, copy a class, store it in a variable, and so on. If C++ were such a language, you could have written code like the following:

```
// Warning-this is NOT C++
// Assumes Class is a class that's also an object
Class Read(const char* fileName);
Document* DocumentManager::OpenDocument(const char* fileName)
{
    Class theClass = Read(fileName);
    Document* pDoc = new theClass;
    ...
}
```

That is, we could pass a variable of type `Class` to the `new` operator. In such a paradigm, passing a known class name to `new` is the same as using a hardcoded constant.

Such dynamic languages trade off some type safety and performance for the sake of flexibility, because static typing is an important source of optimization. C++ took the opposite approach, sticking to a static type system, yet trying to provide as much flexibility as possible in this framework.

The bottom line is that creating object factories is a complicated problem in C++. In C++ there is a fracture between types and values: A value has a type attribute, but a type cannot exist on its own. If you want to create an object in a totally dynamic way, you need a means to express and pass around a "pure" type and build a value from it on demand. Because you cannot do this, you somehow must represent types as objects—integers, strings, and so on. Then, you must employ some trick to exchange the value for the right type, and finally to use that type to create an object. This object-type-object trade is fundamental for object factories in statically typed languages.

We will call the object that identifies a type a *type identifier*. (Don't confuse it with typeid.) The type identifier helps the factory in creating the appropriate type of object. As will be shown, sometimes you make the type identifier–object exchange without knowing exactly what you have or what you will get. It's like a fairy tale: You don't know exactly how the token works (and it's sometimes dangerous to try to figure it out), but you pass it to the wizard, who gives you a valuable object in exchange. The details of how the magic happens must be encapsulated in the wizard . . . the factory, that is.

We will explore a simple factory that solves a concrete problem, try various implementations of it, and then extract the generic part of it into a class template.

8.3 Implementing an Object Factory

Say you write a simple drawing application, allowing editing of simple vectorized drawings consisting of lines, circles, polygons, and so on.[1] In a classic object-oriented manner, you define an abstract Shape class from which all your figures will derive:

```
class Shape
{
public:
    virtual void Draw() const = 0;
    virtual void Rotate(double angle) = 0;
    virtual void Zoom(double zoomFactor) = 0;
    ...
};
```

You might then define a class Drawing that contains a complex drawing. A Drawing essentially holds a collection of pointers to Shape—such as a list, a vector, or a hierarchical structure—and provides operations to manipulate the drawing as a whole. Two typical operations you might want to do are saving a drawing as a file and loading a drawing from a previously saved file.

Saving shapes is easy: Just provide a pure virtual function such as Shape::Save(std:: ostream&). Then the Drawing::Save operation might look like this:

```
class Drawing
{
public:
```

---

[1] This "Hello, world" of design is a good basis for C++ interview questions. Although many candidates manage to conceive such a design, few of them know how to implement the loading of files, which is a rather important operation.

```
    void Save(std::ofstream& outFile);
    void Load(std::ifstream& inFile);
    ...
};

void Drawing::Save(std::ofstream& outFile)
{
    write drawing header
    for (each element in the drawing)
    {
        (current element)->Save(outFile);
    }
}
```

The Shape-Drawing example just described is often encountered in C++ books, including Bjarne Stroustrup's classic (Stroustrup 1997). However, most introductory C++ books stop when it comes to loading graphics from a file, exactly because the nice model of having separate drawing objects breaks. Explaining the gory details of reading objects makes for a big parenthesis, which understandably is often avoided. On the other hand, this is exactly what we want to implement, so we have to bite the bullet. A straightforward implementation is to require each Shape-derived object to save an integral identifier at the very beginning. Each object should have its own unique ID. Then reading the file would look like this:

```
// a unique ID for each drawing object type
namespace DrawingType
{
const int
    LINE = 1,
    POLYGON = 2,
    CIRCLE = 3
}

void Drawing::Load(std::ifstream& inFile)
{
    // error handling omitted for simplicity
    while (inFile)
    {
        // read object type
        int drawingType;
        inFile >> drawingType;

        // create a new empty object
        Shape* pCurrentObject;
        switch (drawingType)
        {
            using namespace DrawingType;
        case LINE:
            pCurrentObject = new Line;
            break;
        case POLYGON:
            pCurrentObject = new Polygon;
            break;
```

```
        case CIRCLE:
            pCurrentObject = new Circle;
            break;
        default:
            handle error—unknown object type
        }
        // read the object's contents by invoking a virtual fn
        pCurrentObject->Read(inFile);
        add the object to the container
    }
}
```

This is indeed an object factory. It reads a type identifier from the file, creates an object of the appropriate type based on that identifier, and invokes a virtual function that loads that object from the file. The only problem is that it breaks the most important rules of object orientation:

- It performs a `switch` based on a type tag, with the associated drawbacks, which is exactly what object-oriented programs try to eliminate.
- It collects in a single source file knowledge about all `Shape`-derived classes in the program, which again you must strive to avoid. For one thing, the implementation file of `Drawing::Load` must include all headers of all possible shapes, which makes it a bottleneck of compile dependencies and maintenance.
- It is hard to extend. Imagine adding a new shape, such as `Ellipse`, to the system. In addition to creating the class itself, you must add a distinct integral constant to the namespace `DrawingType`, you must write that constant when saving an `Ellipse` object, and you must add a label to the `switch` statement in `Drawing::Load`. This is an awful lot more than what the architecture promised—total insulation between classes—and all for the sake of a single function!

We'd like to create an object factory that does the job without having these disadvantages. One practical goal worth pursuing is to break the `switch` statement apart—so that we can put the `Line` creation statement in the file implementation for `Line`—and do the same for `Polygon` and `Circle`.

A common way to keep together and manipulate pieces of code is to work with pointers to functions, as discussed at length in Chapter 5. The unit of customizable code here (each of the entries in the `switch` statement) can be abstracted in a function with the signature

```
Shape* CreateConcreteShape();
```

The factory keeps a collection of pointers to functions with this signature. In addition, there has to be a correspondence between the IDs and the pointer to the function that creates the appropriate object. Thus, what we need is an *associative collection*—a map. A map offers access to the appropriate function given the type identifier, which is precisely what the `switch` statement offers. In addition, the map offers the scalability that the `switch` statement, with its fixed compile-time structure, cannot provide. The map can grow at runtime—you can add entries (tuples of IDs and pointers to functions) dynamically, which is exactly what we need. We can start with an empty map and have each Shape-derived object add an entry to it.

Why not use a vector? IDs are integral numbers, so we can keep a vector and have the ID be the index in the vector. This would be simpler and faster, but a map is better here. The map doesn't require its indices to be adjacent, plus it's more general—vectors work only with integral indices, whereas maps accept any ordered type as an index. This point will become important when we generalize our example.

We can start designing a ShapeFactory class, which has the responsibility of managing the creation of all Shape-derived objects. In implementing ShapeFactory, we will use the map implementation found in the standard library, std::map:

```
class ShapeFactory
{
public:
    typedef Shape* (*CreateShapeCallback)();
private:
    typedef std::map<int, CreateShapeCallback> CallbackMap;
public:
    // Returns 'true' if registration was successful
    bool RegisterShape(int shapeId,
        CreateShapeCallback createFn);
    // Returns 'true' if the shapeId was registered before
    bool UnregisterShape(int shapeId);
    Shape* CreateShape(int shapeId);
private:
    CallbackMap callbacks_;
};
```

This is a basic design of a scalable factory. The factory is scalable because you don't have to modify its code each time you add a new Shape-derived class to the system. Shape-Factory divides responsibility: Each new shape has to register itself with the factory by calling RegisterShape and passing it its integral identifier and a pointer to a function that creates an object. Typically, the function has a single line and looks like this:

```
Shape* CreateLine()
{
    return new Line;
}
```

The implementation of Line also must register this function with the ShapeFactory that the application uses, which is typically a globally accessible object.[2] The registration is usually performed with startup code. The whole connection of Line with the Shape Factory is as follows:

```
// Implementation module for class Line
// Create an anonymous namespace
//  to make the function invisible from other modules
namespace
```

---

[2] This brings us to the link between object factories and singletons. Indeed, more often than not, factories *are* singletons. Later in this chapter is a discussion of how to use factories with the singletons implemented in Chapter 6.

```
    {
        Shape* CreateLine()
        {
            return new Line;
        }
        // The ID of class Line
        const int LINE = 1;
        // Assume TheShapeFactory is a singleton factory
        // (see Chapter 6)
        const bool registered =
            TheShapeFactory::Instance().RegisterShape(
                LINE, CreateLine);
    }
```

Implementing the ShapeFactory is easy, given the amenities std::map has to offer. Basically, ShapeFactory member functions forward only to the callbacks_ member:

```
    bool ShapeFactory::RegisterShape(int shapeId,
        CreateShapeCallback createFn)
    {
        return callbacks_.insert(
            CallbackMap::value_type(shapeId, createFn)).second;
    }

    bool ShapeFactory::UnregisterShape(int shapeId)
    {
        return callbacks_.erase(shapeId) == 1;
    }
```

If you're not very familiar with the std::map class template, the previous code might need a bit of explanation:

- std::map holds pairs of keys and data. In our case, keys are integral shape IDs, and the data consists of a pointer to function. The type of our pair is std::pair<const int, CreateShapeCallback>. You must pass an object of this type when you call insert. Because that's a lot to write, it's better to use the typedef found inside std::map, which provides a handy name—value_type—for that pair type. Alternatively, you can use std::make_pair.
- The insert member function we called returns another pair, this time containing an iterator (which refers to the element just inserted) and a bool that is true if map didn't contain a pair having an equivalent key, and false otherwise. The .second field access after the call to insert selects this bool and returns it in a single stroke, without our having to create a named temporary.
- erase returns the number of elements erased.

The CreateShape member function simply fetches the appropriate pointer to a function for the ID passed in, and calls it. In the case of an error, it throws an exception. Here it is:

```
    Shape* ShapeFactory::CreateShape(int shapeId)
    {
        CallbackMap::const_iterator i = callbacks_.find(shapeId);
```

```
        if (i == callbacks_.end())
        {
            // not found
            throw std::runtime_error("Unknown Shape ID");
        }
        // Invoke the creation function
        return (i->second)();
    }
```

Let's see what this simple class brought us. Instead of relying on the large, know-it-all switch statement, we obtained a dynamic scheme requiring each type of object to register itself with the factory. This moves the responsibility from a centralized place to each concrete class, where it belongs. Now whenever you define a new Shape-derived class, you can just *add* files instead of *modifying* files.

8.4 Type Identifiers

The only problem that remains is the management of type identifiers. Still, adding type identifiers requires a fair amount of discipline and centralized control. Whenever you add a new shape class, you must check all the existing type identifiers and add one that doesn't clash with them. If a clash exists, the second call to RegisterShape for the same ID fails, and you won't be able to create objects of that type.

We can solve this problem by choosing a more generous type than int for expressing the type identifier. Our design doesn't require integral types, only types that can be keys in a map, that is, types that support operator== and operator<. (That's why we can be happy we chose maps instead of vectors.) For example, we can store type identifiers as strings and establish the convention that each class is represented by its name: Line's identifier is "Line", Polygon's identifier is "Polygon", and so forth. This minimizes the chance of clashing names because class names are unique.

If you enjoy spending your weekends studying C++, maybe the previous paragraph rang a bell for you. Let's use type_info! The std::type_info class is part of the runtime type information (RTTI) provided by C++. You get a reference to a std::type_info by invoking the typeid operator on a type or an expression. What seems nice is that std::type_info provides a name member function that returns a const char* pointing to a human-readable name of the type. For your compiler, you might have seen that typeid(Line).name() points to the string "class Line", which is exactly what we wanted.

The problem is, this does not apply to all C++ compiler implementations. The way type_info::name is defined makes it unsuitable for anything other than debugging purposes (such as printing it in a debug console). There is no guarantee that the string is the actual class name, and worse, there is no guarantee that the string is unique throughout the application. (Yes, you can have two classes that have the same name according to std::type_info::name.) And the shotgun argument is that there's no guarantee that the type name will be unique in *time*. There is no guarantee that typeid(Line).name() points to the same string when the application is run twice. Implementing persistence is an important application of factories, and std::type_info::name is *not* persistent. All this makes `std::type_info` deceptively close to being useful for our object factory, but it is not a real solution.

Back to the management of type identifiers. A decentralized solution for generating type identifiers is to use a unique value generator—for instance, a random number or random string generator. You would use this generator each time you add a new class to the program, then hardcode that random value in the source file and never change it.[3] This sounds like a brittle solution, but think of it this way: If you have a random string generator that has a 10^{-20} probability of repeating a value in a thousand years, you get a rate of error smaller than that of a program using a "perfect" factory.

The only conclusion that can be drawn here is that type identifier management is not the business of the object factory itself. Because C++ cannot guarantee a unique, persistent type ID, type ID management becomes an extra-linguistic issue that must be left to the programmers.

We have described all the elements in a typical object factory, and we have a prototype implementation. It's time now for the next step—the step from concrete to abstract. Then, enriched with new insights, we'll go back to concrete.

8.5 Generalization

Let's enumerate the elements involved in our discussion of object factories. This gives us the intellectual workout necessary for putting together a generic object factory.

- *Concrete product.* A factory delivers some product in the form of an object.
- *Abstract product.* Products inherit a base type (in our example, `Shape`). A product is an object whose type belongs to a hierarchy. The base type of the hierarchy is the abstract product. The factory behaves polymorphically in the sense that it returns a pointer to the abstract product, without conveying knowledge of the concrete product type.
- *Product type identifier.* This is the object that identifies the type of the concrete product. As discussed, you have to have a type identifier to create a product because of the static C++ type system.
- *Product creator.* The function or functor is specialized for creating exactly one type of object. We modeled the product creator using a pointer to function.

The generic factory will orchestrate these elements to provide a well-defined interface, as well as defaults for the most used cases.

It seems that each of the notions just enumerated will transform into a template parameter of a `Factory` template class. There's only one exception: The concrete product doesn't have to be known to the factory. Had this been the case, we'd have different

---

[3]Microsoft's COM factory uses such a method. It has an algorithm for generating unique 128-bit identifiers (called globally unique identifiers, or GUIDs) for COM objects. The algorithm relies on the uniqueness of the network card serial number or, in the absence of a card, the date, time, and other highly variable machine states.

Factory types for each concrete product we're adding, and we are trying to keep Factory insulated from the concrete types. We want only different Factory types for different abstract products.

This being said, let's write down what we've grabbed so far:

```cpp
template
<
    class AbstractProduct,
    typename IdentifierType,
    typename ProductCreator
>
class Factory
{
public:
    bool Register(const IdentifierType& id, ProductCreator creator)
    {
        return associations_.insert(
            AssocMap::value_type(id, creator)).second;
    }
    bool Unregister(const IdentifierType& id)
    {
        return associations_.erase(id) == 1;
    }
    AbstractProduct* CreateObject(const IdentifierType& id)
    {
        typename AssocMap::const_iterator i =
            associations_.find(id);
        if (i != associations_.end())
        {
            return (i->second)();
        }
        handle error
    }
private:
    typedef std::map<IdentifierType, ProductCreator>
        AssocMap;
    AssocMap associations_;
};
```

The only thing left out is error handling. If we didn't find a creator registered with the factory, should we throw an exception? Return a null pointer? Terminate the program? Dynamically load some library, register it on the fly, and retry the operation? The actual decision depends very much on the concrete situation; any of these actions makes sense in some cases.

Our generic factory should let the user customize it to do any of these actions and should provide a reasonable default behavior. Therefore, the error handling code should be pulled out of the CreateObject member function into a separate **FactoryError** policy (see Chapter 1). This policy defines only one function, OnUnknownType, and Factory gives that function a fair chance (and enough information) to make any sensible decision.

The policy defined by **FactoryError** is very simple. **FactoryError** prescribes a template of two parameters: `IdentifierType` and `AbstractProduct`. If `FactoryErrorImpl` is an implementation of **FactoryError**, then the following expression must apply:

```
FactoryErrorImpl<IdentifierType, AbstractProduct> factoryErrorImpl;
IdentifierType id;
AbstractProduct* pProduct = factoryErrorImpl.OnUnknownType(id);
```

`Factory` uses `FactoryErrorImpl` as a last-resort solution: If `CreateObject` cannot find the association in its internal map, it uses `FactoryErrorImpl<IdentifierType, Abstract-Product>::OnUnknownType` for fetching a pointer to the abstract product. If `OnUnknownType` throws an exception, the exception propagates out of `Factory`. Otherwise, `CreateObject` simply returns whatever `OnUnknownType` returned.

Let's code these additions and changes (shown in bold):

```
template
<
    class AbstractProduct,
    typename IdentifierType,
    typename ProductCreator,
    template<typename, class>
        class FactoryErrorPolicy
>
class Factory
    : public FactoryErrorPolicy<IdentifierType, AbstractProduct>
{
public:
    AbstractProduct* CreateObject(const IdentifierType& id)
    {
        typename AssocMap::const_iterator i = associations_.find(id);
        if (i != associations_.end())
        {
            return (i->second)();
        }
        return OnUnknownType(id);
    }
private:
    ... rest of functions and data as above ...
};
```

The default implementation of **FactoryError** throws an exception. This exception's class is best made distinct from all other types so that client code can detect it separately and make appropriate decisions. Also, the class should inherit one of the standard exception classes so that the client can catch all kinds of errors with one `catch` block. **DefaultFactoryError** defines a nested exception class (called `Exception`)[4] that inherits `std::exception`.

---

[4]There is no need to make the name distinctive (like `FactoryException`), because the type is already inside class template `DefaultFactoryError`.

```
        template <class IdentifierType, class ProductType>
        class DefaultFactoryError
        {
        public:
            class Exception : public std::exception
            {
            public:
                Exception(const IdentifierType& unknownId)
                    : unknownId_(unknownId)
                {
                }
                virtual const char* what()
                {
                    return "Unknown object type passed to Factory.";
                }
                const IdentifierType& GetId()
                {
                    return unknownId_;
                };
            private:
                IdentifierType unknownId_;
            }
        protected:
            static ProductType* OnUnknownType(const IdentifierType& id)
            {
                throw Exception(id);
            }
        };
```

Other, more advanced implementations of FactoryError can look up the type identifier and return a pointer to a valid object, return a null pointer (if the use of exceptions is undesirable), throw some exception object, or terminate the program. You can tweak the behavior by defining new FactoryError implementations and specifying them as the fourth argument of Factory.

8.6 Minutiae

Actually, Loki's Factory implementation does not use std::map. It uses a drop-in replacement for map, AssocVector, which is optimized for rare inserts and frequent lookups, the typical usage pattern of Factory. AssocVector is described in detail in Chapter 11.

In an initial draft of Factory, the map type was customizable by virtue of its being a template parameter. However, often AssocVector fits the bill exactly; in addition, using standard containers as template template parameters is not, well, standard. This is because implementers of standard containers are free to add more template arguments, as long as they provide defaults for them.

Let's focus now on the ProductCreator template parameter. Its main requirement is that it have functional behavior (accept operator() and take no arguments) and return a pointer convertible to AbstractProduct*. In the concrete implementation shown earlier,

`ProductCreator` was a simple pointer to a function. This suffices if all we need is to create objects by invoking `new`, which is the most common case. Therefore, we choose

```
AbstractProduct* (*)()
```

as the default type for `ProductCreator`. The type looks a bit like a confusing emoticon because its name is missing. If you put a name after the asterisk within the parentheses,

```
AbstractProduct* (*PointerToFunction)()
```

the type reveals itself as a pointer to a function taking no parameters and returning a pointer to `AbstractProduct`. If this still looks unfamiliar to you, you may want to refer to Chapter 5, which includes a discussion on pointers to functions.

By the way, speaking of that chapter, there is a very interesting template parameter you can pass to `Factory` as `ProductCreator`, namely `Functor<AbstractProduct*>`. If you choose this, you gain great flexibility: You can create objects by invoking a simple function, a member function, or a functor, and bind appropriate parameters to any of them. The glue code is provided by `Functor`.

Our `Factory` class template declaration now looks like this:

```
template
<
    class AbstractProduct,
    class IdentifierType,
    class ProductCreator = AbstractProduct* (*)(),
    template<typename, class>
        class FactoryErrorPolicy = DefaultFactoryError
>
class Factory;
```

Our `Factory` class template is now ready to be of use.

8.7 Clone Factories

Although genetic factories producing clones of the universal soldier are quite a scary prospect, cloning C++ objects is a harmless and useful activity most of the time. Here the goal is slightly different from what we have dealt with so far: We no longer have to create objects from scratch. We have a pointer to a polymorphic object, and we'd like to create an exact copy of it. Because we don't exactly know the type of the polymorphic object, we don't exactly know what new object to create, and this is the actual issue.

Because we do have an object at hand, we can apply classic polymorphism. Thus, the usual idiom used for object cloning is to declare a virtual `Clone` member function in the base class and to have each derived class override it. Here's an example using our geometric shapes hierarchy:

```
class Shape
{
```

```
public:
    virtual Shape* Clone() const = 0;
    ...
};
class Line : public Shape
{
public:
    virtual Line* Clone() const
    {
        return new Line(*this);
    }
    ...
};
```

The reason that Line::Clone does not return a pointer to Shape is that we took advantage of a C++ feature called *covariant return types*. Because of covariant return types, you can return a pointer to a derived class instead of a pointer to the base class from an overridden virtual function. From now on, the idiom goes, you must implement a similar Clone function for each concrete class you add to the hierarchy. The contents of the functions are the same: You create a Polygon, you return a new Polygon(*this), and so on.

This idiom works, but it has a couple of major drawbacks:

- If the base class wasn't designed to be cloneable (didn't declare a virtual function equivalent to Clone) and is not modifiable, the idiom cannot be applied. This is the case when you write an application using a class library that requires you to derive from its base classes.
- Even if all the classes are changeable, the idiom requires a high degree of discipline. Forgetting to implement Clone in some derived classes will remain undetected by the compiler and may cause runtime behavior ranging from bizarre to pernicious.

The first point is obvious; let's discuss the second one. Imagine you derived a class DottedLine from Line and forgot to override DottedLine::Clone. Now say you have a pointer to a Shape that actually points to a DottedLine, and you invoke Clone on it:

```
Shape* pShape;
...
Shape* pDuplicateShape = pShape->Clone();
```

The Line::Clone function will be invoked, returning a Line. This is a very unfortunate situation because you assume pDuplicateShape to have the same dynamic type as pShape, when in fact it doesn't. This might lead to a lot of problems, from drawing unexpected types of lines to crashing the application.

There's no solid way to mitigate this second problem. You can't say in C++: "I define this function, and I require any direct or indirect class inheriting it to override it." You must shoulder the painful, repetitive task of overriding Clone in every shape class, and you're doomed if you don't.

If you agree to complicate the idiom a bit, you can get an acceptable runtime check.

Make Clone a public nonvirtual function. From inside it call a *protected virtual* function called, say, DoClone, and then enforce the equality of the dynamic types. The code is simpler than the explanation:

```
class Shape
{
   ...
public:
   Shape* Clone() const  //nonvirtual
   {
      // delegate to DoClone
      Shape* pClone = DoClone();
      // Check for type equivalence
      // (could be a more sophisticated test than assert)
      assert(typeid(*pClone) == typeid(*this));
      return pClone;
   }
protected:
   virtual Shape* DoClone() const = 0; // protected
};
```

The only downside is that you can no longer use covariant return types.

Shape derivees would always override DoClone, leave it protected so that clients cannot call it, and leave Clone alone. Clients use Clone only, which performs the runtime check. As you have certainly figured out, programming errors, such as overriding Clone or making DoClone public, can still sneak in.

Don't forget that, no matter what, if you cannot change all the classes in the hierarchy (the hierarchy is *closed*) and if it wasn't designed to be cloneable, you don't have any chance of implementing this idiom. This is quite a dismissive argument in many cases, so we should look for alternatives.

Here a special object factory may be of help. It leads to a solution that doesn't have the two problems mentioned earlier, at the cost of a slight performance hit—instead of a virtual call, there is a map lookup plus a call via a pointer to a function. Because the number of classes in an application is never really big (they are written by people, aren't they?), the map tends to be small, and the hit should not be significant.

It all starts from the idea that in a clone factory, the type identifier and the product have the same type. You receive as a type identifier the object to be duplicated and pass as output a new object that is a copy of the type identifier. To be more precise, they're not quite the same type: A cloning factory's IdentifierType is a *pointer to* AbstractProduct. The exact deal is that you pass a pointer to the clone factory, and you get back another pointer, which points to a cloned object.

But what's the key in the map? It can't be a pointer to AbstractProduct because you don't need as many entries as the objects we have. You need only one entry per *type* of object to be cloned, which brings us again to the std::type_info class. The type identifier passed when the factory is asked to create a new object is different from the type identifier that's stored in the association map, and that makes it impossible for us to reuse the code we've written so far. Another consequence is that the product creator now needs the pointer to the object to be cloned; in the factory we created earlier from scratch, no parameter was needed.

Let's recap. The clone factory gets a pointer to an `AbstractProduct`. It applies the `typeid` operator to the pointed-to object and obtains a reference to a `std::type_info` object. It then looks up that object in its private map. (The `before` member function of `std::type_info` introduces an ordering over the set of `std::type_info` objects, which makes it possible to use a map and perform fast searches.) If an entry is not found, an exception is thrown. If it is found, the product creator will be invoked, with the pointer to the `AbstractProduct` passed in by the user.

Because we already have the `Factory` class template handy, implementing the `Clone-Factory` class template is a simple exercise. (You can find it in Loki.) There are a few differences and new elements:

- `CloneFactory` uses `TypeInfo` instead of `std::type_info`. The class `TypeInfo`, discussed in Chapter 2, is a wrapper around a pointer to `std::type_info`, having the purpose of defining proper initialization, assignment, `operator==`, and `operator<`, which are all needed by the map. The first operator delegates to `std::type_info::operator==`; the second operator delegates to `std::type_info::before`.
- There is no longer an `IdentifierType` because the identifier type is implicit.
- The `ProductCreator` template parameter defaults to `AbstractProduct*(*)(Abstract-Product*)`.
- The `IdToProductMap` is now `AssocVector<TypeInfo, ProductCreator>`.

The synopsis of `CloneFactory` is as follows:

```
template
<
    class AbstractProduct,
    class ProductCreator =
        AbstractProduct* (*)(AbstractProduct*),
    template<typename, class>
        class FactoryErrorPolicy = DefaultFactoryError
>
class CloneFactory
{
public:
    AbstractProduct* CreateObject(const AbstractProduct* model);
    bool Register(const TypeInfo&,
        ProductCreator creator);
    bool Unregister(const TypeInfo&);
private:
    typedef AssocVector<TypeInfo, ProductCreator>
        IdToProductMap;
    IdToProductMap associations_;
};
```

The `CloneFactory` class template is a complete solution for cloning objects belonging to closed class hierarchies (that is, class hierarchies that you cannot modify). Its simplicity and effectiveness stem from the conceptual clarifications made in the previous sections and from the runtime type information that C++ provides through typeid and std::type_info. Had RTTI not existed, clone factories would have been much more awkward to implement—in fact, so awkward that putting them together wouldn't have made much sense in the first place.

8.8 Using Object Factories with Other Generic Components

Chapter 6 introduced the SingletonHolder class, which was designed to provide specific services to your classes. Because of the global nature of factories, it is natural to use Factory with SingletonHolder. They are very easy to combine by using typedef. For instance:

```
typedef SingletonHolder< Factory<Shape, std::string> > ShapeFactory;
```

Of course, you can add arguments to either SingletonHolder or Factory to choose different trade-offs and design decisions, but it's all in one place. From now on, you can isolate a bunch of important design choices in one place and use ShapeFactory throughout the code. Within the simple type definition just shown, you can select the way the factory works and the way the singleton works, thus exploiting all the combinations between the two. With a single line of declarative code, you direct the compiler to generate the right code for you and nothing more, just as at runtime you'd call a function with various parameters to perform some action in different ways. Because in our case it all happens at compile time, the emphasis is more on design decisions than on runtime behavior. Of course, runtime behavior is affected as well, but in a more global and subtle way. By writing "regular" code, you specify what's going to happen at runtime. When you write a type definition such as the one above, you specify what's going to happen during compile time—in fact, you kind of call code-generation functions at compile time, passing arguments to them.

As alluded to in the beginning of this chapter, an interesting combination is to use Factory with Functor:

```
typedef SingletonHolder
<
    Factory
    <
        Shape, std::string, Functor<Shape*, NullType>
    >
>
ShapeFactory;
```

This gives you great flexibility in creating objects, by leveraging the power of Functor (for which implementation we took great pains in Chapter 5). You can now create Shapes in almost any way imaginable by registering various Functors with the Factory, and the whole thing is a Singleton.

8.9 Summary

Object factories are an important component of programs that use polymorphism. Object factories help in creating objects when their types are either not available or are available only in a form that's incompatible for use with language constructs.

Object factories are used mostly in object-oriented frameworks and libraries, as well as in various object persistence and streaming schemes. The latter case was analyzed in depth with a concrete example. The solution essentially distributes a switch of type across multiple implementation files, thus achieving low coupling. Although the factory remains a central authority that creates objects, it doesn't have to collect knowledge about all the static types in a hierarchy. Instead, it's the responsibility of each type to register itself with the factory. This marks a fundamental difference between the "wrong" and the "right" approach.

Type information cannot be easily transported at runtime in C++. This is a fundamental feature of the family of languages to which C++ belongs. Because of this, type identifiers that represent types have to be used instead. They are associated with creator objects that are callable entities, as described in Chapter 5 on generalized functors (pointers to functions or functors). A concrete object factory starting from these ideas was implemented and was then generalized into a class template.

Finally, we discussed clone factories (factories that can duplicate polymorphic objects).

8.10 Factory Class Template Quick Facts

• Factory declaration:

```
template
<
    class AbstractProduct,
    class IdentifierType,
    class ProductCreator = AbstractProduct* (*)(),
    template<typename, class>
        class FactoryErrorPolicy = DefaultFactoryError
>
class Factory;
```

• `AbstractProduct` is the base class of the hierarchy for which you provide the object factory.
• `IdentifierType` is the type of the "cookie" that represents a type in the hierarchy. It has to be an ordered type (able to be stored in a `std::map`). Commonly used identifier types are strings and integral types.
• `ProductCreator` is the callable entity that creates objects. This type must support `operator()`, taking no parameters and returning a pointer to `AbstractProduct`. A `ProductCreator` object is always registered together with a type identifier.
• `Factory` implements the following primitives:

```
bool Register(const IdentifierType& id, ProductCreator creator);
```

Registers a creator with a type identifier. Returns true if the registration was successful; false otherwise (if there already was a creator registered with the same type identifier).

```
bool Unregister(const IdentifierType& id);
```

Unregisters the creator for the given type identifier. If the type identifier was previously registered, the function returns true.

```
AbstractProduct* CreateObject(const IdentifierType& id);
```

Looks up the type identifier in the internal map. If it is found, it invokes the corresponding creator for the type identifier and returns its result. If the type identifier is not found, the result of FactoryErrorPolicy<IdentifierType, AbstractProduct>:: OnUnknown-Type is returned. The default implementation of FactoryErrorPolicy throws an exception of its nested type Exception.

8.11 CloneFactory Class Template Quick Facts

* CloneFactory declaration:

```
template
<
    class AbstractProduct,
    class ProductCreator =
        AbstractProduct* (*)(const AbstractProduct*),
    template<typename, class>
        class FactoryErrorPolicy = DefaultFactoryError
>
class CloneFactory;
```

* AbstractProduct is the base class of the hierarchy for which you want to provide the clone factory.
* ProductCreator has the role of duplicating the object received as a parameter and returning a pointer to the clone.
* CloneFactory implements the following primitives:

```
bool Register(const TypeInfo&, ProductCreator creator);
```

Registers a creator with an object of type TypeInfo (which accepts an implicit conversion constructor from std::type_info). Returns true if the registration was successful; false otherwise.

```
bool Unregister(const TypeInfo& typeInfo);
```

Unregisters the creator for the given type. If the type was previously registered, the function returns true.

```
AbstractProduct* CreateObject(const AbstractProduct* model);
```

Looks up the dynamic type of model in the internal map. If it is found, it invokes the corresponding creator for the type identifier and returns its result. If the type identifier is not found, the result of FactoryErrorPolicy<OrderedTypeInfo, AbstractProduct>::OnUnknownType is returned.

9

Abstract Factory

This chapter discusses a generic implementation of the Abstract Factory design pattern (Gamma et al. 1995). An abstract factory is an interface for creating a family of related or dependent polymorphic objects.

Abstract factories can be an important architectural component because they ensure that the right concrete objects are created throughout a system. You don't want a `Funky-Button` to appear on a `ConventionalDialog`; you can use the Abstract Factory design pattern to ensure that a `FunkyButton` can appear only on a `FunkyDialog`. You do this by controlling a small piece of code; the rest of the application works with the abstract types `Dialog` and `Button`.

After reading this chapter, you will

- Understand the area of applicability of the Abstract Factory design pattern
- Know how to define and implement Abstract Factory components
- Know how to use the generic Abstract Factory facility provided by Loki and how to extend it to suit your needs

9.1 The Architectural Role of Abstract Factory

Let's say you are in the enviable position of designing a "find 'em and kill 'em" game, like Doom or Quake.

You want to entice regular taxpayers to enjoy your game, so you provide an Easy level. On the Easy level, the enemy soldiers are rather dull, the monsters move like molasses, and the super-monsters are quite friendly.

You also want to entice hardcore gamers to play your game, so you provide a Diehard level. On this level, enemy soldiers fire three times a second and are karate pros, monsters are cunning and deadly, and really bad super-monsters appear once in a while.

A possible modeling of this scary world would include defining a base class `Enemy` and deriving the refined interfaces `Soldier`, `Monster`, and `SuperMonster` from it. Then, you derive `SillySoldier`, `SillyMonster`, and `SillySuperMonster` from these interfaces for the Easy level. Finally, you implement `BadSoldier`, `BadMonster`, and `BadSuperMonster` for the Diehard level. The resulting inheritance hierarchy is shown in Figure 9.1.

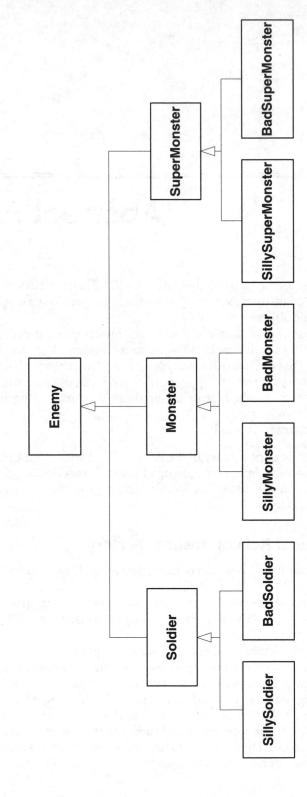

Figure 9.1: A hierarchy for a game with two levels of difficulty

It is worth noting that in your game, an instantiation of BadSoldier and an instantiation of SillyMonster never "live" at the same time. It wouldn't make sense; the player plays either the easy game with SillySoldiers, SillyMonsters, and SillySuperMonsters, or the tough game in the company of BadSoldiers, BadMonsters, and Bad SuperMonsters.

The two categories of types form two families; during the game, you always use objects in one of the two families, but you never combine them.

It would be nice if you could enforce this consistency. Otherwise, if you're not careful enough throughout the application, the beginner happily punching SillySoldiers could suddenly meet a BadMonster around the corner, get whacked, and exercise that money-back guarantee.

Because it's better to be careful once than a hundred times, you gather the creation functions for all the game objects into a single interface, as follows:

```
class AbstractEnemyFactory
{
public:
   virtual Soldier* MakeSoldier() = 0;
   virtual Monster* MakeMonster() = 0;
   virtual SuperMonster* MakeSuperMonster() = 0;
};
```

Then, for each play level, you implement a concrete enemy factory that creates enemies as prescribed by the game strategy.

```
class EasyLevelEnemyFactory : public AbstractEnemyFactory
{
public:
   Soldier* MakeSoldier()
   { return new SillySoldier; }
   Monster* MakeMonster()
   { return new SillyMonster; }
   SuperMonster* MakeSuperMonster()
   { return new SillySuperMonster; }
};

class DieHardLevelEnemyFactory : public AbstractEnemyFactory
{
public:
   Soldier* MakeSoldier()
   { return new BadSoldier; }
   Monster* MakeMonster()
   { return new BadMonster; }
   SuperMonster* MakeSuperMonster()
   { return new BadSuperMonster; }
};
```

Finally, you initialize a pointer to AbstractEnemyFactory with a pointer to an object of appropriate concrete class:

```
class GameApp
{
```

```
    ...
    void SelectLevel()
    {
        if (user chooses the Easy level)
        {
            pFactory_ = new EasyLevelEnemyFactory;
        }
        else
        {
            pFactory_ = new DieHardLevelEnemyFactory;
        }
    }
private:
    // Use pFactory_ to create enemies
    AbstractEnemyFactory* pFactory_;
};
```

The advantage of this design is that it keeps all the details of creating and properly matching enemies inside the two implementations of AbstractEnemyFactory. Because the application uses pFactory_ as the only object creator, consistency is enforced by design. This is a typical usage of the Abstract Factory design pattern.

The Abstract Factory design pattern prescribes collecting creation functions for families of objects in a unique interface. Then you must provide an implementation of that interface for each family of objects you want to create.

The product types advertised by the abstract factory interface (Soldier, Monster, and SuperMonster) are called *abstract products.* The product types that the implementation actually creates (SillySoldier, BadSoldier, SillyMonster, and so on) are called *concrete products.* These terms should be familiar to you from Chapter 8.

The main disadvantage of Abstract Factory is that it is type intensive: The abstract factory base class (AbstractEnemyFactory in the example) must know about every abstract product that's to be created. In addition, at least in the implementation just provided, each concrete factory class depends on the concrete products it creates.

You can reduce dependencies by applying the techniques described in Chapter 8. There, you created a concrete object not by knowing its type but by knowing its type identifier (such as an int or a string). Such a dependency is much weaker.

However, the more you reduce dependencies, the more you also reduce type knowledge, and consequently the more you undermine the type safety of your design. This is yet another instance of the classic dilemma of better type safety versus lesser dependencies that often appears in C++.

As often happens, getting the right solution involves a trade-off between competing benefits. You should choose the setting that best suits your needs. As a rule of thumb, try to go with a static model when you can, and rely on a dynamic model when you must.

The generic implementation of Abstract Factory presented in the following sections sports an interesting feature that reduces static dependencies without compromising type safety.

9.2 A Generic Abstract Factory Interface

As hinted in Chapter 3, the Typelist facility makes implementing generic Abstract Factories a slam-dunk. This section describes how to define a generic AbstractFactory interface with the help of typelists.

The example shown in the previous section is a typical use of the Abstract Factory design pattern. To recap:

- You define an abstract class (the abstract factory class) that has one pure virtual function for each product type. The virtual function corresponding to type T usually returns a T*, and its name is CreateT, MakeT, or something similar.
- You define one or more concrete factories that implement the interface defined by the abstract factory. You implement each member function by creating a new object of a derived type, usually by invoking the new operator.

All this seems simple enough, but as the number of products created by the abstract factory grows, the code becomes less and less maintainable. Furthermore, at any moment you might decide to plug in an implementation that uses a different allocation, or a prototype object.

A generic Abstract Factory would be of help here, but only if it's flexible enough to easily accommodate things such as custom allocators and passing arguments to constructors.

Recall the class template GenScatterHierarchy from Chapter 3. GenScatterHierarchy instantiates a basic template—provided by the user—with each type in a typelist. By its structure, the resulting instantiation of GenScatterHierarchy inherits all the instantiations of the user-provided template. In other words, if you have a template Unit and a typelist TList, GenScatterHierarchy<TList,Unit> is a class that inherits Unit<T> for each type T in TList.

GenScatterHierarchy can be very useful for defining an abstract factory interface   you define an interface that can create objects of one type, and then you apply that interface to multiple types with GenScatterHierarchy.

The "unit" interface, which can create objects of a generic type T, is as follows.

```
template <class T>
class AbstractFactoryUnit
{
public:
   virtual T* DoCreate(Type2Type<T>) = 0;
   virtual ~AbstractFactoryUnit() {}
};
```

This little template looks perfectly kosher—virtual destructor and all[1]—but what's that Type2Type business? Recall from Chapter 2 that Type2Type is a simple template whose unique purpose is to disambiguate overloaded functions. Okay, but then where are those ambiguous functions? AbstractFactoryUnit defines only *one* DoCreate function. There will be several AbstractFactoryUnit instantiations in the same inheritance hierarchy, as you'll see in a moment. The Type2Type<T> helps in disambiguating the various DoCreate overloads generated.

The generic AbstractFactory interface uses GenScatterHierarchy in conjunction with AbstactFactoryUnit, as follows:

---

[1] See Chapter 4 for an extended discussion of virtual destructors.

```
template
<
    class TList,
    template <class> class Unit = AbstractFactoryUnit
>
class AbstractFactory : public GenScatterHierarchy<TList, Unit>
{
public:
    typedef TList ProductList;
    template <class T> T* Create()
    {
        Unit <T>& unit = *this;
        return unit.DoCreate(Type2Type<T>());
    }
};
```

Aha, there's Type2Type in action to make it clear which DoCreate function is called by Create. Let's analyze what happens when you type the following:

```
// Application code
typedef AbstractFactory
<
    TYPELIST_3(Soldier, Monster, SuperMonster)
>
AbstractEnemyFactory;
```

As Chapter 3 explains, the AbstractFactory template generates the hierarchy depicted in Figure 9.2. AbstractEnemyFactory inherits AbstractFactoryUnit<Soldier>, AbstractFactoryUnit<Monster>, and AbstractFactoryUnit<SuperMonster>. Each defines one pure virtual member function DoCreate, so AbstractEnemyFactory has three DoCreate overloads. In a nutshell, AbstractEnemyFactory is pretty much equivalent to the abstract class of the same name defined in the previous section.

The template member function Create of AbstractFactory is a dispatcher that routes the creation request to the appropriate base class:

```
AbstractEnemyFactory* p = ...;
Monster* pOgre = p->Create<Monster>();
```

One important advantage of the automatically generated version is that Abstract-EnemyFactory is a highly *granular* interface. You can automatically convert a reference to an AbstractEnemyFactory to a reference to an AbstractFactoryUnit<Soldier>, Abstract-FactoryUnit<Monster>, or AbstractFactoryUnit<SuperMonster>. This way, you can pass only small subunits of the factory to various parts of your application. For instance, a certain module (Surprises.cpp) needs only to create SuperMonsters. You can communicate to that module in terms of pointers or references to AbstractFactoryUnit<SuperMonster>, so that Surprises.cpp is not coupled with Soldier and Monster.

Using AbstractFactory's granularity, you can reduce the coupling that affects the Abstract Factory design pattern. You gain this decoupling without sacrificing the safety of your abstract factory interface because only the interface, not the implementation, is granular.

This brings us to the implementation of the interface. The second important advantage

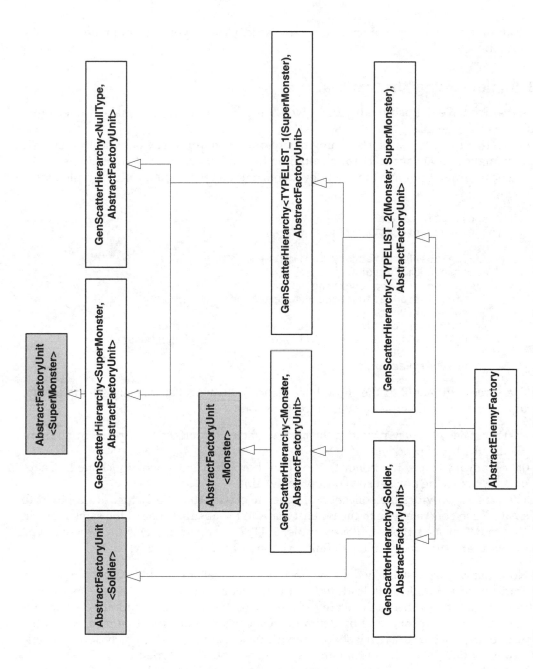

Figure 9.2: The class hierarchy generated for AbstractEnemyFactory

of the automatically generated `AbstractEnemyFactory` is that you can automate the implementation, too.

9.3 Implementing `AbstractFactory`

Now that we have defined the interface, we should look into ways to make implementation as easy as possible.

Given the use of typelists in defining the interface, a natural way of building a generic implementation of `AbstractFactory` would be to employ typelists of concrete products. In practical terms, building the Easy level concrete factory should be as simple as the following:

```
// Application code
typedef ConcreteFactory
<
    // The abstract factory to implement
    AbstractEnemyFactory,
    // The policy for creating objects
    // (for instance, use the new operator)
    OpNewFactoryUnit,
    // The concrete classes that this factory creates
    TYPELIST_3(SillySoldier, SillyMonster, SillySuperMonster)
>
EasyLevelEnemyFactory;
```

The three arguments to the (now hypothetical) `ConcreteFactory` class template are enough information to implement a complete factory:

* `AbstractEnemyFactory` provides the abstract factory interface to implement and, implicitly, the list of products.
* `OpNewFactoryUnit` is the policy that dictates how objects are actually created. (Chapter 1 discusses the policy class concept in detail.)
* The typelist provides the collection of concrete classes that the factory is supposed to create. Each concrete type in the typelist maps to the abstract type of the same index in `AbstractFactory`'s typelist. For example, `SillyMonster` (index 1) is the concrete type for `Monster` (same index in the definition of `AbstractEnemyFactory`).

Now that we have established the synopsis of `ConcreteFactory`, let's figure out how we can implement it. Simple math leads us to the conclusion that there should be as many pure virtual function overrides as there are definitions. (Otherwise we wouldn't be able to instantiate `ConcreteFactory`, and by definition, `ConcreteFactory` must be ready to serve.) Consequently, `ConcreteFactory` should inherit `OpNewFactoryUnit` (which is responsible for implementing `DoCreate`) instantiated with every type in the typelist.

Here the `GenLinearHierarchy` class template, which complements `GenScatterHierarchy` (see Chapter 3), can be of great use because it takes care of all the details of generating the instantiations for us.

`AbstractEnemyFactory` must be the root of the hierarchy. All `DoCreate` implementations and ultimately `EasyLevelEnemyFactory` must derive from it. Each instantiation of

OpNewFactoryUnit overrides one of the three DoCreate pure virtual functions defined by AbstractEnemyFactory.

Let's proceed by defining OpNewFactoryUnit. Obviously, OpNewFactoryUnit is a class template having the type to create as a template parameter. In addition, GenLinear-Hierarchy requires that OpNewFactoryUnit accept an additional template parameter and derive from it. (GenLinearHierarchy uses this second parameter to generate the string-shaped inheritance hierarchy shown in Figure 3.6.)

```
template <class ConcreteProduct, class Base>
class OpNewFactoryUnit : public Base
{
    typedef typename Base::ProductList BaseProductList;
protected:
    typedef typename BaseProductList::Tail ProductList;
public:
    typedef typename BaseProductList::Head AbstractProduct;
    ConcreteProduct* DoCreate(Type2Type<AbstractProduct>)
    {
        return new ConcreteProduct;
    }
};
```

OpNewFactoryUnit must do only some type calculations for figuring out which abstract product to implement.

Each OpNewFactoryUnit instantiation is a component in a food chain. Each OpNew-FactoryUnit instantiation "eats" the head of the product list by overriding the appropriate DoCreate function, and passes the beheaded ProductList down the class hierarchy. Thus, the topmost OpNewFactoryUnit instantiation (the one just below AbstractEnemyFactory) implements DoCreate(Type2Type<Soldier>), and the bottommost OpNewFactoryUnit instantiation implements DoCreate(Type2Type<SuperMonster>).

Let's recap how OpNewFactoryUnit honors its position in the food chain. First, Op-NewFactoryUnit imports the ProductList type from its base class and renames it Base-ProductList. (If you look at AbstractFactory's definition, you'll see that indeed it exports the ProductList type.) The abstract product that OpNewFactoryUnit implements is the head of BaseProductList, hence AbstractProduct's definition. Finally, OpNewFactoryUnit reexports BaseProductList::Tail as ProductList. This way the remaining list is passed down the inheritance hierarchy.

Notice that OpNewFactoryUnit::DoCreate does not return a pointer to Abstract-Product, as its pure counterpart does. Instead, OpNewFactoryUnit::DoCreate returns a pointer to a ConcreteProduct object. Does it still qualify as an implementation of the pure virtual function? The answer is yes, thanks to a C++ language feature called *covariant return types*. C++ allows you to override a function that returns a pointer to a *base* class with a function that returns a pointer to a *derived* class. It makes a lot of sense. With covariant return types, you either know the exact type of the concrete factory and you get maximum type information, or you know only the base type of the factory and you get lesser type information.

ConcreteFactory must generate a hierarchy using GenLinearHierarchy. Its implementation is straightforward:

```
template
<
    class AbstractFact,
    template <class, class> class Creator = OpNewFactoryUnit,
    class TList
>
class ConcreteFactory
    : public GenLinearHierarchy<
        typename TL::Reverse<TList>::Result, Creator, AbstractFact>
{
public:
    typedef typename AbstractFact::ProductList ProductList;
    typedef TList ConcreteProductList;
};
```

The class hierarchy that GenLinearHierarchy generates for ConcreteFactory is shown in Figure 9.3.

There is only one twist: ConcreteFactory must reverse the concrete product list when passing it to GenLinearHierarchy. Why? Well, we have to go back to Figure 3.6, which shows how GenLinearHierarchy generates a hierarchy. GenLinearHierarchy distributes types in the typelist to its Unit template argument from the bottom up; the first element in the typelist is passed to the Unit instantiation that's at the bottom of the class hierarchy. However, OpNewFactoryUnit implements the DoCreate overloads in a top-down fashion. In conclusion, ConcreteFactory reverses the typelist TList using the TL::Reverse compile-time algorithm (see Chapter 3) before passing it to GenLinearHierarchy.

If, at this point, you still find AbstractFactory and ConcreteFactory a bit confusing or too complicated, take heart. It is because the two class templates make nonchalant use of typelists. Typelists themselves are likely a new concept to you, and it will take some time to get used to them. If you think of typelists as a black-box concept—"typelists are to types what regular lists are to values"—the implementations in this chapter are very simple. And once you *truly* get used to typelists, the sky's the limit. Unconvinced? Read on.

9.4 A Prototype-Based Abstract Factory Implementation

The Prototype design pattern (Gamma et al. 1995) describes a method for creating objects starting from a *prototype,* an archetypal object. You obtain new objects by cloning the prototype. And the gist of it all is that the cloning function is virtual.

As Chapter 8 discusses in detail, the essential problem in creating polymorphic objects is the *virtual constructor dilemma:* Creation from scratch requires knowledge about the type of object being created, yet polymorphism fosters *not* knowing the exact type.

The Prototype pattern avoids the dilemma by using a prototype object. If you have one object—a prototype—you can take advantage of virtual functions. The virtual constructor dilemma still applies to the prototype itself, but it's much more localized.

A prototype-based approach to building enemies for the game in our example would

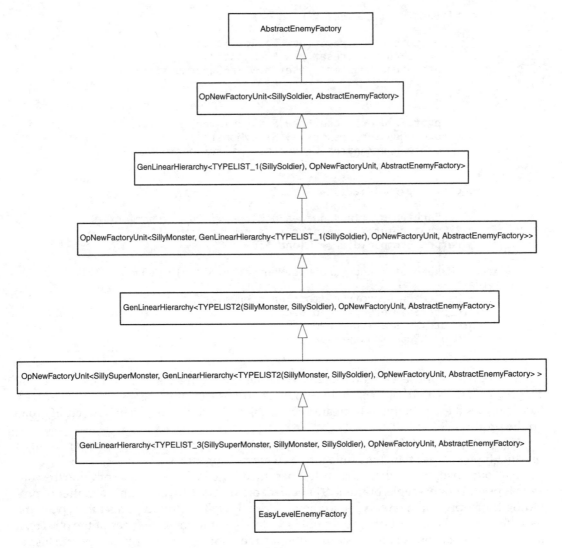

Figure 9.3: The class hierarchy generated for EasyLevelEnemyFactory

prescribe holding pointers to the base classes Soldier, Monster, and SuperMonster. Then we would write code like the following:[2]

```
class GameApp
{
    ...
    void SelectLevel()
    {
```

[2] Warning—this code has trouble with exception safety. Fixing it is left as an exercise for the reader.

```
        if (user chooses Diehard level)
        {
            protoSoldier_.reset(new BadSoldier);
            protoMonster_.reset(new BadMonster);
            protoSuperMonster_.reset(new BadSuperMonster);
        }
        else
        {
            protoSoldier_.reset(new SillySoldier);
            protoMonster_.reset(new SillyMonster);
            protoSuperMonster_.reset(new SillySuperMonster);
        }
    }
    Soldier* MakeSoldier()
    {
        // Each enemy class defines a Clone virtual function
        // that returns a pointer to a new object
        return protoSoldier_->Clone();
    }
    ... MakeMonster and MakeSuperMonster similarly defined ...
private:
    // Use these prototypes to create enemies
    auto_ptr<Soldier> protoSoldier_;
    auto_ptr<Monster> protoMonster_;
    auto_ptr<SuperMonster> protoSuperMonster_;
};
```

Of course, real-world code would better separate the interface and the implementation. The basic idea is that GameApp holds pointers to base enemy classes—the prototypes. GameApp uses these prototypes to create enemy objects by calling the virtual function Clone on the prototypes.

A prototype-based Abstract Factory implementation would collect a pointer for each product type and use the Clone function to create new products.

In a ConcreteFactory that uses prototypes, there's no longer a need to provide the concrete types. In our example, building SillySoldiers or BadSoldiers is only a matter of providing the appropriate prototypes to the factory object. The prototype's static type is the base (Soldier) class. The factory does not have to know the concrete types of the objects; it just calls the Clone virtual member function for the appropriate prototype object. This reduces the concrete factory's dependency on the concrete types.

For the GenLinearHierarchy expansion mechanism to work correctly, however, there has to be a typelist. Recall ConcreteFactory's declaration:

```
template
<
    class AbstractFact,
    template <class, class> class Creator,
    class TList
>
class ConcreteFactory;
```

TList is the concrete product list. In the EasyLevelEnemyFactory, TList was TYPE-LIST_3(SillySoldier,SillyMonster,SillySuperMonster). If we use the Prototype design pattern, TList becomes irrelevant. However, GenLinearHierarchy needs TList for generating one class for each product in the abstract product list. What to do?

In this case, a natural solution is to pass ConcreteFactory the *abstract product list* as the TList argument. Now GenLinearHierarchy generates the right number of classes, and there's no need to change ConcreteFactory's implementation.

ConcreteFactory's declaration now becomes

```
template
<
    class AbstractFact,
    template <class, class> class Creator,
    class TList = typename AbstractFact::ProductList
>
class ConcreteFactory;
```

(Recall from AbstractFactory's definition in Section 9.2 that it defines the inner type ProductList.)

Let's now implement PrototypeFactoryUnit, the unit template that holds the prototype and calls Clone. The implementation is straightforward and is actually simpler than OpNew-FactoryUnit. This is because OpNewFactoryUnit had to maintain *two* typelists (the abstract products and the concrete products), whereas PrototypeFactoryUnit deals only with the abstract product list.

```
template <class /*AbstractProduct*/, class Base>
class PrototypeFactoryUnit : public Base
{
    typedef typename Base::ProductList BaseProductList;
protected:
    typedef typename Base::ProductList::Tail ProductList;
public:
    typedef typename Base::ProductList::Head AbstractProduct;
    PrototypeFactoryUnit(AbstractProduct* p = 0)
        :pPrototype_(p)
    {}
    friend void DoGetPrototype(const PrototypeFactoryUnit& me,
        AbstractProduct*& pPrototype)
    {
        pPrototype = me.pPrototype_;
    }
    friend void DoSetPrototype(PrototypeFactoryUnit& me,
        AbstractProduct* pObj)
    {
        me.pPrototype_=pObj;
    }
    template <class U>
    void GetPrototype(U*& p)
    {
        return DoGetPrototype(*this, p);
    }
    template <class U>
    void SetPrototype(U* pObj)
    {
```

```
        DoSetPrototype(*this, pObj);
    }
    AbstractProduct* DoCreate(Type2Type<AbstractProduct>)
    {
        assert(pPrototype_);
        return pPrototype_->Clone();
    }
private:
    AbstractProduct* pPrototype_;
};
```

The PrototypeFactoryUnit class template makes some assumptions that may or may not apply to your concrete situation. First, PrototypeFactoryUnit doesn't own its prototype; sometimes, you might want SetPrototype to delete the old prototype before reassigning it. Second, PrototypeFactoryUnit uses a Clone function that supposedly clones the product. In your application you might use a different name, either because you are constrained by another library or because you prefer another naming convention.

If you need to customize your prototype-based factory, you need only write a template similar to PrototypeFactoryUnit. You can inherit PrototypeFactoryUnit and override only the functions you want. For example, say you want to implement DoCreate so that it returns a null pointer if the prototype pointer is null.

```
template <class AbstractProduct, class Base>
class MyFactoryUnit
    : public PrototypeFactoryUnit<AbstractProduct, Base>
{
public:
    // Implement DoCreate so that it accepts a null prototype
    // pointer
    AbstractProduct* DoCreate(Type2Type<AbstractProduct>)
    {
        return pPrototype_ ? pPrototype_->Clone() : 0;
    }
};
```

Let's get back to our game example. To define a concrete prototype-based factory, all you have to write in the application code is the following:

```
// Application code
typedef ConcreteFactory
<
    AbstractEnemyFactory,
    PrototypeFactoryUnit
>
EnemyFactory;
```

To conclude, the AbstractFactory/ConcreteFactory duo offers you the following features:

- You can easily define factories with the help of typelists.
- Because AbstractFactory inherits each of its units, the interface is very granular. You can pass individual "creator units" (pointers or references to AbstractFactoryUnit<T> subobjects) to different modules, thus reducing coupling.

- You can use `ConcreteFactory` to implement the `AbstractFactory` by providing a policy template that dictates the creation method. For statically bound creation policies (such as `OpNewFactoryUnit`, which uses the `new` operator), you need to pass the typelist of concrete products that the factory creates.
- A popular creation policy is to apply the Prototype design pattern; you can easily use Prototype with `ConcreteFactory` by using the canned `PrototypeFactoryUnit` class template.

Try to obtain all these benefits with a handcrafted implementation of the Abstract Factory design pattern.

9.5 Summary

The Abstract Factory design pattern fosters an interface for creating a family of related or dependent polymorphic objects. Using Abstract Factory, you can divide implementation classes into disjoint families.

It is possible to implement a generic abstract factory interface by using typelists and policy templates. The typelists provide the product list (both concrete and abstract) and the policy templates.

The `AbstractFactory` class template provides a skeleton for defining abstract factories and works in conjunction with the `AbstractFactoryUnit` class template. `AbstractFactory` requires a user-provided abstract product typelist. Internally, `AbstractFactory` uses `GenScatter-Hierarchy` (see Chapter 3) to generate a granular interface that inherits `AbstractFactoryUnit<T>` for each product T in the abstract product typelist. This structure gives you the opportunity to reduce coupling by passing only individual factory units to various parts of an application.

The `ConcreteFactory` template helps with implementing the `AbstractFactory` interface. `ConcreteFactory` uses a FactoryUnit policy for creating objects. Internally, `Concrete Factory` uses `GenLinearHierarchy` (see Chapter 3). Loki provides two predefined implementations of the FactoryUnit policy: `OpNewFactoryUnit`, which creates objects by calling the `new` operator, and `PrototypeFactoryUnit`, which creates objects by cloning a prototype.

9.6 `AbstractFactory` and `ConcreteFactory` Quick Facts

- `AbstractFactory` synopsis:

```
template
<
    class TList,
    template <class> class Unit = AbstractFactoryUnit
>
class AbstractFactory;
```

where `TList` is the typelist of abstract products that the factory creates, and `Unit` is the template that defines the interface for each type in `TList`. For example,

```
typedef AbstractFactory<TYPELIST_3(Soldier, Monster, SuperMonster)>
    AbstractEnemyFactory;
```

defines an abstract factory capable of creating `Soldier`s, `Monster`s, and `Super-Monster`s.

- AbstractFactoryUnit<T> defines an interface consisting of a pure virtual function with the signature T* DoCreate(Type2Type<T>). Usually you don't call DoCreate directly; instead, you use AbstractFactory::Create.

- AbstractFactory exposes a Create template function. You can instantiate Create with any of the types of the abstract products. For example:

```
AbstractEnemyFactory *pFactory = ...;
Soldier *pSoldier = pFactory->Create<Soldier>();
```

- For implementing the interface that AbstractFactory defines, Loki provides the ConcreteFactory template. ConcreteFactory's synopsis is

```
template
<
    class AbstractFact,
    template <class, class> class FactoryUnit = OpNewFactoryUnit,
    class TList = AbstractFact::ProductList
>
class ConcreteFactory;
```

where AbstractFact is the instantiation of AbstractFactory that is to be implemented, FactoryUnit is the implementation of the FactoryUnit creation policy, and TList is the typelist of concrete products.

- The FactoryUnit policy implementation has access to both the abstract product and the concrete product that it must create. Loki defines two Creator policies: OpNew-FactoryUnit (Section 9.3) and PrototypeFactoryUnit (Section 9.4). They can also serve as examples for implementing custom implementations of the FactoryUnit policy.

- OpNewFactoryUnit uses the new operator for creating objects. If you use OpNewFactory-Unit, you must provide a concrete product typelist as the third parameter to Concrete-Factory. For example:

```
typedef ConcreteFactory
<
    AbstractEnemyFactory,
    OpNewFactoryUnit,
    TYPELIST_3(SillySoldier, SillyMonster, SillySuperMonster)
>
EasyLevelEnemyFactory;
```

- PrototypeFactoryUnit stores pointers to abstract product types and creates new objects by calling the Clone member function of their respective prototypes. This implies that PrototypeFactoryUnit requires each abstract product T to define a virtual member function Clone that returns a T* and whose semantics is to duplicate the object.

- When using PrototypeFactoryUnit with ConcreteFactory, you don't provide the third template argument to ConcreteFactory. For example:

```
typedef ConcreteFactory
<
    AbstractEnemyFactory,
    PrototypeFactoryUnit
>
EnemyFactory;
```

10

Visitor

This chapter discusses generic components that use the Visitor design pattern (Gamma et al. 1995). Visitor is a powerful—if controversial—design pattern that changes the dependency trade-offs involved in class design.

Visitor gives you a surprising amount of flexibility in a certain area: You can add virtual functions to a class hierarchy without recompiling them or their existing clients. However, this flexibility comes at the expense of disabling features that designers take for granted: You cannot add a new leaf class to the hierarchy without recompiling the hierarchy and all its clients. Therefore, Visitor's operational area is limited to very stable hierarchies (you seldom add new classes) and heavy processing needs (you often add new virtual functions).

Visitor goes against programmers' intuition; therefore, a careful implementation and rigorous discipline are essential to using it successfully. This chapter's goal is to craft a dependable generic implementation of Visitor that leaves as little burden on the application programmer as possible.

After reading this chapter, you will

- Understand how Visitor works
- Know when to apply the Visitor pattern and, equally important, when not to
- Understand the basic implementation of a visitor (the GoF implementation)
- Know how to overcome some drawbacks of the GoF Visitor implementation
- Learn how most of the decisions that pertain to implementing Visitor can be moved up to a library
- Be armed with powerful generic components that will help you greatly in implementing visitors that specifically solve your problems

10.1 Visitor Basics

Let's consider a class hierarchy whose functionality you want to enhance. To do this, you can either add new classes or add new virtual member functions.

Adding new classes is easy. You derive from a class and implement the needed virtual functions. You don't need to change or recompile any existing classes. It's code reuse at its best.

In contrast, adding new virtual functions is difficult. To be able to manipulate objects polymorphically (via pointers to the root class), you must add virtual member functions to the root class, and possibly to many other classes in the hierarchy. This is a major operation. It modifies the root class on which all the hierarchy and clients are dependent. As the ultimate result, you have to recompile the world.

In a nutshell, from a dependency standpoint, new classes are easy to add, and new virtual member functions are difficult to add.

But suppose that you have a hierarchy to which you seldom add new classes, but to which you often need to add virtual member functions. In this case, you have an advantage that you don't need, namely, the ease of adding classes. You also have a drawback that's annoying, namely, the difficulty of adding new virtual member functions. Here's where Visitor can be of help. Visitor trades the advantage you don't care about for an advantage you need. Visitor enables you to add new virtual functions to a hierarchy easily, while also making it more difficult to add new classes. The runtime cost of this wizardry is at least an extra virtual call, as you will see.

Visitor applies best when operations on objects are distinct and unrelated. The "state and operations" paradigm for each class becomes of little relevance. A view that *separates* types from operations is more appropriate. For such cases, it makes more sense to keep various implementations of a conceptual operation together, rather than spread them over the class hierarchy.

Suppose, for example, that you develop a document editor. Document elements such as paragraphs, vector drawings, and bitmaps are represented as classes derived from a common root, say, `DocElement`. The document is a structured collection of pointers to `DocElement`s. You need to iterate through this structure and perform operations such as spell checking, reformatting, and statistics gathering. In an ideal world, you should implement those operations mostly by adding code, not by modifying existing code. Furthermore, you ease maintenance if you put all the code pertaining to, say, getting document statistics in one place.

Document statistics may include the number of characters, nonblank characters, words, and images. These would naturally belong to a class called `DocStats`.

```cpp
class DocStats
{
    unsigned int
        chars_,
        nonBlankChars_,
        words_,
        images_;
    ...
public:
    void AddChars(unsigned int charsToAdd)
    {
        chars_ += charsToAdd;
    }
    ...similarly defined AddWords, AddImages...
    // Display the statistics to the user in a dialog box
    void Display();
};
```

If you used a classic object-oriented approach to grabbing statistics, you would define a virtual function in DocElement that deals with gathering statistics.

```
class DocElement
{
    ...
    // This member function helps the "Statistics" feature
    virtual void UpdateStats(DocStats& statistics) = 0;
};
```

Then each concrete document element would define the function in its own way. For example, class Paragraph and class RasterBitmap, which are derived from DocElement, would implement UpdateStats as follows:

```
void Paragraph::UpdateStats(DocStats& statistics)
{
    statistics.AddChars(number of characters in the paragraph);
    statistics.AddWords(number of words in the paragraph);
}

void RasterBitmap::UpdateStats(DocStats& statistics)
{
    // A raster bitmap counts as one image
    // and nothing else (no characters etc.)
    statistics.AddImages(1);
}
```

Finally, the driver function would look like this:

```
void Document::DisplayStatistics()
{
    DocStats statistics;
    for (each DocElement in the document)
    {
        element->UpdateStats(statistics);
    }
    statistics.Display();
}
```

This is a fairly good implementation of the Statistics feature, but it has a number of disadvantages.

- It requires DocElement and its derivees to have access to the DocStats definition. Consequently, every time you modify DocStats, you must recompile the whole DocElement hierarchy.
- The actual operations of gathering statistics are spread throughout the UpdateStats implementations. A maintainer debugging or enhancing the Statistics feature must search and edit multiple files.
- The implementation technique does not scale with respect to adding other operations that are similar to gathering statistics. To add an operation such as "increase font size

by one point," you will have to add another virtual function to DocElement (and suffer all of the hassles that this implies).

A solution that breaks the dependency of DocElement on DocStats is to move all operations into the DocStats class and let it figure out what to do for each concrete type. This implies that DocStats has a member function void UpdateStats(DocElement&). The document then simply iterates through its elements and calls UpdateStats for each of them.

This solution effectively makes DocStats invisible to DocElement. However, now DocStats depends on each concrete DocElement that it needs to process. If the object hierarchy is more stable than its operations, the dependency is not very annoying. Now the problem is that the implementation of UpdateStats has to rely on the so-called *type switch*. A type switch occurs whenever you query a polymorphic object on its concrete type and perform different operations with it depending on what that concrete type is. DocStats::UpdateStats is bound to do such a type switch, as in the following:

```
void DocStats::UpdateStats(DocElement& elem)
{
    if (Paragraph* p = dynamic_cast<Paragraph*>(&elem))
    {
        chars_ += p->NumChars();
        words_ += p->NumWords();
    }
    else if (dynamic_cast<RasterBitmap*>(&elem))
    {
        ++images_;
    }
    else ...
    add one 'if' statement for each type of object you inspect
}
```

(The definition of p inside the if test is legal because of a little-known addition to C++. You can define and test a variable right in an if statement. The lifetime of that variable extends to that if statement and its else part, if any. Although it's not an essential feature and writing cute code per se is not recommended, the feature was invented especially to support type switches, so why not reap the benefits?)

Whenever you see something like this, a mental alarm bell should go off. Type switching is not at all a desirable solution. (Chapter 8 presents a detailed argument.) Code that relies on type switching is hard to understand, hard to extend, and hard to maintain. It's also open to insidious bugs. For example, what if you put the dynamic_cast for a base class before the dynamic_cast for a derived class? The first test will match derived objects, so the second one will never succeed. One of the goals of polymorphism is to eliminate type switches because of all the problems they have.

Here's where the Visitor pattern can be helpful. You need new functions to act virtual, but you don't want to add a new virtual function for each operation. To effect this, you must implement a *unique bouncing virtual function* in the DocElement hierarchy, a function that "teleports" work to a different hierarchy. The DocElement hierarchy is called the *visited* hierarchy, and the operations belong to a new *visitor* hierarchy.

Each implementation of the bouncing virtual function calls a *different* function in the visitor hierarchy. That's how visited types are selected. The functions in the visitor hierarchy called by the bouncing function are virtual. That's how operations are selected.

Following are a few lines of code to illustrate this idea. First, we define an abstract class DocElementVisitor that defines an operation for each type of object in the DocElement hierarchy.

```
class DocElementVisitor
{
public:
   virtual void VisitParagraph(Paragraph&) = 0;
   virtual void VisitRasterBitmap(RasterBitmap&) = 0;
   ... other similar functions ...
};
```

Next we add the bouncing virtual function, called Accept, to the class DocElement hierarchy, one that takes a DocElementVisitor& and invokes the appropriate VisitXxx function on its parameter.

```
class DocElement
{
public:
   virtual void Accept(DocElementVisitor&) = 0;
   ...
};

void Paragraph::Accept(DocElementVisitor& v)
{
   v.VisitParagraph(*this);
}

void RasterBitmap::Accept(DocElementVisitor& v)
{
   v.VisitRasterBitmap(*this);
}
```

Now here's DocStats in all its splendor:

```
class DocStats : public DocElementVisitor
{
public:
   virtual void VisitParagraph(Paragraph& par)
   {
      chars_ += par.NumChars();
      words_ += par.NumWords();
   }
   virtual void VisitRasterBitmap(RasterBitmap&)
   {
      ++images_;
   }
   ...
};
```

(Of course, a real-world implementation would likely pull out the functions' implementations from the class definition to a separate source file.)

This small example also illustrates a drawback of Visitor: You don't really add virtual member functions. True virtual functions have full access to the object for which they're defined, whereas from inside `VisitParagraph` you can access only the public part of `Paragraph`.

The driver function `Document::DisplayStatistics` creates a `DocStats` object and invokes `Accept` on each `DocElement`, passing that `DocStats` object as a parameter. As the `DocStats` object visits various concrete `DocElements`, it gets nicely filled up with the appropriate data—no type switching needed!

```
void Document::DisplayStatistics()
{
    DocStats statistics;
    for (each DocElement in the document)
    {
        element->Accept(statistics);
    }
    statistics.Display();
}
```

Let's analyze the resulting context. We have added a new hierarchy, rooted in `DocElementVisitor`. This is a *hierarchy of operations*—each of its classes is actually an operation, like `DocStats`. Adding a new operation becomes as easy as deriving a new class from `DocElementVisitor`. No element of the `DocElement` hierarchy needs to be changed.

For instance, let's add a new operation, `IncrementFontSize`, as a helper in implementing an Increase Font Size hot key or toolbar button.

```
class IncrementFontSize : public DocElementVisitor
{
public:
    virtual void VisitParagraph(Paragraph& par)
    {
        par.SetFontSize(par.GetFontSize() + 1);
    }
    virtual void VisitRasterBitmap(RasterBitmap&)
    {
        // nothing to do
    }
    ...
};
```

That's it. No change to the `DocElement` class hierarchy is needed, and there is no change to the other operations. You just add a new class. `DocElement::Accept` bounces `IncrementFontSize` objects just as well as it bounces `DocStats` objects. The resulting class structure is represented in Figure 10.1.

Recall that, by default, new classes are easy to add, whereas new virtual member functions are not easy. We transformed classes into functions by bouncing back from the `DocElement` hierarchy to the `DocElementVisitor` hierarchy; thus, `DocElementVisitor`'s derivatives are objectified functions. This is how the Visitor design pattern works.

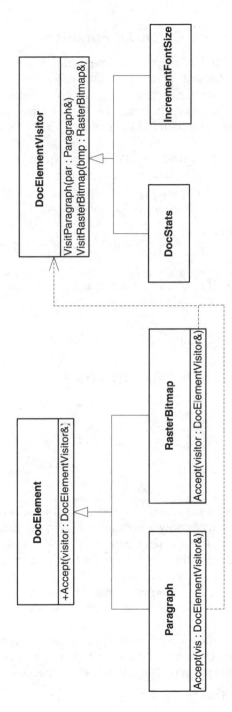

Figure 10.1: The visitor and visited hierarchies, and how operations are teleported

10.2 Overloading and the Catch-All Function

Although not germane to the Visitor pattern, leveraging C++ overloading (or not) has a tremendous impact on implementing designs that use Visitor.

In `DocElementVisitor`, we defined one member function per type visited: `Visit-Paragraph(Paragraph&)`, `VisitRasterBitmap(RasterBitmap&)`, and so on. These functions foster a kind of redundancy. The name of the element visited is also encoded in the function name.

Usually it's best to avoid redundancy. We can get rid of it by leveraging C++ overloading. We simply name all the functions `Visit` and leave it to the compiler to figure out which overload of `Visit` to call based on the type of the parameter passed to it. So an alternative `DocElementVisitor` definition looks like this:

```
class DocElementVisitor
{
public:
    virtual void Visit(Paragraph&) = 0;
    virtual void Visit(RasterBitmap&) = 0;
    ... other similar functions ...
};
```

It also becomes simpler to define all the `Accept` member functions. They now exhibit a nice uniformity.

```
void Paragraph::Accept(DocElementVisitor& v)
{
    v.Visit(*this);
}

void RasterBitmap::Accept(DocElementVisitor& v)
{
    v.Visit(*this);
}
```

They look so similar that you might be tempted to factor them out in the base class `DocElement`. Wrong. The similarity is only a mirage. Actually, the functions are quite different: The static type of `*this` in `Paragraph::Accept` is `Paragraph&`, and in `RasterBitmap::Accept` it's `RasterBitmap&`. It is this static type that helps the compiler figure out which overload of `DocElementVisitor::Visit` to call. If you implement `Accept` in `DocElement`, the static type of `*this` would be `DocElement&`, which doesn't provide the compiler with the needed type information. So base class factoring is not an option. It actually invalidates our design.

Using overloading introduces an interesting idea. Let's assume that all `DocElement` derivatives implement `Accept` by simply bouncing to `DocElementVisitor::Visit`. Then we can provide `DocElementVisitor` with the following catch-all overload.

```
class DocElementVisitor
{
public:
    ... as above ...
```

```
    virtual void Visit(DocElement&) = 0;
};
```

When will this overload be called? If you directly derive a new class from DocElement and don't provide an appropriate Visit overload for it in DocElementVisitor, then over-loading rules and automatic derived-to-base conversions come into play. The reference to the unknown class will be automatically converted to a reference to the DocElement base class, and the catch-all member function will be called. If you don't put the catch-all in there, you'll get a compile-time error. Whether you prefer this way or the other depends on the concrete situation.

You can do a lot of things inside the catch-all overload. Refer, for example, to John Vlissides' work (Vlissides 1998, 1999). You can take contingency measures, do something very generic, or fall back to a type switch (hack by using dynamic_cast) to find out the ac-tual type of the DocElement.

10.3 An Implementation Refinement: The Acyclic Visitor

So you have decided to use Visitor. Let's get pragmatic. In a real-life project, how should you organize the code?

A dependency analysis of the earlier example reveals the following:

* For the DocElement class definition to compile, it must know about the DocElement-Visitor because DocElementVisitor appears in the DocElement::Accept member function signature. A forward declaration would suffice.
* For the DocElementVisitor class definition to compile, it has to know about *all* the con-crete classes (at least) in the DocElement hierarchy because the class names appear in DocElementVisitor's Visit*Xxx* member functions.

This type of dependency is called a *cyclic dependency*. Cyclic dependencies are well-known maintenance bottlenecks. DocElement needs DocElementVisitor, and DocElement-Visitor needs all of DocElement's hierarchy. Consequently, DocElement depends on its own subclasses. Actually, this is a *cyclic name dependency*; that is, the class definitions de-pend only on their *names* in order to compile. Thus, a sensible division of classes into files would look like this:

```
// File DocElementVisitor.h
class DocElement;
class Paragraph;
class RasterBitmap;
... forward declarations for all DocElement derivatives ...

class DocElementVisitor
{
public:
   virtual void VisitParagraph(Paragraph&) = 0;
...
};
```

```
// File DocElement.h
class DocElementVisitor;

class DocElement
{
public:
    virtual void Accept(DocElementVisitor&) = 0;
    ...
};
```

Furthermore, each one-line `Accept` implementation needs the definition of `DocElement-Visitor`, and each concrete visitor has to include its classes of interest. All this leads to an intricate map of dependencies.

What becomes *really* cumbersome is adding new derivatives to `DocElements`. But hold on, we're not supposed to add any new elements to the `DocElement` hierarchy. Visitor applies best to stable hierarchies to which you want to add operations without touching them. Recall, however, that Visitor can do this for you at the expense of making it hard to add derivatives to the visited hierarchy (in our example, the hierarchy rooted in `DocElement`).

But life is change. Let's face it, here on Earth, there's no such thing as a stable hierarchy. Occasionally you *will* have to add a new class to the `DocElement` hierarchy. For the previous example, here's what you must do to add a class `VectorGraphic` derived from `DocElement`:

- Go to `DocElementVisitor.h` and add a new forward declaration for `VectorGraphic`.
- Add a new pure overload to `DocElementVisitor`, as follows:

    ```
    class DocElementVisitor
    {
        ... as before ...
        virtual void VisitVectorGraphic(VectorGraphic&) = 0;
    };
    ```

- Go to every concrete visitor and implement `VisitVectorGraphic`. Depending on the task, the function can be a do-nothing function. Alternatively, you can define `DocElementVisitor::VisitVectorGraphic` as a do-nothing, as opposed to a pure virtual function, but in this case, the compiler won't remind you if you don't implement it in concrete visitors.
- Implement `Accept` in the `VectorGraphic` class. *Don't forget to do this.* If you derive directly from `DocElement` and forget to implement `Accept`, there's no problem—you'll get a compile-time error. But if you derive from another class, such as `Graphic`, and if that class defines `Accept`, the compiler won't utter a word about your forgetting to make `VectorGraphic` visitable. This bug won't be detected until runtime, when you notice that your Visitor framework refuses to call any implementation of `VisitVectorGraphic`. Quite a nasty bug to deal with.

Corollary: All of the `DocElement` and `DocElementVisitor` hierarchies will be recompiled, and you need to add a considerable amount of mechanical code, all simply to keep things working. Depending on the size of the project, this requirement could range from being annoying to being totally unacceptable.

Robert Martin (1996) invented an interesting variation of the Visitor pattern that leverages dynamic_cast to eliminate cyclicity. His approach defines a strawman base class, BaseVisitor, for the visitor hierarchy. BaseVisitor is only a carrier of type information. It doesn't have any content; therefore, it is totally decoupled. The visited hierarchy's Accept member function accepts a reference to BaseVisitor and applies dynamic_cast against it to detect a matching visitor. If Accept finds a match, it jumps from the visited hierarchy to the visitor hierarchy.

This might sound weird at first, but it's very simple. Let's see how we can implement an acyclic visitor for our DocElement/DocElementVisitor design. First, we define a visitor archetypal base class, the strawman.

```
class DocElementVisitor
{
public:
   virtual ~DocElementVisitor() {}
};
```

The do-nothing virtual destructor does two important things. First, it gives Doc-ElementVisitor RTTI (runtime type information) capabilities. (Only types with at least one virtual function support dynamic_cast.) Second, the virtual destructor ensures correct polymorphic destruction of DocElementVisitor objects. A polymorphic hierarchy without virtual destructors engenders undefined behavior if a derived object is destroyed via a pointer to a base object. Thus, we nicely solve two dangerous problems with one line of code.

The DocElement class definition remains the same. Of interest to us is its definition of the Accept(DocElementVisitor&) pure virtual function.

Then, for each derived class in the visited hierarchy (the one rooted in DocElement), we define a small visiting class that has only one function, Visit*Xxxx*. For instance, for Paragraph, we define the following:

```
class ParagraphVisitor
{
public:
   virtual void VisitParagraph(Paragraph&) = 0;
};
```

The Paragraph::Accept implementation looks like this:

```
void Paragraph::Accept(DocElementVisitor& v)
{
   if (ParagraphVisitor* p =
      dynamic_cast<ParagraphVisitor*>(&v))
   {
      p->VisitParagraph(*this);
   }
   else
```

```
    {
        optionally call a catch-all function
    }
}
```

The prima donna here is dynamic_cast, which enables the runtime system to figure out whether v is actually a subobject of an object that also implements ParagraphVisitor and, if so, to obtain a pointer to that ParagraphVisitor.

RasterBitmap and the other DocElement-derived classes define similar implementations of Accept. Finally, a concrete visitor derives from DocElementVisitor and the archetypal visitors of all classes that are of interest to it. For instance:

```
class DocStats :
    public DocElementVisitor,   // Required
    public ParagraphVisitor,    // Wants to visit Paragraph objects
    public RasterBitmapVisitor  // Wants to visit RasterBitmap
                                // objects
{
public:
    void VisitParagraph(Paragraph& par)
    {
        chars_ += par.NumChars();
        words_ += par.NumWords();
    }
    void VisitRasterBitmap(RasterBitmap&)
    {
        ++images_;
    }
};
```

The resulting class structure is presented in Figure 10.2. The horizontal dotted lines depict dependency layers, and the vertical ones depict the insulation between hierarchies. Notice how dynamic_cast provides the means to jump magically from one hierarchy to the other by leveraging the strawman DocElementVisitor class.

The described structure encompasses a lot of details and interactions. However, the basic structure is simple. Let's recap everything by analyzing an event flow. We assume that we have a pointer, pDocElem, to a DocElement whose dynamic ("real") type is Paragraph. Then we do the following:

```
DocStats stats;
pDocElem->Accept(stats);
```

The following events happen, in order.

1. The stats object is automatically converted to a reference to DocElementVisitor because it inherits this class publicly.
2. The virtual function Paragraph::Accept is called.
3. Paragraph::Accept attempts a dynamic_cast<ParagraphVisitor*> against the address of the DocElementVisitor object that it received. Because that object's dynamic type is

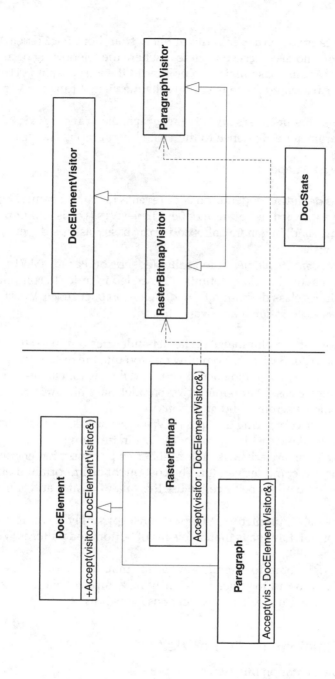

Figure 10.2: Class structure for an acyclic visitor

DocStats and because DocStats inherits publicly from both DocElementVisitor and ParagraphVisitor, the cast succeeds. (Here is where the teleporting occurs!)

4. Now Paragraph::Accept has obtained a pointer to the ParagraphVisitor part of the DocStats object. Paragraph::Accept will invoke the virtual function VisitParagraph on that pointer.

5. The virtual call reaches DocStats::VisitParagraph. DocStats::VisitParagraph also receives as its parameter a reference to the visited paragraph. The visit is completed.

Let's examine the new dependency chart.

- DocElement's class definition depends on DocElementVisitor by name. Dependency by name means that a forward declaration of DocElementVisitor is enough.
- ParagraphVisitor—and, in general, all *Xxx*Visitor base classes—depends by name on the classes that it visits.
- The Paragraph::Accept implementation fully depends on ParagraphVisitor. Full dependency means that the full class definition is needed in order to compile the code.
- Any concrete visitor's class definition fully depends on DocElementVisitor and on all of the base visitors *Xxx*Visitor that it wants to visit.

The Acyclic Visitor pattern eliminates cyclic dependencies but in exchange leaves you with even more work to do. Basically, from now on, you must maintain *two* parallel sets of classes: the visited hierarchy rooted in DocElement; and the visitor classes *Xxx*Visitor, one for each concrete visited class. Maintaining two parallel class hierarchies is not desirable because it requires much discipline and attention.

A note on efficiency in comparing the "plain" Visitor with the Acyclic Visitor: In the latter, there's one extra dynamic cast in the path. Its cost in time might be constant or might increase logarithmically or linearly with the number of polymorphic classes in the program, depending on your compiler vendor. The cost might be important if efficiency is an issue. So in some cases you might be forced to use the "plain" Visitor and to maintain cyclic dependencies.

Because of this overall grim picture, Visitor is, unsurprisingly, a controversial pattern. Even Erich Gamma of GoF fame says that on his list of bottom-ten patterns, Visitor is at the very bottom (Vlissides 1999).

Visitor is clumsy, rigid, hard to extend, and hard to maintain. However, with perseverance and diligence we can put together a Visitor library implementation that is win-win: easy to use, extend, and maintain. The next sections show how.

10.4 A Generic Implementation of Visitor

Let's divide the implementation into two major units:

- *Visitable classes.* These are the classes belonging to the hierarchy that we want to visit (add operations to).
- *Visitor classes.* These classes define and implement the actual operations.

Table 10.1: Component Names

Name	Belongs To	Represents
BaseVisitable	Library	The root of all hierarchies that can be visited
Visitable	Library	A mix-in class that confers visitable properties to a class in the visitable hierarchy
DocElement	Application	A sample class—the root of the hierarchy we want to make visitable
Paragraph, RasterBitmap	Application	Two sample visitable concrete classes, derived from DocElement
Accept	Library and application	The member function that's called for visiting the visitable hierarchy
BaseVisitor	Library	The root of the visitor hierarchy
Visitor	Library	A mix-in class that confers visitor properties to a class in the visitor hierarchy
Statistics	Application	A sample visitor concrete class
Visit	Library and application	The member function that is called back by the visitable elements, for its visitors

The approach is simple and consistent: We try to factor out as much code as possible into the library. If we succeed in doing that, we will be rewarded with simplified dependencies. That is, instead of the two parts—visitor and visitable—depending on each other, both will depend on the library. This is good because the library is supposed to be much more immutable than the application.

We first try to implement a generic Acyclic Visitor, since it has better behavior with regard to dependency and insulation. Later, we'll tweak it for performance. In the end, we return to implementing a classic GoF Visitor that is speedier at the expense of some flexibility.

In the discussion on implementation, the names listed and defined in Table 10.1 apply. Some of the names in the table actually describe class templates, or, better said, will *become* class templates as we increasingly make our code more generic. For now, it's important to define the entities that the names represent.

Let's focus on the visitor hierarchy first. Here things are quite simple—we must provide some base classes for the user, classes that define a Visit operation for a given type. In addition, we must provide the strawman class that's used by the dynamic cast as required by the Acyclic Visitor pattern. Here it is:

```
class BaseVisitor
{
public:
    virtual ~BaseVisitor() {}
};
```

That's not a lot of reuse, but somebody has to write this little class.

Now we provide a simple class template Visitor. Visitor<T> defines a pure virtual function for visiting an object of type T.

```
template <class T>
class Visitor
{
public:
    virtual void Visit(T&) = 0;
};
```

In the general case, Visitor<T>::Visit might return something other than void. Visitor<T>::Visit can pass a useful result via Visitable::Accept. Consequently, let's add a second template parameter to Visitor:

```
template <class T, typename R = void>
class Visitor
{
public:
    typedef R ReturnType;
    virtual ReturnType Visit(T&) = 0;
};
```

Whenever you want to visit a hierarchy, you first derive your SomeVisitor from BaseVisitor, and as many Visitor instantiations as types you want to visit.

```
class SomeVisitor :
    public BaseVisitor // required
    public Visitor<RasterBitmap>,
    public Visitor<Paragraph>
{
public:
    void Visit(RasterBitmap&); // visit a RasterBitmap
    void Visit(Paragraph &);   // visit a Paragraph
};
```

The code looks clean, simple, and easy to use. Its structure makes it clear which classes your code visits. Even better, the compiler does not allow you to instantiate Some-Visitor if you don't define all the Visit functions. There is a name dependency between SomeVisitor's class definition and the names of the classes it visits (RasterBitmap and Paragraph). This dependency is quite understandable, because SomeVisitor *knows* about these types and *needs* to do specific operations on them.

We have now concluded the visitor side of the implementation. We defined a simple base class that acts as the root for dynamic_cast (BaseVisitor) and a class template (Visitor) that generates a pure virtual function (Visit) for each visited type.

The code we have written so far, in spite of its small quantity, has fairly good reuse potential. The Visitor class template generates a separate type for each visited class. The library client is relieved of the burden of littering the implementation with all those little classes such as ParagraphVisitor and RasterBitmapVisitor. The types generated by the Visitor class template will ensure the link with the Visitable classes.

This brings us to the visitable hierarchy. As discussed in the previous section, the visitable hierarchy in an Acyclic Visitor implementation has the following responsibilities:

- Declare a pure virtual Accept function that takes a reference to a BaseVisitor in the base class.
- Override and implement that Accept function in each derived class.

To carry the first responsibility we add a pure virtual function to the BaseVisitable class and require DocElement—and in general any root of a visitable hierarchy in the application space—to inherit from it. BaseVisitable looks like this:

```
template <typename R = void>
class BaseVisitable
{
public:
   typedef R ReturnType;
   virtual ~BaseVisitable() {}
   virtual ReturnType Accept(BaseVisitor&) = 0;
};
```

Trivial. Things become interesting when we try to carry the second responsibility, that is, to implement Accept in the library (not in the client). The Accept function implementation is not big, but it's annoying to have each client class take care of it. It would be nice if its code belonged to the library. As prescribed by the Acyclic Visitor pattern, if T is a visited class, T::Accept's implementation applies dynamic_cast<Visitor<T>*> to the BaseVisitor. If the cast succeeds, T::Accept bounces back to Visitor<T>::Visit. However, as mentioned in Section 10.2, simply defining Accept in the BaseVisitable class does not work, because the static type of *this in BaseVisitable does not provide the appropriate information to visitors.

We need a way to implement Accept in the library and to inject this function into the application's DocElement hierarchy. Alas, C++ has no such direct mechanism. There are workarounds that use virtual inheritance, but they are less than stellar and have non-negligible costs. We have to resort to a macro and require each class in the visitable hierarchy to use that macro inside the class definition.

Using macros, with all the clumsiness they bring, is not an easy decision to make, but any other solution does not add much commodity, at considerable expense in time and space. Because C++ programmers are known to be practical people, efficiency is reason enough for relying on macros from time to time instead of using esoteric but ineffective techniques.

The single most important rule in defining a macro is to let it do as little as possible by itself and to forward to a "real" entity (function, class) as quickly as possible. We define the macro for visitable classes as follows:

```
#define DEFINE_VISITABLE() \
    virtual ReturnType Accept(BaseVisitor& guest) \
    { return AcceptImpl(*this, guest); }
```

The client must insert DEFINE_VISITABLE() in each class of the visitable hierarchy. DEFINE_VISITABLE() defines the Accept member function to forward to another function—AcceptImpl. AcceptImpl is a template function parameterized with the type of *this. This way AcceptImpl gains access to the much-needed static type. We define AcceptImpl in the very base of the hierarchy, in BaseVisitable. This way, all derivatives will have access to it. Here's the changed BaseVisitable class:

```
template <typename R = void>
class BaseVisitable
{
public:
    typedef R ReturnType;
    virtual ~BaseVisitable() {}
    virtual ReturnType Accept(BaseVisitor&) = 0;
protected: // Give access only to the hierarchy
    template <class T>
    static ReturnType AcceptImpl(T& visited, BaseVisitor& guest)
    {
        // Apply the Acyclic Visitor
        if (Visitor<T>* p = dynamic_cast<Visitor<T>*>(&guest))
        {
            return p->Visit(visited);
        }
        return ReturnType();
    }
};
```

The fact that we have managed to move AcceptImpl to the library is important. It's not only a matter of automating the client's job. The presence of AcceptImpl in the library gives us the opportunity to adjust its implementation depending on various design constraints, as will become clear later.

The resulting design of Visitor/Visitable hides a great many details from the user, doesn't have annoying usage caveats, and works like a charm. Here's the current codebase for our generic Acyclic Visitor implementation.

```
// Visitor part
class BaseVisitor
{
public:
    virtual ~BaseVisitor() {}
};
template <class T, typename R = void>
class Visitor
{
public:
```

```cpp
      typedef R ReturnType; // Available for clients
      virtual ReturnType Visit(T&) = 0;
};

// Visitable part
template <typename R = void>
class BaseVisitable
{
public:
   typedef R ReturnType;
   virtual ~BaseVisitable() {}
   virtual R Accept(BaseVisitor&) = 0;
protected:
   template <class T>
   static ReturnType AcceptImpl(T& visited, BaseVisitor& guest)
   {
      // Apply the Acyclic Visitor
      if (Visitor<T, R>* p =
         dynamic_cast<Visitor<T, R>*>(&guest))
      {
         return p->Visit(visited);
      }
      return ReturnType();
   }
};

#define DEFINE_VISITABLE() \
   virtual ReturnType Accept(BaseVisitor& guest) \
   { return AcceptImpl(*this, guest); }
```

Ready for a test drive? Here it is:

```cpp
class DocElement : public BaseVisitable<>
{
public:
   DEFINE_VISITABLE()
};

class Paragraph : public DocElement
{
public:
   DEFINE_VISITABLE()
};

class MyConcreteVisitor :
   public BaseVisitor,  // required
   public Visitor<DocElement>,// visits DocElements
   public Visitor<Paragraph>    // visits Paragraphs
{
public:
   void Visit(DocElement&) { std::cout << "Visit(DocElement&) \n"; }
   void Visit(Paragraph&) { std::cout << "Visit(Paragraph&) \n"; }
};
```

```
int main()
{
    MyConcreteVisitor visitor;
    Paragraph par;
    DocElement* d = &par;   // "hide" the static type of 'par'
    d->Accept(visitor);
}
```

This little program will output

```
Visit(Paragraph&)
```

which means that everything works just fine.

Of course, this toy example doesn't show very much about the power of the codebase we've put together. However, given all the pains we've been through in implementing visitors from scratch in the previous sections, it's clear we now have a device that makes it easy to create visitable hierarchies correctly and to visit them.

Let us review the actions you must carry out to define a visitable hierarchy.

- Derive the root of your hierarchy from BaseVisitable<YourReturnType>.
- Add to each class SomeClass in the visitable hierarchy the DEFINE_VISITABLE() macro. (By now your hierarchy is ready to be visited—however, no dependency of any Visitor class is in sight!)
- Derive each concrete visitor SomeVisitor from BaseVisitor. Also, for each class X that you need to visit, derive SomeVisitor from Visitor<X,YourReturnType>. Provide overrides for the Visit member function for each visited type.

The resulting dependency chart is simple. The class definition of SomeVisitor depends by name on each visited class. The implementations of the Visit member functions fully depend on the classes they manipulate.

That's pretty much it. Compared with the previously discussed implementations, this one leaves us much better off. With the help of our Visitor implementation, we now have an ordered way to make visitable hierarchies, and we have reduced client code and dependencies to the bare necessity.

In special cases, you might prefer to implement Accept directly rather than to use the DEFINE_VISITABLE macro. Suppose you define a Section class, derived from DocElement, which contains several Paragraphs. For a Section object, you would like to visit each Paragraph in that Section. In this case, you might want to implement Accept manually:

```
class Section : public DocElement
    // Won't use the DEFINE_VISITABLE() macro
    // because it's going to implement Accept by itself
    {
        ...
        virtual ReturnType Accept(BaseVisitor& v)
        {
            for (each paragraph in this section)
            {
                current_paragraph->Accept(v);
```

```
                }
            }
      };
```

As you can see, there's nothing you *cannot* do when you use the Visitor implementation. The code we defined only frees you from the grunt work you would have to do if you started from scratch.

We have finished defining the kernel Visitor implementation, which includes pretty much anything that is germane to basic visiting needs. But read on, there's a lot more to come.

10.5 Back to the "Cyclic" Visitor

The generic Acyclic Visitor implementation defined in the previous section should be satisfactory in most situations. However, if you are developing a speed-hungry application, that dynamic cast in `Accept` might render you pensive and your speed measurements could make you downright depressed. Here's why. If you use `dynamic_cast` against some object, the runtime support has quite a few things to do. The RTTI code must figure out whether the conversion to the target type is legal and, if it is, must compute a pointer to that target type.

Let's detail a bit how a compiler writer can achieve this. One reasonable solution is to assign a unique integral identifier to each type in the program. The integral identifier also comes in handy when it comes to exception handling, so it's quite a wise integrating solution. Then in each class's virtual table, the compiler puts (a pointer to) a table of identifiers of all its subtypes. Together with these identifiers, the compiler has to store the offsets of the relative positions of the subobjects within the big object. This would be enough information to perform a dynamic cast correctly. When a `dynamic_cast <T2*>(p1)` occurs and `p1` is of type "pointer to `T1`," the runtime support code walks through the table of types for `p1`. If a match with `T2` is found, the runtime support code will perform the needed pointer arithmetic and pass back the result. Otherwise, the result is a null pointer. Details—such as multiple inheritance—render the dynamic cast code even more complicated and slower.

The solution just outlined has $O(n)$ complexity with respect to the number of base classes of a class. In other words, the time taken by a dynamic cast increases linearly as you use deeper and broader inheritance hierarchies.

Another solution is to use hash tables, thus offering increased speed at the expense of memory use. Yet another solution might use a big matrix for the whole application, thus making the dynamic cast take constant time, but at a significant cost in size, especially for programs with many classes. (A possible idea would be to compress that matrix; all this reveals the wonderful life of C++ compiler writers.)

The bottom line is that `dynamic_cast` does have a cost, which is unpredictable and can become unacceptable for some particular needs of an application. This means we should extend our Visitor implementation to accommodate the GoF "cyclic" Visitor, which is faster because it doesn't use `dynamic_cast`, but is harder to maintain.

Recall from the opening of this chapter how the GoF Visitor works. The following list summarizes the main differences between the GoF Visitor and the Acyclic Visitor as implemented by Loki.

- The BaseVisitor class is no longer a strawman; it defines one Visit pure virtual member function for each visited type (assuming we decide to rely on overloading).
- The AcceptImpl function must change. Ideally, the DEFINE_VISITABLE() macro remains unchanged.

Now, it all boils down to this: We have a collection of types we want to visit. Say they are DocElement, Paragraph, and RasterBitmap. How can we express and manipulate a collection of types? The question is a transparent hint to refer to Chapter 3, which describes typelists in detail and defines a complete typelist facility.

Typelists are exactly what we need here. We want to pass a typelist to a Cyclic-Visitor template as a template argument, thus saying, "I want this CyclicVisitor to be able to visit the following types." It would be elegant to say

```
// Forward declarations needed by the typelist below
class DocElement;
class Paragraph;
class RasterBitmap;

// Visits DocElement, Paragraph, and RasterBitmap
typedef CyclicVisitor
<
    void, // return type
    TYPELIST_3(DocElement, Paragraph, RasterBitmap)
>
MyVisitor;
```

MyVisitor depends by name on DocElement, Paragraph, and RasterBitmap.

Let's see which additions we need to make to the current codebase. We use the same procedure we used in Chapter 9 for defining a generic Abstract Factory implementation:

```
// Consult Visitor.h for the definition of Private::VisitorBinder<R>
template <typename R, class TList>
class CyclicVisitor : public GenScatterHierarchy<TList,
    Private::VisitorBinder<R>::Result>
{
    typedef R ReturnType;
    template <class Visited>
    ReturnType Visit(Visited& host)
    {
        Visitor<Visited>& subObj = *this;
        return subObj.Visit(host);
    }
};
```

Remarkably, CyclicVisitor uses Visitor as a building block. Refer to Chapter 3 for the technique and to Chapter 9 for a similar example. Essentially, CyclicVisitor inherits a Visitor<T> for each type T in the typelist TList.

The net effect is that if you pass CyclicVisitor a typelist, it ends up inheriting from Visitor instantiated with every type in that typelist, thus declaring one Visit pure virtual function per type. In other words, it's functionally equivalent to the base Visitor as prescribed by the GoF Visitor pattern.

After you specify your `CyclicVisitor` of choice through a typedef, say `MyVisitor`, all you have to do is use the `DEFINE_CYCLIC_VISITABLE(MyVisitor)` macro (similar to `DEFINE_VISITABLE()`) in your visitable classes appropriately. For example:

```
typedef CyclicVisitor
<
    void, // return type
    TYPELIST_3(DocElement, Paragraph, RasterBitmap)
>
MyVisitor;

class DocElement
{
public:
    virtual void Accept(MyVisitor&) = 0;
};

class Paragraph : public DocElement
{
public:
    DEFINE_CYCLIC_VISITABLE(MyVisitor);
};
```

That's it! Just as in a handmade implementation of the GoF Visitor, you still have to contribute some discipline. The difference now is that the number of things you have to remember and implement yourself is much smaller. To make a hierarchy visitable with our GoF Visitor implementation, do the following:

- Forward declare all the classes in the hierarchy.
- Write a `typedef` for `CyclicVisitor`, instantiated with the return type and with the list of the types you want to visit. (Let's call it `MyVisitor`.)
- Define a virtual pure function `Accept` for your base class.
- Add `DEFINE_CYCLIC_VISITABLE(MyVisitor)` to each class of your hierarchy, or implement `Accept` by hand for classes that you want to sport a different behavior.
- Have each of your concrete visitors inherit from `MyVisitor`.
- Update the `MyVisitor` template instantiation (the `typedef`) whenever you add a new class to the visitable hierarchy, then—sigh—recompile.

Compared with a handmade GoF Visitor implementation, the generic approach is cleaner. The number of points of maintenance is reduced to your `MyVisitor` type definition.

As a practical piece of advice for designing with Visitor, it's best to start with the Acyclic Visitor, which is easier to maintain, and switch to the GoF Visitor only if you really must optimize. The nice part is that the generic componentry makes it very easy to experiment—you need change only one declaration. There's no code to hack into. The details of implementing Visitor are in the library. You need adjust only the declarative link between the client and library in order to achieve two different implementations of Visitor.

10.6 Hooking Variations

Visitor has a number of variations and customizations. This section is dedicated to mapping the hooks that you might need so that you can add these to the implementation that we've put in place.

10.6.1 The Catch-All Function

We discussed the catch-all function in Section 10.2. A Visitor may encounter an unknown type derived from the base class (in our example, DocElement). In this case, you may want either a compile-time error to occur or a default action to be carried out at runtime.

Let's analyze the catch-all issue for the GoF Visitor and the Acyclic Visitor implementations provided by our generic components.

For the GoF Visitor, things are quite simple. If you include the root class of your hierarchy in the typelist you pass to CyclicVisitor, then you give yourself the opportunity to implement the catch-all function. Otherwise, you take the compile-time error route. The following code illustrates the two options:

```
// Forward declarations needed for the GoF Visitor
class DocElement; // Root class
class Paragraph;
class RasterBitmap;
class VectorizedDrawing;

typedef CyclicVisitor
<
    void, // Return type
    TYPELIST_3(Paragraph, RasterBitmap, VectorizedDrawing)
>
StrictVisitor; // No catch-all operation;
               // will issue a compile-time error if you try
               // visiting an unknown type

typedef CyclicVisitor
<
    void, // return type
    TYPELIST_4(DocElement, Paragraph, RasterBitmap,
        VectorizedDrawing)
>
NonStrictVisitor; // Declares Visit(DocElement&), which will be
                  // called whenever you try visiting
                  // an unknown type
```

All this was quite easy. Now let's talk about the catch-all function within our Acyclic Visitor generic implementation.

In Acyclic Visitor an interesting twist occurs. Although essentially catch-all is all about visiting an unknown class by a known visitor, the problem appears reversed: An unknown visitor visits a known class!

Let's look again at our `AcceptImpl` implementation for Acyclic Visitor.

```cpp
template <typename R = void >
class BaseVisitable
{
   ... as above ...
   template <class T>
   static ReturnType AcceptImpl(T& visited,
      BaseVisitor& guest)
   {
      if (Visitor<T>* p =
         dynamic_cast<Visitor<T>*>(&guest))
      {
         return p->Visit(visited);
      }
      return ReturnType(); // Attention here!
   }
};
```

Suppose you add a `VectorizedDrawing` to your `DocElement` hierarchy in a sneaky way—you don't notify any concrete visitors about it. Whenever `VectorizedDrawing` is visited, the dynamic cast to `Visitor<VectorizedDrawing>` fails. This is because your existing concrete visitors are not aware of the new type, so they didn't derive from `Visitor-<VectorizedDrawing>`. Because the dynamic cast fails, the code takes the alternate route and returns the default value of `ReturnType`. Here's the exact place where the catch-all function can enter into action.

Because our `AcceptImpl` function hardcodes the `return ReturnType()` action, it quite rigidly imposes a design constraint without leaving room for variation. Therefore, let's put a policy in place that dictates the catch-all behavior:

```cpp
template
<
   typename R = void,
   template <typename, class> class CatchAll = DefaultCatchAll
>
class BaseVisitable
{
   ... as above ...
   template <class T>
   static ReturnType AcceptImpl(T& visited,
      BaseVisitor& guest)
   {
      if (Visitor<T>* p =
         dynamic_cast<Visitor<T>*>(&guest))
      {
         return p->Visit(visited);
      }
      // Changed
      return CatchAll<R, T>::OnUnknownVisitor(visited, guest);
   }
};
```

The CatchAll policy can do whatever the design requires. It can return a default value or error code, throw an exception, call a virtual member function for the visited object, try more dynamic casts, and so on. The implementation of OnUnknownVisitor depends largely on the concrete design needs. In some cases, you might want to enforce visitation for all the types in the hierarchy. In other cases, you might want to visit some types freely and to ignore all others silently. The Acyclic Visitor implementation favors the second approach, so the default CatchAll looks like this:

```
template <class R, class Visited>
struct DefaultCatchAll
{
   static R OnUnknownVisitor(Visited&, BaseVisitor&)
   {
      // Here's the action that will be taken when
      // there is a mismatch between a Visitor and a Visited.
      // The stock behavior is to return a default value
      return R();
   }
};
```

Should you need a different behavior, all you have to do is plug a different template into BaseVisitable.

10.6.2 Nonstrict Visitation

Maybe it's human nature, but the have-your-cake-and-eat-it-too ideal is every programmer's mantra. If possible, programmers would like a fast, noncoupled, flexible visitor that would read their minds and figure out whether an omission is a simple mistake or a deliberate decision. On the other hand, unlike their customers, programmers are practical, down-to-earth people, with whom you can haggle about trade-offs.

Following this line of thought, the flexibility of CatchAll renders users of GoF Visitor envious. As it is now, the GoF Visitor implementation is strict—it declares one pure virtual function for each type visited. You must derive from BaseVisitor and implement each and every Visit overload, and if you don't, you cannot compile your code.

However, sometimes you don't really want to visit each type in the list. You don't want the framework to be so strict about it. You want options: Either you implement Visit for a type, or OnUnknownVisitor will be automatically called for your CatchAll implementation.

For this kind of situation, Loki introduces a class called BaseVisitorImpl. It inherits BaseVisitor and uses typelist techniques for accommodating typelists. You can look up its implementation in Loki (file Visitor.h).

10.7 Summary

This chapter discussed the Visitor pattern and the problems it addresses. Essentially, Visitor allows you to add virtual functions to a class hierarchy without modifying the classes in that hierarchy. In some cases, Visitor can lead to a clever, extensible design.

However, Visitor has a bunch of problems, to the point that its use with any but the most stable class hierarchies is unjustifiably hard. Acyclic Visitor is of help, at the expense of a decrease in efficiency.

By using careful design and advanced implementation techniques, you can ensure that the generic Visitor components get the best out of the Visitor pattern. Although the implementation fully preserves Visitor's power, it mitigates most of its shortcomings.

In an application, Acyclic Visitor should be the variant of choice, unless you need all the speed you can get. If speed is important, you can use a generic implementation of the GoF Visitor that keeps maintenance low (a single, clear point of maintenance) and compile-time cost reasonable.

The generic implementation leverages advanced C++ programming techniques, such as dynamic casts, typelists, and partial specialization. The outcome is that all the common, repetitive parts of implementing visitors for any concrete need have been absorbed by the library.

10.8 Visitor Generic Components Quick Facts

- To implement the Acyclic Visitor, use `BaseVisitor` (as the strawman base class), `Visitor`, and `Visitable`:

```
class BaseVisitor;

template <class T, typename R = void>
class Visitor;

template
<
    typename R = void,
    template<class, class> CatchAll = DefaultCatchAll
>
class BaseVisitable;
```

- The second template parameter of `Visitor` and the first template parameter of `Base-Visitable` are the return type of the `Visit` and `Accept` member functions, respectively. It defaults to `void` (this is the return type assumed in the GoF book examples and in most Visitor descriptions).
- The second template parameter of `BaseVisitable` is the policy for handling the catch-all issue (see Section 10.2).
- Derive the root of your hierarchy from `BaseVisitable`. Then use the macro `DEFINE_-VISITABLE()` in each class in the hierarchy, or provide a handmade implementation of `Accept(BaseVisitor&)`.
- Derive your concrete Visitor classes from `BaseVisitor`. Also derive your concrete visitor from `Visitor<T>`, for each type T you are interested in visiting.
- For the GoF Visitor, use the `CyclicVisitor` template:

```
template <typename R, class TList>
class CyclicVisitor;
```

- Specify the types visited in the `TList` template argument.

- Use `CyclicVisitor` with your code just as you would use a classic GoF visitor.
- If you need to implement only part of a GoF Visitor (the nonstrict variant), derive your visitor from `BaseVisitorImpl`. `BaseVisitorImpl` implements all the `Visit` overloads to call `OnUnknownVisitor`. You can override part of this behavior.
- The `OnUnknownVisitor` static member function of the **CatchAll** policy provides a catch-all sink for Acyclic Visitor. If you use `BaseVisitorImpl`, it will provide a catch-all for the GoF Visitor, too. The stock implementation of `OnUnknownVisitor` returns a default-constructed value of the return type you chose. You can override this behavior by providing custom implementations of **CatchAll**.

11

Multimethods

This chapter defines, discusses, and implements multimethods in the context of C++.

The C++ virtual function mechanism allows dispatching of a call depending on the dynamic type of one object. The multimethods feature allows dispatching of a function call depending on the types of *multiple* objects. A universally good implementation requires language support, which is the route that languages such as CLOS, ML, Haskell, and Dylan have taken. C++ lacks such support, so its emulation is left to library writers.

This chapter discusses some typical solutions and some generic implementations of each. The solutions feature various trade-offs in speed, flexibility, and dependency management. To describe the technique of dispatching a function call depending on multiple objects, this book uses the terms *multimethod* (borrowed from CLOS) and *multiple dispatch*. A particularization of multiple dispatch for two objects is known as *double dispatch*.

Implementing multimethods is a problem that's as fascinating as it is dreaded, one that has stolen lots of hours of good, healthy sleep from designers and programmers.[1]

The topics of this chapter include

- Defining multimethods
- Identifying situations in which the need for multiobject polymorphism appears
- Discussing and implementing three double dispatchers that foster different trade-offs
- Enhancing double-dispatch engines

After reading this chapter, you will have a firm grasp of the typical situations for which multimethods are the way to go. In addition, you will be able to use and extend several robust generic components, provided by Loki, that implement multimethods.

This chapter limits discussion to multimethods for two objects (double dispatch). You can use the underlying techniques to extend the number of supported objects to three or more. It is likely, though, that in most situations you can get away with dispatching depending on two objects, and therefore you'll be able to use Loki directly.

---

[1] If you have trouble implementing multimethods, you can look at this chapter as a sleep aid—which I hope doesn't mean it has an actual soporific effect.

11.1 What Are Multimethods?

In C++, polymorphism essentially means that a given function call can be bound to different implementations, depending on compile-time or runtime contextual issues.

Two types of polymorphism are implemented in C++:

- Compile-time polymorphism, supported by overloading and template functions[2]
- Runtime polymorphism, implemented with virtual functions

Overloading is a simple form of polymorphism that allows multiple functions with the same name to coexist in a scope. If the functions have different parameter lists, the compiler can differentiate among them at compile time. Overloading is simple syntactic sugar, a convenient syntactic abbreviation.

Template functions are a static dispatch mechanism. They offer more sophisticated compile-time polymorphism.

Virtual member function calls allow the C++ runtime support, instead of the compiler, to decide which actual function implementation to call. Virtual functions bind a name to a function implementation at runtime. The function called depends on the dynamic type of the object for which you make the virtual call.

Let's now see how these three mechanisms for polymorphism scale to multiple objects. Overloading and template functions scale to multiple objects naturally. Both features allow multiple parameters, and intricate compile-time rules govern function selection.

Unfortunately, virtual functions—the only mechanism that implements runtime polymorphism in C++—are tailored for one object only. Even the call syntax—obj.Fun (*arguments*)—gives obj a privileged role over *arguments*. (In fact, you can think of obj as nothing more than one of Fun's arguments, accessible inside Fun as *this. The Dylan language, for example, accepts the dot call syntax only as a particular expression of a general function-call mechanism.)

We define *multimethods* or *multiple dispatch* as the mechanism that dispatches a function call to different concrete functions depending on the dynamic types of multiple objects involved in the call. Because we can take compile-time multiobject polymorphism for granted, we need only implement runtime multiobject polymorphism. Don't be worried; there's a lot left to talk about.

11.2 When Are Multimethods Needed?

Detecting the need for multimethods is simple. You have an operation that manipulates multiple polymorphic objects through pointers or references to their base classes. You would like the behavior of that operation to vary with the dynamic type of more than one of those objects.

Collisions form a typical category of problems best solved with multimethods. For instance, you might write a video game in which moving objects are derived from a Game

---

[2] A more generous view of polymorphism would qualify automatic conversions as the crudest form of polymorphism. They allow, for example, std::sin to be called with an int although it was written for a double. This polymorphism through coercion is only apparent, because the same function call will be issued for both types.

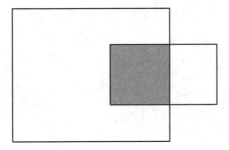

Figure 11.1: Hatching the intersection of two shapes

Object abstract class. You would like their collision to behave differently depending on which two types collide: a space ship with an asteroid, a ship with a space station, or an asteroid with a space station.[3]

For example, suppose you want to mark overlapping areas of drawing objects. You write a drawing program that allows its users to define rectangles, circles, ellipses, polygons, and other shapes. The basic design is an object-oriented classic: Define an abstract class Shape and have all the concrete shapes derive from it; then manipulate a drawing as a collection of pointers to Shape.

Now say the client comes and asks for a nice-to-have feature: If two closed shapes intersect, the intersection should be drawn in a way different from each of the two shapes. For instance, the intersection area could be hatched, as in Figure 11.1.

Finding a single algorithm that will hatch any intersection is difficult. For instance, the algorithm that hatches the intersection between an ellipse and a rectangle is very different (and much more complex) from the one that hatches the intersection between two rectangles. Besides, an overly general algorithm (for instance, one that operates at a pixel level) is likely to be highly inefficient, since some intersections (such as rectangle-rectangle) are trivial.

What you need here is a battery of algorithms, each specialized for two shape types, such as rectangle-rectangle, rectangle-polygon, polygon-polygon, ellipse-rectangle, ellipse-polygon, and ellipse-ellipse. At runtime, as the user moves shapes on the screen, you'd like to pick up and fire the appropriate algorithms, which in turn will quickly compute and hatch the overlapping areas.

Because you manipulate all drawing objects as pointers to Shape, you don't have the type information necessary to select the suitable algorithm. You have to start from pointers to Shape only. Because you have two objects involved, simple virtual functions cannot solve this problem. You have to use double dispatch.

11.3 Double Switch-on-Type: Brute Force

The most straightforward approach to a double dispatch implementation is to implement a double switch-on-type. You try to dynamic cast the first object against each of the possible left-hand types in succession. For each branch, you do the same with the second argument.

---

[3]This example and names were borrowed from Scott Meyers's *More Effective C++* (1996a), Item 31.

When you have discovered the types of both objects, you know which function to call. The code looks like this:

```
// various intersection algorithms
void DoHatchArea1(Rectangle&, Rectangle&);
void DoHatchArea2(Rectangle&, Ellipse&);
void DoHatchArea3(Rectangle&, Poly&);
void DoHatchArea4(Ellipse&, Poly&);
void DoHatchArea5(Ellipse&, Ellipse&);
void DoHatchArea6(Poly&, Poly&);

void DoubleDispatch(Shape& lhs, Shape& rhs)
{
   if (Rectangle* p1 = dynamic_cast<Rectangle*>(&lhs))
   {
      if (Rectangle* p2 = dynamic_cast<Rectangle*>(&rhs))
         DoHatchArea1(*p1, *p2);
      else if (Ellipse p2 = dynamic_cast<Ellipse*>(&rhs))
         DoHatchArea2(*p1, *p2);
      else if (Poly p2 = dynamic_cast<Poly*>(&rhs))
         DoHatchArea3(*p1, *p2);
      else
         Error("Undefined Intersection");
   }
   else if (Ellipse* p1 = dynamic_cast<Ellipse*>(&lhs))
   {
      if (Rectangle* p2 = dynamic_cast<Rectangle*>(&rhs))
         DoHatchArea2(*p2, *p1);
      else if (Ellipse* p2 = dynamic_cast<Ellipse*>(&rhs))
         DoHatchArea5(*p1, *p2);
      else if (Poly* p2 = dynamic_cast<Poly*>(&rhs))
         DoHatchArea4(*p1, *p2);
      else
         Error("Undefined Intersection");
   }
   else if (Poly* p1 = dynamic_cast<Poly*>(&lhs))
   {
      if (Rectangle* p2 = dynamic_cast<Rectangle*>(&rhs))
         DoHatchArea3(*p2, *p1);
      else if (Ellipse* p2 = dynamic_cast<Ellipse*>(&rhs))
         DoHatchArea4(*p2, *p1);
      else if (Poly* p2 = dynamic_cast<Poly*>(&rhs))
         DoHatchArea6(*p1, *p2);
      else
         Error("Undefined Intersection");
   }
   else
   {
      Error("Undefined Intersection");
   }
}
```

Whew! It's been quite a few lines. As you can see, the brute-force approach asks you to write a lot of (allegedly trivial) code. You can count on any dependable C++ programmer to put together the appropriate web of `if` statements. In addition, the solution has the advantage of being fast if the number of possible classes is not too high. From a speed perspective, `DoubleDispatch` implements a linear search in the set of possible types. Because the search is unrolled—a succession of `if-else` statements as opposed to a loop—the speed is very good for small sets.

One problem with the brute-force approach is sheer code size, which makes the code unmaintainable as the number of classes grows. The code just given deals with only three classes, yet it's already of considerable size. The size grows quadratically as you add more classes. Imagine how the code of `DoubleDispatch` would look for a hierarchy of 20 classes!

Another problem is that `DoubleDispatch` is a dependency bottleneck—its implementation must know of the existence of all classes in a hierarchy. It is best to keep the dependency net as loose as possible, and `DoubleDispatch` is a dependency hog.

The third problem with `DoubleDispatch` is that the order of the `if` statements matters. This is a very subtle and dangerous problem. Imagine, for instance, you derive class `RoundedRectangle` (a rectangle with rounded corners) from `Rectangle`. You then edit `DoubleDispatch` and insert the additional `if` statement at the end of each `if-else` statement, right before the `Error` call. You have just introduced a bug.

The reason is that if you pass `DoubleDispatch` a pointer to a `RoundedRectangle`, the `dynamic_cast<Rectangle*>` succeeds. Because that test is before the test for `dynamic_cast<RoundedRectangle*>`, the first test will "eat" both `Rectangle`s and `Rounded Rectangle`s. The second test will never get a chance. Most compilers don't warn about this.

A candidate solution would be to change the tests as follows:

```
void DoubleDispatch(Shape& lhs, Shape& rhs)
{
    if (typeid(lhs) == typeid(Rectangle))
    {
        Rectangle* p1 = dynamic_cast<Rectangle*>(&lhs);
        ...
    }
    else ...
}
```

The tests are now for the exact type instead of the exact or derived type. The `typeid` comparison shown in this code fails if `lhs` is a `RoundedRectangle`, so the tests continue. Ultimately, the test against `typeid(RoundedRectangle)` succeeds.

Alas, this fixes one aspect but breaks another: `DoubleDispatch` is too rigid now. If you didn't add support for a type in `DoubleDispatch`, you would like `DoubleDispatch` to fire on the closest base type. This is what you'd normally expect when using inheritance—by default, derived objects do what base objects do unless you override some behavior. The problem is that the `typeid`-based implementation of `DoubleDispatch` fails to preserve this property. The rule of thumb that results from this fact is that you must still use `dynamic_cast` in `DoubleDispatch` and "sort" the `if` tests so that the most derived classes are tried first.

This adds two more disadvantages to the brute-force implementation of multimethods.

First, the dependency between DoubleDispatch and the Shape hierarchy deepens—Double-Dispatch must know about not only classes but also the inheritance relationships between classes. Second, maintaining the appropriate ordering of dynamic casts puts a supplemental burden on the shoulders of the maintainer.

11.4 The Brute-Force Approach Automated

Because in some situations the speed of the brute-force approach can be unbeatable, it's worth paying attention to implementing such a dispatcher. Here's where typelists can be of help.

Recall from Chapter 3 that Loki defines a typelist facility—a collection of structures and compile-time algorithms that allow you to manipulate collections of types. A brute-force implementation of multimethods can use a client-provided typelist that specifies the classes in the hierarchy (in our example, Rectangle, Poly, Ellipse, etc.). Then a recursive template can generate the sequence of if-else statements.

In the general case, we can dispatch on different collections of types, so the typelist for the left-hand operand can differ from the one for the right-hand operand.

Let's try outlining a StaticDispatcher class template that performs the type deduction algorithm and then fires a function in another class. Explanations follow the code.

```
template
<
    class Executor,
    class BaseLhs,
    class TypesLhs,
    class BaseRhs = BaseLhs,
    class TypesRhs = TypesLhs,
    typename ResultType = void
>
class StaticDispatcher
{
    typedef typename TypesLhs::Head Head;
    typedef typename TypesLhs::Tail Tail;
public:
    static ResultType Go(BaseLhs& lhs, BaseRhs& rhs,
        Executor exec)
    {
        if (Head* p1 = dynamic_cast<Head*>(&lhs))
        {
            return StaticDispatcher<Executor, BaseLhs,
                TypesLhs, BaseRhs, TypeRhs>::DispatchRhs(
                    *p1, rhs, exec);
        }
        else
        {
            return StaticDispatcher<Executor, BaseLhs,
                Tail, BaseRhs, TypesRhs, ResultType>::Go(
                    lhs, rhs, exec);
        }
    }
```

```
        ...
    };
```

If you are familiar with typelists, the workings of StaticDispatcher are seen to be quite simple. StaticDispatcher has surprisingly little code for what it does.

StaticDispatcher has six template parameters. Executor is the type of the object that does the actual processing—in our example, hatching the intersection area. We'll discuss what Executor looks like a bit later.

BaseLhs and BaseRhs are the base types of the arguments on the left-hand side and the right-hand side, respectively. TypesLhs and TypesRhs are typelists containing the possible derived types for the two arguments. The default values of BaseRhs and TypesRhs foster a dispatcher for types in the same class hierarchy, as is the case with the drawing program example.

ResultType is the type of the result of the double-dispatch operation. In the general case, the dispatched function can return an arbitrary type. StaticDispatcher supports this dimension of genericity and forwards the result to the caller.

StaticDispatcher::Go tries a dynamic cast to the first type found in the TypesLhs typelist, against the address of lhs. If the dynamic cast fails, Go delegates to the remainder (tail) of TypesLhs in a recursive call to itself. (This is not a true recursive call, because each time we have a different instantiation of StaticDispatcher.)

The net effect is that Go performs a suite of if-else statements that apply dynamic_-cast to each type in the typelist. When a match is found, Go invokes DispatchRhs. DispatchRhs does the second and last step of the type deduction—finding the dynamic type of rhs.

```
template <...>
class StaticDispatcher
{
    ... as above ...
    template <class SomeLhs>
    static ResultType DispatchRhs(SomeLhs& lhs, BaseRhs& rhs,
        Executor exec)
    {
        typedef typename TypesRhs::Head Head;
        typedef typename TypesRhs::Tail Tail;

        if (Head* p2 = dynamic_cast<Head*>(&rhs))
        {
            return exec.Fire(lhs, *p2);
        }
        else
        {
            return StaticDispatcher<Executor, SomeLhs,
                TypesLhs, BaseRhs, Tail, ResultType>::DispatchRhs(
                    lhs, rhs, exec);
        }
    }
};
```

DispatchRhs performs the same algorithm for rhs as Go applied for lhs. In addition, when the dynamic cast on rhs succeeds, DispatchRhs calls Executor::Fire, passing it the two discovered types. Again, the code that the compiler generates is a suite of if-else statements. Interestingly, the compiler generates one such suite of if-else statements for *each* type in TypesLhs. Effectively, StaticDispatcher manages to generate a polynomial amount of code with two typelists and a fixed codebase. This is an asset, but also a potential danger—too much code can hurt compile times, program size, and total execution time.

To treat the limit conditions that stop the compile-time recursion, we need to specialize StaticDispatcher for two cases: The type of lhs is not found in TypesLhs, and the type of rhs is not found in TypesRhs.

The first case (error on lhs) appears when you invoke Go on a StaticDispatcher with NullType as TypesLhs. This is the sign that the search depleted TypesLhs. (Recall from Chapter 3 that NullType is used to signal the last element in any typelist.)

```
template
<
    class Executor,
    class BaseLhs,
    class BaseRhs,
    class TypesRhs,
    typename ResultType
>
class StaticDispatcher<Executor, BaseLhs, NullType,
    BaseRhs, TypesRhs, ResultType>
{
    static void Go(BaseLhs& lhs, BaseRhs& rhs, Executor exec)
    {
        exec.OnError(lhs, rhs);
    }
};
```

Error handling is elegantly delegated to the Executor class, as you will see later in the discussion on Executor.

The second case (error on rhs) appears when you invoke DispatchRhs on a Static Dispatcher with NullType as TypesRhs. Hence the following specialization:

```
template
<
    class Executor,
    class BaseLhs,
    class TypesLhs,
    class BaseRhs,
    typename ResultType
>
class StaticDispatcher<Executor, BaseLhs, TypesLhs,
    BaseRhs, NullType, ResultType>
{
public:
```

```
        static void DispatchRhs(BaseLhs& lhs, BaseRhs& rhs,
            Executor& exec)
        {
            exec.OnError(lhs, rhs);
        }
    };
```

It is time now to discuss what `Executor` must implement to take advantage of the double-dispatch engine we have just defined.

`StaticDispatcher` deals only with type discovery. After finding the right types and objects, it passes them to a call of `Executor::Fire`. To differentiate these calls, `Executor` must implement several overloads of `Fire`. For example, the `Executor` class for hatching shape intersections is as follows:

```
    class HatchingExecutor
    {
    public:
        // Various intersection algorithms
        void Fire(Rectangle&, Rectangle&);
        void Fire(Rectangle&, Ellipse&);
        void Fire(Rectangle&, Poly&);
        void Fire(Ellipse&, Poly&);
        void Fire(Ellipse&, Ellipse&);
        void Fire(Poly&, Poly&);

        // Error handling routine
        void OnError(Shape&, Shape&);
    };
```

You use `HatchingExecutor` with `StaticDispatcher` as shown in the following code:

```
    typedef StaticDispatcher<HatchingExecutor, Shape,
        TYPELIST_3(Rectangle, Ellipse, Poly)> Dispatcher;
    Shape *p1 = ...;
    Shape *p2 = ...;
    HatchingExecutor exec;
    Dispatcher::Go(*p1, *p2, exec);
```

This code invokes the appropriate `Fire` overload in the `HatchingExecutor` class. You can see the `StaticDispatcher` class template as a mechanism that achieves dynamic overloading—it defers overloading rules to runtime. This makes `StaticDispatcher` remarkably easy to use. You just implement `HatchingExecutor` with the overloading rules in mind, and then you use `StaticDispatcher` as a black box that does the magic of applying overloading rules at runtime.

As a nice side effect, `StaticDispatcher` will unveil any overloading ambiguities at compile time. For instance, assume you don't declare `HatchingExecutor::Fire(Ellipse&, Poly&)`. Instead, you declare `HatchingExecutor::Fire(Ellipse&, Shape&)` and `Hatching-Executor::Fire(Shape&, Poly&)`. Calling `HatchingExecutor::Fire` with an `Ellipse` and a `Poly` would result in an ambiguity—both functions compete to handle the call.

Remarkably, `StaticDispatcher` signals the same error for you and with the same level of detail. `StaticDispatcher` is a tool that's very consistent with the existing C++ overloading rules.

What happens in the case of a runtime error—for instance, if you pass a `Circle` as one of the arguments of `StaticDispatcher::Go`? As hinted earlier, `StaticDispatcher` handles border cases by simply calling `Executor::OnError` with the original (not cast) `lhs` and `rhs`. This means that, in our example, `HatchingExecutor::OnError (Shape&, Shape&)` is the error handling routine. You can use this routine to do whatever you find appropriate—when it's called, it means that `StaticDispatcher` gave up on finding the dynamic types.

As discussed in the previous section, inheritance adds problems to a bruteforce dispatcher. That is, the following instantiation of `StaticDispatcher` has a bug:

```
typedef StaticDispatcher
<
    SomeExecutor,
    Shape,
    TYPELIST_4(Rectangle, Ellipse, Poly, RoundedRectangle)
>
MyDispatcher;
```

If you pass a `RoundedRectangle` to `MyDispatcher`, it will be considered a `Rectangle`. The `dynamic_cast<Rectangle*>` succeeds on a pointer to a `RoundedRectangle`, and because the `dynamic_cast<RoundedRectangle*>` is lower on the food chain, it will never be given a chance. The correct instantiation is

```
typedef StaticDispatcher
<
    SomeExecutor,
    Shape,
    TYPELIST_4(RoundedRectangle, Ellipse, Poly, Rectangle)
>
Dispatcher;
```

The general rule is to put the most derived types at the front of the typelist.

It would be nice if this transformation could be applied automatically, and typelists do support that. We have a means to detect inheritance at compile time (Chapter 2), and typelists can be sorted. This led to the `DerivedToFront` compile-time algorithm in Chapter 3.

All we have to do to take advantage of automatic sorting is to modify the implementation of `StaticDispatcher` as follows:

```
template <...>
class StaticDispatcher
{
    typedef typename DerivedToFront<typename TypesLhs>::Result
        SortedTypesLhs;
    typedef typename SortedTypesLhs::Head Head;
    typedef typename SortedTypesLhs::Tail Tail;
    ... similar typedefs for the right-hand side ...
public:
    ... as above ...
};
```

After all this handy automation, don't forget that all we have obtained is the code generation part. The dependency problems are still with us. Although it makes it very easy to implement brute-force multimethods, StaticDispatcher still has a dependency on all the types in the hierarchy. Its advantages are speed (if there are not too many types in the hierarchy) and nonintrusiveness—you don't have to modify a hierarchy to use StaticDispatcher with it.

11.5 Symmetry with the Brute-Force Dispatcher

When you hatch the intersection between two shapes, you might want to do it differently if you have a rectangle covering an ellipse than if you have an ellipse covering a rectangle. Or, on the contrary, you might need to hatch the intersection area the same way when an ellipse and a rectangle intersect, no matter which covers which. In the latter case, you need a *symmetric* multimethod—a multimethod that is insensitive to the order in which you pass its arguments.

Symmetry applies only when the two parameter types are identical (in our case, BaseLhs is the same as BaseRhs, and LhsTypes is the same as RhsTypes).

The brute-force StaticDispatcher defined previously is asymmetric; that is, it doesn't offer any built-in support for symmetric multimethods. For example, assume you define the following classes:

```
class HatchingExecutor
{
public:
    void Fire(Rectangle&, Rectangle&);
    void Fire(Rectangle&, Ellipse&);
    ...
    // Error handler
    void OnError(Shape&, Shape&);
};

typedef StaticDispatcher
<
    HatchingExecutor,
    Shape,
    TYPELIST_3(Rectangle, Ellipse, Poly)
>
HatchingDispatcher;
```

The HatchingDispatcher does not fire when passed an Ellipse as the left-hand parameter and a Rectangle as the right-hand parameter. Even though from your HatchingExecutor's viewpoint it doesn't matter who's first and who's second, HatchingDispatcher will insist that you pass objects in a certain order.

We can fix the symmetry in the client code by reversing arguments and forwarding from one overload to another:

```
class HatchingExecutor
{
```

```
public:
    void Fire(Rectangle&, Ellipse&);
    // Symmetry assurance
    void Fire(Ellipse& lhs, Rectangle& rhs)
    {
        // Forward to Fire(Rectangle&, Ellipse&)
        //  by switching the order of arguments
        Fire(rhs, lhs);
    }
    ...
};
```

These little forwarding functions are hard to maintain. Ideally, StaticDispatcher would provide itself optional support for symmetry through an additional bool template parameter, which is worth looking into.

The need is to have StaticDispatcher reverse the order of arguments when invoking the callback, for certain cases. What are those cases? Let's analyze the previous example. Expanding the template argument lists from their default values, we get the following instantiation:

```
typedef StaticDispatcher
<
    HatchingExecutor,
    Shape,
    TYPELIST_3(Rectangle, Ellipse, Poly),  // TypesLhs
    Shape,
    TYPELIST_3(Rectangle, Ellipse, Poly),  // TypesRhs
    void
>
HatchingDispatcher;
```

An algorithm for selecting parameter pairs for a symmetric dispatcher can be as follows: Combine the first type in the first typelist (TypesLhs) with each type in the second typelist (TypesRhs). This gives three combinations: Rectangle-Rectangle, Rectangle-Ellipse, and Rectangle-Poly. Next, combine the second type in Types Lhs (Ellipse) with types in TypesRhs. However, because the first combination (Rectangle-Ellipse) has already been made in the first step, this time start with the second element in Types Rhs. This step yields Ellipse-Ellipse and Ellipse-Poly. The same reasoning applies to the next step: Poly in TypesLhs must be combined only with types starting with the third one in TypesRhs. This gives only one combination, Poly-Poly, and the algorithm stops here.

Following this algorithm, you implement only the functions for the selected combination, as follows:

```
class HatchingExecutor
{
public:
    void Fire(Rectangle&, Rectangle&);
    void Fire(Rectangle&, Ellipse&);
    void Fire(Rectangle&, Poly&);
    void Fire(Ellipse&, Ellipse&);
```

```
        void Fire(Ellipse&, Poly&);
        void Fire(Poly&, Poly&);
        // Error handler
        void OnError(Shape&, Shape&);
    };
```

StaticDispatcher must detect all by itself the combinations that were eliminated by the algorithm just discussed, namely Ellipse-Rectangle, Poly-Rectangle, and Poly-Ellipse. For these three combinations, StaticDispatcher must reverse the arguments. For all others, StaticDispatcher forwards the call just as it did before.

What's the Boolean condition that determines whether or not argument swapping is needed? The algorithm selects the types in TypesRhs only at indices *greater than or equal to* the index of the type in TypesLhs. Therefore, the condition is as follows:

> For two types T and U, if the index of U in TypesRhs is less than the index of T in Types-Lhs, then the arguments must be swapped.

For example, say T is Ellipse and U is Rectangle. Then T's index in TypesLhs is 1 and U's index in TypesRhs is 0. Consequently, Ellipse and Rectangle must be swapped before invoking Executor::Fire, which is correct.

The typelist facility already provides the IndexOf compile-time algorithm that returns the position of a type in a typelist. We can then write the swapping condition easily.

First, we must add a new template parameter that says whether the dispatcher is symmetric. Then, we add a simple little traits class template, InvocationTraits, which either swaps the arguments or does not swap them when calling the Executor::Fire member function. Here is the relevant excerpt.

```
    template
    <
        class Executor,
        bool symmetric,
        class BaseLhs,
        class TypesLhs,
        class BaseRhs = BaseLhs,
        class TypesRhs = TypesLhs,
        typename ResultType = void
    >
    class StaticDispatcher
    {
        template <bool swapArgs, class SomeLhs, class SomeRhs>
        struct InvocationTraits
        {
            static ResultType DoDispatch(SomeLhs& lhs, SomeRhs& rhs,
                Executor& exec)
            {
                return exec.Fire(lhs, rhs);
            }
        };
        template <class SomeLhs, class SomeRhs>
        struct InvocationTraits<true, SomeLhs, SomeRhs>
        {
```

```
        static ResultType DoDispatch(SomeLhs& lhs, SomeRhs& rhs,
           Executor& exec)
        {
           return exec.Fire(rhs, lhs); // swap arguments
        }
      }
   public:
      template<class SomeLhs>
      static ResultType DispatchRhs(SomeLhs& lhs, BaseRhs& rhs,
         Executor exec)
      {
         if (Head* p2 = dynamic_cast<Head*>(&rhs))
         {
            enum { swapArgs = symmetric &&
               IndexOf<Head, TypesRhs>::result <
               IndexOf<SomeLhs, TypesLhs>::result };
            typedef InvocationTraits<swapArgs, SomeLhs, Head>
               CallTraits;
            return CallTraits::DoDispatch(lhs, *p2);
         }
         else
         {
            return StaticDispatcher<Executor, BaseLhs,
               TypeLhs, BaseRhs, Tail>::DispatchRhs(
                  lhs, rhs, exec);
         }
      }
   };
```

Support for symmetry adds some complexity to StaticDispatcher, but it certainly makes things much easier for StaticDispatcher's user.

11.6 The Logarithmic Double Dispatcher

If you want to avoid the heavy dependencies accompanying the brute-force solution, you must look into a more dynamic approach. Instead of generating code at compile time, you must keep a runtime structure and use runtime algorithms that help in dynamically dispatching function calls depending on types.

RTTI (runtime type information) can be of further help here because it provides not only dynamic_cast and type identification, but also a runtime ordering of types, through the before member function of std::type_info. What before offers is an ordering relationship on all types in a program. We can use this ordering relationship for fast searches of types.

The implementation here is similar to the one found in Item 31 of Scott Meyers's *More Effective* C++ (1996a), with some improvements: The casting step when invoking a handler is automated, and the implementation herein aims at being generic.

We will avail ourselves of the TypeInfo class, described in Chapter 2. TypeInfo is a wrapper providing exactly the same functionality as std::type_info. In addition, TypeInfo provides value semantics and a caveat-free less-than operator. You can thus store TypeInfo objects in standard containers, which is of interest to this chapter.

Meyers's approach was simple: For each pair of std::type_info objects you want to dispatch upon, you register a pointer to a function with the double dispatcher. The double dispatcher stores the information in a std::map. At runtime, when invoked with two unknown objects, the double dispatcher performs a fast search (logarithmic time) for type discovery, and if it finds an entry, fires the appropriate pointer to a function.

Let's define the structure of a generic engine operating on these principles. We must templatize the engine with the base types of the two arguments (left-hand side and right-hand side). We call this engine BasicDispatcher, because we will use it as the base device for several more advanced double dispatchers.

```
template <class BaseLhs, class BaseRhs = BaseLhs,
    typename ResultType = void>
class BasicDispatcher
{
    typedef std::pair<TypeInfo, TypeInfo>
        KeyType;
    typedef ResultType (*CallbackType)(BaseLhs&, BaseRhs&);
    typedef CallbackType MappedType;
    typedef std::map<KeyType, MappedType> MapType;
    MapType callbackMap_;
public:
    ...
};
```

The key type in the map is a std::pair of two TypeInfo objects. The std::pair class supports ordering, so we don't have to provide a custom ordering functor.

BasicDispatcher can be more general if we templatize the callback type. In general, the callback does not have to be a function. It can be, for example, a functor (refer to the introduction of Chapter 5 for a discussion of functors). BasicDispatcher can accommodate functors by transforming its inner CallbackType type definition into a template parameter.

An important improvement is to change the std::map type to a more efficient structure. Matt Austern (2000) explains that the standard associative containers have a slightly narrower area of applicability than one might think. In particular, a sorted vector in combination with binary search algorithms (such as std::lower_bound) might perform much better, in both space and time, than an associative container. This happens when the number of accesses is much larger than the number of insertions. So we should take a close look at the typical usage pattern of a double-dispatcher object.

Most often, a double dispatcher is a write-once, read-many type of structure. Typically, a program sets the callbacks once and then uses the dispatcher many, many times. This is in keeping with the virtual functions mechanism, which double dispatchers extend. You decide, at compile time, which functions are virtual and which are not.

It seems as if we're better off with a sorted vector. The disadvantages of a sorted vector are linear-time insertions and linear-time deletions, and a double dispatcher is not typically concerned about the speed of either. In exchange, a vector offers about twice the lookup speed and a much smaller working set, so it is definitely a better choice for a double dispatcher.

Loki saves the trouble of maintaining a sorted vector by hand by defining an Assoc-

Vector class template. AssocVector is a drop-in replacement for std::map (it supports the same set of member functions), implemented on top of std::vector. AssocVector differs from a map in the behavior of its erase functions (AssocVector::erase invalidates all iterators into the object) and in the complexity guarantees of insert and erase (linear as opposed to constant). Because of the high degree of compatibility of AssocVector with std::map, we'll continue to use the term *map* to describe the data structure held by the double dispatcher.

Here is the revised definition of BasicDispatcher:

```
template
<
    class BaseLhs,
    class BaseRhs = BaseLhs,
    typename ResultType = void,
    typename CallbackType = ResultType (*)(BaseLhs&, BaseRhs&)
>
class BasicDispatcher
{
    typedef std::pair<TypeInfo, TypeInfo>
        KeyType;
    typedef CallbackType MappedType;
    typedef AssocVector<KeyType, MappedType> MapType;
    MapType callbackMap_;
public:
    ...
};
```

The registration function is easy to define. This is all we need:

```
template <...>
class BasicDispatcher
{
    ... as above ...
    template <class SomeLhs, class SomeRhs>
    void Add(CallbackType fun)
    {
        const KeyType key(typeid(SomeLhs), typeid(SomeRhs));
        callbackMap_[key] = fun;
    }
};
```

The types SomeLhs and SomeRhs are the concrete types for which you need to dispatch the call. Just like std::map, AssocVector overloads operator[] to find a key's corresponding mapped type. If the entry is missing, a new element is inserted. Then operator[] returns a reference to that new or found element, and Add assigns fun to it.

The following is an example of using Add:

```
typedef BasicDispatcher<Shape> Dispatcher;
// Hatches the intersection between a rectangle and a polygon
void HatchRectanglePoly(Shape& lhs, Shape& rhs)
{
    Rectangle& rc = dynamic_cast<Rectangle&>(lhs);
```

```
        Poly& pl = dynamic_cast<Poly&>(rhs);
        ... use rc and pl ...
    }
    ...
    Dispatcher disp;
    disp.Add<Rectangle, Poly>(HatchRectanglePoly);
```

The member function that does the search and invocation is simple:

```
    template <...>
    class BasicDispatcher
    {
        ... as above ...
        ResultType Go(BaseLhs& lhs, BaseRhs& rhs)
        {
            MapType::iterator i = callbackMap_.find(
                KeyType(typeid(lhs), typeid(rhs)));
            if (i == callbackMap_.end())
            {
                throw std::runtime_error("Function not found");
            }
            return (i->second)(lhs, rhs);
        }
    };
```

11.6.1 *The Logarithmic Dispatcher and Inheritance*

BasicDispatcher does not work correctly with inheritance. If you register only Hatch-
RectanglePoly(Shape& lhs,Shape&rhs) with BasicDispatcher, you get proper dispatching only for objects of type Rectangle and Poly—nothing else. If, for instance, you pass
references to a RoundedRectangle and a Poly to BasicDispatcher::Go, BasicDispatcher
will reject the call.

The behavior of BasicDispatcher is not in keeping with inheritance rules, according
to which derived types must by default act like their base types. It would be nice if
BasicDispatcher accepted calls with objects of derived classes, as long as these calls were
unambiguous per C++'s overloading rules.

There are quite a few things you can do to correct this problem, but to date there is
no complete solution. You must be careful to register all the pairs of types with Basic-
Dispatcher.[4]

11.6.2 *The Logarithmic Dispatcher and Casts*

BasicDispatcher is usable, but not quite satisfactory. Although you register a function
that handles the intersection between a Rectangle and a Poly, that function must accept arguments of the base type, Shape&. It is awkward and error-prone to ask client code
(HatchRectanglePoly's implementation) to cast the Shape references back to the correct types.

On the other hand, the callback map cannot hold a different function or functor type for

---

[4]I am convinced there is a solution to the inheritance problem. But, alas, writers of books have deadlines, too.

each element, so we must stick to a uniform representation. Item 31 in *More Effective C++* (Meyers 1996a) discusses this issue, too. No function-pointer-to-function-pointer cast helps because after you exit `BasicDispatcher::Add`, you've lost the static type information, so you don't know what to cast to. (If this sounds confusing, try spinning some code and you'll immediately figure it out.)

We will implement a solution to the casting problem in the context of simple callback functions (not functors). That is, the `CallbackType` template argument is a pointer to a function.

An idea that could help is using a *trampoline function*, also known as a *thunk*. Trampoline functions are small functions that perform little adjustments before calling other functions. They are commonly used by C++ compiler writers to implement features such as covariant return types and pointer adjustments for multiple inheritance.

We can use a trampoline function that performs the appropriate cast and then calls a function of the proper signature, thus making life much easier for the client. The problem, however, is that `callbackMap_` must now store *two* pointers to functions: one to the pointer provided by the client, and one to the pointer to the trampoline function. This is worrisome in terms of speed. Instead of an indirect call through a pointer, we have two. In addition, the implementation becomes more complicated.

An interesting bit of wizardry saves the day. A template can accept a pointer to a function as a nontype template parameter. (Most often in this book, nontype template parameters are integral values.) A template is allowed to accept pointers to global objects, including functions, as nontype template parameters. The only condition is that the function whose address is used as a template argument must have external linkage. You can easily transform static functions into functions with external linkage by removing `static` and putting them into unnamed namespaces. For example, what you would write as

```
static void Fun();
```

in pre-namespace C++, you can write using an anonymous namespace as

```
namespace
{
    void Fun();
}
```

Using a pointer to a function as a nontype template argument means that we no longer need to store it in the map. This essential aspect needs thorough understanding. The reason we don't need to store the pointer to a function is that the compiler has static knowledge about it. Thus, the compiler can hardcode the function address in the trampoline code.

We implement this idea in a new class that uses `BasicDispatcher` as its back end. The new class, `FnDispatcher`, is tuned for dispatching to functions only—not to functors. `FnDispatcher` aggregates `BasicDispatcher` privately and provides appropriate forwarding functions.

The `FnDispatcher::Add` template function accepts three template parameters. Two represent the left-hand-side and the right-hand-side types for which the dispatch is registered

(ConcreteLhs and ConcreteRhs). The third template parameter (callback) is the pointer to a function. The added FnDispatcher::Add overloads the template Add with only two template parameters, defined earlier.

```
template <class BaseLhs, class BaseRhs = BaseLhs,
    typename ResultType = void>
class FnDispatcher
{
    BasicDispatcher<BaseLhs, BaseRhs, ResultType> backEnd_;
    ...
public:
    template <class ConcreteLhs, class ConcreteRhs,
        ResultType (*callback)(ConcreteLhs&, ConcreteRhs&)>
    void Add()
    {
        struct Local // see Chapter 2
        {
            static ResultType Trampoline(BaseLhs& lhs, BaseRhs& rhs)
            {
                return callback(
                    dynamic_cast<ConcreteLhs&>(lhs),
                    dynamic_cast<ConcreteRhs&>(rhs));
            }
        };
        return backEnd_.Add<ConcreteLhs, ConcreteRhs>(
            &Local::Trampoline);
    }
};
```

Using a local structure, we define the trampoline right inside Add. The trampoline casts the arguments to the right types and then forwards to callback. Then, the Add function uses backEnd_'s Add function (defined by BasicDispatcher) to add the trampoline to callbackMap_.

As far as speed is concerned, the trampoline does not incur additional overhead. Although it looks like an indirect call, the call to callback is not. As explained before, the compiler hardwires callback's address right into Trampoline so there is no second indirection. A clever compiler can even inline the call to callback if possible.

Using the newly defined Add function is simple:

```
typedef FnDispatcher<Shape> Dispatcher;

// Possibly in an unnamed namespace
void HatchRectanglePoly(Rectangle& lhs, Poly& rhs)
{
    ...
}

Dispatcher disp;
disp.Add<Rectangle, Poly, HatchRectanglePoly>();
```

Because of its Add member function, FnDispatcher is easy to use. FnDispatcher also exposes an Add function similar to the one defined by BaseDispatcher, so you still can use this function if you need to.[5]

11.7 FnDispatcher and Symmetry

Because of FnDispatcher's dynamism, adding support for symmetry is much easier than it was with the static StaticDispatcher.

All we have to do to support symmetry is to register two trampolines: one that calls the executor in normal order, and one that swaps the parameters before calling. We add a new template parameter to Add, as shown.

```
template <class BaseLhs, class BaseRhs = BaseLhs,
    typename ResultType = void>
class FnDispatcher
{
    ...
    template <class ConcreteLhs, class ConcreteRhs,
        ResultType (*callback)(ConcreteLhs&, ConcreteRhs&),
        bool symmetric>
    void Add()
    {
        struct Local
        {
            ... Trampoline as before ...
            static ResultType TrampolineR(BaseRhs& rhs, BaseLhs& lhs)
            {
                return Trampoline(lhs, rhs);
            }
        };
        Add<ConcreteLhs, ConcreteRhs>(&Local::Trampoline);
        if (symmetric)
        {
            Add<ConcreteRhs, ConcreteLhs>(&Local::TrampolineR);
        }
    }
};
```

Symmetry with FnDispatcher has function-level granularity—for each function you register, you can decide whether or not you want symmetric dispatching.

11.8 Double Dispatch to Functors

As described earlier, the trampoline trick works nicely with pointers to nonstatic functions. Anonymous namespaces provide a clean way to replace static functions with nonstatic functions that are not visible outside the current compilation unit.

---

[5]One case in which you cannot use FnDispatcher::Add is when you need to register dynamically loaded functions. Even in this case, however, you can make slight changes to your design so that you can take advantage of trampolines.

Sometimes, however, you need your callback objects (the CallbackType template parameter of BasicDispatcher) to be more substantial than simple pointers to functions. For instance, you might want each callback to hold some state, and functions cannot hold much state (only static variables). Consequently, you need to register *functors*, and not functions, with the double dispatcher.

Functors (Chapter 5) are classes that overload the function call operator, operator(), thus imitating simple functions in call syntax. Additionally, functors can use member variables for storing and accessing state. Unfortunately, the trampoline trick cannot work with functors, precisely because functors hold state and simple functions do not. (Where would the trampoline hold the state?)

Client code can use BasicDispatcher directly, instantiated with the appropriate functor type.

```
struct HatchFunctor
{
    void operator()(Shape&, Shape&)
    {
        ...
    }
};

typedef BasicDispatcher<Shape, Shape, void, HatchFunctor>
    HatchingDispatcher;
```

HatchFunctor::operator() itself cannot be virtual, because BasicDispatcher needs a functor with value semantics, and value semantics don't mix nicely with runtime polymorphism. However, HatchFunctor::operator() can forward a call to a virtual function.

The real disadvantage is that the client loses some automation that the dispatcher could do—namely, taking care of the casts and providing symmetry.

It seems as if we're back to square one, but only if you haven't read Chapter 5 on generalized functors. Chapter 5 defines a Functor class template that can aggregate any kind of functor and pointers to functions, even other Functor objects. You can even define specialized Functor objects by deriving from the FunctorImpl class. We can define a Functor to take care of the casts. Once the casts are confined to the library, we can implement symmetry easily.

Let's define a FunctorDispatcher that dispatches to any Functor objects. This dispatcher will aggregate a BasicDispatcher that stores Functor objects.

```
template <class BaseLhs, class BaseRhs = BaseLhs,
    typename ResultType = void>
class FunctorDispatcher
{
    typedef Functor<ResultType,
        TYPELIST_2(BaseLhs&, BaseRhs&)>
        FunctorType;
    typedef BasicDispatcher<BaseLhs, BaseRhs, ResultType,
        FunctorType>
        BackEndType;
    BackEndType backEnd_;
```

```
public:
    ...
};
```

FunctorDispatcher uses a BasicDispatcher instantiation as its back end. Basic-Dispatcher stores objects of type FunctorType, which are Functors that accept two parameters (BaseLhs and BaseRhs) and return a ResultType.

The FunctorDispatcher::Add member function defines a specialized FunctorImpl class by deriving from it. The specialized class (Adapter, shown below) takes care of casting the arguments to the right types; in other words, it *adapts* the argument types from BaseLhs and BaseRhs to SomeLhs and SomeRhs.

```
template <class BaseLhs, class BaseRhs = BaseLhs,
    ResultType = void>
class FunctorDispatcher
{
    ... as above ...
    template <class SomeLhs, class SomeRhs, class Fun>
    void Add(const Fun& fun)
    {
        typedef
            FunctorImpl<ResultType, TYPELIST_2(BaseLhs&, BaseRhs&)>
            FunctorImplType;
        class Adapter : public FunctorImplType
        {
            Fun fun_;
            virtual ResultType operator()(BaseLhs& lhs, BaseRhs& rhs)
            {
                return fun_(
                    dynamic_cast<SomeLhs&>(lhs),
                    dynamic_cast<SomeRhs&>(rhs));
            }
            virtual FunctorImplType* Clone() const
            { return new Adapter; }
        public:
            Adapter(const Fun& fun) : fun_(fun) {}
        };
        backEnd_.Add<SomeLhs, SomeRhs>(
            FunctorType((FunctorImplType*)new Adapter(fun)));
    }
};
```

The Adapter class does exactly what the trampoline function did. Because functors have state, Adapter aggregates a Fun object—something that was impossible with a simple trampoline function. The Clone member function, with obvious semantics, is required by Functor.

FunctorDispatcher::Add has remarkably broad uses. You can use it to register not only pointers to functions, but also almost any functor you want, even generalized functors. The only requirements for the Fun type in Add is that it accept the function-call operator with arguments of types SomeLhs and SomeRhs and that it return a type convertible to ResultType. The following example registers two different functors to a Functor-Dispatcher object.

```
typedef FunctorDispatcher<Shape> Dispatcher;
struct HatchRectanglePoly
{
    void operator()(Rectangle& r, Poly& p)
    {
        ...
    }
};
struct HatchEllipseRectangle
{
    void operator()(Ellipse& e, Rectangle& r)
    {
        ...
    }
};
...
Dispatcher disp;
disp.Add<Rectangle, Poly>(HatchRectanglePoly());
disp.Add<Ellipse, Rectangle>(HatchEllipseRectangle());
```

The two functors don't have to be related in any way (as with inheriting from a common base). All they have to do is to implement operator() for the types that they advertise to handle.

Implementing symmetry with FunctorDispatcher is similar to implementing symmetry in FnDispatcher. FunctorDispatcher::Add defines a new ReverseAdapter object that does the casts and reverses the order of calls.

11.9 Converting Arguments: static_cast or dynamic_cast?

All the previous code has performed casting with the safe dynamic_cast. But in the case of dynamic_cast, safety comes at a cost in runtime efficiency.

At registration time, you already know that your function or functor will fire for a pair of specific, known types. Through the mechanism it implements, the double dispatcher *knows* the actual types when an entry in the map is found. It seems a waste, then, to have dynamic_cast check again for correctness when a simple static_cast achieves the same result in much less time.

There are, however, two cases in which static_cast may fail and the only cast to rely on is dynamic_cast. The first occurs when you're using virtual inheritance. Consider the following class hierarchy:

```
class Shape { ... };
class Rectangle : virtual public Shape { ... };
class RoundedShape : virtual public Shape { ... };
class RoundedRectangle : public Rectangle,
    public RoundedShape { ... };
```

Figure 11.2 displays a graphical representation of the relationships between classes in this hierarchy.

This may not be a very smart class hierarchy, but one thing about designing class libraries is that you never know what your clients might need to do. There are definitely

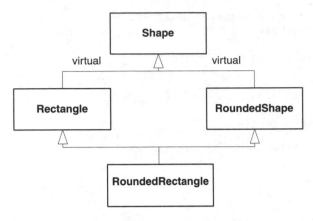

Figure 11.2: A diamond-shaped class hierarchy using virtual inheritance

reasonable situations in which a diamond-shaped class hierarchy is needed, in spite of all its caveats. Consequently, the double dispatchers we defined should work with diamond-shaped class hierarchies.

The dispatchers actually work fine as of now. But if you try to replace the dynamic_casts with static_casts, you will get compile-time errors whenever you try to cast a Shape& to any of Rectangle&, RoundedShape&, and RoundedRectangle&. The reason is that virtual inheritance works very differently from plain inheritance. Virtual inheritance provides a means for several derived classes to share the same base class object. The compiler cannot just lay out a derived object in memory by gluing together a base object with whatever the derived class adds.

In some implementations of multiple inheritance, each derived object stores a pointer to its base object. When you cast from derived to base, the compiler uses that pointer. But the base object does not store pointers to its derived objects. From a pragmatic viewpoint, all this means that after you cast an object of derived type to a virtual base type, there's no compile-time mechanism for getting back to the derived object. You cannot static_cast from a virtual base to an object of derived type.

However, dynamic_cast uses more advanced means to retrieve the relationships between classes and works nicely even in the presence of virtual bases. In a nutshell, you must use dynamic_cast if you have a hierarchy using virtual inheritance.

Second, let's analyze the situation with a similar class hierarchy, but one that doesn't use virtual inheritance—only plain multiple inheritance.

```
class Shape { ... };
class Rectangle : public Shape { ... };
class RoundedShape : public Shape { ... };
class RoundedRectangle : public Rectangle,
    public RoundedShape { ... };
```

Figure 11.3 shows the resulting inheritance graph.

Although the shape of the class hierarchy is the same, the structure of the objects is very different. RoundedRectangle now has two distinct subobjects of type Shape. This means

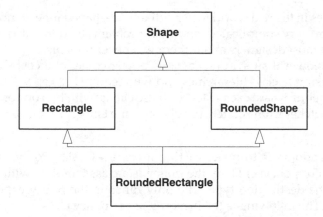

Figure 11.3: A diamond-shaped class hierarchy using nonvirtual inheritance

that converting from RoundedRectangle to Shape is now ambiguous: Which Shape do you mean—that in the RoundedShape or that in the Rectangle? Similarly, you cannot even static cast a Shape& to a RoundedRectangle& because the compiler doesn't know which Shape subobject to consider.

We're facing trouble again. Consider the following code:

```
RoundedRectangle roundRect;
Rectangle& rect = roundRect;            // Unambiguous implicit conversion
Shape& shape1 = rect;
RoundedShape& roundShape = roundRect;   // Unambiguous implicit
                                        // conversion
Shape& shape2 = roundShape;
SomeDispatcher d;
Shape& someOtherShape = ...;
d.Go(shape1, someOtherShape);
d.Go(shape2, someOtherShape);
```

Here, it is essential that the dispatcher use `dynamic_cast` to convert the Shape& to a Rounded-Shape&. If you try to register a trampoline for converting RoundedRectangle& to Shape& a compile-time error occurs due to ambiguity.

There is no trouble at all if the dispatcher uses `dynamic_cast`. A dynamic_cast<Rounded Rectangle&> applied to any of the two base Shape subobjects of a RoundedRectangle leads to the correct object. As you can see, nothing beats a dynamic cast. The `dynamic_cast` operator is designed to reach the right object in a class hierarchy, no matter how intricate its structure is.

The conclusion that consolidates these findings is this: You cannot use `static_cast` with a double dispatcher in a class hierarchy that has multiple occurrences of the same base class, whether or not it is through virtual inheritance.

This might give you a strong incentive to use `dynamic_cast` in all dispatchers. However, there are two supplemental considerations.

- Very few class hierarchies in the real world foster a diamond-shaped inheritance graph. Such class hierarchies are very complicated, and their problems tend to outweigh their advantages. That's why most designers avoid them whenever possible.
- dynamic_cast is much slower than static_cast. Its power comes at a cost. There are many clients who have simple class hierarchies and who require high speed. Committing the double dispatcher to dynamic_cast leaves these clients with two options: Reimplement the whole dispatcher from scratch, or rely on some embarrassing surgery into library code.

The solution that Loki adopts is to make casting a *policy*—CastingPolicy. (Refer to Chapter 1 for a description of policies.) Here, the policy is a class template with two parameters: the source and the destination type. The only function the policy exposes is a static function called Cast. The following is the DynamicCaster policy class.

```
template <class To, class From>
struct DynamicCaster
{
    static To& Cast(From& obj)
    {
        return dynamic_cast<To&>(obj);
    }
};
```

The dispatchers FnDispatcher and FunctorDispatcher use CastingPolicy according to the guidelines described in Chapter 1. Here is the modified FunctorDispatcher class. The changes are shown in bold.

```
template
<
    class BaseLhs,
    class BaseRhs = BaseLhs,
    typename ResultType = void,
    template <class, class> class CastingPolicy = DynamicCaster
>
class FunctorDispatcher
{
    ...
    template <class SomeLhs, class SomeRhs, class Fun>
    void Add(const Fun& fun)
    {
        class Adapter : public FunctorType::Impl
        {
            Fun fun_;
            virtual ResultType operator()(BaseLhs& lhs,
                BaseRhs& rhs)
            {
                return fun_(
                    CastingPolicy<SomeLhs, BaseLhs>::Cast(lhs),
                    CastingPolicy<SomeRhs, BaseRhs>::Cast(rhs));
            }
            ... as before ...
        };
```

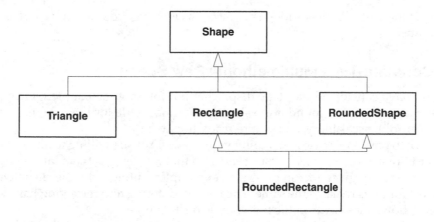

Figure 11.4: A class hierarchy with a diamond-shaped portion

```
    backEnd_.Add<SomeLhs, SomeRhs>(
      FunctorType(new Adapter(fun)));
  }
};
```

Cautiously, the casting policy defaults to DynamicCaster.

Finally, you can do a very interesting thing with casting policies. Consider the hierarchy in Figure 11.4. There are two categories of casts within this hierarchy. Some do not involve a diamond-shaped structure, so static_cast is safe. Namely, static_cast suffices for casting a Shape& to a Triangle&. On the other hand, you cannot static_cast a Shape& to Rectangle& and any of its derivatives; you must use dynamic_cast.

Suppose you define your own casting policy template for this class hierarchy, namely ShapeCaster. You can make it default to dynamic_cast. You can then specialize the policy for the special cases:

```
template <class To, class From>
struct ShapeCaster
{
   static To& Cast(From& obj)
   {
      return dynamic_cast<To&>(obj);
   }
};

template<>
class ShapeCaster<Triangle, Shape>
{
   static Triangle& Cast(Shape& obj)
   {
      return static_cast<Triangle&>(obj);
   }
};
```

You now get the best of both worlds—speedy casts whenever you can, and safe casts whenever you must.

11.10 Constant-Time Multimethods: Raw Speed

Maybe you have considered the static dispatcher but found it too coupled, have tried the map-based dispatcher but found it too slow. You cannot settle for less: You need absolute speed and absolute scalability, and you're ready to pay for it.

The price to pay in this case is changing your classes. You are willing to allow the double dispatcher to plant some hooks in your classes so that it leverages them later.

This opportunity gives a fresh perspective to implementing a double-dispatch engine. The support for casts remains the same. The means of storing and retrieving handlers must be changed, however—logarithmic time is not constant time.

To find a better dispatching mechanism, let's ask ourselves again, What is double dispatching? You can see it as finding a handler function (or functor) in a two-dimensional space. On one axis are the types of the left-hand operator. On the other axis are the types of the right-hand operator. At the intersection between two types, you find their respective handler function. Figure 11.5 illustrates double dispatch for two class hierarchies—one of Shapes and one of DrawingDevices. The handlers can be drawing functions that know how to render each concrete Shape object on each concrete DrawingDevice object.

It doesn't take long to figure out that if you need constant-time searches in this two-dimensional space, you must rely on indexed access in a two-dimensional matrix.

The idea takes off swiftly. Each class must bear a unique integral value, which is the index in the dispatcher matrix. That integral value must be accessible for each class in constant time. A virtual function can help here. When you issue a double-dispatch call, the dispatcher fetches the two indices from the two objects, accesses the handler in the matrix, and launches the handler. Cost: two virtual calls, one matrix indexing operation, and a call through a pointer to a function. The cost is constant.

It seems as if the idea should work quite nicely, but some of its details are not easy to get right. For instance, maintaining indices is very likely to be uncomfortable. For each class, you must assign a unique integral ID and hope that you can detect any duplicates at compile time. The integral IDs must start from zero and have no gaps—otherwise, we would waste matrix storage.

A much better solution is to move index management to the dispatcher itself. Each class stores a static integral variable; initially, its value is −1, meaning "unassigned." A virtual function returns a reference to that static variable, allowing the dispatcher to change it at runtime. As you add new handlers to the matrix, the dispatcher accesses the ID and, if it is −1, assigns the next available slot in the matrix to it.

Here's the gist of this implementation—a simple macro that you must plant in each class of your class hierarchy.

```
#define IMPLEMENT_INDEXABLE_CLASS(SomeClass)\
    static int& GetClassIndexStatic()\
    {\
        static int index = -1;\
        return index;\
```

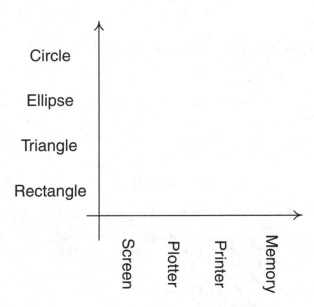

Figure 11.5: Dispatching on Shapes and DrawingDevices

```
}\
virtual int& GetClassIndex()\
{\
    assert(typeid(*this) == typeid(SomeClass));\
    return GetClassIndexStatic();\
}
```

You must insert this macro in the public portion of each class for which you want to support multiple dispatch.[6]

The BasicFastDispatcher class template exposes exactly the same functionality as the previously defined BasicDispatcher but uses different storage and retrieval mechanisms.

```
template
<
    class BaseLhs,
    class BaseRhs = BaseLhs,
    typename ResultType = void,
    typename CallbackType = ResultType (*)(BaseLhs&, BaseRhs&)
>
class BasicFastDispatcher
{
    typedef std::vector<CallbackType> Row;
    typedef std::vector<Row> Matrix;
    Matrix callbacks_;
```

---

[6]Yes, *multiple,* not only double, dispatch. You can easily generalize the index-based solution to support multiple dispatch.

```
        int nextIndex_;
    public:
        BasicFastDispatcher() : nextIndex_(0) {}
        template <class SomeLhs, class SomeRhs>
        void Add(CallbackType pFun)
        {
            int& idxLhs = SomeLhs::GetClassIndexStatic();
            if (idxLhs < 0)
            {
                callbacks_.resize(++nextIndex_);
                idxLhs = callbacks_.size() - 1;
            }
            else if (callbacks_.size() <= idxLhs)
            {
                callbacks_.resize(idxLhs + 1);
            }
            Row& thisRow = callbacks_[idxLhs];
            int& idxRhs = SomeRhs::GetClassIndexStatic();
            if (idxRhs < 0)
            {
                thisRow.resize(++nextIndex_);
                idxRhs = thisRow.size() - 1;
            }
            else if (thisRow.size() <= idxRhs)
            {
                thisRow.resize(idxRhs + 1);
            }
            thisRow[idxRhs] = pFun;
        }
    };
```

The callback matrix is implemented as a vector of vectors of `MappedType`. The `BasicFastDispatcher::Add` function performs the following sequence of actions:

1. Fetches the ID of each class by calling `GetClassIndexStatic`.
2. Performs initialization and adjustments if one or both indices were not initialized. For uninitialized indices, `Add` expands the matrix to accommodate one extra element.
3. Inserts the callback at the correct position in the matrix.

The `nextIndex_` member variable tallies the number of columns added so far. Strictly speaking, `nextIndex_` is redundant; a search for the maximum row length in the matrix would yield the same result. However, `nextIndex_`'s convenience justifies its presence.

The `BasicFastDispatcher::Go` is easy to implement now. The main difference is that `Go` uses the virtual function `GetClassIndex`.

```
    template <...>
    class BasicFastDispatcher
    {
        ... as above ...
        ResultType Go(BaseLhs& lhs, BaseRhs& rhs)
        {
            int& idxLhs = lhs.GetClassIndex();
```

```
            int& idxRhs = rhs.GetClassIndex();
            if (idxLhs < 0 || idxRhs < 0 ||
               idxLhs >= callbacks_.size() ||
               idxRhs >= callbacks_[idxLhs].size() ||
               callbacks_[idxLhs][idxRhs] == 0)
            {
               ... error handling goes here ...
            }
            return callbacks_[idxLhs][idxRhs](lhs, rhs);
         }
      };
```

Let's recap this section. We defined a matrix-based dispatcher that reaches callback objects in constant time by assigning an integral index to each class. In addition, it performs automatic initialization of its support data (the indices corresponding to the classes). Users of BasicFastDispatcher must add a one-macro line, IMPLEMENT_INDEXABLE_CLASS (*YourClass*), to each class that is to use BasicFastDispatcher.

11.11 BasicDispatcher and BasicFastDispatcher as Policies

BasicFastDispatcher (matrix based) is preferable to BasicDispatcher (map based) when speed is a concern. However, the nice advanced classes FnDispatcher and Functor-Dispatcher are built around BasicDispatcher. Should we develop two new classes—FnFastDispatcher and FunctorFastDispatcher—that use BasicFastDispatcher as their back end?

A better idea is to try to adapt FnDispatcher and FunctorDispatcher to use either BasicDispatcher or BasicFastDispatcher, depending on a template parameter. That is, make the dispatcher a *policy* for the class templates FnDispatcher and FunctorDispatcher, much as we did with the casting strategy.

The task of morphing the dispatcher into a policy is eased by the fact that Basic-Dispatcher and BasicFastDispatcher have the same call interface. This makes replacing one with the other as easy as changing a template argument.

The following is the revised declaration of FnDispatcher (FunctorDispatcher's declaration is similar). The changes are shown in bold.

```
template
<
    class BaseLhs,
    class BaseRhs = BaseLhs,
    typename ResultType = void,
    template <class, class>
        class CastingPolicy = DynamicCaster,
    template <class, class, class, class>
        class DispatcherBackend = BasicDispatcher
>
class FnDispatcher; // similarly for FunctorDispatcher
```

Table 11.1 `DispatcherBackend` **Policy Requirements**

Expression	Return Type	Notes
`copy`, `assign`, `swap`, `destroy`		Value semantics.
`backEnd.Add<SomeLhs, SomeRhs>(callback)`	`void`	Add a callback to the `backEnd` object for types `SomeLhs` and `SomeRhs`.
`backEnd.Go(BaseLhs&, BaseRhs&)`	`ResultType`	Performs a lookup and a dispatch for the two objects. Throws `std::runtime_error` if a handler is not found.
`backEnd.Remove<SomeLhs, SomeRhs>()`	`bool`	Removes the callback for the types `SomeLhs` and `SomeRhs`. Returns `true` if there was a callback.
`backEnd.HandlerExists <SomeLhs, SomeRhs>()`	`bool`	Returns `true` if a callback is registered for the types `SomeLhs` and `SomeRhs`. No callback is added.

The two classes themselves undergo very few changes.

Let's clarify the DispatcherBackend policy requirements. First of all, obviously, DispatcherBackend must be a template with four parameters. The parameter semantics are, in order

- Left-hand operand type
- Right-hand operand type
- Return type of the callback
- The callback type

In Table 11.1, `BackendType` represents an instantiation of the dispatcher back-end template, and `backEnd` represents a variable of that type. The table contains functions that we haven't mentioned yet—don't worry. A complete dispatcher must come with functions that remove callbacks and that do a "passive" lookup without calling the callback. These are trivial to implement; you can see them in Loki's source code, file `MultiMethods.h`.

11.12 Looking Forward

Generalization is right around the corner. We can take our findings regarding double dispatch and apply them to implementing true generic multiple dispatch.

It's actually quite easy. This chapter defines three types of double dispatchers:

- A static dispatcher, driven by two typelists
- A map-based dispatcher, driven by a map keyed by a pair of std::type_info objects[7]
- A matrix-based dispatcher, driven by a matrix indexed with unique numeric class IDs

It's easy to generalize these dispatchers as follows. You can generalize the static dispatcher to one driven by a typelist of typelists, instead of two typelists. Yes, you can define a typelist of typelists because any typelist is a type. The following typedef defines a typelist of three typelists, possible participants in a triple-dispatch scenario. Remarkably, the resulting typelist is actually easy to read.

```
typedef TYPELIST_3
(
    TYPELIST_3(Shape, Rectangle, Ellipse),
    TYPELIST_3(Screen, Printer, Plotter),
    TYPELIST_3(File, Socket, Memory)
)
ListOfLists;
```

You can generalize the map-based dispatcher to one that is keyed by a vector of TypeInfo objects (as opposed to a std::pair). That vector's size will be the number of objects involved in the multiple-dispatch operation. A possible synopsis of a generalized BasicDispatcher is as follows:

```
template
<
    class ListOfTypes,
    typename ResultType,
    typename CallbackType
>
class GeneralBasicDispatcher;
```

The ListOfTypes template parameter is a typelist containing the base types involved in the multiple dispatch. For instance, our earlier example of hatching intersections between two shapes would have used a TYPELIST_2(Shape, Shape).

You can generalize the matrix-based dispatcher by using a multidimensional array. You can build a multidimensional array with a recursive class template. The existing scheme of assigning numeric IDs to types works just as it is. This has the nice effect that if you modify a hierarchy once to support double dispatch, you don't have to modify it again to support multiple dispatch.

All these possible extensions need the usual amount of work to get all the details right. A particularly nasty problem related to multiple dispatch and C++ is that there's no uniform way to represent functions with a variable number of arguments.

As of now, Loki implements double dispatch only. The interesting generalizations just suggested are left in the dreaded form of the exercise for . . . you know.

---

[7]Dressed as TypeInfo to ease comparisons and copying.

11.13 Summary

Multimethods are generalized virtual functions. Whereas the C++ runtime support dispatches virtual functions on a per-class basis, multimethods are dispatched depending on multiple classes simultaneously. This allows you to implement virtual functions for collections of types instead of one type at a time.

By their nature, multimethods are best implemented as a language feature. C++ lacks such a feature, but there are several ways to implement it in libraries.

Multimethods are needed in applications that call algorithms that depend on the type of two or more objects. Typical examples include collisions between polymorphic objects, intersections, and displaying objects on various target devices.

This chapter limits discussion to the defining of multimethods for two objects. An object that takes care of selecting the appropriate function to call is called a double dispatcher. The types of dispatchers discussed are as follows:

- *The brute-force dispatcher.* This dispatcher relies on static type information (provided in the form of a typelist) and does a linear unrolled search for the correct types. Once the types are found, the dispatcher calls an overloaded member function in a handler object.
- *The map-based dispatcher.* This uses a map keyed by `std::type_info` objects. The mapped value is a callback (either a pointer to a function or a functor). The type discovery algorithm performs a binary search.
- *The constant-time dispatcher.* This is the fastest dispatcher of all, but it requires you to modify the classes on which it acts. The change is to add a macro to each class that you want to use with the constant-time dispatcher. The cost of a dispatch is two virtual calls, a couple of numeric tests, and a matrix element access.

On top of the last two dispatchers, higher-level facilities can be implemented:

- *Automated conversions.* (Not to be confused with automatic conversions.) Because of their uniformity, the dispatchers above require the client to cast the objects from their base types to their derived types. A casting layer can provide a trampoline function that takes care of these conversions.
- *Symmetry.* Some double-dispatch applications are symmetric in nature. They dispatch on the same base type on both sides of the double-dispatch operation, and they don't care about the order of elements. For instance, in a collision detector it doesn't matter whether a spaceship hits a torpedo or a torpedo hits a spaceship—the behavior is the same. Implementing support for symmetry in the library makes client code smaller and less exposed to errors.

The brute-force dispatcher supports these higher-level features directly. This is possible because the brute-force dispatcher has extensive type information available. The other two dispatchers use different methods and add an extra layer to implement automated conversions and symmetry. Double dispatchers for functions implement this extra layer differently (and more efficiently) than double dispatchers for functors.

Table 11.2 compares the three dispatcher types defined in this chapter. As you can see,

Table 11.2: Comparison of Various Implementations of Double Dispatch

	Static Dispatcher (Static-Dispatcher)	Logarithmic Dispatcher (Basic-Dispatcher)	Constant-Time Dispatcher (BasicFast-Dispatcher)
Speed for few classes	Best	Modest	Good
Speed for many classes	Low	Good	Best
Dependency introduced	Heavy	Low	Low
Alteration of existing classes needed	None	None	Add a macro to each class
Compile-time safety	Best	Good	Good
Runtime safety	Best	Good	Good

none of the presented implementations is ideal. You should choose the solution that best fits your needs for a given situation.

11.14 Double Dispatcher Quick Facts

- Loki defines three basic double dispatchers: StaticDispatcher, BasicDispatcher, and BasicFastDispatcher.
- StaticDispatcher's declaration:

```
template
<
    class Executor,
    class BaseLhs,
    class TypesLhs,
    bool symmetric = true,
    class BaseRhs = BaseLhs,
    class TypesRhs = TypesLhs,
    typename ResultType = void
>
class StaticDispatcher;
```

where

BaseLhs is the base left-hand type.

TypesLhs is a typelist containing the set of concrete types involved in the double dispatch on the left-hand side.

symmetric controls whether the dispatch is symmetric or not.

BaseRhs is the base right-hand type.

TypesRhs is a typelist containing the set of concrete types involved in the double dispatch on the right-hand side.

Executor is a class that provides the functions to be invoked after type discovery. Executor must provide an overloaded member function Fire for each combination of types in TypesLhs and TypesRhs.

ResultType is the type returned by the Executor::Fire overloaded functions. The returned value will be forwarded as the result of StaticDispatcher::Go.

- Executor must provide a member function OnError(BaseLhs&, BaseRhs&) for error handling. StaticDispatcher calls Executor::OnError when it encounters an unknown type.

- Example (assume Rectangle and Ellipse inherit Shape, and Printer and Screen inherit OutputDevice):

```
struct Painter
{
    bool Fire(Rectangle&, Printer&);
    bool Fire(Ellipse&, Printer&);
    bool Fire(Rectangle&, Screen&);
    bool Fire(Ellipse&, Screen&);
    bool OnError(Shape&, OutputDevice&);
};

typedef StaticDispatcher
<
    Painter,
    Shape,
    TYPELIST_2(Rectangle, Ellipse), false,
    OutputDevice,
    TYPELIST_2(Printer, Screen),
    bool
>
Dispatcher;
```

- StaticDispatcher implements the Go member function, which takes a BaseLhs&, a BaseRhs&, and an Executor&, and executes the dispatch. Example (using the previous definitions):

```
Dispatcher disp;
Shape* pSh = ...;
OutputDevice* pDev = ...;
bool result = disp.Go(*pSh, *pDev, Painter());
```

- BasicDispatcher and BasicFastDispatcher implement dynamic dispatchers that allow users to add handlers at runtime.

- BasicDispatcher finds a handler in logarithmic time. BasicFastDispatcher finds a handler in constant time but requires the user to change the definitions of all dispatched classes.

- Both classes implement the same interface, illustrated here for BasicDispatcher.

```
template
<
    class BaseLhs,
    class BaseRhs = BaseLhs,
    typename ResultType = void,
```

```
        typename CallbackType = ResultType (*)(BaseLhs&, BaseRhs&)
    >
    class BasicDispatcher;
```

where

> CallbackType is the type of object that handles the dispatch.
> BasicDispatcher and BasicFastDispatcher store and invoke objects of this type.
> All other parameters have the same meaning as for StaticDispatcher.

- The two dispatchers implement the functions described in Table 11.1.
- In addition to the three basic dispatchers, Loki also defines two advanced layers: Fn-Dispatcher and FunctorDispatcher. They use one of BasicDispatcher or BasicFast-Dispatcher as a policy.
- FnDispatcher and FunctorDispatcher have similar declarations, as shown here.

```
    template
    <
        class BaseLhs,
        class BaseRhs = BaseLhs,
        ResultType = void,
        template <class To, class From>
            class CastingPolicy = DynamicCast
        template <class, class, class, class>
            class DispatcherBackend = BasicDispatcher
    >
    class FnDispatcher;
```

where

> BaseLhs and BaseRhs are the base classes of the two hierarchies involved in the double dispatch.
>
> ResultType is the type returned by the callbacks and the dispatcher.
>
> CastingPolicy is a class template with two parameters. It must implement a static member function Cast that accepts a reference to From and returns a reference to To. The stock implementations DynamicCaster and StaticCaster use dynamic_cast and static_cast, respectively.
>
> DispatcherBackend is a class template that implements the same interface as BasicDispatcher and BasicFastDispatcher, described in Table 11.1.

- Both FnDispatcher and FunctorDispatcher provide an Add member function for their primitive handler type. For FnDispatcher the primitive handler type is ResultType-(*)(BaseLhs&, BaseRhs&). For FunctorDispatcher, the primitive handler type is Functor<ResultType,TYPELIST_2(BaseLhs&, Base Rhs&)>. Refer to Chapter 5 for a description of Functor.
- In addition, FnDispatcher provides a template function to register callbacks with the engine:

```
    void Add<SomeLhs, SomeRhs,
        ResultType (*callback)(SomeLhs&, SomeRhs&),
        bool symmetric>();
```

- If you register handlers with the Add member function shown in the previous code, you benefit from automated casting and optional symmetry.
- FunctorDispatcher provides a template Add member function:

```
template <class SomeLhs, class SomeRhs, class F>
void Add(const F& fun);
```

- F can be any of the types accepted by the Functor object (see Chapter 5), including another Functor instantiation. An object of type F must accept the function-call operator with arguments of types BaseLhs& and BaseRhs& and return a type convertible to ResultType.
- If no handler is found, all dispatch engines throw an exception of type std::-runtime_error.

Appendix

A Minimalist
Multithreading Library

A multithreaded program has multiple points of execution at the same time. Practically, this means that in a multithreaded program you can have multiple functions running at once. On a multiprocessor computer, different threads might run literally simultaneously. On a single-processor machine, a multithreading-capable operating system will apply *time slicing*—it chops each thread at short time intervals, suspends it, and gives another thread some processor time. Multithreading gives the user the impression that multiple things happen at once. For instance, a word processor can verify grammar while letting the user enter text.

Users don't like to see the hourglass cursor, so we programmers must write multithreaded programs. Unfortunately, as pleasing as it is to users, multithreading is traditionally very hard to program, and even harder to debug. Moreover, multithreading pervades application design. Making a library work safely in the presence of multiple threads cannot be done from the outside; it must be built in, even if the library does not use threads of its own.

It follows that the components provided in this book cannot ignore the threading issue. (Well, they actually could, in which case most of them would be useless in the presence of multiple threads.) Because modern applications increasingly use multithreaded execution, it would be a pity to sweep multithreading under the rug out of laziness.

This appendix provides tools and techniques that establish a sound ground for writing portable multithreaded object-oriented applications in C++. It does not provide a comprehensive introduction to multithreaded programming—a fascinating domain in itself. Trying to discuss a complete threading library *en passant* in this book would be a futile, doomed effort. The focus here is on figuring out the minimal abstractions that allow us to write multithreaded components.

Loki's threading abilities are scarce compared with the host of amenities that a modern operating system provides, because its concern is only to provide thread-safe components. On the bright side, the synchronization concepts defined in this appendix are higher level than the traditional mutexes and semaphores and might help in the design of any object-oriented multithreaded application.

A.1 A Critique of Multithreading

The advantages of multithreading on multiprocessor machines are obvious. But when executed on a single processor, multithreading may seem a bit silly. Why would you want to slow down the processor with time-slicing algorithms? Obviously, you won't get any net gain. No miracle can occur—there's still only one processor, so overall multithreading will actually slightly reduce efficiency because of the additional swapping and bookkeeping.

The reason that multithreading is important even on single-processor machines is *efficient resource use*. In a typical modern computer, there are many more resources than the processor. You have devices such as disk drives, modems, network cards, and printers. Because they are physically independent, these resources can work at the same time. For instance, there is no reason why the processor cannot compute while the disk spins and while the printer prints. However, this is exactly what would happen if your application and operating system committed exclusively to a single-threaded execution model. And you wouldn't be happy if your application didn't allow you to do anything while transferring data from the Internet through the modem.

In the same vein, even the processor might be unused for extended periods of time. As you are editing a 3D image, the short intervals between your mouse moves and clicks are little eternities to the processor. It would be nice if the drawing program could use those idle times to do something useful, such as ray tracing or computing hidden lines.

The main alternative to multithreading is *asynchronous execution*. Asynchronous execution fosters a callback model: You start an operation and register a function to be called when the operation completes. The main disadvantage of asynchronous execution compared with using multithreading is that it leads to state-rich programs. By using asynchronous execution, you cannot follow an algorithm from one point to another; you can only store a state and let the callbacks change that state. Maintaining such state is troublesome in all but the simplest operations.

True threads don't have this problem. Each thread has an implicit state given by its execution point (the statement where the thread currently executes). You can easily follow what a thread does because it's just like following a simple function. The execution point is exactly what you have to manage by hand in asynchronous execution. (The main question in asynchronous programming is "Where am I now?") In conclusion, multithreaded programs can follow the synchronous execution model, which is good.

On the other hand, threads are exposed to big problems as soon as they start sharing resources, such as data in memory. Because threads can be interrupted at any time by other threads (yes, that's *any* time, including in the middle of an assignment to a variable), operations that you thought were atomic are not. Unorganized access of threads to a piece of data is always lethal to that data.

In single-threaded programming, data health is usually guaranteed at the entry and at the exit of a function. For instance, the assignment operator (operator=) of a String class assumes the String object is valid upon entry and at exit of the operator. With multithreaded programming, you must make sure that the String object is valid even *during* the assignment operation, because another thread may interrupt an assignment and do another operation against the String object. Whereas single-threaded programming accustoms you to think of functions as atomic operations, in multithreaded programming you must state explicitly which operations are atomic. In conclusion, multithreaded programs have big trouble sharing resources, which is bad.

Most programming techniques for multithreading focus on providing *synchronization objects* that enable you to serialize access to shared resources. Whenever you do an operation that must be atomic, you lock a synchronization object. If other threads try to lock the same synchronization object, they are put on hold. You modify the data (and leave it in a coherent state) and then unlock the synchronization object. At that moment, some other thread will be able to lock the synchronization object and gain access to the data. This effectively makes every thread work on consistent data.

The following sections define various locking objects. The synchronization objects provided herein are not comprehensive, yet you can do a great deal of multithreaded programming by using them.

A.2 Loki's Approach

To deal with threading issues, Loki defines the ThreadingModel policy. ThreadingModel prescribes a template with one argument. That argument is a C++ type for which you need to access threading amenities:

```
template <typename T>
class SomeThreadingModel
{
    ...
};
```

The following sections progressively fill ThreadingModel with concepts and functionality. Loki defines a single threading model that is the default for most of Loki.

A.3 Atomic Operations on Integral Types

Assuming x is a variable of type int, consider this statement:

```
++x;
```

It might seem awkward that a book focused on design analyzes a simple increment statement, but this is the thing with multithreading—little issues affect big designs.

To increment x, the processor has to do three operations:

1. Fetch the variable from memory.
2. Increment the variable inside the arithmetic logic unit (ALU) of the processor. The ALU is the only place where an operation can take place; memory does not have arithmetic capabilities of its own.
3. Write the variable back to memory.

Because the first operation reads, the second modifies, and the third writes the data, this troika is known as a *read-modify-write (RMW) operation*.

Now suppose this increment happens in a multiprocessor architecture. To maximize efficiency, during the modify part of the RMW operation the processor unlocks the memory bus. This way another processor can access the memory while the first increments the variable, leading to better resource use.

Unfortunately, another processor can start an RMW operation against the same integer. For instance, assume there are two increments on x, which initially has value 0, performed by two processors P1 and P2 in the following sequence:

1. P1 locks the memory bus and fetches x.
2. P1 unlocks the memory bus.
3. P2 locks the memory bus and fetches x (which is still 0). At the same time, P1 increments x inside its ALU. The result is 1.
4. P2 unlocks the memory bus.
5. P1 locks the memory bus and writes 1 to x. At the same time, P2 increments x inside its ALU. Because P2 fetched a 0, the result is, again, 1.
6. P1 unlocks the memory bus.
7. P2 locks the memory bus and writes 1 to x.
8. P2 unlocks the memory bus.

The net result is that although two increment operations have been applied to x starting from 0, the final value is 1. This is an erroneous result. Worse, neither processor (thread) can figure out that the increment failed and will retry it. In a multithreaded world, nothing is atomic—not even a simple increment of an integer.

There are a number of ways to make the increment operation atomic. The most efficient way is to exploit processor capabilities. Some processors offer locked-bus operations—the RMW operation takes place as described previously, except that the memory bus is locked throughout the operation. This way, when P2 fetches x from memory, it will be after its increment by P1 has completed.

This low-level functionality is usually packaged by operating systems in C functions that provide atomic increment and atomic decrement operations.

If an OS defines atomic operations, it usually does so for the integral type that has the width of the memory bus—most of the time, int. The threading subsystem of Loki (file Threads.h) defines the type IntType inside each ThreadingModel implementation.

The primitives for atomic operations, still inside ThreadingModel, are outlined in the following:

```
template <typename T>
class SomeThreadingModel
{
public:
    typedef int IntType; // or another type as dictated by the platform
    static IntType AtomicAdd(volatile IntType& lval, IntType val);
    static IntType AtomicSubtract(volatile IntType & lval, IntType val);
    ... similar definitions for AtomicMultiply, AtomicDivide,
    ... AtomicIncrement, AtomicDecrement ...
    static void AtomicAssign(volatile IntType & lval, IntType val);
    static void AtomicAssign(IntType & lval, volatile IntType & val);
};
```

These primitives get the value to change as the first parameter (notice the pass by non-const reference and the use of volatile), and the other operand (absent in the case of unary operators) as the second parameter. Each primitive returns a copy of the `volatile` destination. The returned value is very useful when you're using these primitives because you can inspect the actual result of the operation. If you inspect the `volatile` value after the operation,

```
volatile int counter;
...
SomeThreadingModel<Widget>::AtomicAdd(counter, 5);
if (counter == 10) ...
```

then your code does not inspect `counter` immediately after the addition because another thread can modify `counter` between the call to `AtomicAdd` and the `if` statement. Most of the time, you need to see what value `counter` has immediately after *your* call to `AtomicAdd`, in which case you write

```
if (AtomicAdd(counter, 5) == 10) ...
```

The two `AtomicAssign` functions are necessary because even the copy operation can be nonatomic. For instance, if your machine bus is 32 bits wide and `long` has 64 bits, copying a `long` value involves two memory accesses.

A.4 Mutexes

Edsger W. Dijkstra has proven that in the presence of multithreading, the thread scheduler of the operating system must provide certain synchronization objects. Without them, writing correct multithreaded applications is impossible.

Mutexes are fundamental synchronization objects that allow threads to access shared resources in an ordered manner. This section defines the notion of a mutex. The rest of Loki does not use mutexes directly; instead, it defines higher-level means of synchronization that can be easily implemented with mutexes.

Mutex is a collocation of **Mut**ual **Ex**clusion, a phrase that describes the functioning of this primitive object: A mutex allows threads mutually exclusive access to a resource.

The basic functions of a mutex are `Acquire` and `Release`. Each thread that needs exclusive access to a resource (such as a shared variable) acquires the mutex. Only one thread can acquire the mutex. After one thread acquires it, all other threads that invoke `Acquire` block in a wait state (the function `Acquire` does not return). When the thread that owns the mutex calls the `Release` function, the thread scheduler chooses one of the threads that is in a wait state on the same mutex and gives that thread the ownership of the mutex.

The observable effect is that mutexes are access serialization devices: The portion of code between a call to `mtx.Acquire()` and a call to `mtx.Release()` is atomic with respect to the `mtx` object. Any other attempt to acquire the `mtx` object must wait until the atomic operation finishes.

It follows that you should allocate one mutex object for each resource you want to share between threads. The resources you might want to share include, notably, C++ objects. Every nonatomic operation with these resources must start with acquiring the mutex and end with releasing the mutex. The nonatomic operations that you might want to perform include, notably, non-`const` member functions of thread-safe objects.

For instance, imagine you have a `BankAccount` class that provides functions such as `Deposit` and `Withdraw`. These operations do more than add to and subtract from a `double` member variable; they also log additional information regarding the transaction. If `BankAccount` is to be accessed from multiple threads, the two operations must certainly be atomic. Here's how you can do this:

```
class BankAccount
{
public:
   void Deposit(double amount, const char* user)
   {
      mtx_.Acquire();
      ... perform deposit transaction ...
      mtx_.Release();
   }
   void Withdraw(double amount, const char* user)
   {
      mtx_.Acquire();
      ... perform withdrawal transaction ...
      mtx_.Release();
   }
   ...
private:
   Mutex mtx_;
   ...
};
```

As you probably have figured out (if you didn't know already), failing to call `Release` for each `Acquire` you issue has deadly effects. You lock the mutex and leave it locked—all other threads trying to acquire it block forever. In the previous code, you must implement `Deposit` and `Withdraw` very carefully with regard to exceptions and premature returns.

To mitigate this problem, many C++ threading APIs define a `Lock` object that you can initialize with a mutex. The `Lock` object's constructor calls `Acquire`, and its destructor calls `Release`. This way, if you allocate a `Lock` object on the stack, you can count on correct pairing of `Acquire` and `Release`, even in the presence of exceptions.

For portability reasons, Loki does not define mutexes on its own. It's likely you already use a multithreading library that defines its own mutexes. It would be awkward to duplicate their functionality. Instead, Loki relies on higher-level locking semantics that are implemented in terms of mutexes.

A.5 Locking Semantics in Object-Oriented Programming

Synchronization objects are associated with shared resources. In an object-oriented program, resources are objects. Therefore, in an object-oriented program, synchronization objects are associated with application objects.

It follows that each shared object should aggregate a synchronization object and lock it appropriately in every mutating member function, much as the `BankAccount` example does. This is a correct way to structure an object supporting multithreading. The structure fostering one synchronization object per object is known as *object-level locking*.

However, sometimes the size and the overhead of storing one mutex per object are too big. In this case, a synchronization strategy that keeps only one mutex per class can help.

Consider, for example, a `String` class. From time to time, you might need to perform a locking operation on a `String` object. However, you don't want each `String` to carry a mutex object; that would make `String`s big and their copying costly. In this case, you can use a static mutex object for all `String`s. Whenever a `String` object performs a locking operation, that operation will block all locking operations for all `String` objects. This strategy fosters *class-level locking*.

Loki defines two implementations of the **ThreadingModel** policy: `ClassLevelLockable` and `ObjectLevelLockable`. They encapsulate class-level locking and object-level locking semantics, respectively. The synopsis is presented here.

```
template <typename Host>
class ClassLevelLockable
{
public:
    class Lock
    {
    public:
        Lock();
        Lock(Host& obj);
        ...
    };
    ...
};

template <typename Host>
class ObjectLevelLockable
{
public:
    class Lock
    {
    public:
        Lock(Host& obj);
        ...
    };
    ...
};
```

Technically, `Lock` keeps a mutex locked. The difference between the two implementations is that you cannot construct an `ObjectLevelLockable<T>::Lock` without passing a T object to it. The reason is that `ObjectLevelLockable` uses per-object locking.

The `Lock` nested class locks the object (or the entire class, in the case of `ClassLevelLockable`) for the lifetime of a `Lock` object.

In an application, you inherit one of the implementations of **ThreadingModel**. Then you use the inner class `Lock` directly. For example,

```
class MyClass : public ClassLevelLockable <MyClass>
{
    ...
};
```

Table A.1: Implementations of ThreadingModel

Class Template	Semantics
SingleThreaded	No threading strategy at all. The Lock and ReadLock classes are empty mock-ups.
ObjectLevelLockable	Object-level locking semantics. One mutex per object is stored. The Lock inner class locks the mutex (and implicitly the object).
ClassLevelLockable	Class-level locking semantics. One mutex per class is stored. The Lock inner class locks the mutex (and implicitly all objects of a type).

The exact locking strategy depends on the ThreadingModel implementation you choose to derive from. Table A.1 summarizes the available implementations.

You can define synchronized member functions very easily, as outlined in the following example:

```
class BankAccount : public ObjectLevelLockable<BankAccount>
{
public:
   void Deposit(double amount, const char* user)
   {
      Lock lock(*this);
      ... perform deposit transaction ...
   }
   void Withdraw(double amount, const char* user)
   {
      Lock lock(*this);
      ... perform withdrawal transaction ...
   }
   ...
};
```

You no longer have any problem with premature returns and exceptions; the correct pairing of lock/unlock operations on the mutex is guaranteed by language invariants.

The uniform interface supported by the dummy interface SingleThreaded gives syntactic consistency. You can write your code assuming a multithreading environment, and then easily change design decisions by modifying the threading model.

The ThreadingModel policy is used in Chapter 4 (Small-Object Allocation), Chapter 5 (Generalized Functors), and Chapter 6 (Implementing Singletons).

A.6 Optional volatile Modifier

C++ provides the volatile type modifier, with which you should qualify each variable that you share with multiple threads. However, in a single-threaded model, it's best not to use volatile because it prevents the compiler from performing some important optimizations.

That's why Loki defines the inner class VolatileType. Inside SomeThreadingModel-<Widget>, VolatileType evaluates to volatile Widget for ClassLevelLockable and ObjectLevelLockable, and to plain Widget for SingleThreaded. You can see VolatileType at work in Chapter 6.

A.7 Semaphores, Events, and Other Good Things

Loki's support for multithreading stops here. General multithreading libraries provide a richer set of synchronization objects and functions such as semaphores, events, and memory barriers. Also, the function that starts a new thread is conspicuously absent from Loki—witness to the fact that Loki aims to be thread safe but not to use threads itself.

It is possible that a future version of Loki will provide a complete threading model. Multithreading is a domain that can greatly benefit from generic programming techniques. However, competition is heavy here—check out ACE (Adaptive Communication Environment) for a great, very portable multithreading library (Schmidt 2000).

A.8 Summary

Threads are absent from standard C++. However, synchronization issues in multithreaded programs pervade application and library design. The trouble is, the threading models supported by various operating systems are very different. Therefore, Loki defines a high-level synchronization mechanism having a minimal interaction with a threading model provided from the outside.

The ThreadingModel policy and the three class templates that implement Threading-Model define a platform for building generic components that support different threading models. At compile time, you can select support for object-level locking, class-level locking, or no locking at all.

The object-level locking strategy allocates one synchronization object per application object. The class-level locking strategy allocates one synchronization object per class. The former strategy is faster; the second uses a smaller amount of resources.

All implementations of ThreadingModel support a unique syntactic interface. This makes it easy for the library and for client code to use a uniform syntax. You can adjust locking support for a class without incurring changes to its implementation. For the same purpose, Loki defines a do-nothing implementation that supports a single-threaded model.

Bibliography

Alexandrescu, Andrei. 2000a. Traits: The else-if-then of types. C++ *Report*, April.

———. 2000b. On mappings between types and values. C/C++ *Users Journal*, October.

Austern, Matt. 2000. The standard librarian. C++ *Report*, April.

Ball, Steve, and John Miller Crawford. 1998. Channels for inter-applet communication. *Dr. Dobb's Journal*, September. Available at http://www.ddj.com/articles/1998/9809/9809a/9809a.htm.

Boost. The Boost C++ Library. http://www.boost.org.

Coplien, James O. 1992. *Advanced C++ Programming Styles and Idioms*. Reading, MA: Addison-Wesley.

———. 1995. The column without a name: A curiously recurring template pattern. C++ *Report*, February.

Czarnecki, Krzysztof, and Ulrich Eisenecker. 2000. *Generative Programming: Methods, Tools, and Applications*. Reading, MA: Addison-Wesley.

Gamma, Erich, Richard Helm, Ralph Johnson, and John Vlissides. 1995. *Design Patterns: Elements of Reusable Object-Oriented Software*. Reading, MA: Addison-Wesley.

Järvi, Jaakko. 1999a. *Tuples and Multiple Return Values in C++*. TUCS Technical Report No. 249, March.

———. 1999b. The Lambda Library. http://lambda.cs.utu.fi.

Knuth, Donald E. 1998. *The Art of Computer Programming*. Vol. 1. Reading, MA: Addison-Wesley.

Koenig, Andrew, and Barbara Moo. 1996. *Ruminations on C++*. Reading, MA: Addison-Wesley.

Lippman, Stanley B. 1994. *Inside the C++ Object Model*. Reading, MA: Addison-Wesley.

Martin, Robert. 1996. Acyclic Visitor. Available at http://objectmentor.com/publications/acv.pdf.

Meyers, Scott. 1996a. *More Effective C++*. Reading, MA: Addison-Wesley.

———. 1996b. Refinements to smart pointers. C++ *Report*, November–December.

———. 1998a. *Effective C++*, 2nd ed. Reading, MA: Addison-Wesley.

———. 1998b. Counting objects in C++. C/C++ *Users Journal*, April.

———. 1999. auto_ptr update. Available at http://www.awl.com/cseng/titles/0-201-63371-X/auto_ptr.html. Note: The Colvin/Gibbons trick is not described as-is in any paper. Meyers's notes on `auto_ptr` are the most accurate description of the solution that Greg Colvin and Bill Gibbons found. The trick uses `auto_ptr` to solve the function return problem.

Schmidt, D. 1996. Reality check. C++ *Report*, March. Available at http://www.cs.wustl.edu/~schmidt/editorial-3.html.

————. 2000. The ADAPTIVE Communication Environment (ACE). Available at http://www.cs.wustl.edu/~schmidt/ACE.html.

Stevens, Al. 1998. Undo/Redo redux. *Dr. Dobb's Journal*, November.

Stroustrup, Bjarne. 1997. *The* C++ *Programming Language*, 3rd ed. Reading, MA: Addison-Wesley.

————. 2000. Wrapping calls to member functions. C++ *Report*, June.

Sutter, Herb. 2000. *Exceptional* C++: *47 Engineering Puzzles, Programming Problems, and Solutions.* Reading, MA: Addison-Wesley.

Van Horn, Kevin S. 1997. Compile-time assertions in C++. C/C++ *Users Journal*, October. Available at http://www.xmission.com/~ksvhsoft/ctassert/ctassert.html.

Veldhuizen, Todd. 1995. Template metaprograms. C++ *Report*, May. Available at http://extreme.indiana.edu/~tveldhui/papers/Template-Metaprograms/meta-art.html.

Vlissides, John. 1996. To kill a singleton. C++ *Report*, June. Available at http://www.stat.cmu.edu/~lamj/sigs/c++-report/cppr9606.c.vlissides.html.

————. 1998. *Pattern Hatching.* Reading, MA: Addison-Wesley.

————. 1999. Visitor in frameworks. C++ *Report*, November–December.

Index

A

Abstract Factory design pattern, 69, 40–51
  architectural role of, 219–222
  basic description of, 219–234
  implementing, 226–233
  interface, generic, 223–226
  quick facts, 233–234
AbstractEnemyFactory, 221–222, 224–227
AbstractFactory, 219–234
AbstractProduct, 209–214, 216–217
abstract products, 209–214, 216–217, 222, 231
Accept, 240–251, 254
AcceptImpl, 252, 256, 259
ACE, 309
Acquire, 161–162, 305, 306
Action, 100
Adapter, 284
Add, 278–282, 284, 300
address-of, 170–171
after, 16
AbstactFactoryUnit, 223–226
Alexandrescu, Andrei, 29
algorithms
  copy, 40
  compile-time, 76
  linear search, 56
  operating on typelists, 76
Allocate, 83, 85
Allocated, 82
allocation, small-object. *See also* allocators
  basic description of, 77–96
  default free store allocators and, 78
  fixed-size allocators and, 84–87
  hat trick and, 89–91

  memory chunks and, 81–84
  quick facts, 94–95
allocators. *See also* allocation, small-object
  default free store, 78
  fixed-size, 84–87
  memory chunks and, 81–84
  workings of, 78–79
allocChunk_, 85, 87
AllowConversion, 192–193
ALU (arithmetic logic unit), 303
AnotherDerived, 197
APIs (application program interfaces), 161, 306
Append, 57–58, 76
Application, 100
arguments, 114–115, 285–290
Array policy, 19–20
arrays, 19–20, 183–184
ArrayStorage, 189–190
assert, 193
AssertCheck, 193
AssertCheckStrict, 193
assertions, compile-time, 23–26
associative collections, 203
AssocVector, 210, 277–278
asynchronous execution, 302
atexit, 134–139, 142–143, 149
ATEXIT_FIXED, 139
AtExitFn, 144–145
AtomicAdd, 305
AtomicAssign, 305
AtomicDecrement, 186
AtomicIncrement, 186
auto_ptr, 108, 159, 170
available_, 79

B

backEnd_, 281, 294
BackendType, 294
BadMonster, 219–222
BadSoldier, 219–222, 230
BadSuperMonster, 219–221
BankAccount, 306
Bar, 139
Base, 63, 90, 91, 176
BASE_IF, 37
BaseLhs, 272, 299
BaseProductList, 227
BaseRhs, 272, 284, 299
BaseSmartPtr, 46
BaseVisitable, 249, 251, 254
BaseVisitor, 245, 249–250, 252, 254, 256, 261
BaseVisitorImpl, 260, 262
BasicDispatcher, 277–284, 292–294, 297–299
BasicFastDispatcher, 291–294, 297, 298–299
before, 16
BinderFirst, 121
BindFirst, 121, 127–128
binding, 119–121, 127–128
BitBlast, 40–41, 44–46
blocksAvailable_, 81–83
blockSize_, 82
bookkeeping data level, 185–187
bool, 105, 174–175, 177, 191
_buffer, 135
bulk allocation, 86
butterfly allocation, 86
Button, 50, 61–62, 219–221

C

callable entities, 103–104
callbackMap_, 280
callbacks, 103–104, 205, 280–281
callbacks_, 205, 281
CallbackType, 277, 280, 299
CastingPolicy policy, 288, 299
CatchAll policy, 260, 262
Chain, 122, 128
chaining requests, 122
char, 35, 38, 114–115
checking issues, 181–182
checkingImpl, 193
Checking policy, 15–16, 188, 193–194
chunks, of memory, 81–87
chunkSize, 88

Circle, 203
class(es). See also inheritance; policy classes
    base, 228
    client, 153–154
    decomposing, 19–20
    derived, 228
    final, 29
    generating, with typelists, 64–75
    -level locking operations, 187
    local, 28–29
    object factories and, 200–201
    visitable, 248–255
    visitor, 248–255
Class, 200
ClassLevelLockable, 153, 307–309
Clone, 30, 107, 123, 164, 211–213, 230, 232, 234, 284
CloneFactory, 214–218
clone object factories, 211–215
CLOS, 263
columns_, 292
COM (Component Object Model), 133, 192
command(s). See also Command design pattern
    active, 102
    forwarding, 102
Command, 100
Command design pattern, 99–104
    basic description of, 100–102
    in the real world, 102–103
comparison operators, 178–181
compile-time
    assertions, 23–26
    detecting convertibility and inheritance at, 34–37
CompileTimeChecker, 25–26
CompileTimeError, 25
COMRefCounted, 192
ConcreteCommand, 100, 102
ConcreteFact, 232, 234
ConcreteFactory, 226–228, 230–231, 233–234
ConcreteLifetimeTracker, 144–145
concrete products, 222, 227
const, 44, 114–115, 182–183
constant(s)
    mapping integral, to types, 29–31
    -time multimethods, 290–293
ConventionalDialog, 219–221
conversion
    argument, 114–115, 285–290
    binding as, 119–121
    implicit, to raw pointer types, 171–173
    return type, 114–114
    user-defined, 172

Conversion policy, 36–37, 188, 192–193
convertibility, detecting, at compile time,
     35–37
copy
   construction, eliding of, 123
   deep, 123, 162–164, 192
   destructive, 168–170
   on write (COW), 165
Copy, 40, 45
copy_backward, 144
copyAlgo, 45
CORBA (Common Object Request Broker
     Architecture), 115, 133
counting, reference, 165–167
covariant return types, 212–213
Create, 9, 11–12, 14, 31–32, 198, 224, 234
CreateButton, 50
CreateDocument, 199
CreateObject, 208–209
CreateScrollBar, 50
CreateShape, 205–206
CreateShapeCallback, 205
CreateStatic, 153
CreateT, 223
CreateUsingMalloc, 153
CreateUsingNew, 153
CreateWindow, 50
Creation policy, 151, 153
Creator policy, 7–9, 11–14, 149, 154, 156
cyclic
   dependencies, 243–248
   references, 168
CyclicVisitor, 255–257, 261
Czarnecki, Krzysztof, 54

D

dead reference problem, 135–142
Deallocate, 82–87
deallocChunk_, 86–87
deep copy, 123, 163–164, 192
DeepCopy, 192
DEFAULT_CHUNK_SIZE, 93–94, 95
default free store allocator, 78
DefaultLifetime, 153
DEFAULT_THREADING, 94
#define preprocessor directive, 93, 139
DEFINE_CYCLIC_VISITABLE, 257
DEFINE_VISITABLE, 252, 254, 256
delete, 12, 89–91, 94, 108, 132, 143, 159, 172–178
delete[], 184, 189–190
DeleteChar, 125

dependency, circular, 141
DependencyManager, 141
Deposit, 306
dereference, checking before, 182
Derived, 90, 197–198
DerivedToFront algorithm, 63–65, 76, 272
design patterns
   Abstract Factory pattern, 69, 49–51, 219–
     234
   Command pattern, 99–104
   Double-Checked Locking pattern, 146–147,
     149
   Prototype design pattern, 228–233
   Strategy design pattern, 8
Destroy policy, 20
destroyed_, 136, 138
_DestroySingleton, 135
DestructiveCopy, 192
destructors, 12–13
detection, dead-reference, 135–137
Dialog, 219–221
Dijkstra, Edgar, 305–306
DisallowConversion, 192–193
DispatcherBackend policy, 294
DispatchRhs, 269–270
Display, 135–142, 169
DisplayStatistics, 230
do-it-all interface, failure of, 4–5
DocElement, 236–248, 249, 251, 256, 259
DocElementVisitor, 239–248
DocElementVisitor.h, 243–244
DoClone, 213
DoCreate, 223–224, 227, 232
DocStats, 236–237, 240–242, 246–247, 248
Document, 198
DocumentManager, 198–199
DottedLine, 212
double, 306
Double-Checked Locking pattern, 146–147,
     149
DoubleDispatch, 267, 268
double dispatcher, logarithmic, 263, 276–285,
     297–300
double switch-on-type, 264–268
Dr. Dobb's Journal, 125
Drawing, 201–203
DrawingDevices, 290
DrawingType, 203
Dylan, 263
dynamic_cast, 238, 243, 246, 251, 255, 267,
     285–290, 299
   cost of, 255–256
DynamicCaster, 288, 289

E

EasyLevelEnemyFactory, 227, 229, 231
Effective C++ (Meyers), 132
efficient resource use, 302
Eisenecker, Ulrich, 54
ElementAt, 20
Ellipse, 203, 271, 273
else, 238
EmptyType, 39–40, 48, 110
encapsulation, 99
EnforceNotNull, 15, 18
enum, 45
equality, 173–178
erase, 278
Erase, 58–59, 76
EraseAll, 76, 59
error(s)
    messages, compile-time assertions and, 24
    reporting, 181–182
EventHandler, 71
events, 71, 309
exceptions, 209
Execute, 100, 102
Executor, 269–272
exists2Way, 36
ExtendedWidget, 18, 164

F

factor(ies)
    basic description of, 197–218
    classes and, 200–201
    generalization and, 207–210
    implementing, 201–206
    need for, 198–200
    quick facts, 216–217
    templates, 216–218
    type identifiers and, 206–207
    using, with generic components, 215
Factory, 207–208, 215–217
FactoryErrorImpl, 209
FactoryError policy, 208–209, 217–218, 234
FactoryErrorPolicy, 217–218, 234
FastWidgetPtr, 17
Field, 67–70, 74–75
Fire, 275, 270, 271
firstAvailableBlock_, 81–83
FixedAllocator, 80–81, 84–95
FnDispatcher, 280–282, 285, 288, 293–294, 299–300

FnDoubleDispatcher, 280
Foo, 103, 139
forwarding functions, cost of, 122–124
free, 143, 189–190
fun_, 113, 115
functionality, optional, through incomplete
    instantiation, 13–14
functions
    forwarding, cost of, 122–124
    static, singletons and, 130
functor(s)
    argument type conversions and, 114–115
    basic description of, 99–128
    binding and, 119–121
    chaining requests and, 122
    command design pattern and, 100–102
    double dispatch to, 282–285
    generalized, 99–128
    handling, 110–112
    heap allocation and, 124–125
    implementing Undo and Redo with,
        125–126
    multimethods and, 282–285
    quick facts, 126–128
    real-world issues and, 122–125
    return type conversions and, 114–115
Functor1, 106
Functor2, 106
FunctorDispatcher, 283–285, 288, 293,
    299–300
FunctorHandler, 110–112, 117–119, 126
Functor template, 99–108, 114, 117, 120, 125–126,
    215
FunctorImpl, 107–112, 123–124, 128, 283, 284
FunctorType, 284
FunkyDialog, 219–221

G

GameApp, 230
Gamma, Ralph, 248
generalization, 207–210. *See also* generalized
    functors
generalized functors. *See also* functors
    argument type conversions and, 114–115
    basic description of, 99–128
    binding and, 119–121
    chaining requests and, 122
    Command design pattern and, 100–102
    handling, 110–112
    heap allocation and, 124–125
    implementing Undo and Redo with, 125–126

quick facts, 126–128
real-world issues and, 122–125
return type conversions and, 114–115
GenLinearHierarchy, 71–75, 227, 230, 231
GenScatterHierarchy, 64–75, 223–226, 227–228
geronimosWork, 117
GetClassIndex, 292–293
GetClassIndexStatic, 292
GetImpl, 162, 173, 183, 190
GetImplRef, 162, 190
GetLongevity, 154
GetPrototype, 12, 14
Go, 269, 270, 272, 279
GoF (Gang of Four) book, 100, 122, 125, 199, 235, 248–249, 255–262
granular interfaces, 224
GraphicButton, 61–62
GUI (graphical user interface), 102

H

handles, 161
Harrison, Tim, 146
Haskell, 263
hat trick, 89–91
HatchingDispatcher, 272
HatchingExecutor, 271
HatchRectanglePoly, 279
header files
  DocElementVisitor.h, 243–244
  Multimethods.h, 294
  Typelist.h, 51, 55, 75
  SmallAlloc.h, 93–95
heaps, 124–125, 189–190
HeapStorage, 189–190
hierarchies
  linear, 70–74
  scattered, 64–70
HTMLDocument, 198

I

IdentifierType, 209, 213, 215
IdToProductMap, 214
#ifdef preprocessor directive, 138–139
if-else statements, 29, 267, 268, 270
if statements, 238, 267, 305
IMPLEMENT_INDEXABLE_CLASS, 293

implicit conversion, to raw pointer types, 171–173
IncrementFontSize, 240, 241
indexed access, 55
IndexOf, 56, 76, 275
inequality, 173–178
inheritance
  detecting, at compile time, 34–37
  logarithmic dispatcher and, 279
  multiple, 5–6
INHERITS, 37
InIt, 40, 82
initialization
  checking, 181–182
  dynamic, 132
  lazy, 182
  object factories and, 197
  static, 132
insert, 205
InsertChar, 120, 122, 125–126
Instance, 131–132, 135–137, 146, 151
instantiation, 13–14, 120, 272, 274
int, 159
Int2Type, 29–31, 68–69
interface(s)
  Abstract Factory design pattern, 223–226
  application program (APIs), 161, 306
  do-it-all, failure of, 4–5
  granular, 224
  graphical user (GUI), 102
  separation, 101
intrusive reference counting, 167. *See also* reference counting
IntType, 186, 304
InvocationTraits, 275
isConst, 47
isPointer, 47
isReference, 41, 47
isStdArith, 47
isStdFloat, 47
isStdFundamental, 42–43, 47
isStdIntegral, 47
isStdSignedInt, 47
isStdUnsignedInt, 47
isVolatile, 47

K

KDL problem, 135–142, 155
Keyboard, 135–142, 155
KillPhoenixSingleton, 138
Knuth, Donald E., 77, 78

L

Lattanzi, Len, 77
Length, 76
less, 180–181
LhsTypes, 272
Lifetime policy, 149–153
LifetimeTracker, 142–143
LIFO (last in, first out), 134
Line, 203, 204, 212–213
linking, reference, 167–168
LISP, 52
ListOfTypes, 295
Lock, 146, 184, 306
LockedStorage, 189–190
locking
   class-level, 307
   object-level, 306–308
   pattern, double-checked, 146–147, 149
   semantics, 306–308
LockingProxy, 184–185
Log, 135–142
logarithmic double dispatcher, 263, 276–285,
      297–300
logic_error, 152
Loki, 70, 77, 91–92, 210, 303, 309
   multimethods and, 263, 268, 277–278, 288,
      295–300
   mutexes and, 306
   smart pointers and, 163
long double data type, 35
longevity, 139–145, 149, 151
lower_bound, 277

M

MacroCommand, 122
macros, 122, 251–252, 254, 256–257, 261
"maelstrom effect," 170
MAKE_VISITABLE, 261
MakeAdapter, 28–29
MakeCopy, 164
MakeT, 223
malloc, 143
map, 204–205, 210, 277, 278
mapping
   integral constants to types, 31–32
   type-to-type, 31–33
Martin, Robert, 245
maxObjectSize, 88
MAX_SMALL_OBJECT_SIZE, 93–94, 95

MemControlBlock, 78–79
MemFunHandler, 117–119, 126
memory
   allocators, workings of, 78–80
   chunks of, 81–87
   heaps, 124–125, 189–190
   RMW (read-modify-write) operation, 303–304
Meyers, Scott, 77, 133–134, 276, 280
Meyers singleton, 133–134
ML, 263
ModalDialog, 27
Monster, 219–222, 224, 229
More Effective C++ (Meyers), 276, 280
MostDerived, 63, 76
multimethods
   arguments and, 285–290
   basic description of, 263–300
   constant-time, 290–293
   double switch-on-type and, 265–268
   logarithmic double dispatcher and, 276–285
   need for, 264–265
   quick facts, 297–300
   symmetry and, 273–74
Multimethods.h, 294
MultiThreaded, 6
MultiThreadedRefCounting, 186–187
multithreading, 145–148, 302–306
   at the bookkeeping data level, 185–187
   critique of, 302–303
   library, 301–309
   mutexes and, 305–306
   at the pointee object level, 184–185
   reference counting and, 186
   reference tracking and, 186–187
   smart pointers and, 184–187
mutex_, 146
mutexes, 146–147, 305–306
MyController, 27
MyOnlyPrinter, 130
MyVisitor, 257

N

name, 206
name cyclic dependency, 243
new[], 183
next_, 187
NiftyContainer, 28–30, 33–34
NoChecking, 15, 18–19
NoCopy, 192
NoDestroy, 153
NoDuplicates, 60–61, 76

NonConstType, 47
nontemplated operators, 176–177
NonVolatileType, 47
NoQualifiedType, 47
NullType, 39–41, 48, 52, 54–56, 62–63, 270

O

object factor(ies)
  basic description of, 197–218
  classes and, 200–201
  generalization and, 207–210
  implementing, 201–206
  need for, 198–200
  quick facts, 216–217
  templates, 216–218
  type identifiers and, 206–207
  using, with generic components, 215
ObjectLevelLockable, 307–309
OnDeadReference, 136–139, 150
OnError, 272
OnEvent, 70–71
OnUnknownVisitor, 260, 262
operators
  operator.*, 104, 116–117
  operator!=, 174, 176, 178
  operator(), 103–113, 116, 122–127, 283, 285
  operator->, 157, 160–162, 165, 182–185
  operator->*, 104, 116–117
  operator*, 157, 161–162, 178–179, 182
  operator<, 144
  operator<=, 178–179
  operator=, 162
  operator==, 176–177, 178
  operator>, 178–179
  operator>=, 178–179
  operator[], 55, 183, 278
  operator T*, 172
OpNewCreator, 10
OpNewFactoryUnit, 226, 227, 231, 234
OrderedTypeInfo, 217, 276–277
orthogonal policies, 20
OutIt, 40
ownership-handling strategies, 163–170
Ownership policy, 183–184, 186, 188, 190–192

P

Paragraph, 237, 241, 247, 249, 254, 256
ParagraphVisitor, 246, 247, 248, 251

parameter(s)
  template, 10–11, 64, 105
  types, optimized, 43–44
ParameterType, 43–44, 47, 123
ParentFunctor, 111, 120–121
Parm1, 111
Parm2, 111
ParmN, 109
Parrot, 117–119
pattern(s)
  Abstract Factory pattern, 69, 49–51, 219–
    234
  Command pattern, 99–104
  Double-Checked Locking pattern, 146–147, 149
  Prototype design pattern, 228–233
  Strategy design pattern, 8
Pattern Hatching (Vlissides), 133
pData_, 86
pDocElem, 246
pDuplicateShape, 212
pDynObject, 140
pFactory_, 222
Phoenix Singleton, 137–142, 149, 153
pimpl idiom, 78
pInstance_, 131–132, 136, 138, 146–148, 151
placement new, 138
pLastAlloc_, 89
POD (plain old data) structure, 45–46
Point3D, 70
pointee_, 160, 161, 178, 183
PointeeType, 41–42, 47, 160–161
pointee object level, 184–185
pointer(s)
  address-of operator and, 170–171
  arrays and, 183–184
  basic description of, 157–195
  checking issues and, 181–182
  copy on write (COW) and, 165
  deep copy and, 163–164
  destructive copy and, 168–170
  equality and, 173–178
  error reporting and, 181–182
  failure of the do-it-all interface and, 5
  handling, to member functions, 115–119
  implicit conversion and, 171–173
  inequality and, 173–178
  multithreading and, 184–187
  ordering comparison operators and, 178–181
  ownership-handling strategies, 163–170
  quick facts, 194–195
  raw, 171–173
  reference counting and, 165–167, 186
  reference linking and, 166–168
  reference tracking and, 186–187

traits of, implementing, 41–42
types, implicit conversion, 171–173
PointerToObj, 118
PointerTraits, 41–42
PointerType, 160, 190–191
policies. *See also* policy classes
  basic description of, 3, 7–11
  BasicDispatcher and, 293–294
  BasicFastDispatcher and, 293–294
  compatible, 17–18
  decomposing classes in, 19–20
  enriched, 12
  multimethods and, 293–294
  noncompatible, 17–18
  orthogonal, 20
  singletons and, 149–150, 152–153
  stock, 152–153
policies (listed by name). *See also* policies
  Array policy, 19–20
  CastingPolicy policy, 288, 299
  CatchAll Policy, 260, 262
  Checking policy, 15–16, 188, 193–194
  Conversion policy, 36–37, 188, 192–193
  Creation policy, 151, 153
  Creator policy, 8–9, 11–14, 149, 155, 156
  Destroy policy, 20
  DispatcherBackend policy, 294
  FactoryError policy, 208–209, 217–218, 234
  Lifetime policy, 149–153
  Ownership policy, 183–184, 186, 188, 190–
    192
  Storage policy, 17, 185, 188, 189–190
  Structure policy, 16–17
  ThreadingModel policy, 16, 149, 151–153, 186,
    303–309
policy classes. *See also* classes
  basic description of, 3–22
  combining, 14–16
  customizing structure with, 16–17
  destructors of, 12–13
  implementing, 10–11
Poly, 271, 279
Polygon, 203, 212
polymorphism, 78, 163–164
  Abstract Factory implementation and,
    228–229
  multimethods and, 264
  object factories and, 197–200, 211–212
prev_, 187
Printer, 161–162
printf, 105
printingPort_, 130
priority_queue, 142–145

ProductCreator, 210–211, 216–217
Prototype design pattern, 228–233
PrototypeFactoryUnit, 231–232, 234
prototypes, 228–233
pTrackerArray, 143

Q

qualifiers, stripping, 44

R

RasterBitmap, 237, 241, 247, 249, 256
RasterBitmapVisitor, 247, 251
realloc, 143
Receiver, 100
Rectangle, 267, 279, 289
RectanglePoly, 279
Redo, 125–126
RefCounted, 6, 192
RefCountedMT, 192
reference(s)
  counting, 165–167, 186
  linking, 167–168, 186–187
ReferencedType, 41–42, 47
RefLinked, 192
RegisterShape, 206
RejectNull, 194
RejectNullStatic, 193–194
RejectNullStrict, 194
Release, 161–162, 192, 305, 306
Replace, 76
ReplaceAll, 61, 76
Reset, 162
resource leaks, 133
Result, 55
ResultType, 111, 269, 284
return type(s)
  conversion, 114–115
  covariant, 228
  generalized functors and, 114–115
RISC processors, 148
RMW (read-modify-write) operation, 303–
  304
RoundedRectangle, 272, 286–287, 289
RoundedShape, 286–287, 289
runtime_error, 137, 209–210, 300
runtime type information (RTTI), 215, 245, 255,
  276

S

safe_reinterpret_cast, 26
SafeWidgetPtr, 17
sameType, 36
Save, 201–203
scanf, 105
ScheduleDestruction, 149–150
Schmidt, Douglas, 146–147
Scroll, 122
ScrollBar, 50, 61–62
Secretary, 5
Section, 254
Select, 33–34, 62
semantics
    failure of the do-it-all interface and, 4–5
    functors and, 99
    locking, 306–308
semaphores, 309
SetLongevity, 140–145, 149
SetPrototype, 12, 14, 232
Shape, 201–202, 265, 268, 279, 286–289
ShapeCast, 289
ShapeFactory, 204–205, 215
Shapes, 290
SillyMonster, 219–222, 226
SillySoldier, 219–222, 230
SillySuperMonster, 219–222
SingleThreaded, 153, 308
singleton(s). See also SingletonHolder
    basic C++ idioms supporting, 131–132
    dead reference problem and, 135–142
    destroying, 133–135
    Double-Checked Locking pattern and, 146–147
    failure of the do-it-all interface and, 4–5
    implementing, 129–154
    longevity and, 139–145
    Meyers singleton, 133–134
    multithreading and, 145–148
    Phoenix, 137–142, 149, 153
    static functions and, 130
    uniqueness of, enforcing, 132–133
SingletonHolder, 3, 91, 129–130, 148–153, 215.
        See also singletons
    assembling, 150–152
    decomposing, 149–150
    quick facts, 155–156
    working with, 153–156
SingletonWithLongevity, 153, 154
sizeof, 25, 34–35, 82, 90–91
size_t, 36, 79
skinnable programs, 103

SmallAlloc.h, 93–95
small-object allocation
    basic description of, 77–96
    default free store allocators and, 78
    fixed-size allocators and, 84–87
    hat trick and, 89–91
    memory chunks and, 81–84
    quick facts, 94–95
SmallObjAllocator, 80–81, 87–89, 92–95
SmallObject, 80–81, 89, 91–95, 123–124
smart pointer(s)
    address-of operator and, 170–171
    arrays and, 183–184
    basic description of, 157–195
    checking issues and, 181–182
    copy on write (COW) and, 165
    deep copy and, 163–164
    destructive copy and, 168–170
    equality and, 173–178
    error reporting and, 181–182
    failure of the do-it-all interface and, 5
    implicit conversion and, 171–173
    inequality and, 173–178
    multithreading and, 184–187
    ordering comparison operators and, 178–181
    ownership-handling strategies, 163–170
    quick facts, 194–195
    raw, 171–173
    reference counting and, 165–167, 186
    reference linking and, 167–168
    reference tracking and, 186–187
    types, implicit conversion, 171–173
SmartPtr, 3, 6–7, 14–19, 44, 87, 157–195
Soldier, 219–222, 224, 229–230
SomeLhs, 278, 284
SomeRhs, 278, 284
SomeThreadingModel, 309
SomeVisitor, 250, 254
spImpl_, 112
statements
    if, 238, 267, 305
    if-else, 29, 267, 268, 270
static, 280
static_cast, 114, 285–290, 299
STATIC_CHECK, 25
StaticDispatcher, 268–276, 297–298
static manipulation, 6
Statistics, 249
stats, 246–247
STL, 115, 171
StorageImpl, 189, 190
Storage policy, 17, 185, 188, 189–190
Strategy design pattern, 8

String, 302–303, 307
Stroustrup, Bjarne, 202
struct, 45
structure(s)
  customizing, with policy classes, 16–17
  POD (plain old data), 45–46
  specialization of, 7
Structure policy, 16–17
SuperMonster, 219–222, 229
SUPERSUBCLASS, 37, 62
Surprises.cpp, 224
Sutter, Herb, 77
switch, 203
SwitchPrototype, 13–14
symmetry, 273–74
synchronization objects, 303

T

template(s)
  advantages of, 6–7
  implementing policy classes with, 11
  skeleton, Functor class, 104–108
  specialization, partial, 53–54
  template parameters, 10–11, 64, 105
templated operators, 176–177
TemporarySecretary, 5
Tester, 178
Tester*, 178
TestFunction, 113–115
TextDocument, 198
ThreadingModel policy, 16, 149, 151–153, 186,
  303–309
time
  separation, 101
  slicing, 201
TList, 53–65, 75, 120, 127, 223, 231–234, 261
Tools menu, 102
trampoline functions (thunks), 280–283
Trampoline, 281
translation units, 132
Triangle, 289
tuples, generating, 70
type(s)
  atomic operations on, 303–304
  conversions, generalized functors and,
    114–115
  detection of fundamental, 42–43
  identifiers, 201, 206–207
  integral, 303–305
  modifiers, 308–309
  multiple inheritance and, 6

multithreading and, 303–305
parameters, optimized, 43–44
replacing an element in, 60–61
safety, loss of static, 4
selection, 33–34
-to-type mapping, 31–33
traits, 38–46
Type2Type, 32–33, 223
TypeAt, 55, 76
TypeAtNonStrict, 55, 76, 109
typedef, 14, 19, 51, 54, 215, 295
typeid, 38, 267
type_info, 37–39, 54, 206–207, 213–215, 276–277,
  295
TypeInfo, 38–39, 48
TYPELIST, 295
Typelist.h, 51, 55, 75
typelists, 223, 268, 272
  appending to, 57–58
  basic description of, 49–76
  calculating length and, 53–54
  class generation with, 64–75
  compile-time algorithms operating on, 76
  creating, 52–53
  defining, 51–52
  detecting fundamental types and, 42–43
  need for, 49–41
  partially ordering, 61–64
  quick facts, 75
  searching, 56–57
TypesLhs, 269–270, 274
TypesRhs, 269, 270, 274
TypeTraits, 41–48, 123, 183

U

UCHAR_MAX, 83
Undo, 125–126
unique bouncing virtual functions, 238
Unlock, 184
UpdateStats, 237–238
upper_bound, 144
use_Size, 91

V

ValueType, 33
vector, 183
VectorGraphic, 244

VectorizedDrawing, 259
Veldhuizen, Todd, 54
virtual
    constructor dilemma, 229
    functions, 238
Visit, 249–250, 254, 256
Visitable, 249, 251, 252–254
Visitor design pattern
    acyclic, 243–248
    basic description of, 235–262
    catch-all function and, 242–243, 258–259
    cyclic, 243–248, 254–257
    generic implementation of, 248–255
    hooking variations, 258–260
    nonstrict visitation and, 261
    quick facts, 261–262
VisitParagraph, 240, 242
VisitRasterBitmap, 242
VisitVectorGraphic, 244
Vlissides, John, 133
void*, 172

volatile, 151, 308–309, 308–309
VolatileType, 151, 309

W

Widget, 26–32, 38, 44, 61–62, 159, 164, 184, 309
WidgetEventHandler, 71–74
WidgetFactory, 49–51
WidgetInfo, 65–67
WidgetManager, 9–14, 19–20
Window, 50
Withdrawal, 306

X

X Windows, 103

The C++ In-Depth Series

Bjarne Stroustrup, Series Editor

Modern C++ Design
Generic Programming and Design Patterns Applied
By Andrei Alexandrescu
0201704315
Paperback
352 pages
© 2001

Accelerated C++
Practical Programming by Example
By Andrew Koenig and
Barbara E. Moo
020170353X
Paperback
352 pages
© 2000

Essential C++
By Stanley B. Lippman
0201485184
Paperback
304 pages
© 2000

C++ Network Programming, Volume 1
Mastering Complexity with ACE and Patterns
By Douglas C. Schmidt and
Stephen D. Huston
0201604647
Paperback
336 pages
© 2002

The Boost Graph Library
User Guide and Reference Manual
By Jeremy G. Siek, Lie-Quan Lee, and
Andrew Lumsdaine
0201729148
Paperback
352 pages
© 2002

Exceptional C++
47 Engineering Puzzles, Programming Problems, and Solutions
By Herb Sutter
0201615622
Paperback
240 pages
© 2000

More Exceptional C++
40 New Engineering Puzzles, Programming Problems, and Solutions
By Herb Sutter
020170434X
Paperback
304 pages
© 2002

C++ Network Programming, Volume 2
Systematic Reuse with ACE and Frameworks
By Douglas C. Schmidt and
Stephen D. Huston
0201795256
Paperback
384 pages
© 2003

Applied C++
Practical Techniques for Building Better Software
By Philip Romanik and Amy Muntz
0321108949
Paperback
352 pages
© 2003

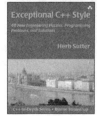

Exceptional C++ Style
40 New Engineering Puzzles, Programming Problems, and Solutions
By Herb Sutter
0201760428
Paperback
352 pages
© 2005

Also Available

The C++ Programming Language, Special Edition
By Bjarne Stroustrup
0201700735
Hardcover | 1,040 pages | © 2000

Written by the creator of C++, this is the most widely read and most trusted book on C++.

inform**IT**.com THE TRUSTED TECHNOLOGY LEARNING SOURCE

Learn**IT** at **Inform**IT

Looking for a book, eBook, or training video on a new technology? Seeking timely and relevant information and tutorials? Looking for expert opinions, advice, and tips? **InformIT has the solution.**

- Learn about new releases and special promotions by subscribing to a wide variety of newsletters.
  Visit **informit.com/newsletters**.

- Access FREE podcasts from experts at **informit.com/podcasts**.

- Read the latest author articles and sample chapters at **informit.com/articles**.

- Access thousands of books and videos in the Safari Books Online digital library at **safari.informit.com**.

- Get tips from expert blogs at **informit.com/blogs**.

Visit **informit.com/learn** to discover all the ways you can access the hottest technology content.

Are You Part of the **IT** Crowd?

Connect with Pearson authors and editors via RSS feeds, Facebook, Twitter, YouTube, and more! Visit **informit.com/socialconnect**.